BEHOLD A PALE FARCE

Cyberwar, Threat Inflation, & the Malware Industrial Complex

BILL BLUNDEN
AND
VIOLET CHEUNG

Published by:
Trine Day LLC
PO Box 577
Walterville, OR 97489
1-800-556-2012
www.TrineDay.com
publisher@TrineDay.net

Library of Congress Control Number: 2014932890

Blunden, Bill and Cheung, Violet
Behold A Pale Farce–1st ed.
p. cm.
Includes index and references.
Epud (ISBN-13) 978-1-937584-81-8
Mobi (ISBN-13) 978-1-937584-82-5
Print (ISBN-13) 978-1-937584-80-1
1. Information warfare 2. Information warfare -- Psychological aspects 3. Computer security -- United States. 4. Computer networks -- Security measures -- United States. 5. Cyberspace -- Security measures -- United States. 6. Political Science -- Political Freedom & Security -- International Security. 7. United States -- Military policy -- History -- 21st century. I. Blunden, Bill and Cheung, Violet II. Title

FIRST EDITION
10 9 8 7 6 5 4 3 2 1

Printed in the USA
Distribution to the Trade by:
Independent Publishers Group (IPG)
814 North Franklin Street
Chicago, Illinois 60610
312.337.0747
www.ipgbook.com

A functioning republic requires *well informed* citizens who exercise *sound judgment.*

Hence, this book is dedicated to:

Deborah Natsios and John Young

For showing how secrecy undermines democracy.

Noam Chomsky and Edward Herman

For their research on the propaganda model.

War is a way of shattering to pieces, or pouring into the stratosphere, or sinking in the depths of the sea, materials which might otherwise be used to make the masses too comfortable, and hence, in the long run, too intelligent.

–George Orwell, *1984*

Table of Contents

Preface

Media Massage

And I will utter my judgments against them touching all their wickedness ...

−Jeremiah 1:16 King James Bible

I think it's wrong that – that newspaper reporters have all these documents, 50,000 or whatever they have, and are selling them and giving them out as if these – you know, it just doesn't make sense. We ought to come up with a way of stopping it. I don't know how to do that. That's more of the courts and the policymakers. But from my perspective, it's wrong, and to allow this to go on is wrong.

−General Keith Alexander[1]

In an ideal world, the media would serve as a watchdog of sorts, where those in power must tolerate constant, and rigorous, scrutiny by an aggressive press which reports to an engaged and knowledgeable populace. This is what's known as the *Jeffersonian model* for analyzing the role of the media. An alternative model is the *Propaganda model*, where the major news outlets distort information in a manner that defends the agendas of the people who control society.

Guardian journalist Glenn Greenwald has characterized these two models in terms of David Halberstam and Bill Keller. Halberstam was a reporter who was kicked out of the *New York Times* after persistently challenging official government narratives during the Vietnam War. Keller, the former *New York Times* editor, oversaw the publication of documents released by WikiLeaks only after receiving approval for each document from the Obama administration:

David Halberstam viewed the measurement of good journalism as defined by how much you anger the people in power that you're covering whereas Bill Keller defines good journalism – and I think most modern establishment journalists define it this way as well – by how much you please the people in power that you're covering.[2]

In the late 1980s, Noam Chomsky and Edward Herman analytically demonstrated that the large, agenda-setting, news outlets largely adhere to the Propaganda model in their book *Manufacturing Consent*.[3] This should come as no surprise, as the major outlets, like the *Wall Street Journal*, are part of large publicly traded corporations. Being publicly traded, the agenda-setters are beholden to the desires of Wall Street, where investors measure their value as a function of the profit that they generate.

The *Wall Street Journal* sells millions of papers every day,[4] and advertisement revenue is so large that the executives who control the outlet have even considered simply giving away online content for free.[5] What this demonstrates is that major news sources like the *Wall Street Journal* have a product (their readers) that they sell to the buyers in the market (the advertisers).

As it turns out, the profit margin in this market can be pretty good. This is because papers like the *Wall Street Journal* maintain a channel to a valuable commodity: society's decision makers. In other words, many of the people who read the *Wall Street Journal* also represent America's one percent. According to ABC News, the average household income of the *Wall Street Journal*'s subscribers in 2007 was approximately $235,000.[6]

So what's going on is that you have one large corporation selling its product to other large corporations, where the product is the eyes and ears of the top tier. It only makes sense that the ideas put forth will be those that cater to the economic desires and political inclinations of the parties involved. In fact, this kind of distortion is exactly what Noam Chomsky and Edward Herman discovered while studying the nature of the mass media.

Canadian scholar Marshall McLuhan once observed:

> One thing about which fish know exactly nothing is water, since they have no anti-environment which would enable them to perceive the element they live in.[7]

Because it's immersed in water every minute of its life a fish is less likely to recognize the significance of water's presence. Such is the effect of propaganda. Society is overwhelmed by spin often without being aware of it. Because the Constitution of the United States includes provisions regarding the freedom of speech, ideas can compete with one another. As a result propaganda has to be more subtle and sophisticated, so that people don't necessarily feel like they're being overtly influenced.

Firsthand Experience

While we've read about the many filtering mechanisms of the Propaganda model and witnessed its operation from afar, We never thought that We'd encounter them directly. This changed in late 2011 when, out of the blue, Bill Blunden received an e-mail from a senior editor at a well-known technical publisher located South of Market in downtown San Francisco. Having viewed his slides on cyberwar from SFSU's National Cybersecurity Awareness Event,[8] the editor wanted to know if he was interested in authoring a book on the topic. Shortly after the editor's initial query Bill signed a contract and feverishly began the process of putting material together.

Four or five months later the editor ominously summoned your author and co-author to his office for a meeting. He announced that both he and the founder of the publishing house were very concerned about the tone of the book. The editor complained at length about the potential hazards of *push back*, particularly with regard to the coverage of former Director of National Intelligence Mike McConnell. We were sending a message that would directly challenge the narrative being spread by powerful interests, and there was a serious threat of retaliation. He also protested rather loudly that there were some things he *couldn't sell*. Then, to top off his list of complaints, he began to make pointed references to the outcome of the 2012 United States Presidential Election with regard to the book's publication date.

It became clear that we were being asked to significantly alter, if not eliminate, material. The editor seemed to be giving me a thinly veiled ultimatum. Either we get on board and do things his way or he'd negate the contract. At one point, he even suggested that we change the focus of the manuscript away from cyberwar and write an entirely different book.

This is what happens when you sign on with a publishing house where the higher ups believe in "deep editing." Given the effort involved in the project, we were hesitant to walk away. Though that's exactly what we should've done; the minute that he mentioned the 2012 Presidential Election. Instead we adopted a strategy of gentle resistance, a sort of quicksand approach, where we persistently challenged the editor's comments by supplying counter-arguments and then requesting feedback. Unfortunately he decided not to engage in dialogue. As months passed, the editor became unresponsive. Then, after almost a year of work, the publisher abruptly canceled the contract.

As you can see, we were eventually able to find a new publisher to work with. Indeed, we applaud TrineDay for having the courage to back this project at a time when other mainstream publishers, being confronted with a reality that made them just a bit uncomfortable, scurried back into the woodwork. Such are the risks of speaking truth to power.

The Public Relations Industry

The 20th century has been characterized by three developments of great political importance: The growth of democracy; the growth of corporate power; and the growth of corporate propaganda as a means of protecting corporate power against democracy.

– Alex Carey[9]

America has no functioning democracy.

– Former President Jimmy Carter[10]

In the lead up to World War I, President Woodrow Wilson found himself in a difficult position. By maintaining a stance of neutrality during his first term as President, he won his second term with the campaign slogan "He kept us out of war." Shortly after the launch of his second term he pulled a 180-degree turn and decided that the United States needed to enter the war. How could he convince the population to go along with him when they'd already given a mandate for continued neutrality?

To move the American public into his corner, President Wilson formed the Committee on Public Information, also known as the *Creel Committee* (after its chair, journalist George Creel). The Creel Committee headed up a massive campaign to influence public opinion. For example, it amassed a division of some 75,000 "Four Minute Men," a group of volunteers who were given talking points and sent out to give speeches.[11] Their presentations tended to be about four minutes in length, somewhere in the neighborhood of the purported average attention span.

To demonize the enemy, Germans were depicted as bloodthirsty Huns.[12] In particular, the Creel Committee fabricated a story about "Corpse Utilization Plants," which claimed that the Germans were taking the bodies of their own dead soldiers and boiling them down to manufacture pig food and munitions.[13] This story was bolstered by alleged eyewitness accounts appearing in other news sources, who described the gory details of the factories operations.

One member of the Creel Committee, Edward Bernays, is seen as the grandfather of modern propaganda. Bernays is credited with inventing the term *public relations* (aka PR). He did so admittedly to avoid the stigma associated with the word "propaganda."[14] More recently, people within the public relations industry have begun to call what they do as *perception management*. But these are just pleasant sounding euphemisms.

In the discipline of economics they have what's called the *efficient market hypothesis* (EMH) which is a concept used to help describe how markets work.[15] The EMH is founded on the premise that in a properly functioning market, people have access to accurate information and think rationally (see Figure 1).

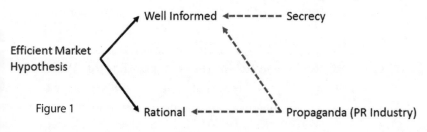

Figure 1

5

In economic markets, the public relations industry at times works assiduously to subvert this scenario, to prevent things from operating efficiently. Those who disseminate propaganda don't necessarily want people to have access to good information. Rather, the architects of propaganda have been known to employ tactics that appeal to people on an emotional level rather than a rational one. To see these tactics in action all you have to do is inspect a couple of beer commercials.

The emphasis on primal responses is no accident. Bernays, as it turns out, was the nephew of Sigmund Freud and he was heavily influenced by his uncle's theory of the mind. Drawing from the subject of psychoanalysis, Bernays argued that people were driven by unconscious and irrational forces that, if not reined in, could tear society apart. As a result, he believed that large-scale manipulation of public opinion was not only possible, but necessary:

> The conscious and intelligent manipulation of the organized habits and opinions of the masses is an important element in democracy society. Those who manipulate this unseen mechanism of society constitute an invisible government which is the true ruling power of our country.[16]

Bernays called his approach, *the engineering of consent*.[17] He applied his tools of on behalf of corporate titans like General Electric and the American Tobacco Corporation. In the 1950s, as the Cold War was kicking into high gear, Bernays led a propaganda campaign at the behest of the United Fruit Corporation (UFC). UFC had land holdings in Guatemala that were threatened by nationalization. Bernays utilized the press to create the perception of a Communist threat, inciting a brutal military coup.[18]

In addition to his Uncle Sigmund, Bernays' ideas were shaped by another prominent thinker: Walter Lippmann. Lippmann was a celebrated journalist and a founder of *The New Republic* magazine. During World War I he was an advisor to President Wilson and was involved in the composition of Wilson's "Fourteen Points" speech. He was also the general secretary of a clandestine quasi-intelligence outfit called "The Inquiry" which was set up by President Wilson for the sake of "drawing up the embryonic outlines of the postwar world."[19]

In his 1922 book entitled *Public Opinion*, Lippmann claimed that the complexities of governance were too much for normal people, such that the "common interest" wasn't always obvious. Instead, the process must be managed by a "specialized class" of elite technocrats who knew what they were doing:

> The common interests very largely elude public opinion entirely, and can be managed only by a specialized class whose personal interests reach beyond the locality.

Lippmann's worldview was later echoed by American political scientist Harold Lasswell:

> The modern propagandist, like the modern psychologist, recognizes that men are often poor judges of their own interests, flitting from one alternative to the next without solid reason.
>
> Democracy in America has compelled a whole new technique of control, largely through propaganda because of the ignorance and superstition of the masses.[20]

Lippmann believed that this specialized class, having identified policies that benefited the common interest, could then generate support for their decisions by *manufacturing consent* (Bernays' idea of engineering consent is derived from this concept). In a nutshell, Lippmann advocated that the specialized class make decisions and then convince society to go along after the fact, using propaganda.

Looking at these formative years, it's clear that the foundations of modern propaganda were established by people who believed that society generally wasn't capable of governing itself. They postulated that people couldn't be trusted to make good decisions and that they would be better off leaving the work to government technocrats who then generated support for their decisions using the tools of public relations. This scheme for democracy was embraced, and propaganda has become the primary means through which the elite communicate with the rest of society.[21]

Historically the American elite have been known to shun democracy in matters of global dominion. Such that public opinion is a mere peripheral issue. For example, speaking to Richard Nixon on the need to depose Chilean President Salvador Allende, Henry Kissinger advised:

> Allende is now president. The State Department thinks we can coexist with him, but I want you to make sure you tell everybody in the U.S. government that we cannot, that we cannot let him succeed, because he has legitimacy. He is democratically elected. And suppose other governments decide to follow in his footstep, like a government like Italy? What are we going to do then? What are we going to say when other countries start to democratically elect other Salvador Allendes? We will – the world balance of power will change ... [22]

Here's another instance where an elite spokesman lets the truth slip out. In August of 2013, at the American Legislative Exchange Council (ALEC) conference in Chicago, one right-wing think-tank fellow made the following statement about the necessary ingredients required to amend the Constitution:

> Oh, well, you really don't need people to do this. You just need control over the legislature and you need money, and we have both. [23]

In democratic forms of governance, where the population is supposed to participate in decision making, citizens need access to good information in order to properly exercise sound judgment. This is in line with Karl Popper's concept of an *open society*. Given the capacity of PR to obfuscate facts and rely on emotionally potent appeals, it can be a powerful means to subvert democracy (see Figure 2). Financial columnist Igor Greenwald comments:

> Corporations lie more convincingly than individuals. They have the resources to hire experts and lobbyists. They can buy any overt advertising they might require from wholly-owned media subsidiaries. [24]

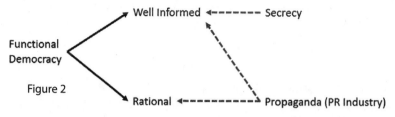

Figure 2

Secrecy can likewise play a similar role in terms of undermining the decision making process, even in presumably democratic political systems. In this regard, national security is a near universal pretext that leaders turn to when they want to keep the public in the dark.[25]

Both of these tools, propaganda and secrecy, will be on display in this book.

Behold a Pale Farce

And I looked, and behold a pale horse: and his name that sat on him was Death, and Hell followed with him.

–Revelations 6:8 King James Bible

Figure 3

The reason why we've devoted so much bandwidth in this preface to propaganda and media studies is that the people promoting the concept of cyberwar rely heavily on tactics honed by the PR industry. As we'll demonstrate, the notion of cyberwar is accompanied by a slew of doomsday scenarios: altogether farcical tales of the end times. We personally doubt very much that these vivid worst-case scenarios are intended to encourage logical thought, hence this book's title.

The primary outcome of the cyberwar campaign is mass anxiety, where people become so apprehensive and uneasy that they'll accept any solution to feel safe again. This is convenient because the solutions being proposed by the cyberwar crowd harken back to the Cold War. There's a heavy emphasis on massive retaliation and Orwellian surveillance schemes, neither of which are constructive approaches. These supposed remedies would only channel vast sums of money to the defense industry and further infringe on our civil liberties by enhancing government control.

There's a very real effort afoot to create the perception of an imminent and grave threat. A public that feels panicky will pay dearly to make the anxiety go away, much to the benefit of the same people stoking the coals of alarm. What society needs to do is to collectively step back, take a deep breath, and approach the topic from a more rational frame of mind.

As far as the domain of politics is concerned, propaganda and secrecy will always exist as means to sabotage decision making. In countries like the United States, however, which have provisions for freedom of speech, there are opportunities to shed light on complicated topics.

In a nutshell: that's what this book is all about.

Organization

This book is divided into four parts. In the first part we present a sampling of cyberwar hyperbole that's received media coverage, identify a couple of the more prominent actors, and follow the policies that have been enacted. Next, we'll take a closer look at China to provide some context against which assertions in the first chapter can be judged. Finally, we set up the second part of the book by developing a cataloguing scheme for cyber incidents. To treat an ailment you first need an accurate diagnosis. Our goal is to establish precise definitions so that we can cultivate an accurate picture of what's actually going on.

In the second part of the book we survey a number of high-profile cyber incidents and classify them according to definitions established at the end of the first part. What we discovered was an overwhelming preponderance of crime and espionage. We didn't, however, encounter any cyber incidents that could be interpreted as cyberwar. Yet cyberwar has been portrayed as an impending threat, one which is certain to transpire. Hence, at the end of part two we introduce the concept of *threat inflation* to expose the underlying dynamics at work.

In the third part of the book we examine solutions that have been offered to protect the United States from the threat of cyberwar. Specifically, the Cold War strategy of deterrence is explored at length and, in lieu of its failings, we wade into the details of the rising surveillance state. Neither of these options is attractive or even feasible. Yet they would both waste vast amounts of money and sacrifice our liberty on the altar of national security. This leads to part four of the book.

In part four we mull over the factors that actually allow cyber-attacks to succeed and steps that can be taken to mitigate them. When it comes to security breaches there are a number of factors working together on various levels. But all factors aren't equal and some factors are actually used by the software industry to obscure more central ones. In light of this we focus primarily on the crisis of poor software design and the market forces that drive it. We also recommend re-orienting our national security strategy towards developing truly resilient software and deploying it at a grass-roots level.

Acknowledgments

We have an executive, a Department of Justice, that's unwilling to prosecute high officials who lied to Congress and the country on camera, but they'll stop at nothing to persecute someone who told them the truth.

– Edward Snowden[26]

This book was composed over what could be characterized as a long forced march. Despite the obstacles, dead ends, ambushes, constant frustration, and hostile environment that beset the project, we stubbornly pressed onward. As in any demanding situation, persistence and optimism were the keys to success.

The stakes are high. Society is being deluged with a perception of threat, a misdiagnosis that has been inflated well beyond what it deserves, in an effort to promote solutions which will undermine our collective security. We have faith that by presenting people with evidence-based conclusions, by appealing to reason, the debate can be shifted away from hyperbole and towards effective broad-based security measures.

There have been many people who offered their assistance during the writing process. In particular we'd like to express our gratitude to George Ledin at UC Sonoma for his support and encouragement. George is one of the very few professors in the United State, who openly lecture on malware designs and his willingness to charge headlong into this nascent field of study is commendable.

Norm Matloff is a professor at UC Davis who works tirelessly to counteract the growing trend of outsourcing (i.e. global labor arbitrage). It's a topic, very much like cyberwar, were corporate-funded propaganda has taken root and holds a disproportionate amount of sway. Norm's activism in this area, to expose the lies and fabrications of corporate spin masters, does a great service to computer scientists all over the country.

We'd also like thank George Smith, a Senior Fellow at GlobalSecurity.org who coined the phrase *Cult of Cyberwar*. George has been tracking this topic for years, and his thoughts on cyberwar have been vital.

That goes double for John Young and Deborah Natsios, who manage the leaks site *Cryptome*. They have consistently offered the world their uncensored view of the security industry. For years John skeptically claimed that the intelligence services had systematically compromised technology across the board. Some people have dismissed his observations as the ranting of a paranoid geezer, "art as evidence" they say. It turns out the grouchy old cynic was right on the money.

Canadian filmmaker Scott Noble also deserves credit for directing a series of powerful, well-researched documentaries that were a significant source of inspiration for this book. Scott's work covers topics like public relations, government secrecy, clandestine operations, and other insidious tools of social control. His films provide a backdrop for what you'll read herein, and can be viewed online for free.[27] It's time very well spent, nay transformative.

Three cheers for Noam Chomsky over on the East Coast, the ideological epicenter of the progressive movement. Noam is a voice of conscience who asks that in the realm of foreign policy we apply to ourselves the same standards that we apply to others. It's this aspect of his analysis that fundamentally shaped this book's stance.

On the other side of the country, nigh the hills of Berkeley, poet and scholar Peter Dale Scott writes voluminously on how sources of wealth and violence outside of government – organized crime, NGOs, transnational corporations, lobbyists, big oil, drug cartels, arms manufacturers, and global financiers – use their influence to exercise state policy. That is, Peter deftly reveals the nature and dealings of the *Deep State*. It's a term that resonates with us as we see our formal institutions as being driven primarily by subtle currents that typically flow beneath the surface of ordinary political discourse.

We'd like to tip our hat to Glenn Greenwald at the *Guardian*. When we discovered that Glenn had been targeted by a goon squad (known as *Team Themis*: HBGary Federal, Palantir, and Berico) on behalf of a major financial institution, we knew it was a sure sign that his journalism had merit. Though, in an effort to inoculate against reflexive ovation, we've begun haunting a blog known as *The Rancid Honeytrap*.[28]

A number of whistleblowers have sacrificed both their careers and their well-being to publicize government programs that pose an enormous threat to our Constitutional liberties. They've also revealed our government officials as a collection of pathological liars. In particular, we're referring to patriots like Philip Agee, Daniel Ellsberg, Chris Pyle, John Stockwell, Ray McGovern, Thomas Tamm, Mark Klein, Thomas Drake, William Binney, Russell Tice, Chelsea Manning, John Kiriakou and Edward Snowden. This book owes these whistleblowers a tremendous debt of gratitude. By virtue of their disclosures, they provided direct, and often damning, evidence to back conclusions that otherwise could only be alluded to with circumstantial evidence.

Then there are publishers like *WikiLeaks* who channel this information to the public. Julian Assange has done the world a service by demonstrating just how subservient the mainstream media outlets have become. The various interests promoting the idea of cyberwar have been able to propagate their message in part because of their connections with the press. Such are the hazards of organizations that monetize information under the rubric of public service. What this shows is that cyberwar propaganda isn't just late-night geek fodder, it says something significant about the current state of journalism.

Make no mistake about it, the aggressive prosecution of whistleblowers and efforts to hobble journalists ultimately translate into a fundamental attack on democracy.[29] While heads of government may publicly intimate[30] that harsher measures will be taken if newspapers fail to show the necessary "social responsibility," the spies aren't anywhere near as coy:

> You've had your fun. Now we want the stuff back.[31]

Finally, we'd like to show some love to all of the professionals at TrineDay who dutifully applied their expertise to make this book happen. Kris Millegan has devoted his life to exposing the intrigues of a relatively small group of plutocrats who relentlessly purchase influence on behalf of their own narrow financial interests. After reading the foreword which he wrote to Daniel Estulin's *Shadow Masters*, we knew that Kris wouldn't back down as the original publisher did. There's a term for this sort of thing: most people call it *integrity*. A vicious class war is raging in the United States and the Devil takes the hindmost.[32] While our social fabric crumbles, society needs this kind of integrity more than ever.

$\Theta(e^x)$,
Bill Blunden and Violet Cheung

Endnotes

1) Glenn Greenwald, "As Europe erupts over US spying, NSA chief says government must stop media," *Guardian*, October 25, 2013, http://www.theguardian.com/commentisfree/2013/oct/25/europe-erupts-nsa-spying-chief-government.

2) Kevin Gosztola, "Glenn Greenwald's Speech to the Socialism Conference [with Transcript]," *FireDogLake*, June 29, 2013, http://dissenter.firedoglake.com/2013/06/29/glenn-greenwalds-speech-to-the-socialism-conference-with-transcript/.

3) Edward Herman and Noam Chomsky, *Manufacturing Consent: The Political Economy of the Mass Media*, Pantheon Books, 1988.

4) US Newspaper Circulation Averages for the Six Months ended: 9/30/2011, Audit Bureau of Circulations, http://abcas3.accessabc.com/ecirc/newstitlesearchus.asp.

5) Catherine Holahan, "The Case for Freeing the WSJ Online," *BusinessWeek*, August 10, 2007, http://www.businessweek.com/technology/content/aug2007/tc20070810_305348.htm.

6) Scott Mayerowitz, "What Do the Rich and Powerful Read?" ABC News, July 28, 2007, http://abcnews.go.com/Business/IndustryInfo/story?id=3421988&page=1.

7) Marshall McLuhan and Quentin Fiore, *War and Peace In the Global Village: An Inventory of Some of the Current Spastic Situations That Could Be Eliminated by More Feedforward*, Hardwired, 1997.

8) *Cyberwar: Hyperbole and Reality*, SFSU's National Cybersecurity Awareness Event, 2010, http://www.belowgotham.com/SFSU-2010-Blunden-Slides.pdf.

9) Alex Carey, *Taking the Risk out of Democracy*, University of Illinois Press, 1997, chapter 2, page 18.

10) Alberto Riva, "Jimmy Carter: US 'has no functioning democracy,'" *Salon*, July 18, 2013, http://www.salon.com/2013/07/18/jimmy_carter_us_has_no_functioning_democracy_partner/.

11) United States. The White House. *Committee on Public Information. Purpose and Plan of Four Minute Men*. Washington D.C.: Government Printing Office, 1917, http://libcudl.colorado.edu/wwi/pdf/i7178116x.pdf.

12) Thomas Fleming, *The Illusion of Victory: America in World War I*. New York: Basic Books, 2003; pg. 247.

13) Randall Martin, *The Art of Faking Credentials*, MercatorNet, March 26, 2008, http://www.mercatornet.com/articles/view/the_art_of_faking_credentials.

14) *Century of the Self*, directed by Adam Curtis, BBC Four, 2002, http://video.google.com/videoplay?docid=9167657690296627941.

15) Eugene Fama, *Efficient Capital Markets: A Review of Theory and Empirical Work*, The Journal of Finance, Volume 25, Number 2, May 1970, pages 383-417.

16) Edward Bernays, *Propaganda*, Ig Publishing, September 2004. ISBN 0970312598.

17) Edward L. Bernays (1947), *The Engineering of Consent*, The Annals of the American Academy of Political and Social Science, 250 p. 113.

18) Larry Type, *The Father of Spin: Edward L. Bernays and The Birth of Public Relations*, Picador, 2002, ISBN-13: 978-0805067897.

19) Ronald Steel, *Walter Lippmann and the American Century*, Transaction Publishers, 2008, p. 128.

20) Harold Lasswell, "Propaganda," *Encyclopedia of the Social Sciences*, Macmillan, 1954.

21) *Psywar*, Directed by Scott Noble, Metanoia Films, Canada, 2010, http://metanoia-films.org/psywar/.

22) "'Make the Economy Scream': Secret Documents Show Nixon, Kissinger Role Backing 1973 Chile Coup," *Democracy Now!*, September 10, 2013, http://www.democracynow.org/2013/9/10/40_years_after_chiles_9_11#.

23) Theresa Riley, "Inside the 'ALEC Universe'," *Bill Moyers and Company*, August 15, 2013, http://billmoyers.com/category/what-matters-today/the-united-states-of-alec/.

24) Igor Greenwald, "Is Capitalism Dying?" *Forbes*, January 7, 2013, http://www.forbes.com/sites/igorgreenwald/2013/01/07/is-capitalism-dying/print/.

25) Alan Cowell, "Cameron Criticizes The *Guardian* for Publishing Secrets," *New York Times*, October 17, 2013, http://www.nytimes.com/2013/10/17/world/europe/cameron-criticizes-the-guardian-for-publishing-secrets.html.

26) "Edward Snowden Speaks Out Against NSA 'Dragnet Mass Surveillance,'" *Democracy Now!* October 14, 2013, http://www.democracynow.org/2013/10/14/edward_snowden_speaks_out_against_nsa#.

27) http://metanoia-films.org/films/.

28) http://ohtarzie.wordpress.com/.

29) Committee to Protect Journalists, *The Obama Administration and the Press: Leak investigations and surveillance in post-9/11 America*, October 10, 2013, http://cpj.org/reports/2013/10/obama-and-the-press-us-leaks-surveillance-post-911.php.

30) Nicholas Watt, "David Cameron makes veiled threat to media over NSA and GCHQ leaks," *Guardian*, October 28, 2013, http://www.theguardian.com/world/2013/oct/28/david-cameron-nsa-threat-newspapers-guardian-snowden/print.

31) Alan Rusbridger, "David Miranda, schedule 7 and the danger that all reporters now face," *Guardian*, August 19, 2013, http://www.theguardian.com/commentisfree/2013/aug/19/david-miranda-schedule7-danger-reporters.

32) Jacob S. Hacker and Paul Pierson, *Winner-Take-All Politics: How Washington Made the Rich Richer – and Turned Its Back on the Middle Class*, Simon & Schuster, March 15, 2011, ISBN-13: 978-1416588702.

Prologue

The Wonder of it All

Behold a cavalcade of legislators, government officials, and think-tank fellows. They claim that the United States waivers perilously at the brink of catastrophe. These people believe that foreign powers are poised to cripple the U.S. power grid and decimate the banking system. They warn that if we fail to implement the measures which they endorse, we risk a Cyber-Armageddon.

Yet this End Times narrative is a farce, and a pale one at that. These doomsday scenarios serve only to benefit the military-industrial complex. Cyberwar propaganda is an instance of threat inflation. Much as during the run-up to the disastrous global War on Terror. The message of cyberwar is eliciting a crisis mentality. The end result is an anxious public that's susceptible to ill-conceived, but highly profitable, solutions.

Once more, while the apparatchiks sound the alarm about external threats, there are genuine threats emanating from within. America's Deep State is busy executing campaigns of espionage and sabotage in foreign networks. U.S. intelligence agencies are embroiled in covert operations at home and abroad which have been instrumental in the emergence of a sprawling underground industry that develops weaponized malware and Orwellian mass-interception tools. Proponents explain that these developments are necessary to ensure our "national security." The reality is that this decidedly offensive approach is seriously *undermining* our collective security.

In these pages you'll see who is spreading the cyberwar message, the nature of the game being played, the real threats that we're being distracted from, and the often unacknowledged root causes of our growing cyber-insecurity.

Part I – Rampant Hyperbole

Chapter 1

A Backdrop of Metaphors

Today, we are in a stealthy cyber war in America. And we're losing.

– Congressman Mike Rogers[1]

In November of 2011, a security researcher named Joe Weiss blogged[2] about a report released by the Illinois Statewide Terrorism and Intelligence Center[3] earlier in the month. The report procured by Weiss, titled *Public Water District Cyber Intrusion*, claimed that a Russian hacker had succeeded in breaching a SCADA system at an unnamed water utility, destroying a water pump by turning the system on and off repeatedly.

SCADA is an acronym that stands for *Supervisory Control and Data Acquisition*. SCADA systems are specialized computer installations used to monitor and control equipment in an industrial setting (e.g. in a factory or power plant). A SCADA system typically consists of a central host computer, known as the *Master Terminal Unit* (MTU), which communicates over a network with a set of *field data interface devices*, the eyes and ears of the SCADA system (e.g. meters, valve position transmitters). There are a couple of SCADA sub-components that we'll see again. Specifically, SCADA systems use what are known as *Remote Terminal Units* (RTUs) to collect data from field data interface devices. SCADA systems also employ *Programmable Logic Controllers* (PLCs) to automate the operation of field data interface devices. SCADA systems are important because they're ubiquitous; the operation of our infrastructure depends upon them.

The attack described by Weiss was discovered when an outside repairman investigated the broken water pump. The repairman examined the SCADA system's log files and noticed a Russian IP address. He concluded that the system had been breached and routed his alert to the Environmental Protection Agency, which in turn contacted the Illinois Department of Homeland Security fusion center.

This DHS report didn't provide explicit details in its alert about the nature of the SCADA system that was attacked, or any forensic information (e.g. the system vendor, the attack vector, or the owner of the compromised installation). This did little to prevent Weiss from speculating that a successful attack could pose a threat to our nuclear arsenal. He told reporters:

> If this is a [big software vendor], this could be so ugly, because a biggie would have not only systems in water utilities but a biggie could even be [used] in nukes.
>
> Everybody keeps asking how come you don't see attacks on SCADA systems? Well, here it is guys.[4]

Homeland Security representatives inferred that the victim was located in Springfield, Illinois. It was later revealed that the water station in question belonged to the Curran Gardner Public Water District, just outside of Springfield.

Never Mind: False Alarm

Oddly, in a matter of days the DHS began to backtrack on its original announcement. DHS spokesman Peter Boogaard claimed that the DHS and FBI were still "gathering facts" and that:

> At this time there is no credible corroborated data that indicates a risk to critical infrastructure entities or a threat to public safety.[5]

Information provided by utility officials was even more conservative. Don Craven, a trustee of the water district, confirmed that:

> The water district is up and running and things are fine…. The water district has multiple wells, multiple pumps. There's no break in service, no lack of water. No concern of quality of water, safety of water…. I drank the water this morning.

The alleged Russian hacker was actually an engineer named Jim Mimlitz who had been contacted on his cell phone for technical support. At the time of the alleged intrusion, he and his family were on vacation in Russia and so he logged in remotely to lend a hand. The destruction of the water pump was completely unrelated. As Mimlitz explains:

> The system has a lot of logging capability. It logs everything. All of the logs showed that the pump failed for some electrical-mechanical reason. But it did not have anything to do with the SCADA system.[6]

The result of this chain of events was a burst of press releases more inclined towards premature speculation rather than measured deliberation.

The Madness of Crowds

The previous story is a typical example of the kind of overblown rhetoric that has been embodied by a series of metaphors which have appeared in public debate over the past few years. We'll spend much of this chapter looking at a few of these metaphors. The associated hyperbole is dangerous because it strikes a raw nerve in the psychic lattice. With homage to Charles Mackay, it elicits the madness of crowds.

In the aftermath of 9/11, terror has taken center stage as the threat du jour. Consider the following statement by Barack Obama made during his 2008 Presidential campaign:

> Every American depends – directly or indirectly – on our system of information networks. They are increasingly the backbone of our economy and our infrastructure; our national security and our personal well-being. But it's no secret that terrorists could use our computer networks to deal us a crippling blow.[7]

At the end of his first term in office, President Obama ran with the cyber meme and described additional worst-case scenarios:

> In a future conflict, an adversary unable to match our military supremacy on the battlefield might seek to exploit our computer vulnerabilities here at home. Taking down vital banking systems could trigger a financial crisis. The lack of clean water or functioning hospitals could spark a public health emergency. And as we've seen in past blackouts, the loss of electricity can bring businesses, cities and entire regions to a standstill.[8]

Yet again, during his 2013 State of the Union Address, Obama told the country that doomsday is potentially lurking around the corner.

> We know foreign countries and companies swipe our corporate secrets. Now our enemies are also seeking the ability to sabotage our power grid, our financial institutions, and our air traffic control systems.[9]

Humans aren't necessarily rational creatures and they tend to inflate spectacular risks that are rare.[10] This is why people are often more scared of flying than they are of driving. When security wonks, or even the President, make intimations about cyber-terrorists fiddling with hardware in nuclear weapons it only exacerbates this pathology.

This is despite the fact that the State Department reported that in 2010 fewer than 20 U.S. citizens were killed in incidents of terror[11] (as opposed to the 30,196 people who died in automobile accidents in 2010).[12] In fact, in terms of raw probability, you're about as likely to be killed in an act of terrorism as you to be crushed by a heavy piece of furniture.[13]

This is what makes all of this semantically loaded bombast so toxic: it discourages the formal process of objective risk assessment with speculative worst-case scenarios that serve only to fuel anxiety. And it's this sort of distortion that makes it difficult to effectively protect ourselves.

An Electronic Pearl Harbor

Let's rewind all the way back to the summer of 1991, a little more than a year after Microsoft released Windows 3.0, when a security industry personality named Winn Schwartau testified in front of a congressional subcommittee about the overall state of computer security. It was there, in the halls of Capitol Hill, that the *Pearl Harbor* cyberwar metaphor gained traction.

He stated that:

> Government and commercial computer systems are so poorly protected today they can essentially be considered defenseless – an Electronic Pearl Harbor waiting to happen.

In May of 1997, this phrase popped up again when former U.S. Deputy Attorney General Jamie Gorelick was quoted as saying that if we weren't careful we'd have, "a cyber equivalent of Pearl Harbor at some point."[14]

But not everyone accepted this metaphor. For example, in February of 2000, during a photo opportunity with members of the hi-tech industry, then President Bill Clinton ran into the Pearl Harbor metaphor when a nearby reporter asked about a series of high-profile denial of service attacks against Amazon and eBay.

> **Q:** Would you entertain one last question, sir? We've always heard for the last four or five years that it was going to take an electronic Pearl Harbor – many of the people around this table I've interviewed over the last four or five years and they've agreed that's the kind of impact we would need for everybody to play together and work together. Is that what happened last week?
>
> **The President:** Well, I hope not. (Laughter.) I think it was an alarm. I don't think it was Pearl Harbor. We lost our Pacific fleet at Pearl Harbor – I don't think the analogous loss was that great. But I think it—
>
> **Q:** Was it of concern—
>
> **The President:** Look, it's a source of concern, but I don't think we should leave here with this vast sense of insecurity. We ought to leave here with a sense of confidence that this is a challenge that was entirely predictable; it's part of the price of the success of the Internet; and we're all determined to work together to meet it.

All told, this is a remarkably coherent response, especially when compared to the prominent overstatements that you'll encounter in this chapter. While Clinton agreed that there was indeed a threat associated with denial of service attacks, he also acknowledged that the corresponding risk *wasn't on the same scale* as the Japanese bombing of Pearl Harbor.

A closer look at recorded denial of service attacks, like the 2007 incident in Estonia, affirms Clinton's stance. A *Denial of Service* (DoS) *attack* attempts to overwhelm hosts on the Internet by flooding them with client requests. They occur out in the wild when too many people visit the same web site simultaneously. A web server being subjected to an onslaught of web page requests sometimes can't keep up with the demand being placed on it and falters. It's like a waiter at a restaurant trying to service too many tables.

The worst thing that can happen as the result of a denial of service attack is that the targeted server will go down until the network engineers find a way to address the corresponding bandwidth problem, or the attack lets up. The damages incurred are almost always limited to lost revenue due to downtime, in addition to the cost of provisioning equipment and services to resume operation. In the pantheon of recorded cyber-attacks, denial of service incidents have resided on the low-impact side of the scale. None of them have involved the transfer, modification, or destruction of data.

Contrast the Estonia denial-of-service incident against the attack on Pearl Harbor which killed thousands of Americans, sunk four of our eight battleships, and irrevocably altered the course of world history. Anyone who equates a denial of service attack with Pearl Harbor is engaged in contemptible exaggeration that perverts the type of threat that a denial of service attack usually represents. Yet some people would point to denial of service attacks and liken them to out-and-out military assaults.

Looking back at the incident in Estonia, *Wired* columnist Kevin Poulsen observes:

> We see, for example, that Estonia's computer emergency response team responded to the junk packets with technical aplomb and coolheaded professionalism, while Estonia's leadership ... well, didn't. Faced with DDoS [Distributed Denial of Service] and nationalistic, cross-border hacktivism – nuisances that have plagued the rest of the wired world for the better part of a decade – Estonia's leaders lost perspective.[15]

Indeed, Estonia's decision makers took a stance that openly embraced hysteria. In an interview with the press, then speaker of the Estonian parliament, Ene Ergma, breathlessly exclaimed to a reporter:

> When I look at a nuclear explosion and the explosion that happened in our country in May, I see the same thing... Like

nuclear radiation, cyberwar doesn't make you bleed, but it can destroy everything.[16]

Bombast aside, temporary loss of service doesn't have to translate into a calamity, particularly when the service provider is prepared in advance. This isn't an unreasonable expectation, either. Continuity of business measures are standard fare in the enterprise, even if it's something as simple as pulling out a manual credit card imprinter when point-of-sale terminals go down.

It's also possible to take a denial-of-service attack and magnify the consequences to generate the desired visceral response. For example, in November of 2009, security software vendor McAfee released its 2009 Virtual Criminology Report which was entitled *Virtually Here: The Age of Cyber Warfare*.[17] The cover of the report displays a stark black and white photo of a nuclear reactor off in the distance.

Given the absence of genuine cyber catastrophes, the report settles for dwelling on hypotheticals. As such, it extrapolates rather pedestrian Distributed Denial of Service (DDoS) attacks and uses these incidents to make conjectures about just how bad fully fledged cyberwar *might* be.

For example, Scott Borg, the director of the U.S. Cyber Consequences Unit (a think tank), stated that "People were provided with attack tools, targets and timing in the Georgia cyber campaign," referencing Russian defacement and denial of service attacks against official Georgian websites. These attacks accompanied more traditional warfare during the South Ossetia war. By itself, this allegation isn't really that disquieting, as DDoS attacks are commonplace. To elevate the reader's heart rate, Borg took these otherwise ordinary events and used them to hint at something much more menacing. Specifically, he warns that:

> So far this technique has been used in denial-of-service and other similar attacks. In the future it will be used to organize people to commit more devastating attacks.

While the Pearl Harbor metaphor fell out of favor for a while, it was resuscitated by officials in DC to garner support for legislation or derive new sources of funding. During his confirmation hearing for

Secretary of Defense in June of 2011, then CIA chief Leon Panetta advised members of the Senate Armed Services Committee that:

> The next Pearl Harbor we confront could very well be a cyber-attack that cripples our power systems, our grid, our security systems, our financial systems, our governmental systems.

Again, during an interview with *60 Minutes,* he reiterated his doomsday vision:

> The reality is that there is the cyber capability to basically bring down our power grid to create ... to paralyze our financial system in this country to virtually paralyze our country.[18]

In this case, some context might help. Panetta's remarks on *60 Minutes* were made in January of 2012 right, around the same time that President Obama was pushing his vision of a leaner military, which mandated some $487 billion in Defense Budget cuts spread over ten years.[19] Per the Budget Control Act of 2011, the Pentagon also faced another $600 billion in cuts over the next ten years if Congress isn't able to sufficiently reduce federal spending.[20]

A Cyber-Katrina

Of course, many other cyberwar metaphors are also in circulation. On April 1st of 2009, Senators Jay Rockefeller (D-W. Va.) and Olympia Snowe (R-ME) introduced the *Cybersecurity Act of 2009.*[21] During their announcement of the bill, Rockefeller stated that:

> We must protect our critical infrastructure at all costs – from our water to our electricity, to banking, traffic lights and electronic health records.... As a member of the Senate Intelligence Committee, I know the threats we face. Our enemies are real, they are sophisticated, they are determined and they will not rest.[22]

Senator Snowe further cautioned that:

> Our failure to implement effective policies and procedures to protect critical infrastructure, prevent invasive intrusion and conduct an aggressive threat assessment has proven extremely

consequential, putting the American information system at grave risk. It is abundantly clear we must unite on all fronts to confront this monumental challenge, if we fail to take swift action, we, regrettably, risk a cyber-Katrina.

It turns out that Senator Snowe wasn't being original when referring to a cyber-Katrina. If you peruse the initial working draft of the proposed legislation, you'll spot the following endorsement on the fourth page:

> (6) Paul Kurtz, a Partner and chief operating officer of Good Harbor Consulting as well as a senior advisor to the Obama Transition Team for cybersecurity, recently stated that the United States is unprepared to respond to a "cyber-Katrina" and that "a massive cyber disruption could have a cascading, long-term impact without adequate co-ordination between government and the private sector."[23]

Paul Kurtz is one of many recurring characters in the cyberwar milieu. At the tail end of the 1990s, he was the director for counterterrorism in the National Security Council's Office of Transnational Threats. In 2003, he was tapped to serve as the senior director for critical infrastructure protection on the White House's Homeland Security Council. During the Clinton and G.W. Bush administrations he was a member of the National Security Council. That was this guy's bread and butter: infrastructure protection.

After retiring to the private sector, he ended up at a boutique consulting company named Good Harbor. Good Harbor specializes in *risk management,* an official-sounding but nebulous umbrella term that covers everything from airport security to urban planning.

The 2009 Cybersecurity Bill wasn't the first time that Kurtz deployed his cyber-Katrina metaphor, either. A couple months before the act was introduced, Kurtz wielded the term at a computer security conference in Arlington. Sitting in a room full of techies, Kurtz queried:

> Who is in charge [in the event of] a cyber-Katrina? ... Is it the FCC? DHS? Commerce? The White House? ... Is there a FEMA for the Internet?

In a sense, his question is reasonable. Nevertheless, at the same time, he blatantly succumbs to the urge to rely on hyperbole to make his point without stopping to ponder the likelihood of such a cataclysm actually taking place.

The Hiroshima of Cyberwar

In addition to the Pearl Harbor metaphor, another harrowing World War II allegory has also gained traction. Just check out the July 3, 2010 cover of *The Economist*, entitled "Cyberwar: The Threat from the Internet."[24] It features an urban cityscape engulfed by a digitized fireball. Very dramatic, but then again, magazine covers are often intended to get our attention and spur our curiosity rather than offer an accurate depiction of reality.

Nevertheless, the press cannot resist hinting at a nuclear holocaust. For example, at an industry conference in the summer of 2012, former FBI Executive Assistant Director Shawn Henry, representing his new security company CrowdStrike, caught the attention of news outlets when he equated malware with WMDs:

> The threat from computer network exploitation and computer attacks is the most significant threat society faces, other than a weapon of mass destruction going off … [25]

In June of 2010, news broke of a worm called *Stuxnet* which was discovered on industrial control systems all over Europe and Asia. In particular, the worm's malicious payload seemed to be directed precisely at programmable logic controller hardware used in the enrichment of uranium. Over half of the infections were found in Iran (whose enrichment program has drawn considerable condemnation).

It wasn't long before intimations of mass destruction began to stream from various news outlets. One security researcher referred to the malware's discovery as an *Oppenheimer Moment*.[26] Russia's ambassador to NATO, Dmitry Rogozin, claimed that malware like Stuxnet could lead to a *new Chernobyl*.[27] A reporter from *Vanity Fair* called it *the Hiroshima of cyberwar*,[28] then farcically added:

> We have crossed a threshold, and there is no turning back.

Reality check: let's stop for a moment and put things into perspective. The bomb that the United States dropped on Hiroshima killed over 100,000 people and leveled an entire city. To date, the impact of Stuxnet on Iran's nuclear program could best be likened to a digital speed bump that has marginally disrupted an enrichment program. Nobody died.

A Cyber 9/11

The images of the Twin Towers exploding into flames, bodies plummeting toward the earth, and billowing clouds of fluttery ash coalesce into a powerful symbol, an archetype of sorts. Given the sheer depth of the imprint that the terror attacks of 9/11 left on our collective unconscious, it was only a matter of time before the event was brandished to describe cyber threats. In December of 2012 former Director of National Intelligence (DNI), Mike McConnell told the *Financial Times*:

> We have had our 9/11 warning. Are we going to wait for the cyber equivalent of the collapse of the World Trade Centers? ... All of a sudden, the power doesn't work, there's no way you can get money, you can't get out of town, you can't get online, and banking, as a function to make the world work, starts to not be reliable ... [29]

This isn't the first time McConnell has said something like this. He actually has a long history of describing potential calamities to the press. In November of 2009, during a program broadcast of *60 Minutes*, McConnell suggested that:

> If I were an attacker and I wanted to do strategic damage to the United States, I would either take the cold of winter or the heat of summer, I probably would sack electric power on the U.S. East Coast, maybe the West Coast, and attempt to cause a cascading effect. All of those things are in the art of the possible from a sophisticated attacker.

Earlier, in the summer of 2009, McConnell made an even bolder claim:

> If the 19 terrorists who attacked the World Trade Center in 2001 had cyber-attacked one large New York bank and been successful in destroying the bank's data and backup data, we would have had an order of magnitude greater economic impact than 9/11 had on the world ... [30]

What McConnell fails to acknowledge is that major financial institutions tend to have elaborate disaster recovery plans in place. Production sites are buttressed by hot secondary sites that can resume transaction processing if the primary sites go down. Not to mention that it's common to maintain a series of remote data backups in fortified vaults. These vaults are sometimes depleted mines that were converted to storage facilities by companies like Iron Mountain in the early years of the Cold War. In other words, destroying a bank's data and backup data is a pretty tall order.

About half a year later, on February 23, 2010, McConnell gave testimony to the Senate Committee on Commerce, Science, and Transportation. Recall that this is the same committee, chaired by Jay Rockefeller, which gave birth to the *Cybersecurity Act of 2010*. During his testimony McConnell made inferences to cyber terrorism, presaging:

> Of particular concern is the rise of non-state actors who are motivated not by greed or a cause, but by those with a different world view who wish to destroy the information infrastructure which powers much of the modern world – the electric grid, the global financial system, the electronic health care records, the transportation networks.

Just a few days after his Senate Committee testimony, an op-ed piece that McConnell wrote appeared in the *Washington Post*. In this op-ed essay he declares that:

> The United States is fighting a cyberwar today, and we are losing. It's that simple. [31]

One aspect of this op-ed that stands out is that McConnell presents what he believes to be the answer to the problem of cyberwar. Specifically, he suggests that the United States could deal with cyberwar by turning to the Cold War strategy of *deterrence*. In other words, we could use the threat of massive retaliation to discourage other countries from attacking us; our adversaries would know that a cyber-attack on the United States would be met with an overwhelming and cataclysmic response.

The attraction of this approach is obvious given our Cold War history and the fall of the Soviet Union. The thinking goes that if it worked back then to prevent open aggression against NATO allies, perhaps it will also work now. However, there are reasons why the strategy of deterrence isn't as conceptually clean with regard to cyber-attacks, reasons that have to do with the basic assumptions of the deterrence doctrine and the nature of the Internet. We'll spend a significant amount of bandwidth in this book looking at these ideas in later chapters.

Dissenting Voices

The metaphors we've seen so far contrast sharply against the conclusions of a man named Howard Schmidt. He's is the exception to the rule. Schmidt spent a much of his career in law enforcement. He's worked as a beat cop, ran the FBI's Computer Exploitation Team, and served as Chief Security Officer for both Microsoft and eBay. In other words, Schmidt's gotten his hands dirty in the trenches. In the aftermath of 9/11 President Bush put him on the Critical Infrastructure Protection Board and he was also named as the special adviser for cyberspace security. In 2009, President Obama appointed him as the top computer security advisor for the White House.

What makes Schmidt stand out is his opinion on cyberwar. In March 2010, at an RSA conference in San Francisco, Schmidt told *Wired*:

> There is no cyberwar.... I think that is a terrible metaphor and I think that is a terrible concept.

He also added:

> As for getting into the power grid, I can't see that that's realistic.

Keep in mind that this is the guy who chaired the President's Critical Infrastructure Protection Board. This is the same guy who has had the ear of President Obama, who's just as experienced and credible as anyone else (though probably more so, based on his experience), calmly stating that all of the cyberwar doomsayers are full of it.

Once more, there are high-level people in the energy industry who agree with him. At the Reuters Cybersecurity Summit in May of 2013, Gerry Cauley, the chief executive of the North American Electric Reliability Corp (NERC, a national organization of U.S. electrical grid operators) told a reporter that there has never been a destructive cyber-attack on the grid[32] and that he was more concerned about physical threats (e.g. a small group armed with explosives) than he was about cyber threats.

This mindset would appear to be justified. For example, in the fall of 2013 there was a series of physical attacks against the power grid in Arkansas. In one incident someone stole a tractor and used it to take down two power line poles.[33] Police later arrested a self-employed pool maintenance worker in connection with the crimes.[34]

Cauley also stated that current attempts to hack into the power grid were "not that overwhelming" and added:

> Anyone who is smart enough to do those kinds of things has better things to do than shut the lights out ...[35]

In May of 2013, a report prepared by the staff of two congressmen described the results of a survey that included respondents from some 113 utilities. The report excitedly states:

> More than a dozen utilities reported "daily," "constant," or "frequent" attempted cyber-attacks ranging from phishing to malware infection to unfriendly probes. One utility reported that it was the target of approximately 10,000 attempted cyber-attacks each month.[36]

But the people actually running public utilities called the report "overblown," and observed that mandatory standards set by NERC where up to the task. Duane Highley, the chief executive of Arkansas Electric Cooperative Corporation, responded:

> Those are very routine kinds of attacks and we know very well how to protect against those.... Our control systems are not vulnerable to attack ...[37]

This should give one pause. What these dissenting opinions demonstrate, if anything, is that there's something fishy going on. A multitude of alleged experts have told us that we're beset on all sides by state-sponsored hackers who plan to destroy our infrastructure and send us whimpering back to the dark ages. But the President's chosen advisor, the head of NERC, and industry executives say otherwise.

The Executive Responds

The metaphors that we've examined in this chapter also serve as a backdrop against which to understand the general environment in which Cybersecurity policy has been developed over the past decade. Obviously our leaders felt pressure, from a number of sources, to take action and they did. Looking at the measures they implemented, as well as the measures that they didn't implement, is instructive.

CNCI – Part I

During the final days of the G.W. Bush administration, in January of 2008, President Bush launched the *Comprehensive National Cybersecurity Initiative* (CNCI) in an effort to shore up the defenses of government networks. This initiative was started, at least in part, on behalf of the sort of doomsday scenarios this chapter has focused on. Former special adviser Richard Clarke describes the event that got the ball rolling:

> The President's scheduler had booked an hour for the decision briefing. It took five minutes. Bush never saw a covert-action proposal he didn't like. Now, with fifty-five minutes left in the meeting, the Director of National Intelligence, Mike McConnell, saw an opening. All the right people were in the room, senior national security cabinet members. McConnell asked if he could discuss a threat to the financial industry and the U. S. Economy. Given the floor, he talked about cyber war and how vulnerable we were to it. Particularly vulnerable was the financial sector, which would not know how to recover from a data-shredding attack, an attack that could do unimaginable damage to the economy. Stunned, Bush turned to Treasury Secretary Hank Paulson, who agreed with the assessment.
>
> At this point, Bush, who had been sitting behind the large desk in the Oval Office, almost jumped in the air. He moved quickly to

the front of the desk and began gesturing for emphasis as he spoke. "Information technology is supposed to be our advantage, not our weakness. I want this fixed. I want a plan, soon, real soon."[38]

Here we see the hand of DNI Mike McConnell at work on an audience that appears to have been particularly disposed towards suggestions of Armageddon.

The $50 billion CNCI program was established by a classified presidential order, *Homeland Security Presidential Directive 23*, so details were initially difficult to come by. However, in October of 2008 the Bush administration started revealing pieces of information. For example, the Office of Management and Budget (OMB) developed a component of the initiative that's known as the *Trusted Internet Connections* (TIC) program which aimed to decrease the number of links between federal networks and external private sector networks to fewer than 100. The motivating idea behind this scheme was that it would be easier for the government to detect incidents if there were fewer connections to watch.

The TIC program stipulates that network gateways to government networks must be monitored by an intrusion detection system developed by the Department of Homeland Security called *Einstein*. Early incarnations of the system focused on inspecting network traffic and firing off alerts when a suspicious connection was observed. The more recent version of the system currently being developed (i.e. *Einstein 3*) implements intrusion prevention functionality that not only identifies security events but also acts to block them at runtime.

Despite the Bush administration's inclination towards secrecy, one aspect of CNCI was patently clear; this executive mandate was only concerned with *government* networks. That is, networks residing within the .mil, .gov, and .ic Internet domains. The private sector was on its own, as far as security was concerned.

There's a certain degree of irony with this fact. Risk to the financial sector was the basis for McConnell's predictions of "unimaginable damage," but *little was actually done to protect private sector banks* by the CNCI. The same holds for private sector interests, like defense contractors, who are heavily entangled with government initiatives and could effectively serve as "trusted" launch points into sensitive networks.

CNCI Re-Loaded

Bush's work on CNCI created a legacy that extended into the following administration. During the 2008 presidential campaign, at a "21st Century Threats" summit, Obama made it known that cyber-security was an important issue:

> As President, I'll make cyber-security the top priority that it should be in the 21st century. I'll declare our cyber-infrastructure a strategic asset, and appoint a National Cyber Advisor who will report directly to me. We'll coordinate efforts across the federal government, implement a truly national cyber-security policy, and tighten standards to secure information – from the networks that power the federal government, to the networks that you use in your personal lives.

When he took office, Obama ordered the National Security Council, in conjunction with the Homeland Security council, to perform a *60-day review of U.S. Cybersecurity policy*. In May of 2009, the findings of this review were published.[39] Unlike Bush's cyber strategy, this report was made public.

The recommendations of the policy review built upon the existing CNCI, but they didn't forge into new horizons. According to Richard Clarke:

> It was CNCI redux. It also had a military Cyber Command, but not a cyber war strategy, not a major policy or program to defend the private sector, nothing to initiate international dialogue on cyber war. And, déjà vu all over again, the new Democratic President went out of his way to take [private sector] regulation off the table ...[40]

Clarke's observation was reinforced during a speech that Obama gave on the day that the policy review was published:

> The vast majority of our critical information infrastructure in the United States is owned and operated by the private sector.

So let me be very clear: My administration will not dictate security standards for private companies.

Just like the president before him, when it came to cyber-security Obama stayed away from regulating the private sector.

CYBERCOM

In June of 2009, Secretary of Defense Robert Gates ordered the creation of the *United States Cyber Command* (CYBERCOM). CYBERCOM was created to "direct the operations and defense of specified Department of Defense information networks." In other words, this new organization would oversee the day-to-day protection of military networks (e.g. military networks, or .mil). Non-military government networks, (e.g. or.gov), remained the purview of the Department of Homeland Security.

The idea behind CYBERCOM was to integrate existing resources spread out over different branches of the military (e.g. the Army, Navy, Marines, and Air Force), to coordinate them centrally. This makes sense if you consider that there are some 15,000 military networks spread out over 4,000 military bases in 88 countries.[41] As one official told *Wired* Magazine:

> It really doesn't add any significant funding... And really, it's not a significant increase in personnel; we just reorganized the personnel have we had in a smarter and more effective way.[42]

Headquartered at Fort Meade, next door to the National Security Agency (NSA), CYBERCOM was originally staffed by approximately 1,000 troops, most of who were transferred over from other positions.[43] In January of 2013, the Pentagon announced that this force would expand to 4,900 personnel[44] and receive an additional investment of $23 billion.[45]

Note that this augmentation comes at a time when the military is actually trying to cut spending, reinforcing the notion that cyberwar (like drones) is a growth industry.

Defense contractors definitely see this as a growth industry and not without good reason. For example, in July of 2013, the Navy awarded contracts to 13 companies, worth as much as $899.5 million, for services related to cyber operations. The list of selected contractors included Booz Allen Hamilton, General Dynamics, Lockheed Martin, and SAIC.[46]

Running an operation like CYBERCOM would require a level of technical sophistication. So it is only natural that when the decision makers were searching for someone to run CYBERCOM, all they had to do was turn towards Fort Meade, to one of the largest consumers of computer hardware in the world: the NSA. In particular, they considered Keith Alexander, the director of the NSA, to be the ideal candidate. In May of 2010 he was promoted to the rank of general and assumed command of CYBERCOM.

It's interesting to note that Alexander retained his position at the NSA. So, while the NSA and CYBERCOM are distinct entities on paper, they're joined at the top. It would be naive to think that this doesn't influence the interaction of the two organizations. One entity identifies threats and the other develops strategies to deal with them.

Alexander, like many other officials mentioned in this chapter, has demonstrated the ability to mischaracterize threats. In September of 2011, Alexander warned of what could happen as a result of a cyber-attack by referring to a power outage back in the summer of 2003 that impacted millions of people in the Northeast and Midwestern U.S. The outage, which was the second largest in history, was caused by a power line in Ohio that came in contact with nearby trees, resulting in a cascading failure that knocked more than 100 power plants offline.[47]

But what does a temporary power outage have to do with cyberwar? In this case Gen. Alexander was trying to link a natural disaster with a hypothetical cyber-attack. This connection is preposterous on its face value; it's an attempt to breathe life into a hypothetical idea using an existing image. You can bet that if a concrete example existed, he would have used it.

The creation of CYBERCOM can be viewed as the realization of assurances that President Obama made early on. As noted earlier, while he was on the campaign trail in 2008, President Obama made it very clear that cyber-security was a *strategic asset*.[48]

Put another way, he was signaling that this was an area that would receive an infusion of federal money, creating a growth market for the defense contractors. The publication of the 60-day review of cyber-security policy could thus be interpreted a preliminary indicator that concrete action was going to follow.

The Question of Offensive Operations

Two years after CYBERCOM was established, in May of 2011, the Obama administration released a policy paper on its "International Strategy for Cyberspace." In this document, the White House presented its position on how the United States should respond to cyber-attacks.

> We reserve the right to use all necessary means – diplomatic, informational, military, and economic – as appropriate and consistent with applicable international law, in order to defend our Nation, our allies, our partners, and our interests. In so doing, we will exhaust all options before military force whenever we can; will carefully weigh the costs and risks of action against the costs of inaction; and will act in a way that reflects our values and strengthens our legitimacy, seeking broad international support whenever possible.[49]

Within weeks of the President conveying his stance, the Pentagon published its own strategy for operating in Cyberspace. The unclassified version of this document didn't touch on the specifics of responding to cyber-attacks (e.g. what constitutes "use of force," thresholds for a military response, or the rules of engagement). In fact, it didn't even provide the sort of broad brush strokes that the Obama administration provided in its policy paper. Though in a speech that outlined the Pentagon's strategy on the day of its publication, Deputy Secretary of Defense William J. Lynn specified:

> The United States reserves the right, under the laws of armed conflict, to respond to serious cyber attacks with a proportional and justified military response at the time and place of our choosing. [50]

What this means is that while Pentagon spokesmen may insist that CYBERCOM is a defensive initiative and "not about the militarization of cyber,"[51] there may be offensive aspects of the program that are being downplayed. Keep in mind that CYBERCOM is subordinate to the *United States Strategic Command* (STRATCOM), the successor to the Cold War's Strategic Air Command, which is in charge of global strike operations as well as strategic deterrence (i.e. the country's nuclear arsenal). The commander of STRATCOM at the time of CYBERCOM's establishment, General Patrick Chilton, openly stated:

> You don't take any response options off the table from an attack on the United States of America.... Why would we constrain ourselves on how we respond?[52]

In light of this comment, is it unreasonable to assume that CYBERCOM may actually at times assume an aggressive posture? Strictly speaking, CYBERCOM was created to "consolidate and streamline Department of Defense capabilities into a single command."[53] Given STRATCOM's global strike mission, and a mindset that leaves "all options on the table," could some of CYBERCOM's capabilities be offensive?

In time these questions were answered conclusively. In mid-October of 2012, President Obama signed a classified directive known as *Presidential Policy Directive 20,* which we'll look at in more detail later on in this chapter. It explicitly mentioned the use of offensive measures.[54] Right around this same time period, in an act that probably signaled this executive action, Secretary of Defense Leon Panetta publicly claimed that pre-emptive action was necessary:

> If we detect an imminent threat of attack that will cause significant physical destruction in the United States or kill American citizens, we need to have the option to take action against those who would attack us ...[55]

This mindset gained enough traction to put down institutional roots. In early 2013, several months after Panetta's statement, word leaked out about the Pentagon's plan to create three different forces under CYBERCOM:

"National mission forces" to protect computer systems that undergird electrical grids, power plants and other infrastructure deemed critical to national and economic security; "combat mission forces" to help commanders abroad plan and execute attacks or other offensive operations; and "cyber protection forces" to fortify the Defense Department's networks.[56]

So, here we are: after years of couching their language strictly in terms of defense, the Pentagon concedes (to itself at least, in classified internal communication) that it will be engaged in offensive actions. But anyone who followed the outbreak of Stuxnet in 2010 could have told you that the United States is one of the Internet's more prolific actors.

Stuxnet

In March of 2013, General Keith Alexander informed Congress that CYBERCOM would be establishing 13 distinct teams of specialists to carry out offensive operations out on the Internet. He was careful to stipulate that they would only engage the enemy in response to an attack.[57]

This is an offensive team that the Defense Department would use to defend the nation if it were attacked in cyberspace. Thirteen of the teams that we're creating are for that mission alone.

As we'll see, history proves just the opposite: that the United States is more than willing to commit first-use with regard to offensive tools. Though officials try very hard to render aggression, as it's conveyed to the press, as being "defensive."

The actual stance of the United States is reflected in its flourishing arms industry. It's only expected that the United States would be a pioneer in the development of high-grade malware, as the United States is the world's leading arms manufacturer. According to the Stockholm International Peace Research Institute (SIPRI), arms sales by U.S.-based arms manufacturers amounted to over half of the total arms sales.[58] To be more precise, in 2011 the United States completed $66 billion in arms exports deals. This is practically 80 percent of the global market.

Despite the malaise that's gripped the national economy, the United States is witnessing record-breaking profits with regard to weapons sales.[59] Not to mention that the contractors that constitute much of the defense industry (e.g. Raytheon, Booz Allen, SAIC, Lockheed, etc.) have been openly recruiting engineers to develop offensive tools.[60] These signs indicate that the United States sponsors extensive malware development programs.[61]

On July 12, 2010, the world got a glimpse of one such program. A security researcher, Sergey Ulasen at VirusBlokAda, an anti-virus software vendor in Belarus, posted a message at an online forum about a malware sample that he and his coworkers had come across.[62] Shortly after Sergey's initial posting, on this same Internet message board, a German security researcher named Frank Boldewin noticed that the malware contained references to industrial control system (ICS) software developed by Siemens (i.e., SIMATIC WinCC/Step 7) that talks to *programmable logic controllers* (PLCs). PLCs are special-purpose embedded hardware systems used to automate the operation of machinery. They're common in manufacturing environments.

As the investigation progressed, the captured malware was christened *Stuxnet*, a name that arises from text strings that were unearthed from the worm's executable files.[63] VirusBlokAda published a full report on Stuxnet which provided some initial details.[64] For example, they found that the worm used a zero-day exploit (an unpatched software bug) to propagate itself. Specifically, it leveraged a flaw in the way that Windows Explorer handles file shortcuts (i.e. .LNK files) such that a machine would be compromised if a user plugged in an infected USB drive or opened an infected Windows network file share.[65]

Note that this particular vulnerability was observed back in November of 2008.[66] Microsoft didn't patch the problem until August of 2010, almost a month after Ulasen went public.[67]

Now that's something, isn't it? A nontrivial software flaw which enabled a newsworthy cyber-attack was virtually ignored by the vendor. For almost two years it languished as an un-patched bug. How many other such bugs exist and have simply been pushed to the wayside? Was this sheer incompetence on the part of Microsoft or something else? Later on in the book we'll uncover a partial answer.

A Picture Emerges

The process of infection, as studied by VirusBlokAda, installs a couple of drivers which were digitally signed by Realtek Semiconductor (a legitimate hardware manufacturer based in Taiwan). This is remarkable because digitally signed drivers, especially those signed by well-known corporate entities like Realtek, are generally assumed to be valid. It's like an official document embossed with a royal seal. A malicious driver sporting a digital signature like this garners the sort of implicit trust that would make it easy for Stuxnet to spread.

Within days of Ulasen's post, on July 16th Versign revoked the Realtek certificate used to sign the drivers. The attackers responded quickly by switching to a digital signature based on a certificate issued to another Taiwan company, JMicron Technology Corp. Again, on July 22nd, VeriSign revoked JMicron's certificate. The attackers did not switch to a third digital signature.

As events unfolded, researchers at Symantec also took a closer look at Stuxnet. What they discovered was that the worm didn't rely on just a single zero-day exploit. Stuxnet actually wielded *four different exploits* based on *unpatched flaws* in the Windows operating system. Symantec's Liam ÓMurchu commented:

> Not only does Stuxnet use zero-day vulnerabilities, it also uses a variety of other vulnerabilities (such as the Microsoft Windows Server Service RPC Handling Remote Code Execution Vulnerability), which shows the extraordinary sophistication, thought, and planning that went into making Stuxnet.[68]

A closer look at the internals of Stuxnet reveals an intricate set of dance steps. Once Stuxnet has compromised a machine, it looks to see if the machine is connected to a Siemens S7 PLC.[69] If an S7 PLC is present, Stuxnet checks for the presence of certain physical devices connected to a PLC. In particular, it seeks out an unusual configuration of frequency converter drives manufactured by Vacon PLC of Finland and Iranian company Fararo Paya. Frequency converter drives are used to control the rotational speed of attached electric motors. For instance, the drives could be used to regulate the operation of gas centrifuges ... which is valuable for organizations trying to enrich uranium.

If Stuxnet doesn't find what it's looking for, it does nothing. However, if the setup of the hardware being examined matches the targeted fingerprint, Stuxnet will alter the frequency converter drive parameters to sabotage the attached centrifuges. At the same time, in a particularly devious move, Stuxnet feeds bogus status information to the user so that they are unaware of the modification (e.g. the world's first known PLC rootkit).[70]

Another interesting aspect of Stuxnet is that it had a limited shelf-life. Stuxnet expired on June 24, 2012. If the malware's payload executed after this date, it did nothing. This feature was probably intended to limit the worm's ability to spread.

Rumors Abound

There were a number of thought-provoking forensic artifacts that Stuxnet left on the systems that it infected. For example, Stuxnet set a value in the Windows registry to the number "19790509" as a way to signal that a machine had already been infected. In Symantec's Stuxnet dossier, investigators speculated that it may represent May 9, 1979, the day that a leading figure of the Iranian Jewish community was executed. Then again, to highlight the somewhat arbitrary nature of this interpretation, *CNET* columnist Elinor Mills also noted this is also the day that one of the Unabomber's explosives injured a student at Northwestern University.[71]

Another piece of evidence that gained widespread attention was revealed by Alexander Gostev of Kaspersky Lab. He pointed out the following string that was embedded in the Stuxnet driver code:

b:\myrtus\src\objfre_w2k_x86\i386\guava.pdb.[72]

Anyone who works with Microsoft's Visual Studio will recognize this as the file path corresponding to an executable file named guava that's been compiled to run on 32-bit Intel hardware and located inside of a Visual Studio project named myrtus. The naming scheme would seem to make some sense to someone acquainted with botany as a guava is a plant in the *myrtle* family genus *psidium*. The *myrtus* genus also resides under the myrtle family.

Ralph Langner is a German engineer who specializes in the area of control systems. He runs a boutique consulting firm out of Hamburg. In early September of 2010 he Googled words like "Hebrew" and "Myrtus" and hypothesized that Stuxnet might be a gambit to sabotage the Bushehr nuclear power plant in Iran, which had recently suffered from unexplained setbacks.[73]

"Myrtus" is the Latin version of the name "Myrtle," which could be interpreted as a reference to the Persian queen Esther in the Old Testament. In this biblical tale, Esther, who was originally named Hadassah (which is Hebrew for Myrtle), foils a plot to exterminate Persian Jews.

Langner made his suspicions public on September 16, 2010.[74]

> It is hard to ignore the fact that the highest number of infections seems to be in Iran. Can we think of any reasonable target that would match the scenario? Yes, we can. Look at the Iranian nuclear program. Strange – they are presently having some technical difficulties down there in Bushehr.

As an aside, one of your authors suspects that myrtus may instead refer to *MyRTUs* (i.e. My Remote Terminal Units). RTUs, like PLCs, are special-purpose field devices that collect data and transfer it back to a main ICS station.[75]

Within days of Langner's announcement, another German named Frank Rieger wrote a newspaper article where he proposed that Stuxnet, instead of targeting the Bushehr plant, was actually aimed at Iran's Natanz uranium-enrichment facility.[76]

Rieger's assertion correlates with a mysterious posting that appeared at WikiLeaks on the 17th of July:

> Two weeks ago, a source associated with Iran's nuclear program confidentially told WikiLeaks of a serious, recent, nuclear accident at Natanz. Natanz is the primary location of Iran's nuclear enrichment program.

WikiLeaks had reason to believe the source was credible however contact with this source was lost.

WikiLeaks would not normally mention such an incident without additional confirmation, however according to Iranian media and the BBC, today the head of Iran's Atomic Energy Organization, Gholam Reza Aghazadeh, has resigned under mysterious circumstances. According to these reports, the resignation was tendered around 20 days ago.[77]

Black Hat, or Just Old Hat?

While there are several aspects of Stuxnet that are remarkable from a technical perspective (e.g. the use of multiple zero-day exploits, the forged digital certificates, the PLC-related components), there are some features that are oddly dated.

From the standpoint of its stealth capabilities, at least as far as the Windows platform is concerned, the techniques used by Stuxnet were amateurish. As one contributor at Cryptome noted:

> Personally I'd be surprised if a crack team of Israeli software engineers were so sloppy that they relied on outdated rootkit technology (e.g. hooking the Nt*[system] calls used by Kernel32.LoadLibrary ... and using UPX to pack code).[78]

Hooking operating system routines to undermine their functionality is an age-old trick that's been around for more than a decade. It's analogous to altering a movie by splicing in one's own footage. Intercepting routines, via hooking, is easy to implement and even easier to detect. With regard to modifying system logic, there are far more subtle and inconspicuous techniques available for discriminating engineers.[79] We wouldn't expect professional-level malware architects to rely on function hooking.

In addition, the fact that the authors of Stuxnet used *UPX* to armor their binaries is another dead giveaway. UPX is what's known as a *packer*. It compresses files so that they're difficult to examine and recognize. Any malware author worth their salt would have the good sense to build a custom packing gear, as all of the well-known packing tools have been studied to death. Instead, the authors of

Stuxnet decided to use a well-known tool which presents absolutely no obstacle to a forensic investigator.

The fact that Stuxnet's cutting-edge features were mixed in with obsolete and outdated anti-forensic measures implies that multiple parties of varying skill-level were probably involved. For example, this could mean that certain components were outsourced.

Stuxnet as a Joint Venture

The notion that Stuxnet was the result of a scheme involving both Israel and the United States was a popular one. A report supporting the theory about Stuxnet being developed by Israel and the United States was published by the *New York Times* in early 2011. The authors cited unnamed sources who claimed that the Israelis had even gone so far as to set up a test lab out in the Negev desert using the same equipment that the Iranians possessed.[80]

Industry luminaries appeared to be of the same mind. Evgeny Kaspersky, the founder of Kaspersky Lab, stated:

> Israeli intelligence unfortunately doesn't send us any reports. There was a lot of talk – on the Internet and in the media – that Stuxnet was a joint U.S.-Israeli project. I think that's probably the most likely scenario.[81]

At a conference in the spring of 2011, Ralph Langner also announced that Stuxnet was the result of a collaborative effort between the U.S. and Israel.[82]

The U.S-Israeli theory also took root in Iran. In April of 2011, Iranian Brigadier General Gholam Reza Jalali claimed:

> The investigations and research showed that the Stuxnet worm had been disseminated from sources in the U.S. and Israel ...[83]

General Jalali specifically pointed a finger at Siemens:

> Siemens should explain why and how it provided the enemies with the information about the codes of the SCADA software and prepared the ground for a cyber-attack against us.[84]

Thus, it did not come as a huge surprise in June of 2012 when an article written by David Sanger in the *New York Times* revealed that

Stuxnet was indeed a joint project code-named Olympic Games that involved both the NSA and Israel's Unit 8200.[85]

One thing that is surprising is the duration of the project. In February of 2013, researchers from Symantec reported that they had identified an early variant of Stuxnet that was captured in the wild as far back as 2007. Though, even at this early point it was designed to attack centrifuges.[86]

> Stuxnet 0.5 also contains code to attack the valve systems in a uranium enrichment facility rather than modifying centrifuge speeds, as in versions 1.x of Stuxnet.

Another surprising aspect of Stuxnet is its development was kept so highly compartmentalized. The right hand of U.S. intelligence didn't know what they left hand was doing. How else could you explain the fact that the Department of Homeland Security and the Idaho National Laboratory established a lab with control system equipment, devoting significant resources towards reverse engineering the worm?[87]

Impact on Iran's Program

By analyzing traffic to C2 servers in Malaysia and Denmark, Symantec determined that Stuxnet infected roughly 100,000 hosts spread out over 155 countries.[88] The problem with this data is that it doesn't necessarily indicate the extent of the damage done because the worm seeks out a very specific system fingerprint before executing its destructive payload. On October of 2010, Siemens indicated that only fifteen of its customers had actually been affected by the malware.[89] Even then, that doesn't tell us much about what happened in Iran.

In late November of 2010, an Iranian nuclear scientist was killed in a bomb attack perpetrated by unknown assassins on motorcycles. In the *New York Times* article that covered this story, Iranian President Mahmoud Ahmadinejad publicly referenced the Stuxnet attacks. He was quoted as saying:

> They succeeded in creating problems for a limited number of our centrifuges with the software they had installed in electronic parts.[90]

But just how bad was the damage? A report compiled by the Institute for Science and International Security (ISIS) offers what is possibly the most detailed picture:

> Although Stuxnet appears to be designed to destroy centrifuges at the Natanz facility, destruction was by no means total. Moreover, Stuxnet did not lower the production of LEU [low enriched uranium] during 2010. LEU quantities could have certainly been greater, and Stuxnet could be an important part of the reason why they did not increase significantly. Nonetheless, there remain important questions about why Stuxnet destroyed only 1,000 centrifuges. One observation is that it may be harder to destroy centrifuges by use of cyber attacks than often believed.[91]

Thus, while Stuxnet destroyed 1,000 IR-1 centrifuges (there were approximately 9,000 total at Natanz) it didn't seem to alter the production of enriched uranium. All told, it would appear that the Stuxnet campaign, if it was truly directed at Iran, was less successful than intended.[92] In fact, Stuxnet seems to be far more capable of generating stories in the press as opposed to disrupting a nuclear program. Jeffrey Carr, the chief executive of security firm Taia Global, remarked:

> Whoever spent millions of dollars on Stuxnet, Flame, Duqu, and so on – all that money is sort of wasted. That malware is now out in the public spaces and can be reverse engineered ...[93]

DuQu: The Son of Stuxnet?

On October 14, 2011, the Laboratory of Cryptography and System Security (CrySyS) at Budapest University of Technology and Economics notified Symantec that they had identified a malware sample that looked very similar to Stuxnet. The researchers at CrySys called this new malware sample *DuQu* (pronounced dyü-kyü) as it creates files whose named begin with the string "~dq."

Based on timestamps embedded in the malware, researchers at Symantec believed that DuQu had been active, in one form or another, for at least a year (about five months after Stuxnet was first revealed in July of 2010).[94]

Unlike Stuxnet, DuQu wasn't a worm; it didn't self-replicate. Instead, it was Trojan-packaged inside of a malicious Microsoft Word file.[95] The attack vector consisted of a zero-day exploit that targeted a specific bug (i.e. CVE-2011-3402) in the Windows Kernel that handled TrueType font parsing.[96] In November Microsoft released an advisory that offered a workaround to address the bug,[97] though it wasn't until December 2011 that Microsoft released a security update.[98]

While DuQu had a limited shelf-life (i.e. 30 days before self-destructing, by default), as did Stuxnet, Symantec claimed that infections had been confirmed in six unnamed organizations spread across eight different countries.[99] Symantec also asserted that the developers who created DuQu had *access to the source code* used to build Stuxnet (not just the raw, compiled, binaries).[100] These basic conclusions were echoed by researchers at Kaspersky Lab, who speculated that there were at most a couple of dozen infections worldwide.[101]

Another distinguishing feature of DuQu is that it didn't contain code that targeted ICS installations. Instead, its primary payload was a RAT (Remote Administration Tool), leading investigators to conclude that DuQu was designed to perform network reconnaissance and collect information. To this end, DuQu utilized a digitally signed driver. One variant of DuQu used a driver that was digitally signed by a certificate belonging to C-Media Electronics Incorporated, a company based in Taiwan.[102]

Platform Tilded

In December of 2011, researchers at Kaspersky Lab concluded that the drivers used by Stuxnet and DuQu were too similar for it to be a mere coincidence. They hypothesized that the two deliverables were created using a *common source code framework*, referred to as *Tilded* (pronounced tilde-deed) as it displays a tendency towards file names that begin with "~d."[103]

> From the data we have at our disposal, we can say with a fair degree of certainty that the "Tilded" platform was created around the end of 2007 or early 2008 before undergoing its most significant changes in summer/autumn 2010. Those changes were

sparked by advances in code and the need to avoid detection by antivirus solutions. There were a number of projects involving programs based on the "Tilded" platform throughout the period 2007-2011. Stuxnet and Duqu are two of them – there could have been others, which for now remain unknown.

Flame, Gauss, and miniFlame

In May of 2012, Kaspersky Labs announced that it had found an interesting malware specimen while investigating an incident on behalf of UN's International Telecommunication Union. An early analysis of the malware had also been performed by researchers in the Laboratory of Cryptography and System Security (CrySyS) at the Budapest University of Technology and Economics.[104]

What the investigators found was an extensible malware framework, the software equivalent of a multi-purpose Swiss army knife, which implemented a broad range of features using an interchangeable collection of pluggable modules. Each module implements a subset of related features so that modules can be mixed and matched to come up with the right mixture of functionality.

As a side note, this module-based approach is remarkably similar to that employed by the Metasploit's Meterpreter payload.[105] The researchers at Kaspersky named the malware framework after a specific module referred to as *Flame*, a component that's used to scout out new host machines and infect them.[106]

Taken as a whole, the base malware install and all of its extension modules tip the scales at 20 MB, which is whale-sized as far as most worms and viruses are concerned. Then again, given the sheer number of operations that the software supported (data compression, data encryption, data deletion, keystroke logging, screen capturing, Bluetooth connectivity, Secure Shell connectivity, database client components, a built-in virtual machine, etc.) this isn't necessarily a surprise.

Flame is so large and includes so many bells and whistles that it almost resembles some sort of commercial enterprise application. Hence, it makes sense that Flame didn't implement any rootkit features. Instead, it hid in plain sight. This turned out to be a successful strategy, as the malware evaded detection for several years.[107] According to Mikko Hypponen, chief research officer at anti-virus vendor F-Secure:

> Flame was a failure for the antivirus industry. We really should have been able to do better. But we didn't. We were out of our league, in our own game.[108]

This is a significant statement. A big name in the anti-virus industry has openly admitted that they're outgunned! Of course, this isn't news for the developers who create malware. In fact, beating anti-virus software is de rigueur. It's a task that is easily within reach of the average computer science undergraduate.[109] George Ledin, a professor who teaches a course on malware development, lamented:

> The AV [anti-virus] business is, unfortunately, a bizarre combination of janitorial service ("spill in aisle 8") and insurance (but without accident, comprehensive, or liability coverage). It's a sweet business to be in. That's why we have some fifty companies offering this kind of fake "protection."

Initially, investigators didn't see a technical connection between Flame and the Tilded platform (which provides the base architecture for both Stuxnet and DuQu). Then, researchers at Kaspersky realized that an encrypted DLL used by an early variant of Stuxnet was almost identical to a module used by Flame. They were so similar that it's believed that they were derived from the *same source code.*[110]

Roughly three quarters of all Flame infections observed by Kaspersky occurred in Iran and Israel. The rest were scattered in small handfuls among Middle East countries like the Sudan, Syria, Lebanon and Saudi Arabia.

Then there's the matter of forged Microsoft certificates, which allowed Flame to intercept Windows update traffic and spread itself by pretending to be a legitimate operating system update. The engineers who developed flame were able to generate a legitimate code-signing certificate, one that linked to Microsoft's official root digital certificate, by re-purposing a certificate normally used for Terminal Services (i.e. remote desktop) licensing.[111] Doing so involved identifying weaknesses in the cryptographic algorithms used to create these certificates and then finding enough computing power to exploit the weaknesses.[112]

This is a key point: whoever forged the rogue digital certificate had significant computing resources.

This evidence corroborates an article published by the *Washington Post*, in which unnamed U.S. officials asserted that Flame had been developed jointly by the United States and Israel in an effort to scout out Iran's networks and lay the groundwork for the Stuxnet attack.[113] Conversely both U.S. and Israeli officials have loudly denied involvement.[114] Furthermore, while the assumed target of the attacks is the Iranian nuclear program, one blogger has implied that other motives may also be at play:

> My source also tells me that this is the first known instance in which Israeli intelligence has used malware to intrude on Israeli citizens. Within Israel and the Palestinian territories Flame is implemented by the Shin Bet. The "beauty" of it for the secret police is that unlike "legal" eavesdropping on phones or computers, you don't need to ask for judicial approval to infect a computer. [115]

As the researchers at Kaspersky continued to sift through forensic artifacts related to Flame, they made additional discoveries. For example, they found a new malware platform that they called *Gauss*.[116]

> Based on the results of a detailed analysis of Flame, we continued to actively search for new, unknown components. A more in-depth analysis conducted in June 2012 resulted in the discovery of a new, previously unknown malware platform that uses a modular structure resembling that of Flame, a similar code base and system for communicating to C&C servers, as well as numerous other similarities to Flame.
>
> In our opinion, all of this clearly indicates that the new platform which we discovered and which we called "Gauss," is another example of a cyber-espionage toolkit based on the Flame platform.

Shortly afterwards, in July of 2012, Kaspersky announced that they had also unearthed a smaller standalone espionage program that was also based on Flame:

The SPE malware, which we call "miniFlame," is a small, fully functional cyber-espionage malware designed for data theft and direct access to infected systems.

MiniFlame is in fact based on the Flame platform but is implemented as an independent module. It can operate either independently, without the main modules of Flame in the system, or as a component controlled by Flame.[117]

All Roads Lead to Uncle Sam

What we've seen so far is a widespread and intricate series of interrelated malware frameworks that researchers believe to be linked at the source code level (see Figure 1-1). In other words, they believe that the connections between these various software components aren't merely the result of binary files being re-purposed, after they were built, by tweaking a few bits here and there with a hex editor. Rather, they see deep structural commonalities that can only be achieved by having access to the original blueprints, the source code, of the platforms in question.

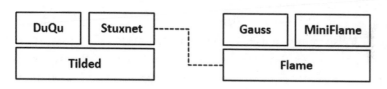

Figure 1-1

Both Stuxnet and DuQu appear to be based on the Tilded platform, which is in turn related to the Flame platform with its Gauss and miniFlame offshoots. Given that United States officials have leaked involvement in designing and deploying Stuxnet, the evidence strongly supports the conclusion that *the U.S. government is running an extensive offensive software program.*

Plan X

There have been other developments that support this conclusion. For example, the Defense Advanced Research

Projects Agency (DARPA) is working on a program called *Plan X*. The goal of this program is to take cyber-attacks, which are currently run as special-purpose operations using a small group of highly-skilled specialists, and industrialize the process so that cyber-attacks can be launched reliably en masse, in a predictable manner, without all of the setup effort. A DARPA announcement on Plan X refers to this as "automatically constructing verifiable and quantifiable cyber operations." This means focusing on:

> Developing high-level mission plans and automatically synthesizing a mission script that is executed through a human-on-the-loop interface, similar to the auto-pilot function in modern aircraft. This process will leverage formal methods to provably quantify the potential battle damage from each synthesized mission plan.[118]

In a nutshell, the military wants to be able to launch offensive operations on an industrial scale.

Presidential Policy Directive 20

While Stuxnet and Plan X are strong indicators that the DoD isn't limiting itself to defensive actions in cyberspace, they're still not entirely conclusive. Definitive evidence, which directly confirms the existence of an offensive cyber program, appeared in June of 2013. This is when a former CIA operative turned whistleblower named Edward Snowden leaked a top-secret document to Glenn Greenwald at the *Guardian*. The leaked document, *Presidential Policy Directive 20*,[119] was issued in October of 2012. Page 9 of this document touches on Offensive Cyber Effects Operations (OCEO):

> The United States Government shall identify potential targets of national importance where OCEO can offer a favorable balance of effectiveness and risk as compared with other instruments of national power.

In other words, Obama explicitly told the Pentagon to draw up a list of targets for cyber-attacks which would serve "U.S. national objectives around the world." As far as our leaders are concerned, they're not limited to merely using offensive tools for retaliation. They believe that attacks can be used proactively when it serves their purposes.

Hacking Foreign Targets for Years

This doesn't mean that U.S.-sponsored cyber-intrusions are a new phenomenon. According to whistleblower Ed Snowden the NSA has run more than 61,000 hacking operations all over the world.[120]

Confidential sources cited by Foreign Policy magazine also point to the NSA's Office of Tailored Access Operations (TAO), which has run rampant through Chinese networks for the past 15 years.[121] TAO is a unit that includes some 600 hackers who work in rotating shifts 24 hours a day all year round, infiltrating foreign computers to extract political, military, and economic data. TAO is also tasked with performing reconnaissance on behalf of cyber-attacks executed by CYBERCOM.

Top-secret documents examined by the Washington Post show that the TAO program is involved in a larger $625 million, 1,870 person, effort code-named GENIE which is geared towards subverting entire foreign networks. By 2011, the GENIE campaign succeeded in compromising nearly 69,000 devices on the Internet and loading them with "implants," allowing the devices to be surreptitiously controlled. Foreign Policy magazine puts TAO's 12-year total for the number of devices it's compromised at over 80,000.[122]

According to the Washington Post, the NSA prefers high-end network hardware to individual computers, as this provides them with access to mass streams of network traffic:

> The NSA unit's software engineers would rather tap into networks than individual computers because there are usually many devices on each network. Tailored Access Operations has software templates to break into common brands and models of "routers, switches and firewalls from multiple product vendor lines," according to one document describing its work.[123]

The NSA seems to have perfected what's known as the Man in the Middle (MITM) attack, where data from a hacked network device is temporarily redirected to the NSA before being routed back to the original destination.[124] This allows the NSA to archive and decrypt the corresponding network traffic without altering the targets under surveillance. On at least one occasion it appears that the NSA has impersonated Google to execute a MITM attack (which implies that there may be some private sector collaboration).[125]

To see where all of this is headed, the NSA has recently brought online a system, code-named *TURBINE*, which is capable of automating the management of millions of implants.

Oz the Great and Powerful

Slogans, headings, headlines and/or other succinct, clear messages should be used wherever possible.

– NATO Allied Joint Doctrine for Psychological
Operations AJP-3.10.1(A)

You may recall a scene from the *Wizard of Oz*, where Dorothy and her cohorts were advised to "pay no attention to the man behind the curtain." To understand what's driving these Hollywood disaster movie screenplays, you've got to recognize that the creation of CNCI and CYBERCOM weren't spontaneous events. They didn't just appear out of thin air. Rather, there are discernible forces at play.

For years we have been told that an existential menace was looming on the horizon, a prophecy of the end times heralded by a long stream of government legislators, retired bureaucrats, generals, and security wonks. There's a *Cyber Cold War* taking place they say[126], and as in our earlier Cold War the United States is living under the perpetual threat of doomsday. Such is the message of the far-reaching public relations campaign, a crusade that involves elements within the defense industry. The sense of anxiety that's stirred up encourages a mental state of susceptibility. This, in turn, enables the advancement of policies and initiatives which often failed to address the very state of insecurity that was used to drive these same policies and initiatives.

Endnotes

1) Mike Rogers, "America is losing the cyber war vs. China," *Detroit News*, February 8, 2013, http://mikerogers.house.gov/news/documentsingle.aspx?DocumentID=319502.

2) Joe Weiss, Water System Hack – The System Is Broken, Unfettered Blog, November 17, 2011, http://community.controlglobal.com/content/water-system-hack-system-broken.

3) ICSB-11-327-01 – Illinois Water Pump Failure Report, ICS-CERT Information Bulletin, November 23, 2011, http://www.us-cert.gov/control_systems/pdf/ICSB-11-327-01.pdf.

4) Kim Zetter, "H(ackers)2O: Attack on City Water Station Destroys Pump," *Wired*, November 18, 2011, http://www.wired.com/threatlevel/2011/11/hackers-destroy-water-pump/.

5) Mike M. Ahlers, "Feds investigating Illinois 'pump failure' as possible cyber attack," *CNN*, November 18, 2011, http://articles.cnn.com/2011-11-18/us/us_cyber-attack-investigation_1_cyber-attack-cyber-security-national-cybersecurity?_s=PM:US.

6) Kim Zetter, "Comedy of Errors Led to False 'Water-Pump Hack' Report," *Wired*, November 30, 2011, http://www.wired.com/threatlevel/2011/11/water-pump-hack-mystery-solved/.

7) Andrew Nusca, "America's cyber czar speaks," *ZDNet*, April 20, 2012, http://www.zdnet.com/blog/btl/americas-cyber-czar-speaks/74832.

8) Barack Obama, "Taking the Cyberattack Threat Seriously," *Wall Street Journal*, July 19, 2012, http://online.wsj.com/article/SB10000872396390444330904577535492693044650.html.

9) Barack Obama, "Obama's 2013 State of the Union Address," *New York Times*, February 12, 2013, http://www.nytimes.com/2013/02/13/us/politics/obamas-2013-state-of-the-union-address.html.

10) Bruce Schneier, "The Psychology of Security," January 18, 2008, http://www.schneier.com/essay-155.html.

11) U.S. Department of State, "Terrorism Deaths, Injuries, Kidnappings of Private U.S. Citizens, 2010," Office of the Coordinator for Counterterrorism, August 18, 2011, http://www.state.gov/j/ct/rls/crt/2010/170267.htm.

12) National Highway Traffic Safety Administration, "Fatality Analysis Reporting System (FARS) Encyclopedia," http://www-fars.nhtsa.dot.gov/Main/index.aspx.

13) Micah Zenko, "How Many Americans Are Killed by Terrorism," Council on Foreign Relations, June 5, 2012, http://blogs.cfr.org/zenko/2012/06/05/how-many-americans-are-killed-by-terrorism/.

14) John Carlin, "A Farewell to Arms," *Wired*, May 1997, http://www.wired.com/wired/archive/5.05/netizen.html.

15) Kevin Poulsen, "'Cyberwar' and Estonia's Panic Attack," *Wired*, August 22, 2007, http://www.wired.com/threatlevel/2007/08/cyber-war-and-e/.

16) Joshua Davis, "Hackers Take Down the Most Wired Country in Europe," *Wired*, August 21, 2007, http://www.wired.com/politics/security/magazine/15-09/ff_estonia?currentPage=all.

17) Paul B. Kurtz, *Virtual Criminology Report 2009: Virtually Here: The Age of Cyber Warfare*, McAfee, http://www.mcafee.com/us/resources/reports/rp-virtual-criminology-report-2009.pdf.

18) Scott Pelley, "Panetta: Cyber warfare could paralyze U.S.," *60 Minutes*, January 5, 2012, http://www.cbsnews.com/2102-18563_162-57353420.html?tag=contentMain;contentBody.

19) *Remarks by the President on the Defense Strategic Review*, Office of the Press Secretary, January 5, 2012, http://www.whitehouse.gov/the-press-office/2012/01/05/remarks-president-defense-strategic-review.

20) Jeremy Herb, "Panetta warns lawmakers against balancing budget with more defense cuts," *The Hill*, February 28, 2012, http://thehill.com/blogs/defcon-hill/budget-approriations/213059-panetta-budget-cant-be-balanced-by-cutting-defense.

21) *S. 773: Cybersecurity Act of 2009*, 111th Congress: 2009-2010, Staff Working Draft, March 31, 2009, http://cdt.org/security/CYBERSEC4.pdf.

22) *Chairman Rockefeller and Senator Snowe Introduce Comprehensive Cybersecurity Legislation*, Democratic Press Office, April 1, 2009, http://commerce.senate.gov/public/index.cfm?p=PressReleases&ContentRecord_id=bb7223ef-1d78-4de4-b1d5-4cf54fc38662&ContentType_id=77eb-43da-aa94-497d-a73f-5c951ff72372&Group_id=4b968841-f3e8-49da-a529-7b18e32fd69d&MonthDisplay=4&YearDisplay=2009.

23) *S. 773: Cybersecurity Act of 2009*, 111th Congress: 2009-2010, Staff Working Draft, March 31, 2009, http://cdt.org/security/CYBERSEC4.pdf.

24) "Cyberwar The Threat From the Internet," *The Economist* July 3rd-9th, 2010, http://www.amazon.com/Economist-3rd-9th-Cyberwar-Threat-Internet/dp/B003V56PFK.

25) Elinor Mills, "Ex-FBI agent tells hackers to 'step up' against cyberattacks," *CNET*, July 25, 2012, http://news.cnet.com/8301-1009_3-57479934-83/ex-fbi-agent-tells-hackers-to-step-up-against-cyberattacks/.

26) Brent Huston, "Welcome to the Post-Zeus/Stuxnet World!," MicroSolved, Inc., January 5, 2011, http://stateofsecurity.com/?p=1262.

27) David Brunnstrom, "Russia says Stuxnet could have caused new Chernobyl," *Reuters*, January 26, 2011, http://www.reuters.com/article/2011/01/26/us-iran-nuclear-russia-idUSTRE70P6WS20110126.

28) Michael Joseph Gross, "A Declaration of Cyberwar," *Vanity Fair*, April 2011, http://www.vanityfair.com/culture/features/2011/04/stuxnet-201104.

29) Paul Taylor, "Former US Spy chief warns on cybersecurity," *Financial Times*, December 2, 2012, http://www.ft.com/intl/cms/s/0/ed7ff098-3c4d-11e2-a6b2-00144feabdc0.html#axzz2LIYX8KIR.

30) Nathan Gardels, "Mike McConnell: An American Spymaster on Cyberwar," *HuffingtonPost.com*, July 8, 2009, http://www.huffingtonpost.com/nathan-gardels/mike-mcconnell-an-america_b_227944.html.

31) Mike McConnell, "Mike McConnell on how to win the cyberwar we're losing," *Washington Post*, February 28, 2010, http://www.washingtonpost.com/wp-dyn/content/article/2010/02/25/AR2010022502493.html.

32) Alina Selyukh and Jim Finkle, "Some U.S. utilities say they're under constant cyber attack," *Reuters*, May 21, 2013, http://www.reuters.com/article/2013/05/21/us-cybersecurity-utilities-idUSBRE94K18V20130521.

33) Alan Blinder, "Power grid Is Attacked in Arkansas," *New York Times*, October 8, 2013, http://www.nytimes.com/2013/10/09/us/power-grid-is-attacked-in-arkansas.html.

34) Alan Blinder, "Arrest in Attacks on Power Grid," *New York Times*, October 14, 2013, http://www.nytimes.com/2013/10/14/us/arrest-in-attacks-on-power-grid.html.

35) Alina Selyukh and Jim Finkle, "REUTERS SUMMIT: Power group more worried about physical than cyber threats," *Reuters*, May 14, 2013, http://uk.reuters.com/article/2013/05/13/cyber-summit-energy-idUKL2N0DQ2R420130513.

36) "Electric Grid Vulnerability: Industry Responses Reveal Security Gaps," A report written by the staff of congressmen Edward J. Markey (D-MA) and Henry A. Waxman (D-CA), May 21, 2013, http://markey.house.gov/sites/markey.house.gov/files/documents/Markey%20Grid%20Report_05.21.13.pdf .

37) Alina Selyukh and Jim Finkle, "Some U.S. utilities say they're under constant cyber attack," *Reuters*, May 21, 2013, http://www.reuters.com/article/2013/05/21/us-cybersecurity-utilities-idUSBRE94K18V20130521.

38) Richard Clarke, *Cyber War: The Next Threat to National Security and What to Do About It*, Ecco, 2012, ISBN-13: 978-0061962240, page 114.

39) *Cyberspace Policy Review*, White House, May 2009, http://www.whitehouse.gov/assets/documents/Cyberspace_Policy_Review_final.pdf.

40) Richard Clarke, *Cyber War: The Next Threat to National Security and What to Do About It*, Ecco, 2012, ISBN-13: 978-0061962240, page 118.

41) Lance Whitney, "U.S. CyberCom launches with first commander," *CNET*, May 24, 2010, http://news.cnet.com/8301-13639_3-20005749-42.html.

42) Noah Shachtman, "Cyber Command: We Don't Wanna Defend the Internet (We Just Might Have To)," *Wired*, May 28, 2010, http://www.wired.com/dangerroom/2010/05/cyber-command-we-dont-wanna-defend-the-internet-but-we-just-might-have-to/.

43) Lance Whitney, "U.S. CyberCom launches with first commander," *CNET*, May 24, 2010, http://news.cnet.com/8301-13639_3-20005749-42.html.

44) Ellen Nakashima, "Pentagon to boost cybersecurity force," *Washington Post*, January 27, 2013, http://www.washingtonpost.com/world/national-security/pentagon-to-boost-cybersecurity-force/2013/01/19/d87d9dc2-5fec-11e2-b05a-605528f6b712_print.html.

45) Thom Shanker, "Pentagon Is Updating Conflict Rules in Cyberspace," *New York Times*, June 27, 2013, http://www.nytimes.com/2013/06/28/us/pentagon-is-updating-conflict-rules-in-cyberspace.html.

46) "Navy earmarks hundreds of millions of dollars for cyber warfare project involving 13 companies," *Military and Aerospace Electronics*, July 17, 2013, http://cryptome.org/2013/07/navy-cyberwar-racket-990m.htm.

47) *Final Report on the August 14, 2003 Blackout in theUnited States and Canada*, U.S.-Canada Power System Outage Task Force, April 2004, https://reports.energy.gov/BlackoutFinal-Web.pdf.

48) Jill Aitoro, "Security Analysts Praise Obama's Pledge for a Cyber Chief," *Nextgov*, July 18, 2008, http://www.nextgov.com/cybersecurity/2008/07/security-analysts-praise-obamas-pledge-for-a-cyber-chief/42264/print/.

49) White House, *International Strategy for Cyberspace*, May 17, 2011, http://www.whitehouse.gov/sites/default/files/rss_viewer/international_strategy_for_cyberspace.pdf.

50) "Remarks on the Department of Defense Cyber Strategy," Deputy Secretary of Defense William J. Lynn, III, National Defense University, Washington, D.C., Thursday, July 14, 2011, http://www.defense.gov/speeches/speech.aspx?speechid=1593.

51) Thom Shanker, "New Military Command for Cyberspace," *New York Times*, June 24, 2009, http://www.nytimes.com/2009/06/24/technology/24cyber.html?_r=1&pagewanted=print.

52) Elaine Grossman, "U.S. General Reserves Right to Use Force, Even Nuclear, in Response to Cyber Attack," *Global Security Newswire*, May 12, 2009, http://www.nti.org/gsn/article/us-general-reserves-right-to-use-force-even-nuclear-in-response-to-cyber-attack/.

53) Thom Shanker, "New Military Command for Cyberspace," *New York Times*, June 24, 2009, http://www.nytimes.com/2009/06/24/technology/24cyber.html?_r=1&pagewanted=print.

54) Ellen Nakashima, "Obama signs secret directive to help thwart cyberattacks," *Washington Post*, November 14, 2012, http://www.washingtonpost.com/world/national-security/obama-signs-secret-cybersecurity-directive-allowing-more-aggressive-military-role/2012/11/14/7bf51512-2cde-11e2-9ac2-1c61452669c3_print.html.

55) Phil Stewart , "U.S. defense chief says pre-emptive action possible over cyber threat," *Reuters*, October 11, 2012, http://www.reuters.com/article/2012/10/12/net-us-usa-cyber-pentagon-idUSBRE89B04Q20121012.

56) Ellen Nakashima, "Pentagon to boost cybersecurity force," *Washington Post*, January 27, 2013, http://www.washingtonpost.com/world/national-security/pentagon-to-boost-cybersecurity-force/2013/01/19/d87d9dc2-5fec-11e2-b05a-605528f6b712_print.html.

57) Mark Mazzetti and David Sanger, "Security Leader Says U.S. Would Retaliate Against Cyberattacks," *New York Times*, March 12, 2013, http://www.nytimes.com/2013/03/13/us/intelligence-official-warns-congress-that-cyberattacks-pose-threat-to-us.html.

58) "Top 100 arms sales decreased in 2011," *SIPRI*, February 18, 2013, http://www.sipri.org/research/armaments/production/Top100/media/pressreleases/2013/AP_PR.

59) "Briefing on Department of State Efforts to Expand Defense Trade," Andrew J. Shapiro, Assistant Secretary, Bureau of Political-Military Affairs, June 14, 2012, http://www.state.gov/r/pa/prs/ps/2012/06/192408.htm.

60) Andy Greenberg, "New Grad Looking For a Job? Pentagon Contractors Post Openings For Black-Hat Hackers," *Forbes*, June 15, 2012, http://www.forbes.com/sites/andygreenberg/2012/06/15/new-grad-looking-for-a-job-pentagon-contractors-post-openings-for-black-hat-hackers-2/.

61) "U.S. Eases Rules on Exporting Military Technology to Secure Role as World's Leading Arms Dealer," *Democracy Now!* October 16, 2013, http://www.democracynow.org/2013/10/16/us_eases_rules_on_exporting_military#.

62) Sergey Ulasen, "Rootkit.TmpHider," *Wilders Security Forum*, July 12, 2010, http://www.wilderssecurity.com/showthread.php?p=1711135#post1711135.

63) Tareq Saade, "The Stuxnet Sting," Microsoft Malware Protection Center, July 16, 2010, http://blogs.technet.com/b/mmpc/archive/2010/07/16/the-stuxnet-sting.aspx.

64) Kupreev Oleg and Ulasen Sergey, "Trojan-Spy.0485 And Malware-Cryptor. Win32.Inject.gen.2 Review," VirusBlokAda, July, 2010, http://www.f-secure.com/weblog/archives/new_rootkit_en.pdf.

65) "Microsoft Security Advisory (2286198), Vulnerability in Windows Shell Could Allow Remote Code Execution," Microsoft Corp., July 16, 2010, http://technet.microsoft.com/en-us/security/advisory/2286198.

66) Nicolas Falliere, Liam O Murchu, and Eric Chien, *W32.Stuxnet Dossier*, Symantec Security Response, February 2011, http://www.symantec.com/content/en/us/enterprise/media/security_response/whitepapers/w32_stuxnet_dossier.pdf.

67) *Microsoft Security Bulletin MS10-046 – Critical Vulnerability in Windows Shell Could Allow Remote Code Execution (2286198)*, Microsoft Corp., August 02, 2010, http://technet.microsoft.com/en-us/security/bulletin/MS10-046.

68) Liam O Murchu, *Stuxnet Using Three Additional Zero-Day Vulnerabilities*, Symantec, September 14, 2010, http://www.symantec.com/connect/blogs/stuxnet-using-three-additional-zero-day-vulnerabilities.

69) Eric Byres, Andrew Ginter, and Joel Langill, "How Stuxnet Spreads – A Study of Infection Paths in Best Practice Systems," Tofino Security, Abterra Technologies, and ScadaHacker.com, February 22, 2011, http://abterra.ca/papers/How-Stuxnet-Spreads.pdf.

70) Eric Chien, *Stuxnet: A Breakthrough*, Symantec, November 16, 2010, http://www.symantec.com/connect/blogs/stuxnet-breakthrough.

71) Elinor Mills, "Stuxnet: Fact vs. Theory," *CNET*, October 5, 2010, http://news.cnet.com/8301-27080_3-20018530-245.html.

72) Alexander Gostev, "Myrtus and Guava, Episode 3," *SecureList*, July 15, 2010, http://www.securelist.com/en/blog/272/Myrtus_and_Guava_Episode_3.

73) Michael Joseph Gross, 'A Declaration of Cyberwar," *Vanity Fair*, April 2011, http://www.vanityfair.com/culture/features/2011/04/stuxnet-201104.

74) Ralph Langner, *Stuxnet Logbook*, September 16, 2010, http://www.langner.com/en/2010/09/16/stuxnet-logbook-sep-16-2010-1200-hours-mesz/#more-217.

75) *SCADA Systems*, Motorola, Inc., http://www.motorola.com/web/Business/Products/SCADA%20Products/_Documents/Static%20Files/SCADA_Sys_Wht_Ppr-2a_New.pdf.

76) Frank Rieger, "Der digitale Erstschlag ist erfolgt," *Frankfurter Allgemeine Zeitung*, September 22, 2010, http://www.faz.net/aktuell/feuilleton/debatten/digitales-denken/trojaner-stuxnet-der-digitale-erstschlag-ist-erfolgt-1578889.html.

77)Julian Assange, "Serious nuclear accident may lay behind Iranian nuke chief's mystery resignation," *WikiLeaks*, July 17, 2009 http://wikileaks.org/wiki/Serious_nuclear_accident_may_lay_behind_Iranian_nuke_chief's_mystery_resignation.

78) Bill Blunden, "Stuxnet Myrtus or MyRTUs?" *Cryptome*, October 1, 2010, http://cryptome.org/0002/myrtus-v-myRTUs.htm.

79) Bill Blunden, *An Uninvited Guest (Who Won't Go Home)*, Black Hat DC 2011, http://www.blackhat.com/presentations/bh-dc-10/Blunden_Bill/Blackhat-DC-2010-Blunden-Uninvited-Guest-wp.pdf.

80) William J. Broad, John Markoff and David E. Sanger, "Israeli Test on Worm Called Crucial in Iran Nuclear Delay," *New York Times*, January 15, 2011, http://www.nytimes.com/2011/01/16/world/middleeast/16stuxnet.html?pagewanted=all.

81) Matthias Schepp and Thomas Tuma, "Anti-Virus Pioneer Evgeny Kaspersky," *Der SPIEGEL*, June 24, 2011, http://www.spiegel.de/international/world/0,1518,770191,00.html.

82) "US and Israel were behind Stuxnet claims researcher," *BBC News*, March 4, 2011, http://www.bbc.co.uk/news/technology-12633240.

83) Gregg Keizer, "Iranian general accuses Siemens of helping U.S., Israel build Stuxnet," *Computerworld*, April 18, 2011, http://www.computerworld.com/s/article/9215901/Iranian_general_accuses_Siemens_of_helping_U.S._Israel_build_Stuxnet.

84) Ibid.

85) David Sanger, "Obama Order Sped Up Wave of Cyberattacks Against Iran," *New York Times*, June 1, 2012, http://www.nytimes.com/2012/06/01/world/middleeast/obama-ordered-wave-of-cyberattacks-against-iran.html.

86) Geoff McDonald, Liam O Murchu, Stephen Doherty, Eric Chien, *Stuxnet 0.5: The Missing Link*, Symantec, February 26, 2013, http://www.symantec.com/content/en/us/enterprise/media/security_response/whitepapers/stuxnet_0_5_the_missing_link.pdf.

87) Tabassum Zakaria, "Idaho laboratory analyzed Stuxnet computer virus," *Reuters*, September 29, 2011, http://www.reuters.com/article/2011/09/30/us-usa-cyber-idaho-idUSTRE78T08B20110930.

88)Nicolas Falliere, Liam O Murchu, and Eric Chien, *W32.Stuxnet Dossier*, Symantec Security Response, February 2011, http://www.symantec.com/content/en/us/enterprise/media/security_response/whitepapers/w32_stuxnet_dossier.pdf.

89) "Cyber worm found at German industrial plants," *The Local*, October 2, 2010, http://www.thelocal.de/national/20101002-30225.html.

90) William Yong and Robert F. Worth, "Bombings Hit Atomic Experts in Iran Streets," *New York Times*, November 29, 2010, http://www.nytimes.com/2010/11/30/world/middleeast/30tehran.html.

91) David Albright, Paul Brannan, and Christina Walrond, *Stuxnet Malware and Natanz: Update of ISIS December 22, 2010 Report*, Institute for Science and International Security, February 15, 2011, http://isis-online.org/uploads/isis-reports/documents/stuxnet_update_15Feb2011.pdf.

92) David Sanger and William Broad, "Iran Is Said to Move to New Machines for Making Nuclear Fuel," *New York Times*, February 21, 2013, http://www.nytimes.com/2013/02/22/world/middleeast/iran-upgrading-nuclear-equipment-inspectors-say.html.

93) David Kushner, "The Real Story of Stuxnet," *IEEE Spectrum*, February 26, 2013, http://beta.spectrum.ieee.org/telecom/security/the-real-story-of-stuxnet.

94) Kim Zetter, "Son of Stuxnet Found in the Wild on Systems in Europe," *Wired*, October 18, 2011, http://www.wired.com/threatlevel/2011/10/son-of-stuxnet-in-the-wild/.

95) Alexander Gostev, "The Duqu Saga Continues: Enter Mr. B. Jason and TV's Dexter," *SecureList*, Novermber 11, 2011, http://www.securelist.com/en/blog/208193243/The_Duqu_Saga_Continues_Enter_Mr_B_Jason_and_TVs_Dexter.

96) *Vulnerability Summary for CVE-2011-3402*, National Vulnerability Database, Novermber 4, 2011, http://web.nvd.nist.gov/view/vuln/detail?vulnId=CVE-2011-3402.

97) Microsoft Security Advisory (2639658), *Vulnerability in TrueType Font Parsing Could Allow Elevation of Privilege*, Microsoft Corp., November 03, 2011, http://technet.microsoft.com/en-us/security/advisory/2639658.

98) Microsoft Security Bulletin MS11-087 – *Critical Vulnerability in Windows Kernel-Mode Drivers Could Allow Remote Code Execution (2639417)*, Microsoft Corp., December 13, 2011, http://technet.microsoft.com/en-us/security/bulletin/ms11-087.

99) Symantec Security Response, *W32.Duqu: The Precursor to the Next Stuxnet*, Symantec, October 24, 2011, http://www.symantec.com/connect/w32_duqu_precursor_next_stuxnet.

100) Ibid.

101) Dennis Fisher, "Researchers 'Convinced' Duqu Written By Same Group as Stuxnet," *Threat Post*, Novermber 16, 2011, https://threatpost.com/en_us/blogs/researchers-convinced-duqu-written-same-group-stuxnet-111611.

102) *Duqu Trojan Questions and Answers*, Dell SecureWorks, October 26, 2011, http://www.secureworks.com/research/threats/duqu/.

103) Alexander Gostev and Igor Soumenkov, "Stuxnet/Duqu: The Evolution of Drivers," *SecureList*, December 28, 2011, http://www.securelist.com/en/analysis/204792208/Stuxnet_Duqu_The_Evolution_of_Drivers.

104) "sKyWIper (a.k.a. Flame a.k.a. Flamer): A complex malware for targeted attacks," Laboratory of Cryptography and System Security (CrySyS Lab), Budapest University of Technology and Economics, Department of Telecommunications, May 31, 2012, http://www.crysys.hu/skywiper/skywiper.pdf.

105) Skape and mmiller@hick.org, "Metasploit Meterpreter," *NoLogin*, December 26, 2004, http://www.nologin.org/Downloads/Papers/meterpreter.pdf.

106) Alexander Gostev, "The Flame: Questions and Answers," *Securelist*. May 28, 2012, http://www.securelist.com/en/blog/208193522/The_Flame_Questions_and_Answers.

107) Mikko Hypponen, "Why Antivirus Companies Like Mine Failed to Catch Flame and Stuxnet," *Wired*, June 1, 2012, http://www.wired.com/threatlevel/2012/06/internet-security-fail/.

108) Ibid.

109) Dancho Danchev, "Today's assignment : Coding an undetectable malware," *ZDNet*, August 6, 2008, http://www.zdnet.com/blog/security/todays-assignment-coding-an-undetectable-malware/1649.

110) Alexander Gostev, "Back to Stuxnet: the missing link," *Securelist*, June 11, 2012, http://www.securelist.com/en/blog?weblogid=208193568.

111) Jonathan Ness, "Microsoft certification authority signing certificates added to the Untrusted Certificate Store," Microsoft, June 3, 2012, http://blogs.technet.com/b/srd/archive/2012/06/03/microsoft-certification-authority-signing-certificates-added-to-the-untrusted-certificate-store.aspx.

112) Alex Sotirov, "Analyzing the MD5 collision in Flame," Trail of Bits, Inc., June 2012, http://trailofbits.files.wordpress.com/2012/06/flame-md5.pdf.

113) Ellen Nakashima, Greg Miller and Julie Tate, "U.S., Israel developed Flame computer virus to slow Iranian nuclear efforts, officials say," *Washington Post*, June 19, 2012, http://www.washingtonpost.com/world/national-security/us-israel-developed-computer-virus-to-slow-iranian-efforts-officials-say/2012/06/19/gJQA6xBPoV_story.html.

114) Dave Lee, "Flame: Israel rejects link to malware cyber-attack," *BBC News*, May 31, 2012, http://www.bbc.com/news/technology-18277555?print=true.

115) Richard Silverstein, "Flame: Israel's New Contribution to Middle East Cyberwar," *Tikun Olam*, May 28, 2012, http://www.richardsilverstein.com/tikun_olam/2012/05/28/flame-israels-new-contribution-to-middle-east-cyberwar/.

116) Global Research and Analysis Team (GReAT), *Guass: Abnormal Distribution*, Kaspersky Lab, August 9, 2012, http://www.securelist.com/en/analysis/204792238/Gauss_Abnormal_Distribution.

117) Global Research and Analysis Team (GReAT), *miniFlame aka SPE: "Elvis and his friends,"* Kaspersky Lab, October 15, 2012, http://www.securelist.com/en/analysis/204792247/miniFlame_aka_SPE_Elvis_and_his_friends.

118) Noah Shachtman, "Darpa Looks to Make Cyberwar Routine With Secret 'Plan X,'" *Wired*, August 21, 2012, http://www.wired.com/dangerroom/2012/08/plan-x/.

119) Presidential Policy Directive/ PPD-20, October 2012, http://s3.documentcloud.org/documents/710230/presidential-policy-directive.pdf.

120) Lana Lam, "Edward Snowden: US government has been hacking Hong Kong and China for years," *South China Morning Post*, June 13, 2013, http://www.scmp.com/news/hong-kong/article/1259508/edward-snowden-us-government-has-been-hacking-hong-kong-and-china.

121) Matthew Aid, "Inside the NSA's Ultra-Secret China Hacking Group," *Foreign Policy*, June 10, 2013, http://www.foreignpolicy.com/articles/2013/06/10/inside_the_nsa_s_ultra_secret_china_hacking_group?print=yes&hidecomments=yes&page=full.

122) Matthew Aid, "The NSA's New Code Breakers," *Foreign Policy*, October 15, 2013, http://www.foreignpolicy.com/articles/2013/10/15/the_nsa_s_new_codebreakers?print=yes&hidecomments=yes&page=full.

123) Barton Gellman and Ellen Nakashima, "U.S. spy agencies mounted 231 offensive cyber-operations in 2011, documents show," *Washington Post*, August 30, 2013, http://www.washingtonpost.com/world/national-security/us-spy-agencies-mounted-231-offensive-cyber-operations-in-2011-documents-show/2013/08/30/d090a6ae-119e-11e3-b4cb-fd7ce041d814_print.html.

124) "NSA Documents Show United States Spied Brazilian Oil Giant," *Globo*, September 8, 2013, http://g1.globo.com/fantastico/noticia/2013/09/nsa-documents-show-united-states-spied-brazilian-oil-giant.html.

125) Edward Moyer, "NSA disguised itself as Google to spy, say reports," *CNET*, September 12, 2013, http://news.cnet.com/8301-13578_3-57602701-38/nsa-disguised-itself-as-google-to-spy-say-reports/.

126) David Sanger, "A New Cold War, in Cyberspace, Tests U.S. Ties to China," *New York Times*, February 24, 2013, http://www.nytimes.com/2013/02/25/world/asia/us-confronts-cyber-cold-war-with-china.html.

Chapter 2

Our Frenemy in Asia

I magine a world where your job and home are assigned by the government. Once a month you show up at a designated government office to pick up commodity stamps which indicate how many pounds of rice, ounces of oil, yards of cloth, and other essentials have been allocated to you. The officials at this government office carefully check your resident permit, which is logged at a central registrar's office. This was how things worked in China roughly 30 years ago under what's known as the *Hukou* (resident permit) and *Liangpiao* (rationing stamps) systems. With the institution of these exacting social controls, people couldn't freely move, as ration coupons were only issued at the government office where their resident permit was registered.

Foreigners were few and far between during this time period. Granted, they didn't need commodity stamps, but their basic economic activities were confined to a small subset of merchants who were authorized to authenticate passports and accept foreign currency.

If China had remained this way, the recent flurry of cyber-attacks attributed to China would have to have been singularly masterminded by the People's Republic of China (PRC) government. No one else, and no other organization, would have the freedom to engage in illegal activity on a local scale, let alone on a global scale. The populace, immobilized by policies like Hukou and Liangpiao, would be subject to extensive neighborhood watch systems, such that the government could quickly track down criminals and squash illegal behavior. This would include badmouthing party officials or expressing opinions that weren't politically correct (i.e. thought crime).

A Plurality of Actors

China's economic development changed the security apparatus dramatically. In 1978, the State loosened restrictions on labor movement to allow farmers, then roughly 76% of the workforce, to seek employment in cities.[1] As a result, between 1978 and 2009, more than 10% of the population (approximately 180 million people) migrated from rural to urban areas. Many of these workers are referred to as "the floating population," as employment tended to shift geographically over time. With the Liangpiao system's demise in 1993, Hukou became increasingly inaccurate; for the first time in Communist history, the State suddenly didn't know the location of each citizen.

As the security apparatus lost its former efficacy, a criminal element emerged. China's leadership initiated the country's economic ascent by throwing off the shackles of Maoist egalitarianism, asserting that they needed "to let some people get rich first."[2] The practical consequence was a widening chasm between the very rich and everybody else. Prominent VIPs began to show off their wealth with sports cars and high fashion. Behind all of the celebratory glitz is a pervasive, murky, backdrop of venality. The alleged crimes of Communist official Bo Xilai and his associates (e.g. bribery, racketeering, offshore gambling, and even murder) do not at all come as a surprise to the locals.[3] By the time the trial concluded in September 2013, the judge said Bo's embezzlement and bribery was over $4 million.[4] One particular instance that came to light was a $100,000 trip to Africa taken by Bo's son and his friends.

Most Chinese assume a priori that their leaders enjoy special treatments. It is common knowledge that even the strictest rules have wide latitude of interpretation if the perpetrator happens to be someone powerful. To be fair, in light of the 2008 economic collapse in the United States, this is hardly a phenomenon unique to China alone.[5]

While China boasts almost 100 billionaires,[6] the working class struggles. The dream of owning a house is out of reach for the bulk of the population. For example, the starting salary for college graduates in Beijing is 2,500 yuan per month (about $400)[7] and the average price of houses in Beijing is 1.7 million yuan (about $250,000).[8] This means that a starting college graduate in Beijing worries about housing prospects in the same way that a part-time waiter does in Denver. The financial pressure on normal citizens to manage the basics of life (e.g. a house, marriage, children, taking care of ailing parents, health care) is practically overwhelming.

This is exactly this sort of income inequality that stimulates crime. The rich thrive by forging allegiances with allies in the government. The poor get a piece of the action with the tacit guarantee that the law will look the other way. The nature of Internet crime, as we'll see, is chaotic and decentralized in a manner reminiscent of the Wild West. Informal arrangements between bounty hunters, corrupt politicians, and greedy corporate interests are the general rule... not organized armies.

The idea that cyber-attacks from China are part of an all-encompassing campaign by the Chinese government is what psychologists call *out-group homogeneity bias*. It's human nature for the American public to ignore the nuances of social dynamics in a foreign country like China but at the same time recognize the variability in the United States. In reality each country has its own intricate framework of moving parts, especially a country as vast as China. Though it suits the Pentagon quite well to ceaselessly point to the East and leverage our innate tendency to see one great big united hoard of Chinese hackers.

The sheer size of the Chinese government guarantees that independent outfits will, at some point, intersect with other groups. An unidentified Chinese hacker interviewed by the *New York Times* stated:

> I don't think the West understands... China's government is so big. It's almost impossible to not have any crossover with the government.[9]

There are also foreigners in China who are believed to be engaged in organized criminal activity. Officials have admitted that there is a lack of oversight of this population.[10] Beijing, for instance, has about 200,000 foreigners and the government only has adequate records on 721 of them, people who hold Chinese green cards. The remaining foreigners are cause for concern.

All told, there are a lot of different criminal operators in China, people who have the motivation, means, and opportunity to commit cyber-attacks. A given attack originating from China could be the work of a cash-strapped outlaw trying to get ahead, a well-funded organized crime syndicate, a high-ranking party official sponsoring an operation for his own personal gain, an opportunistic foreign visitor with money to burn, or a state-sponsored government agent from another country running a false-flag campaign from a launch pad within the PRC.

Internal threats have overwhelmed the government. Yet, all too widely, the sprawling ecosystem in China is viewed as a singular entity without recognizing the inescapable plurality of a country that maintains a population which hovers above a billion.

Rule of Law Breaks Down

Anyone who has done business in Hong Kong knows that, despite the rapid economic growth of mainland China, Hong Kong still has one ace up its sleeve: regulatory infrastructure, a legacy of the British colonialists. Specifically, we are talking about the legal and administrative oversight.

If you want to do business with the Chinese, it's generally less risky to do so in Hong Kong because there are a significant number of *checks and balances* in place to safeguard buyers and sellers. In fact, it's fairly common for merchants from the mainland to travel to Hong Kong for this very reason. Simply put, there's better supervision and less room for monkey business. If someone tries to rip you off, there are business associations and government authorities that you can go to. In Hong Kong there's rule of law with little deviation.

In contrast, with regard to law and order, mainland China is in a state of disarray. Such is the conclusion of Chen Gaungcheng, a well-known political activist who was granted permission to study in the United States after escaping house arrest in Shandong. Based on his work on abortion cases in China as well as his firsthand experience on the infringement of his own human rights, this self-taught lawyer asserts:

The fundamental question the Chinese government must face
is lawlessness. China does not lack laws, but the rule of law.[11]

The economic and political reforms that began in China during
the years of Deng Xiaoping transferred power to local officials and
resulted in extensive abuse. In fact, outside observers question the
extent to which the central leadership can exercise their authority
to reform their system and impose rule of law.[12] Such were the
primary conclusions of He Qinglian in her celebrated book *The
Pitfalls of Modernization.*[13]

The Chinese have an ancient colloquialism:

The king is less adequate than the immediate manager.

县官不如现管

This is commonly used in the context of political corruption.
When you want to sidestep the law, you have to choose a target.
This maxim cautions against bribing a national leader as it's usually
more effective to find the local official charged with direct oversight
and bribe him.

To get an idea for how bad things have gotten, mainland China
(PRC) is becoming a popular haven for white collar fugitives from
Taiwan.[14] Although most outlaws disappear into the nation's teeming
masses, some of the more prominent fugitives have been brazen
enough to open businesses and start new careers. For example, a
businessman named Chen Youhao was charged with stealing about
800 million New Taiwan dollars from a subsidiary of the Tuntex
Group in Taiwan. He subsequently escaped to the mainland and
established one of the top ten businesses in a city named Xiamen.

The Internet's Frontier Town

With economic development came the Internet and the online
economy. These developments pose additional challenges to
the ailing rule of law. "China's networks are wide open" concluded
Dillon Beresford, a researcher from NSS Labs who spent the better
part of 18 months navigating his way through the far reaches of

China's governmental, military, and university networks. Just how bad is it? Beresford stated:

> The amount of data I have found that is not intended for public consumption is amazing. I stopped after three terabytes. These systems are not maintained and are all vulnerable to attacks… They don't have the manpower or even the knowledge to maintain them. And, in many ways, China is still playing catch up with the U.S. They're an aggressor in cyberspace, but their own networks are very weak and poorly designed.[15]

Beresford also observes that China doesn't even have a policy framework in place:

> One of the things I thought about with my research is the issue of transparency. This is an issue in China and, I would guess, other authoritarian regimes … in China, the government runs everything and there's no clear policy for cyber-security.[16]

In addition to the policy vacuum China's copyright infringements aren't helping either. According to a Brookings report on cyber-security the prevalence of pirated software is an Achilles heel as far as network security is concerned:

> Even more, many believe that China's systems are more vulnerable than are America's. This assertion has merit, in part because greater use of "pirated" software by Chinese companies and institutions means that their systems typical do not get the same upgrades of protection to evolving cyber threats that nominal buyers receive.[17]

In 2010, China's *National Computer Network Emergency Response Team* (CNCERT) reported that over ten million machines alone were compromised by Trojan software and that these machines were being managed by almost half a million command-and-control (C&C) servers. Nevertheless, at the end of 2010 the Ministry of Public Security admitted that they had only arrested 460 people on hacking charges.[18]

Take a moment to digest this fact and put it into context. China is a nation with more than a billion people. A sprawling city of several million is seen as a "town." There are thousands of cyber out-laws, and that's probably an understatement. This is a nation that is admittedly unable to effectively rein in tax evasion.[19] Something as essential as collecting taxes (an activity that offers direct and concrete benefits to the government) eludes China thanks to per-vasive bribery and a dysfunctional bureaucracy. The government can't even handle tasks that are definitely in its best interests. To understand the depth of the problem, consider that there's a vast underground market in China for fake receipts, despite the fact that the crime is sometimes punishable by death.[20]

Never mind the staggering amount of air pollution,[21] which is so bad that wearing a mask is practically mandatory, or the fact that Chinese parents have so little faith in the quality of local products that the number of arrests for smuggling baby formula at the border with Hong Kong has exceeded the number of arrests for heroin smuggling.[22]

Let's not forget the new ID system. Starting in 2005, China deployed a new generation of digital ID cards. Unfortunately, in contrast to their western counterparts, the designers failed to im-plement a disabling feature, such that cards can't be canceled in the event of theft or loss. Hence, the new ID cards are prized proces-sions for criminals. Today, genuine ID cards are a booming busi-ness online, sorted by age, sex and other physical attributes, at a price tag of about $65 each.[23]

China is not an expanding imperial power bent on hegemony. Rather, China is a country that's *struggling simply to function*, much less function properly. This is a consequence of systemic corruption which prevents the government from competently delivering necessary services. As a testimony to this, the number of protests in China doubled between 2006 and 2010, peaking at 180,000 recorded "mass incidents."[24]

Given the non-stop array of gaffes, how could you expect the PRC leaders to effectively deal with outlaws on their stretch of the Internet? Corruption is so ubiquitous, and rule of law is often so tenuous, that China is fertile ground for criminal activity. If you ever wondered why there are so many servers in China that host criminal activity, now you know why.[25]

Bribery is commonplace, and suffice it to say that all of the related officials have been given financial incentives to look the other way. *If the Internet seems a bit lawless in China, that's because it is.*

Despite what the military types may say, what goes on in China is not necessarily the result of some grand 1000-year plan on behalf of the PRC's top leadership, but rather the *logical end-result of their waning control and the emergence of rogue elements* that have found refuge in the relative disorder of China's networks.

Let me put it to you this way: If an Eastern European intelligence officer were running a covert operation based somewhere in Europe, he or she would be well advised to launch their attacks from China to mislead forensic investigators. Anti-forensics is a blossoming discipline in the field of computer security.[26] Elaborate ruses involving forgery, deception, and impersonation are as old as espionage. Any intelligence operator worth his salt will go to great lengths to pivot his attack through another country while making sure to use tools, operational signatures, and planted artifacts that implicated a third-party. It's a matter of standard tradecraft.

Welcome to the *wilderness of mirrors*.

The knee-jerk response of everyone in the media, in the military, and in Washington is to reflexively blame the PRC. Not for a single moment do any of the commentators on the nightly news, or alleged experts from the myriad of beltway think tanks, presume to suspect someone else (e.g. corporate-based, state-sponsored, or organized crime).

Opposing Models for Reform

One solution that the PRC is contemplating is to copy the Hong Kong system. This school of thought is embodied by what's called the *Guangdong model*, as Hong Kong borders the Mainland province of Guangdong and the two neighbors share a common dialect (Cantonese). The Guangdong model favors liberalization of economic policies coupled with greater political openness, with an emphasis on rule of law based on due process. China's new leader Xi Jinping is charging ahead in this direction. For example, the availability of transcripts regarding the trial of Bo Xilai is unprecedented.

Hardliners in the Communist Party argue that the country is straying from its traditional socialist values, and all it simply needs is a security apparatus that's on par with China's economic boom. They point back to the era of Mao, where society was relatively secure because the government knew almost everything about each of its citizens, and then did what was necessary to maintain security. It's somewhat akin to the authoritarian, J. Edgar Hoover, school of thought. From this vantage point, due process and individual rights are sacrificed in the name of expediency and results.

Bo Xilai, a figurehead of this authoritarian camp, launched brutal crackdowns on organized crime. Because Mr. Bo was the head of the Communist Party in Chongqing region, this alternative model for change has been dubbed the *Chongqing model*. The fall of Mr. Bo doesn't necessarily signal the end of the Chongqing movement, as it is stylistically consistent with the Tiananmen Square massacre and Falun Gong persecutions. Without a doubt, this approach still has powerful supporters in the government.

In search of solutions to growing disorder, the Chinese government is operating with a split personality, pulled into two opposite directions by the Guangdong model and Chongqing model.

Ironically, as Western commentators question the long-term viability of Chongqing model, it's interesting to note that the J. Edgar Hoover style of safeguarding national security has also seen revival in the U.S. post 9/11. Specifically, we are alluding to the *Patriot Act*, the *2012 National Defense Authorization Act*, warrantless wiretaps, drone strikes, and the ongoing campaign to entrench government secrecy. What's different is that the U.S. is a fairly young republic founded on the ideals of freedom. China, on the other hand, is accustomed to authoritarian power structures which have recurred in various forms for thousands of years.

In the end, China and the United States suffer from common problems originating from the Internet (e.g. cybercrime, espionage) and both nations have pondered solutions. Though heavy-handed tactics wielded by strong leaders may possess the lure of a simple-sounding cure, it would behoove both countries to focus on imposing rule of law without taking shortcuts that impinge upon individual rights or short-circuit due process.

The Extent of China's Capabilities

While trying to manage Internet threats, China has recently made gestures towards defending its networks. In July of 2010, more than a year after the formation of CYBERCOM, China announced the creation of its *Information Security Base*, a department dedicated to tackling cyber war threats. An officer from the Chinese General Staff Headquarters, who requested to remain anonymous, told a reporter from the *Global Times*: "It is a defensive base for information security, not an offensive headquarters for cyber war."[27]

That's not to say that China hasn't developed offensive capability. China has almost certainly been working on its offense since 2003, when the People's Liberation Army (PLA) openly stated that it would be deploying information warfare units.[28] Strategists like General Dai Qingmin expounded on the merits of pre-emptive measures in the domain of electronic warfare:

> Actions such as intelligence warfare, psychological warfare, and campaign deception in advance of combat seem to be even more important to the unimpeded implementation of planning and ensuring war. For this reason, information warfare must be started in advance of other combat actions before making war plans and while making war plans.[29]

Yet, despite the theoretical emanations of ambitious Chinese generals, it may be that China's bark is worse than its bite. At least, that's the opinion of Desmond Ball, a professor in the Strategic and Defense Studies Centre located at the Australian National University. In a 2011 article, he concluded:

> There is no evidence that China's cyber-warriors can penetrate highly secure networks or covertly steal or falsify critical data. They would be unable to systematically cripple selected command and control, air defence and intelligence networks and databases of advanced adversaries, or to conduct deception operations by secretly manipulating the data in these networks. The gap between the sophistication of the anti-virus and network security programs available to China's cyber-war-

riors as compared to those of their counterparts in the more open, advanced IT societies, is immense. China's cyber-warfare authorities must despair at the breadth and depth of modern digital information and communications systems and technical expertise available to their adversaries.[30]

These conclusions are in stark contrast to the torrent of reports published by the American press. Most cyberwar pieces that find their way to print depict China as technical juggernaut, a horde of ultra-sophisticated invaders which has infiltrated its way into the heart of our information infrastructure and likely installed some sort of system-wide doomsday device. Voices that fail to adhere to this basic message, and its tone, are outnumbered.

In early 2013 a computer security vendor, Mandiant Corporation, provided the *New York Times* with a report on a series of espionage operations that appeared to originate out of China. Mandiant believes that the Chinese military, through an obscure command referred to as Unit 61398, was responsible, and furthermore investigators voiced concern that these attacks were targeting American critical infrastructure.[31]

Joined at the Hip

With the end of the Cold War, officials have begun to rely on China as a convenient boogeyman. Faced with a litany of claims that China intends to infiltrate and destroy our infrastructure, it might be useful to consider the nature of the economic realities that bind China to the United States.

Consider this: the *United States is China's largest trading partner* such that the Chinese economy depends heavily on American consumers as a source of revenue.[32] Likewise, *the Chinese own more of our debt, in terms of Treasury securities, than anyone else.*[33] In fact, they own more than fifteen percent of our total public debt, nothing to sneeze it.

In the meantime, while the Pentagon and the defense contractors hyper-ventilate about the PLA's plans to cripple our networks, the State Department is busy trying to sell China jetliners made by defense contractor Boeing.[34] How's that for cognitive dissonance?

Given this level of economic interdependency, all of the various doomsday scenarios begin to lose their hue of legitimacy. If the United States went down in a blaze of cyber glory what would happen to China's export market? Even worse, how would China recoup the trillion dollar investment it made in Treasury securities?

Strategically, what does China gain from obliterating our infrastructure?

Considering these questions, in a statement that directly contradicts statements made by a myriad of other high-ranking government officials, Defense Intelligence Agency Director Army Lt. Gen. Michael T. Flynn told a reporter:

> We should not view China as an adversary.[35]

The Chinese would be shooting themselves in the foot if they crippled the U.S. It should be patently clear to anyone that it's in China's best interest to keep the U.S. economy humming right along. This state of affairs strongly suggests that the likelihood of *a mass-scale infrastructure attack by China is about as realistic as a land invasion.*

This reality says something about the people stoking doomsday scenarios that involve China: government officials, think-tank "experts," retired military officers, and corporate information security front men. Keep this in mind every time you hear them raise the alarm.

Both Sides Keep the Other in Business

In light of their somewhat tenuous grip on their networks, it's probably not that far a stretch to conclude that the Chinese are just as worried about us as we seem to be about them (if not more so). In June of 2011, the official newspaper of the Chinese Military, the *Liberation Army Daily*, stated:

> The U.S. military is hastening to seize the commanding military heights on the Internet, and another Internet war is being pushed to a stormy peak …. Their actions remind us that to protect the nation's Internet security, we must accelerate Internet defense development and accelerate steps to make a strong Internet army.[36]

Like their counterparts overseas, Chinese military figures are prone to dramatic proclamations. For instance, in June of 2011 army officials made the following claim in an article published by the *China Youth Daily*:

> Just as nuclear warfare was the strategic war of the industrial era, cyber-warfare has become the strategic war of the information era, and this has become a form of battle that is massively destructive and concerns the life and death of nations.[37]

In March of 2013, China's state news agency reported that over the course of the first two months of 2013 more than fifty percent of all cyber-attacks emanated from the United States, and that servers located in the United States were controlling 1.29 million infected machines in China.[38]

Wait a minute. Does this sound oddly familiar?

The Chinese military claims that China faces an existential threat from the United States and they need to build up their cyber capabilities. Retired spymaster Michael Hayden, with a certain amount of bravado, infers that there's merit to this idea:

> The Chinese, with some legitimacy, will say, "You spy on us." And as former director of the NSA I'll say, "Yeah, and we're better at it than you are."[39]

At the same time, you could invert the names of the two countries and come up with a valid statement. The United States military, facing budget cuts and furloughs,[40] claims that America faces an existential threat from China and we need to build up our cyber capabilities. Both militaries point at each other and howl for funding. Such is the nature of a self-perpetuated arms race.

The two sides keep each other in business.

Then again, this is what military officers and defense contractors are preoccupied with: war, breaking things and killing people. It's what they do. Though, they prefer to call it "defense" because it sounds less hostile. Of course if you look for them it's only expected that you'd unearth hundreds of military publications in both China and the United States that dwell on the vagaries of cyberwar.

Cyberwar proponents like to point to military publications as proof that the other side is gunning for us and infer that anyone who thinks otherwise isn't paying attention (they'll moan "don't you see, we're asleep at the wheel, they're laughing at us!"). However, the question arises as to whether the views expressed by these same military publications actually reflect those of their civilian leaders or are simply appeals directed at them from below, subtle admonishments to provide more tax money?

The #1 Threat to Economic Security?

With respect to federal funding it's interesting to see how narrow financial interests often try to manufacture ways to align themselves with broader public concerns. In an annual report on China published in 2013, the Pentagon stated that the Chinese government "appeared" to be siphoning off intellectual property from the United States and that the acquired intelligence could potentially benefit China's hi-tech industry and threaten the U.S. economy.[41]

Former White House Advisor Richard Clarke took this narrative a step further by explicitly claiming that Chinese spying is costing American jobs.[42]

Mike Rogers, the Republican congressman from Michigan who currently chairs the House Intelligence Committee, pulled out all the stops and went flat-out full bore. During a video segment released on CNBC he brazenly stated that cyber-attacks from China are the *number one threat to U.S. economic security.*[43]

Could Congressman Rogers (who, by the way, has received a healthy infusion of campaign donations from the likes of Boeing, General Dynamics, Lockheed Martin, Raytheon, and SAIC) be correct? Let's pause for a moment and reflect on this notion. Does Chinese cyber espionage actually represent this sort of existential threat?

As a side note, Mike Rogers was an FBI special agent before being elected to the Michigan Senate in 1995.[44]

George Smith, a senior fellow at GlobalSecurity.org, believes that globalization in the form of offshore outsourcing has done more damage to the average American worker.[45]

American business ceded its property to the Chinese industrial base for immediate profit in pursuit of the very cheapest unprotected manpower. This was long before Chinese espionage became an issue the national security megaplex decided to exploit for the purpose of parasitic rent-seeking.

Who are you going to find on the street who cares if Chinese cyberwarriors from a building in Shanghai are into American businesses? They've already lost their jobs or much of their earning power. And their access to the Internet is a smartphone made in China.

Take a day off from the memes. Corporate America isn't hiring, haven't you heard? It's not because of mass Chinese cyber-spying.

There are acknowledged experts on this topic, like Norm Matloff at UC Davis, who agree with this conclusion.[46] Outsourcing has done significant damage to American workers in addition to yielding crucial strategic assets. The short-term financial interests of the corporate elite are disrupting society's long-term interests.

Smith's core message, that there are serious economic threats that we're being distracted from with overstated tales of Chinese cyber-espionage, is not difficult to corroborate. Researchers from the Federal Reserve Bank of Dallas have studied the recent financial crisis and calculated the damage wrought on behalf of banks which have been deemed too big to fail. It's somewhere on the order of the U.S. annual GDP:

> We conservatively estimate that 40 to 90 percent of one year's output ($6 trillion to $14 trillion, the equivalent of $50,000 to $120,000 for every U.S. household) was foregone due to the 2007-09 recession ...[47]

Having said that, now take a look at the graph displayed in Figure 2-1. It's based on data collected by the St. Louis Federal Reserve Bank. It compares average hourly earnings for production and nonsupervisory employees[48] against corporate profits (after taxes).[49] For the sake of clarity, data has been indexed at 100 starting on January 1, 2009.

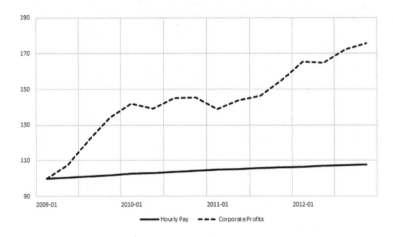

Figure 2-1

Glancing over the graph it's pretty clear that wages have stagnated and corporate profits have soared, nearly doubling. *This, dear reader, is not the result of Chinese cyber espionage.* It's the result of oligarchic state capture.

Please note, *we are not arguing that cyber-security isn't a serious issue.* It definitely is. Rather, we contend that Chinese cyber espionage isn't the existential threat that people like Mike Rogers are making it out to be.

The upper echelons of the income scale, people who also happen to hold the bulk of their wealth in the financial markets, are thriving. Thanks in no small part to global labor arbitrage, the decade-spanning assault on unions, monetary policy that favors stockholders (e.g. quantitative easing), and impressive increases in worker productivity. The average person, conversely, hasn't shared in this windfall.[50] In fact, one could argue that the American middle class is essentially being *strip mined* by the people at the top.

Endnotes

1) Jialu Liu, Virginia Harper Ho, and Lu Zhang, "Chinese Workers: Under Threat or a Threat to American Workers," *Working Paper #2*, July 2010, http://www.indiana.edu/~rccpb/Working_Paper/Workers_Symposium_RCCPB_WP2_July_2010.pdf.

2) "To each according to his abilities," *The Economist*, May 31, 2001, http://www.economist.com/node/639652.

3) "Bo's butler confessed to Chinese officials," *World News*. May 24, 2012.

4) "Going Down Fighting," *The Economist*, August 31, 2013, http://www.economist.com/news/china/21584367-china-has-been-gripped-extraordinary-courtroom-drama-going-down-fighting.

5) "The Untouchables," *FRONTLINE*, January 22, 2013, http://www.pbs.org/wgbh/pages/frontline/untouchables/.

6) "The World's Billionaries," *Forbes*, http://www.forbes.com/billionaires/.

7) "Average starting pay of Chinese college grads hits 2,500 yuan," *People's Daily Online*, May 24, 2011, http://english.people.com.cn/90001/90776/90882/7389879.html.

8) "Average age of Beijing first-home buyers is 27," *China Economic Net*, August 28, 2010, http://en.ce.cn/Industries/Property/201008/28/t20100828_21770552.shtml.

9) Edward Wong, "Hackers Find China Is Land of Opportunity," *New York Times*, May 22, 2013, http://www.nytimes.com/2013/05/23/world/asia/in-china-hacking-has-widespread-acceptance.html.

10) "Foreigners in Beijing," *Sing Tao Daily*, May 27, 2012.

11) Chen Guangchen, "How China Flouts Its Laws," *New York Times*, May 29, 2012, http://www.nytimes.com/2012/05/30/opinion/how-china-flouts-its-laws.html.

12) "The emperor does know," *The Economist*, May 12, 2012, http://www.economist.com/node/21554561.

13) Qinglian He, Xian dai hua di xian jing: Dang dai Zhongguo di jing ji she hui wen ti, Xin hua shu dian jing xiao, 1998, ISBN: 7507209083.

14) "Taiwan's key economic fugitives in the Mainland," *Sing Tao Daily*, May 14, 2012.

15) Paul Roberts, "Glass Dragon: China's Cyber Offense Obscures Woeful Defense," *Threat Post*, April 27, 2011.

16) Ibid.

17) Kenneth Lieberthal and Peter W. Singer, "Cybersecurity and U.S.-China Relations," Brookings Institute, February of 2012, http://www.brookings.edu/research/papers/2012/02/23-cybersecurity-china-us-singer-lieberthal.

18) Iain Mills, "China's Faltering Cyber-Security Efforts Offer Chance for Engagement," *World Politics Review*, December 9, 2010.

19) William Gamble, "The Middle Kingdom Runs Dry: Tax Evasion in China," *Foreign Affairs*, November/December 2000.

20) David Barboza, "Coin of Realm in China Graft: Phony Receipts," *New York Times*, August 3, 2012, http://www.nytimes.com/2013/08/04/business/global/coin-of-realm-in-china-graft-phony-receipts.html.

21) Edward Wong, "Air Pollution Linked to 1.2 Million Premature Deaths in China," *New York Times*, April 1, 2013, http://www.nytimes.com/2013/04/02/world/asia/air-pollution-linked-to-1-2-million-deaths-in-china.html.

22) Liza Lin and Julie Cruz, "Milk Smugglers Top Heroin Courier Arrests in Hong Kong," *Bloomberg*, April 26, 2013, http://www.bloomberg.com/news/print/2013-04-25/milk-smugglers-top-heroin-courier-arrests-in-hong-kong.html.

23) "Crooks strike rich with ID card you can't cancel," *Shanghai Daily*, August 14, 2013, http://www.china.org.cn/china/2013-08/14/content_29710947.htm.

24) "Rising Protests in China," *Atlantic*, February 17, 2012, http://www.theatlantic.com/infocus/2012/02/rising-protests-in-china/100247/.

25) Robert McMillan, "In China, $700 Puts a Spammer in Business," *IDG News Service*, May 08, 2009.

26) Bill Blunden, *The Rootkit Arsenal: Escape and Evasion in the Dark Corners of the System*, Jones and Bartlett, 2nd Edition, ISBN-13: 978-1449626365.

27) Peng Pu, "PLA unveils nation's first cyber center," *Global Times*, July 22, 2010.

28) "PLA to Organize First Information Warfare Units," *Mingpao* News, March 12, 2003.

29) Colonel Timothy L. Thomas, "China's Electronic Long-Range Reconnaissance," *Military Review*, November-December 2008.

30) Desmond Ball, "China's Cyber Warfare Capabilities," *Security Challenges*, Volume 7, Number 2, pp. 81-103.

31) David E. Sanger, David Barboza And Nicole Perlroth, "Chinese Army Unit Is Seen as Tied to Hacking Against U.S.," *New York Times*, February 18, 2013, http://www.nytimes.com/2013/02/19/technology/chinas-army-is-seen-as-tied-to-hacking-against-us.html.

32) "Top 10 trading partners of the Chinese mainland," *China Daily*, February 19, 2014, http://europe.chinadaily.com.cn/business/2014-02/19/content_17290585.htm.

33) *Major Foreign Holders Of Treasury Securities* (in billions of dollars), U.S. Department of Treasury, http://www.treasury.gov/resource-center/data-chart-center/tic/Documents/mfh.txt.

34) Eric Lipton, Nicola Clark and Andrew W. Lehren, "Diplomats Help Push Sales of Jetliners on the Global Market," *New York Times*, January 2, 2011, http://www.nytimes.com/2011/01/03/business/03wikileaks-boeing.html.

35) J.J. Green, "Inside the Looking Glass: The staggering pace of change," *WTOP*, October 24, 2013, http://www.wtop.com/807/3490243/Inside-the-Looking-Glass-The-staggering-pace-of-change.

36) Chris Buckley, "China military paper urges steps against U.S. cyber war threat," *Reuters*, June 16, 2011.

37) Chris Buckley, "China PLA officers call Internet key battleground," *Reuters*, June 3, 2011.

38) Sui-Lee Wee, "China says U.S. is top source of hacking attacks on country," *Reuters*, March 10, 2013, http://www.reuters.com/article/2013/03/10/us-china-hacking-idUSBRE92902F20130310.

39) Joseph Menn, "Analysis – The near impossible battle against hackers everywhere," *Reuters*, February 24, 2013, http://uk.reuters.com/article/2013/02/24/uk-cybersecurity-battle-idUKBRE91N03720130224.

40) Sarah Wheaton, "Pentagon Warns of Widespread Civilian Furloughs," *New York Times*, February 20, 2013, http://www.nytimes.com/2013/02/21/us/pentagon-warns-of-widespread-civilian-furloughs.html.

41) Office of the Secretary of Defense, "Military and Security Developments Involving the People's Republic of China 2013," May 2013, http://www.defense.gov/pubs/2013_china_report_final.pdf.

42) Richard Clarke, "How China Steals Our Secrets," *New York Times*, April 2, 2012, http://www.nytimes.com/2012/04/03/opinion/how-china-steals-our-secrets.html.

43) Karen McVeigh and Dominic Rushe, "House passes Cispa cybersecurity bill despite warnings from White House," *Guardian*, April 18, 2013, http://www.guardian.co.uk/technology/2013/apr/18/house-representatives-cispa-cybersecurity-white-house-warning/print.

44) U.S. Rep. Mike Rogers (MI-08) biography, http://mikerogers.house.gov/biography/.

45) George Smith, "The nebulous Menace: Shoeshine at its best," *Dick Destiny Blog*, May 7, 2013, http://dickdestiny.com/blog1/2013/05/07/the-nebulous-menace-shoeshine-at-its-best/.

46) Norman Matloff, "Globalization and the American IT Worker," *Communications of the ACM*, November 2004/Volume 47, Number 11, http://heather.cs.ucdavis.edu/CACM.pdf.

47) Tyler Atkinson, David Luttrell and Harvey Rosenblum, "How Bad Was It? The Costs and Consequences of the 2007–09 Financial Crisis," *Dallas Federal Reserve Staff Papers*, Number 20, July 2013, http://dallasfed.org/assets/documents/research/staff/staff1301.pdf.

48) Federal Reserve Economic Data, Average Hourly Earnings of Production and Nonsupervisory Employees: Total Private (AHETPI), http://research.stlouisfed.org/fred2/series/AHETPI/.

49) Federal Reserve Economic Data, Corporate Profits After Tax (CP), http://research.stlouisfed.org/fred2/series/CP/.

50) Richard Fry and Paul Taylor, *A Rise in Wealth for the Wealthy; Declines for the Lower 93%*, Pew Research, April 23, 2013, http://www.pewsocialtrends.org/2013/04/23/a-rise-in-wealth-for-the-wealthydeclines-for-the-lower-93/.

Chapter 3

Cyberwar as a Misdiagnosis

Don't you see that the whole aim of Newspeak is to narrow the range of thought? ... Every concept that can ever be needed, will be expressed by exactly one word, with its meaning rigidly defined and all its subsidiary meanings rubbed out and forgotten.

– George Orwell, *1984*

Everyone is playing word games.... No one is telling the truth ...

– Bruce Schneier[1]

The vision of cyberwar that's habitually conveyed to the public is an apocalyptic nightmare similar to the aftermath of Pearl Harbor, Hiroshima, Chernobyl and Katrina. Doomsayers prophesize that banks will fail, power grids will black out, and chaos will ensue. Cyberwar in its most severe incarnation is referred to by certain elements in the media as *Cyber-Armageddon*.[2]

While the exact odds of this happening have not been quantified, people are being presented with the message that it could happen.[3] Once more, rather than focus on the actual likelihood of a Cyber-Armageddon, alleged experts prefer to focus on how horrific the consequences will be. As we mentioned earlier, while it's possible that you could win a state lottery, it's not necessarily wise to make personal financial decisions based on the expectation of winning, regardless of how wonderful it would be.

One reason this message has been so effective is that authorities and alleged experts have been artfully exploiting the English language. In George Orwell's 1947 essay *Politics and the English Language*, he discusses how language can be manipulated to mislead.[4] Orwell shows how political control is related to the corruption of language. For instance, he explains how euphuisms can conceal unpleasant consequences by using words that do not evoke disturbing mental imagery:

> Defenseless villages are bombarded from the air, the inhabitants driven out into the countryside, the cattle machine-gunned, the huts set on fire with incendiary bullets: this is called *pacification*.
>
> Millions of peasants are robbed of their farms and sent trudging along the roads with no more than they can carry: this is called transfer of population or *rectification of frontiers*.
>
> People are imprisoned for years without trial, or shot in the back of the neck or sent to die of scurvy in Arctic lumber camps: this is called *elimination of unreliable elements*.

Orwell also observes:

> If thought corrupts language, language can also corrupt thought. A bad usage can spread by tradition and imitation, even among people who should and do know better.

Such is the dynamic at work with the term *cyberwar*, which has been used expansively to refer to a broad range of different security incidents (e.g. espionage, crime, etc.). This conflation of different threats allows the pundits to frame everything that's happening out on the Internet using the rhetoric of war, thus lending credence to their proposed solutions.

In his 2010 *Washington Post* op-ed piece, former DNI Mike McConnell asserts that the United States is losing a cyberwar. He backs this claim by directing the reader's attention to Operation Aurora, where a number of high-profile corporations like Google and Adobe were attacked in an effort to access and steal intellectual property. But this wasn't war. In fact, it sounds a lot more like industrial espionage. Industrial espionage isn't war; they represent distinct ideas, yet blurry logic allows the concepts to merge, as if to claim that 2+2 = 5.

Likewise, when *USA Today*[5] and the *Christian Science Monitor*[6] cover the antics of the LulzSec hacking collective, which clearly violate a multitude of Federal and local criminal laws, their actions are referred to as cyberwar.

There are those in the corporate stratum who advise that we should consider a definition of war conceived by the Chinese military.[7] In particular, a definition which officers of the People's Liberation Army have called "unrestricted warfare" in which:

> Warfare can be military, or it can be quasi-military, or it can be non-military. It can use violence, or it can be non-violent. It can be a confrontation between professional soldiers, or one between newly emerging forces consisting primarily of ordinary people or experts.... The battlefield is everywhere and war may be conducted in areas where military actions do not dominate ...

Given such a sprawling definition, one might almost be tempted to ask these Chinese officers what unrestricted war isn't. Unrestricted war is everywhere and all the time. In the background we can clearly hear the Inner Party of Oceania chanting their mantra: WAR IS PEACE. Honestly, what kind of formulation would you expect from military leaders in an authoritarian regime that censors the Internet and regularly jails political dissidents?

George Orwell, in his book *1984*, described a side-effect of this sort of rhetorical conflation:

> You think, I dare say, that our chief job is inventing new words. But not a bit of it! We're destroying words – scores of them, hundreds of them, every day. We're cutting the language down to the bone.

What's happening is that the meaning of the word *war* is being expanded to swallow up other words (like espionage, crime, sabotage,. etc.). As Orwell explained, language is being used to corrupt thought. Events which are clearly acts of espionage or crime, and unrelated to any ongoing military hostilities, are being depicted as acts of war because *military problems naturally lend themselves to military solutions.*

It doesn't matter if terms are confused furtively or if the proponents of cyberwar explicitly advocate switching to more "holistic" (i.e. conflated) definitions of the word "war." By framing cyber-attacks using the language of war, tacit assumptions come into play that direct our decision makers towards a specific kind of approach to address cyber-attacks.

In matters of war, who do you turn to?

Most people would answer: The Department of Defense.

Dialing 911

This begs a question: are military solutions the optimal way to deal with common problems like crime, espionage, and sabotage? Most functioning societies maintain police departments to deal with lawbreakers and civilian-based security services like the FBI to catch spies.[8] The core mission of an army is vastly different from that of domestic law enforcement. Should the military be charged with maintaining law-and-order online?

One way to debunk the notion that we should rely on the Pentagon to solve all of our cyber-security problems (militarize the Internet) is to methodically classify incidents into distinct categories.

As any doctor or plumber will tell you, *effective treatment is based on a correct diagnosis.* You don't begin an aggressive regime of chemotherapy without first confirming that a patient has a form of cancer that will respond to treatment. To move towards constructive solutions that address our cyber-security ailments, we first need to observe and classify the corresponding symptoms.

Investigative categories are standard procedure for law enforcement agencies. Whether incident categories are developed to match the divisions of the security apparatus, or the security apparatus has been adapted to incident categories, an incident-response table exists. If you visit the FBI's website on Famous Cases and Criminals, you'll see this approach at work.[9] Investigations are filed under terrorism, organized crime, espionage, public corruption, white collar crime, etc.

Put another way, if you dial up 911, the operator will first determine the nature of your emergency and then dispatch the appropriate resources.

One concern that stems out of this is that areas of jurisdiction in national security have become muddled. An article in *The*

Economist, published in April of 2009, indicates the Department of Defense is pushing to expand its role with regard to cyber-security. In other words, there's a battle going on behind the scenes for scope of authority, control and funding:

> The most likely explanation for the sudden spate of scare stories is rather more mundane: a turf war between American government agencies over who should oversee the nation's cyber-security. In one corner is the Department of Homeland Security, which operates the National Cyber Security Center (NCSC), a body set up to co-ordinate America's various cyber-security efforts. In the other corner is the National Security Agency (NSA), which thinks it ought to be in charge. At stake are tens of billions of dollars in funding promised for a multi-year cyber-security initiative.[10]

Given the risks of a misdiagnosis or an inappropriate response, there's the compounded potential of a misdiagnosis coupled simultaneously with an inappropriate response. A stomach transplant simply won't do much for arthritis, it will only waste a load of money and put the patient at greater risk from resulting complications. Yet this is *exactly* the sort of situation that the Cult of cyberwar would put society in.

To correctly diagnose the cyber threats at hand, let's look at generally accepted definitions of war, terrorism, espionage, and crime. The resulting analysis will provide a springboard for the rest of the book.

War

In the early 1800s, the German military strategist Carl von Clausewitz described war as:

> A real political instrument, a continuation of political commerce, a carrying out of the same by other means.

In other words, when ordinary political tools like diplomacy falter, our leaders call in the generals. War, he asserted is violent coercion driven by political necessity.

Thomas Rid, a researcher in the Department of War Studies at King's College London, distilled Clausewitz's extensive analysis down into three tightly coupled ingredients. Specifically, Rid views war as being: violent, instrumental, and political. In other words, war is the employment of violence as a means (an instrument) to force opposition to concede to demands that are rooted in attributable and expressed political motivations.[11]

The definition used by the DoD also builds upon the one established by Clausewitz. In particular, the DoD's Joint Publication 1, Doctrine for the Armed Forces of the United States, defines war as "socially sanctioned violence to achieve a political purpose" and adds that war is "characterized as a confrontation between nation states or coalitions/alliances of nation-states."

The latter clause is notable because it explicitly stipulates the involvement of nation-states. In other words, the identities of the participants are evident and correspond to sovereign entities. There has to be attribution. This is why soldiers wear marked uniforms and battleships fly flags. If war is a way to achieve political aims, how can a nation under attack make the necessary concessions if they don't know who is attacking them?

Given that many of the high-profile people who talk in terms of cyberwar are, or have been, government officials, it only makes sense that we would give them the benefit of adopting the government's definition of war. In light of DoD's definition we can identify basic characteristics of war:

- Violence
- Perpetrated by nation-states
- Wielded as a tool that serves political goals

Hence, it's not enough to merely identify political intentions mingled in with international intrigue. There must also be *violence*. Specifically, we mean *acts of force* which result in the sort of human carnage that occur when countries unleash the full might of their armed forces against each other.

In light of the previous definition of war, we arrive naturally at a definition for cyberwar:

Cyberwar: a violent act of force, perpetrated by a nation-state, which serves to realize political goals through the use of malware.

As things stand now, there have been no cyber incidents that are anywhere near on par with our military campaigns in Iraq or Afghanistan, let alone World Wars I and II. Thomas Rid observes in his 2011 paper:

> The world never experienced an act of cyberwar, which would have to be violent, instrumental, and – most importantly – politically attributed. No attack on record meets all of these criteria.

We would tend to agree with him. In the survey of incidents that we performed, we didn't come across any attacks that satisfied all of the aforementioned criteria for cyberwar.

Terrorism

Terrorism also entails politically motivated violence, and hence may be confused with war. The *Code of Federal Regulations* (Title 28, Section 0.85) defines terrorism as:

> The unlawful use of force and violence against persons or property to intimidate or coerce a government, the civilian population, or any segment thereof, in furtherance of political or social objectives.

Recognized experts who study this area have established even more detailed criteria. Martha Crenshaw is a political scientist at Stanford who has studied terrorism for the past 30 years. According to Crenshaw:

1. Terrorism is part of a revolutionary strategy – a method used by insurgents to seize political power from an existing government.
2. Terrorism is manifested in acts of socially and politically unacceptable violence.
3. There is a consistent pattern of symbolic or representative selection of the victims or objects of acts of terrorism.

4. The revolutionary movement deliberately intends these actions to create a psychological effect on specific groups and thereby to change their political behavior and attitudes.[12]

Cyber-terrorism is terrorism that's executed through malicious software. The main difference between cyber-terrorism and cyber-war (as defined by criteria 1 and 3) stems from the fact that *terrorism* is the weapon of insurgents, as opposed to *terror*, which national governments sometimes wield.

Concrete examples of state-sponsored terror abound. The ongoing campaign of U.S. drone strikes in the Middle East is an acute example of state-sponsored terror[13] as were the dropping of atomic bombs on Japan.[14] In both cases the recipients of state violence have included large numbers of innocent civilians.[15]

Terrorists typically don't have the resources to systematically overrun a country, a capability normally reserved for superpower militaries. Instead, they choose a small subset of symbolic targets to achieve the greatest bang for the buck in order to disseminate their message, so to speak. What terrorists hope for is that the sustained pressure of their attacks will wear away at the resolve of the targeted group.

When fear takes over (and hence the term *terror-ism*), the intended audience may decide to give in and comply with terrorist demands. Therefore, the basic mechanism of change is very different between terrorism and war.

Gary Brecher describes this process as "nerf" war:

> Nerf wins – low-casualty, high-cost performance-art style guerrilla bombings. And Al Qaeda style maximum-splatter is for hotheaded idiots who forget that the real job of a guerrilla force is to stay in existence, lean on the enemy, wear him out and bankrupt him.[16]

There are those who see the Anonymous hacking collective as a group of cyber terrorists. For example, Keith Alexander, the head of CYBERCOM, has warned that Anonymous could launch attacks that target the power grid.[17]

Contrast this against the conclusions of Robert Mueller, the director of the FBI. He believes that genuine instances of cyber terror have been conspicuously absent. At the RSA Security Conference in 2012, Mueller remarked that:

> To date, terrorists have not used the Internet to launch a full-scale cyber attack.[18]

Former White House advisor Richard Clarke concurs:

> To date, terrorists haven't so much attacked the Internet or used the Internet to attack physical systems as they have used it to plan and coordinate attacks ... [19]

Incidents of cyber-terror, as delineated by Crenshaw's criteria, are as scarce. In addition, the U.S. government has not responded to Anonymous by calling in air strikes. Instead, it has relied on law enforcement and international cooperation to capture hackers and relegated judgment to the judicial system.

This kind of response is in line with the standard U.S. counter-terrorist strategy that was consistently applied between 1972 and the Clinton Administration. The four key principles of this strategy were refusing to concede to terrorist demands, the imposition of diplomatic and economic sanctions, the enforcement of the rule of law by bringing terrorists to trial and multilateral cooperation.[20]

For a textbook example of this approach, recall how the Japanese government responded to the 1995 Sarin nerve gas attacks perpetrated by the Aum Shinrikyo cult in Tokyo's subway system. One blogger sums it up neatly:

> They didn't implement a vast system of domestic surveillance. They didn't suspend basic civil rights. They didn't begin to capture, torture, and kill without due process. They didn't, in other words, allow themselves to be terrorized. Instead, they addressed the threat. They investigated and arrested the cult's leadership. They tried them in civilian courts and earned convictions through due process.[21]

The post 9/11 military invasions in the Middle East are uncommon responses to terrorism. Waging war against an entire country in an effort to combat a small group of terrorists is an incredibly reckless, wasteful, and destructive option. Countless thousands of innocent people needlessly paid the price for this approach with their lives in Iraq and Afghanistan.[22] In fact, there is a very strong argument that using this brutal approach only creates more terrorists.[23] The CIA's former head of counterterrorism, Robert Grenier, has stated:

> We have gone a long way down the road of creating a situation where we are creating more enemies than we are removing from the battlefield. We are already there with regards to Pakistan and Afghanistan ...[24]

Espionage

Collecting data surreptitiously is an age-old vocation. Unlike war, espionage is all about information and the misappropriation thereof. Cyber-espionage is merely espionage conducted via digital infiltration.

Espionage is a well-defined term, legally speaking. The exact details are spelled out (at length) in Title 18 United States Code, Sections 792-798. These sections were, historically, the result of the Espionage Act of 1917. The Department of Defense offers a more bite-size definition in Joint Publication 1-02. Specifically, the Pentagon views espionage as:

> The act of obtaining, delivering, transmitting, communicating, or receiving information about the national defense with an intent, or reason to believe, that the information may be used to the injury of the United States or to the advantage of any foreign nation.[25]

Note the emphasis on national defense. The topic of industrial espionage is actually addressed by the Economic Espionage Act of 1996, which is governed by sections 1831(a) and 1832 in Title 18 of the United States Code. These sections deal primarily with trade secrets which are stolen, duplicated, traded in, or purchased to "benefit any foreign government, foreign instrumentality, or foreign agent."

Violence is not part of the equation as far as espionage, in and of itself, is concerned. While it's true that espionage does sometime occur during war, not many of the incidents of cyber-espionage surveyed by this book occurred within the context of an ongoing military engagement. Furthermore, there are very few, if any, instances in recorded modern history where a nation state initiated full-blown military aggression against another country in response to an act of espionage. You don't call in an airstrike when you uncover a spy; you hand over matters to domestic security services. Since the Espionage Act of 1917, the FBI (originally the Bureau of Investigation, or BOI) has been charged with investigating cases of espionage within the United States.

Crime

Crimes are a violation of public law, which is defined by a myriad of statutes at the local, state, and federal level. Gambling for example is *legal* in the U.S. at the federal level, though it is often prohibited at the state level. Both Colorado and Washington State have legalized the cultivation and sale of marijuana. In other locales, however, possession of marijuana is a misdemeanor (see California Health and Safety Code, sections 11357-11362.9) and in certain places possession of marijuana is a straight up felony (see Utah Code, Title 58, Section 8 of Chapter 37). It's all a matter of codification. Strictly speaking, as we've shown, espionage is a federal crime. Though, as a matter of popular usage, when people refer to cybercrime they're talking about something other than espionage (e.g. identity theft, bank fraud, extortion, the destruction of property, etc.).

Depending on jurisdiction, crimes may be investigated by one of the many agencies in the Department of Justice, the Department of Homeland Security, an agency run by a state government, or a municipal police department. Regardless of who responds, criminal activity is the purview of law enforcement officials. Judgment and sentencing are, with few exceptions, left to civilian courts. In other words, *this is largely outside the normal purview of the United States military.*

Looking Ahead

There's been a concerted effort to make the notion of cyberwar as all-encompassing as possible, to lump together as many high-profile incidents as they can, in conjunction with a deluge of hypothetical worst-case scenarios, so that commentators can point to our general state of cyber-insecurity and loudly exclaim that a cyberwar is transpiring. By depicting the bulk of all cyber incidents as acts of war, the defense industry sets itself up to provide solutions. As we mentioned earlier, it's only natural to turn over matters of war to the Department of Defense.

The most effective countermeasure against this Orwellian manipulation is to sort incidents into their respective categories. Take a good hard look at what's happening and call a spade a spade. Recognizing the various distinctions that we've spelled out makes it clear that instances of crime, or espionage, or terrorism are not equivalent to acts of war. Instead, they are perennial phenomena that will always plague society regardless of whether a war is transpiring or not.

For example, espionage may occur during a war to gather intelligence, but that doesn't make it equivalent to an act of war, because it fails to meet the criterion that the Department of Defense itself has spelled out. Collecting information isn't a potentially lethal act of force, and as Thomas Rid observes:

> Espionage is not directly instrumental; its main purpose is not achieving a goal but to gather the information that may be used to design more concrete instruments or policies.[26]

Crime and espionage, in particular, are pervasive in the online domain, as we'll show in the following chapters. But the survey of incidents we'll examine doesn't reveal any cases of cyberwar. This, in turn, brings into question the wisdom of using the military to address the problems posed by online security threats. Furthermore, if military solutions aren't optimal, then what sorts of solutions are appropriate?

Endnotes

1) Anne Flaherty, Jack Gillum, Matt Apuzzo, and Stephen Braun, "Secret to Prism program: Even bigger data seizure," *Associated Press*, June 15, 2013.

2) Robert Lucky, "Cyber Armageddon," *IEEE Spectrum*, September 2010, http://spectrum.ieee.org/telecom/security/cyber-armageddon.

3) "Cyber Fear Echo Chamber," Southern Virginia Security, December 2, 2009, http://www.sovasec.com/2009/12/cyfear-echo-chamber-co-the-usual-suspects/.

4) George Orwell, *Politics and the English Language*, http://mla.stanford.edu/Politics_&_English_language.pdf.

5) Byron Acohido, "LulzSec, Anonymous declare war against governments, corporations," *USA Today*, June 20, 2011, http://content.usatoday.com/communities/technologylive/post/2011/06/lulzsec-anonymous-declare-war-against-governments-corporations/1#.UABh5vUX7Mo.

6) James Bosworth, "LulzSec, Anonymous show Latin America unprepared for cyberwarfare," *Christian Science Monitor*, June 23, 2011, http://www.csmonitor.com/World/Americas/Latin-America-Monitor/2011/0623/LulzSec-Anonymous-show-Latin-America-unprepared-for-cyberwarfare.

7) "Cyber-warfare: Is the risk of cyber-warfare overrated?" *The Economist*, July 29, 2013, http://www.economist.com/debate/days/view/998.

8) Federal Bureau of Investigation, Counterintelligence, http://www.fbi.gov/about-us/investigate/counterintelligence.

9) Federal Bureau of Investigation, Famous Cases and Criminals, http://www.fbi.gov/about-us/history/famous-cases.

10) "Cyberwar: Battle is joined," *Economist*, April 23, 2009, http://www.economist.com/node/13527677/print.

11) Thomas Rid, "Cyber War Will Not Take Place," *Journal of Strategic Studies*, 2011, 1–28.

12) Martha Crenshaw, *Explaining Terrorism: Causes, Processes, and Consequences*. Routledge, 2010, p. 23.

13) *Democracy Now!*, "Yemeni Activist Farea al-Muslimi Urges U.S. to Stop the Drone War on His Country," April 25, 2013, http://www.democracynow.org/2013/4/25/yemeni_activist_farea_al_muslimi_urges.

14) Sean Malloy, *Atomic Tragedy: Henry L. Stimson and the Decision to Use the Bomb against Japan*, Cornell University Press, 2010, ISBN-13: 978-0801476297.

15) *Counting Drone Strike Deaths*, Columbia Law School, Human Rights Clinic, http://web.law.columbia.edu/sites/default/files/microsites/human-rights-institute/COLUMBIACounting%20Drone%20Strike%20DeathsSUMMARY.pdf.

16) Gary Brecher, "WN 38 IRA vs. Al Qaeda: I was Wrong," *The Exiled*, April 27, 2011, http://exiledonline.com/wn-38-ira-vs-al-qaeda-i-was-wrong/.

17) Siobhan Gorman, "Alert on Hacker Power Play," *Wall Street Journal*, February 21, 2012.

18) Robert Mueller, Speech given at RSA Security Conference, March 1, 2012, San Francisco, http://www.fbi.gov/news/speeches/combating-threats-in-the-cyber-world-outsmarting-terrorists-hackers-and-spies.

19) Richard A. Clark and Robert K. Knake, *Cyber War: The Next Threat to National Security and What to Do About It*, Ecco, 2010, page 136.

20) Martha Crenshaw, *Explaining Terrorism: Causes, Processes, and Consequences*. Routledge, 2010, p. 23.

21) Freddie, "to understand terrorism and threat assessment, look to Aum," *L'Hôte*, June 10, 2013, http://lhote.blogspot.com/2013/06/to-understand-terrorism-and-threat.html.

22) Brad Knickerbocker, "Iraq war 10 years later: Was it worth it?," *Christian Science Monitor*, March 17, 2013, http://www.csmonitor.com/USA/Military/2013/0317/Iraq-war-10-years-later-Was-it-worth-it.

23) Jeremy Egner, "His Target Is Assassinations," *New York Times*, June 6, 2013, http://www.nytimes.com/2013/06/09/movies/jeremy-scahill-on-his-documentary-dirty-wars.html?_r=0&pagewanted=print.

24) Paul Harris, "Drone attacks create terrorist safe havens, warns former CIA official," *Guardian*, June 5, 2012, http://www.theguardian.com/world/2012/jun/05/al-qaida-drone-attacks-too-broad/print.

25) US Department of Defense, Joint Publication 1-02 Department of Defense Dictionary of Military and Associated Terms, February 2012, http://www.dtic.mil/doctrine/new_pubs/jp1_02.pdf.

26) Thomas Rid, "Cyber War Will Not Take Place," *Journal of Strategic Studies*, 2011, 1–28.

PART II

A SERIES OF UNFORTUNATE EVENTS

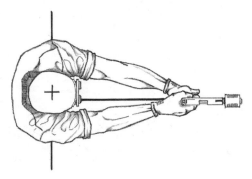

Chapter 4
Cybercrime

Chapter 5
Espionage

Chapter 6
The Scope of U.S. Espionage

Chapter 7
The Infrastructure

Chapter 8
Threat Inflation

Chapter 4

Cybercrime

In this chapter we're going to traverse a catalogue of genuine incidents that have been publicly reported both by the media and open source intelligence services. The general idea is to develop a view of reality that's based on hard evidence and discernible trends instead of hypothetical worst-case scenarios. Rather than dwell on what *could* happen, We're going to develop a baseline that's founded on what's *actually* happening.

If you were to look out over the past few years' worth of cyber-incidents and partition them up using the classification scheme established in the previous chapter, you'd end up with mostly crime and espionage. This is what has been re-packaged to manufacture the perception of cyberwar. To graphically substantiate my counter-claim we've provided a large set of corroborating events that demonstrates the ubiquity of crime and the dearth of war. In this chapter we will focus on cybercrime, which over the past three decades has evolved from teenage mischief to a sprawling and profitable criminal ecosystem.

The Ecosystem

The illicit profits generated by the drug trade have fueled the creation of intricate criminal syndicates. The scale of production has reached such levels that organizations have been forced to rely on the division of labor to achieve efficiencies.[1] Ron Brooks, who oversees a drug task force in Northern California, states that if a cartel is going to survive:

> There's got to be a network. That means facilitation of stash houses, of communications, people that rent the cell phones, people that drive the trucks, people that sell this marijuana at the wholesale and retail level, people that get the money

bulk transferred back to Mexico, which is where the command-and-control is for many of these organizations. You're
talking about a very big organization.[2]

Similar forces are at work in the milieu of cybercrime. The profits have become so immense that the demand for entry into the
market is tremendous. Crooks everywhere see a less risky way to
make a fast buck and they want in on the action. Although the basic
dance steps of the average cyber theft are the same as those traditionally used by burglars, the actual process of implementing these
steps is relatively complicated and involves a variety of rarified
skills. As in the domain of narcotics trafficking, criminal organizations have begun to specialize and rely on division of labor.

Before we look into specific instances of cybercrime, we're going to survey the general process to develop the requisite vocabu-
lary and background. In particular, we'll show how online crooks
identify and pilfer data from unsuspecting users, fence the goods
to turn them into cash, and evade law enforcement.

Breaking In

Locating potential victims and infecting their machines can be a
challenge for the uninitiated. To save time and resources, *Pay-Per-
Install* (PPI) services have emerged. These allow cyber criminals to
outsource the distribution of their malware. They simply contact
a PPI provider and specify the number of systems they need
infected and the geographic regions they wish to target. Rates are
surprisingly affordable. For example, infecting 1,000 computers in
the U.S. or Europe can cost between $100 and $200.[3]

PPI services facilitate the creation of botnets. A *botnet* is a large
collection of compromised machines that are steered en masse by
people known as *bot herders*. These infected computers are known
as *zombies* because they are secretly being controlled from afar. Bot
herders issue marching orders to their computer minions using
intermediary machines known as *command and control* (C&C)
servers, which are often compromised machines themselves. C&C
servers not only disseminate commands, they also collect data
funneled back up by the infected machines in the trenches.

In December of 2009, researcher Gunter Ollman published information on a provider called FurioGaming that offers the following PPI sales pitch:

> Having a hard time spreading your bot? Let us do all the work! We have a lot of experience when it comes to bot spreading and we know like no other how much time it can costs before your finally able to host boot, so now we offer Turbo bot Spreading for those who want bots FAST and cheap! In less then 24 hours you're all set to start host booting.
>
> We spread all type of bots although we prefer the BBO bot because it connects on all operation systems and the BBO bot gets you the best possible spreading results, plus if you want us to spread your BBO bot we will do the crypting for free!
>
> We can spread your bot for as long as you want and we will provide you the download link so you can keep track of the downloads your bot is getting.[4]

As Ollman points out, FurioGaming even has a help desk system for customers to request assistance from the company when they have an issue. As with most commercial software products, customers having problems with their bots can open a ticket and get technical support.

PPI services tend to install "droppers" on the machines they compromise. Droppers exist to receive software payloads from command and control servers and install them on the infected host (this is basically a low-tech variation of what anti-forensic people call a *User-Mode Exec.*). This way the outlaw employing the PPI service can decide how to leverage the compromised machine (e.g. send spam, collect passwords, perform a DDoS, etc.). The downloader merely provides a generic level of access.

PPI providers often act as middlemen, sub-contracting out the actual infection process to affiliates who concentrate on specific infection vectors (e.g. drive-by downloads, phishing, file-sharing, etc.). An affiliate may just be a bot herder who, rather than searching out new machines to infect, hands over a subset of machines already under his control. Managing a large botnet like this can be a profitable venture. A 27-year-old hacker from the Netherlands purportedly made $139,000 a month from leasing out his Bredolab botnet to spammers.[5]

Fencing the Goods

Once a crook has stolen valuable information, they have to find a way to convert it into cash (i.e. they've got to *monetize* the illicit data). As you might expect, there's a whole sub-economy dedicated to this task. For example, there's literally an online commodity market of sorts for the computer underground, hosted on what are known as *Carding sites*. Carding sites are basically web-based message boards where outlaws can buy and sell stolen data (e.g. credit and debit card numbers, social security numbers, driver licenses, etc.). Crooks who deal in various aspects of bank fraud all over the world can congregate at these sites and do business.

In the lower levels of this commodity market, where data is turned into cash, are countless informal networks of money mules.[6] Money mules bridge the online world with the physical world. The more sophisticated shops will fabricate counterfeit credit/debit cards and distribute the cards to *cashers*, people who'll use the fake plastic to withdraw cash from ATMs or purchase expensive items (e.g. a $4,000 high-end laptop with all the trimmings) which are then resold on legitimate exchanges like eBay.

In an effort to minimize their exposure, some mule outfits use *drop-addresses*. A drop address is a physical (i.e. snail-mail) address which mules use as a shipping destination when buying merchandise online with stolen account numbers.

Mules take a cut of the money they collect and can profit handsomely, but they also assume the most risk. This is why money mules are viewed as the weak links in the cybercrime food chain. They have a notably short half-life, so to speak, because they have a habit of being photographed by ATM cameras and falling into patterns that law enforcement can capitalize on. To manage this high turnover, there are dedicated recruiters who run the equivalent of mule temp agencies in an effort to provide the market with a fresh stream of workers.

Evading Capture

The best way to stay out of jail is to avoid detection in the first place. To this end, malware detection services like virtest.com offer a way for malware developers to ensure that their code won't be recognized by anti-virus software.

There are legitimate/official services, like ThreatExpert.com and VirusTotal.com, which offer malware scanning free of charge. From the standpoint of a malware developer, the problem is that these legitimate services share their findings with the broader security community. Specifically, when they identify a malicious application they openly publish its signature so that discovered threats can be recognized by everyone else. This works to the advantage of the average user, but not for crooks (who don't want their malware to be recognized as such). The underground services claim not to share their findings with anyone else.

Building an online malware detection service is pretty straightforward and may be preferable for truly paranoid specialists. In a nutshell, you buy licensed copies of as many security suites as possible, crank them up to the maximum degree of heuristic sensitivity, and then create a web-based front end so that users can submit executable files for scanning. The specifics on how to do this are detailed at length in the *Malware Analyst's Cookbook and DVD*.[7]

Another way to keep a low profile is to operate from a covert outpost within the vicinity of your target. In particular, accessing a bank account from a faraway location often indicates a fraudulent transaction, so cyber thieves prefer using a local proxy. To this end, bot herders have started engineering their botnets to offer anonymity services. A hacker using this sort of service would connect to the botnet and have their Internet traffic routed through dozens of compromised hosts before being routed to the intended target.

The TDSS botnet is a well-documented example on the Windows platform.[8] Compromised zombies load a module named Socks.dll (as in TCP/IP Sockets) into an instance of svchost.exe, a common host process for Windows services. This rogue DLL implements a proxy server of sorts that can forward network requests on behalf of another machine.

Get enough of these proxies to talk to each other, and the resulting network path becomes a Gordian knot that's difficult to trace. According to researchers at Kaspersky, botnet herders charge around $100 per month to use an anonymity service. To make the technology easier to use, some botnet developers have even gone so far as to create a Firefox web browser plug-in for their anonymity service. To browse anonymously, simple enable the plug-in to channel web traffic through the botnet.

Sometimes the authorities succeed in tracking the original destination of an attack; many crooks prepare for this contingency by relying on bullet-proof hosting. This is provided by hosting services that are willing to look the other way when people start complaining about SPAM and malware. The Russian Business Network (RBN) is a textbook example, where cyber miscreants could rent a server for $600 a month and do whatever they wanted. China is another well-known refuge that offers a similar pricing scheme (roughly $700 per month).[9]

To see how bullet-proof hosting works, it helps to understand how IP addresses are managed. At a very high-level, IP addresses are allocated by a nonprofit corporate entity known as a *Regional Internet Registry* (RIR).[10] There are currently five RIRs worldwide. For example, the *American Registry for Internet Numbers* (ARIN) is the RIR for the United States and Canada. Each RIR hands out addresses in blocks to *Local Internet Registries* (LIRs), which are mostly backbone ISPs, large enterprises, or academic institutions. LIRs can, in turn, allocate blocks of addresses from their pools and assign them to downstream ISPs, who do the same for smaller ISPs lower down on the food chain.

On paper, LIRs and downstream ISPs have to navigate through a formal screening process, where they answer a bunch of questions and provide supporting documentation to demonstrate that they're legitimate. But there have been instances where criminal organizations have capitalized on countries where regulation is lax; hence, bullet-proof hosting. It's not so much a technical problem as it is a political and bureaucratic phenomenon. As the Secretary General of Interpol explains:

> It is clear that organized cybercrime has taken root in countries that don't have response mechanisms, laws, infrastructure and investigative support set up to respond to the threat quickly.[11]

A Snapshot of Cybercrime

Now that we've examined the basic environment in which online crooks operate, let's look at a series of well-known incidents. From these case studies we will be able to distill some general conclusions about the true nature of the Internet-based threats that society faces on a day-to-day basis. There's a lot of crime, but no war. This hasn't stopped cyberwar PR from encouraging people to confuse the two, to associate relatively high-risk incidents with cyberwar and fuel anxiety. The end result is akin to someone who worries that a bomb will land on the house rather than that a burglar will break into it, and who looks towards the military for solutions rather than to law enforcement.

The TJX Hack

Back in 2003, a young hacker named Albert Gonzalez was arrested by the U.S. Secret Service for making fraudulent ATM withdrawals. At the time he was a system administrator for a carding site named *ShadowCrew*. Given his level of access to the ShadowCrew site, the Secret Service made a deal with him to work as a paid informant.

Gonzalez agreed to help them entice other criminals who frequented ShadowCrew by convincing them to use an allegedly secure VPN (virtual private network). This dedicated connection was then monitored by the Secret Service, allowing them to collect evidence. The sting, dubbed *Operation Firewall*, culminated in a series of raids during the fall of 2004 where authorities collared some 28 suspects from seven different countries. The Secret Service estimates that the forum trafficked in at least 1.7 million stolen credit cards, costing financial institutions more than $4.3 million.[12]

As ShadowCrew vanished, Gonzalez began searching for a new score, despite the fact that he was still working as a paid informant. Specifically, he and his confederates identified a Marshalls store in the vicinity of St. Paul, Minnesota, that was using an outdated, and conspicuously insecure, encryption protocol (i.e. WEP) to protect wireless network traffic in the store. Using WEP to protect wireless network traffic is like trying to secure a bank vault with a screen door. It may be a deterrent to honest people but a determined thief would make quick work of it.

Using a high-powered antenna, they captured data broadcast to cash registers and other computers by hand-held price-checking devices. They used this data to crack the WEP encryption and then intercept user credentials as employees logged into the central database managed by TJX, the company that owned the store. They eventually set up their own accounts in the TJX database system and started to pilfer a veritable mother-load of credit card data. At the time of the intrusion, Gonzalez was pulling down $75,000 a year as an informant for the U.S. Secret Service.

In January of 2007, TJX admitted that it had been the victim of an "unauthorized intrusion" sometime in December of 2006.[13] Sherry Lang, a spokesperson for the company declared that TJX had identified a "limited number" of credit card holders affected by the intrusion. As she put it, the number of customers affected was "substantially less than millions."[14]

This turned out to be an understatement. Gonzalez and his partners in crime compromised 45.7 million credit- and debit-card numbers. In other words, this crime affected more people than the population of the entire state of New York. In a 2009 SEC filing, TJX stated that the breach cost the company $200 million.[15] It was estimated that the banks that issued the compromised cards would end up spending more than $300 million to replace them.[16]

The feds pursued the TJX case for the better part of a year before coming to the realization in May of 2008 that the perpetrator was their own informant. Gonzalez was caught and, in March of 2010, sentenced to 20 years in prison for his part in the TJX Hack. Without a doubt, the TJX hack was a criminal act that was handled by law enforcement.

Another factor that we see in the instance of the TJX hack is just how dangerous outdated technology really is, especially when it's used to control network access. In this case it was an insecure wireless standard deployed at a major retail outlet. Hundreds of millions of dollars lost because someone failed to recognize and remediate an obviously weak link in the defensive perimeter. This is not the last time that we'll see this sort of problem.

The Heartland Payment Systems Breach

Gonzalez had been pretty busy while working as an informant for the Secret Service. In addition to pulling the TJX caper, Gonzalez and two co-conspirators from Eastern Europe hacked into a slew of other databases belonging to companies like Heartland Payment Systems, 7-Eleven, and the Hannaford Brothers supermarket chain.

The intrusions took place during the summer and fall of 2007. The attackers started with a list a Fortune 500 companies. After identifying a potential target they'd take a field trip to a local store to see what sort of payment processing software was installed on the checkout computers. For good measure they might also visit the company's website to glean additional intelligence.

They launched their operations from a set of geographically dispersed servers located in New Jersey, California, Illinois, Latvia, and the Ukraine. Naturally, these servers were leased under assumed names. The attack vector of choice was SQL injection, which entails manipulating an input query sent to a database server in order to get the database software to do something it shouldn't (like open up a back door or peek at valuable data).

In August of 2009 Gonzalez was indicted on charges of hacking. According to prosecutors the group made off with data for more than 134 million credit and debit cards. Heartland claimed that it suffered losses resulting from the breach on the order of $12.6 million.[17] Almost a year later, in March of 2010, Gonzalez was sentenced. The 20-year stretch that he received for the Heartland job was scheduled to run concurrently with his earlier TJX sentence, adding only a single day to the total amount of time that he'd serve.

In this case, the weak link that the intruders exploited was provided by poorly designed software, which proved vulnerable to SQL injection. Such applications make the unintentional mistake of accepting, and processing, arbitrary database commands. This provides the opportunity to subvert a database server by injecting malicious logic into an existing stream of database commands. In 2010 the Open Web Application Security Project (OWASP) ranked SQL injection as one of their top ten attack methods.[18]

The DarkMarket Sting

A tried and true means of countering an opposing group is to play a fundamental role in its creation, so that it may be controlled and monitored from the inside. In other words, if you can manage both sides of a conflict, you can control its outcome. In the early days of the Soviet Republic, from 1921 until 1926, the government's State Political Directorate (the secret police) ran a counterintelligence program known as *Operation Trust*. The basic idea was to mobilize counter-revolutionary forces loyal to the former Czarist Empire and incite them to establish an anti-Bolshevik society. The Russians used Operation Trust to capture and execute Sidney Reilly, the legendary British spy that Ian Fleming used as one his models for James Bond.

Such was the basis for the FBI's success with its DarkMarket Sting: surreptitious control from the inside. In an operation that was launched in 2006, Special Agent J. Keith Mularski spent the better part of two years infiltrating a carding web site called DarkMarket, which boasted a membership of 2,500 outlaws

Mularksi positioned himself as a Polish spammer. With some help from the Spamhaus Project, he was listed as a prolific offender. Slowly he built up his credibility until he was a discussion moderator at DarkMarket. At one point, DarkMarket came under a denial-of-service (DoS) attack from a rival site.

This presented an opportunity for Mularski to increase his level of access. He volunteered to bolster security by moving the forum to his server. The feds now had a unique vantage point; they controlled the machine that hosted the forum and, unbeknownst to the outlaws who used it, could secretly monitor everything that happened.

Mularski closed the site down in September of 2008. Ironically, in his farewell message he told site members that he was worried the cops were closing in on him. The FBI's operation, which involved extensive assistance from law enforcement in other countries, salvaged information on more than 100,000 credit cards and is believed to have saved financial institutions $70 million in potential losses. Worldwide, the DarkMarket Sting resulted in 60 arrests.[19]

What this story shows is the sheer scale of the online market for stolen data. DarkMarket was just one of many outlaw data-marts that lurk in the dark corners of the Internet. No doubt there are tens of thousands of operators out there who are actively trading. Data theft isn't a niche market anymore. It has gone mainstream and the career criminals have all jumped onboard.

This operation also demonstrates the importance of traditional police work. Though the lure of an easy fix may seem possible, strictly technical means are insufficient. Breaking online crime rings involves the same tedious measures that have traditionally been used against criminals in the past (e.g. informants, gradual long-term infiltration, patiently waiting for opportunities, etc.).

Torpig Takedown

In the 1964 movie *Fail-Safe*, a bomber that's part of the U.S. Strategic Air Command accidentally receives orders to nuke Moscow and follows through with the mission (forcing American leaders to give the Russians a free shot at an American city).

As the U.S. bomber achieves a certain proximity to its target, the pilots are prohibited from accepting new orders under the assumption that the Russians may try to trick pilots by impersonating American officials. There's something to be said for this defense, and one can only wonder what sort of devious disinformation both sides cooked up during the height of the Cold War.

Masquerading as the enemy was the driving idea behind a gambit that researchers at UC Santa Barbara employed to commandeer the Torpig botnet for a period of roughly ten days.

At the time, Torpig was a prolific botnet that consisted of hundreds of thousands of infected computers spread all over the planet. By 2009, experts estimate that it had successfully harvested over half a million online bank accounts and credit card numbers.[20]

One of the distinguishing features of Torpig is its level of sophistication. Getting infected with Torpig is an elaborate multi-stage process. Typically the user will be a victim of a drive-by-download attack, where a browser flaw is used to download a tiny installer application. This installer, in turn, downloads and configures the Mebroot rootkit which embeds itself on a host by replacing the machine's Master Boot record (MBR).

115

The UCSB team was able to hijack the Torpig botnet by giving zombie machines the impression that they were speaking to a legitimate Command and Control (C&C) server, but they weren't. They were actually interacting with a mock C&C server that was staged by the researchers. This put the researchers in a position where they could issue bogus commands and intercept data that the zombies collected.

The researchers at UCSB estimate that the botnet under their control consisted of roughly 183,000 machines. Over the ten day period, Torpig siphoned off more than 70 gigabytes of data and extracted credentials for more than 8,000 accounts at 410 financial institutions. Topping the list were PayPal (1,770 accounts), Poste Italiane (765 accounts), Capital One (314 accounts), E*Trade (304 accounts), and Chase (217 accounts).[21]

According to George Ledin, a Professor at Sonoma State University who teaches a class on malware, one thing that interests the government researchers is the ability of malware to spread quickly. Take Conficker, for example, a worm that multiplied rapidly and, oddly enough, did so without really destroying anything. Its primary feature was its ability to proliferate.

The RBS WorldPay Attack

In November of 2008, RBS WorldPay, the U.S.-based payment processing arm of the Royal Bank of Scotland, was breached by hackers. The intruders initially got in by capitalizing on a software exploit. Then they located a card processing server and succeeded in cracking the encryption used to secure gift card data. The hackers raised their value limits and then manufactured a set of 44 counterfeit debit cards, which they distributed to a network of "cashers" who used the cards to withdraw cash from ATMs. They also filched the social security numbers of approximately 1.1 million account holders.[22]

In just 12 hours the cashers hit 2,100 ATMs in 280 cities worldwide, making off with $9 million. The sheer scale of this operation, and the organization it entailed, is impressive. Roughly a month later, in December, WorldPay publicly disclosed the incident.

Thanks to far-reaching international cooperation between law enforcement agencies, in November of 2009, the four Eastern European men who spearheaded the hack were indicted by a federal grand jury in Atlanta, Georgia.

This is robbery on a whole new scale, all thanks to buggy software. This is why cybercrime is so attractive. It involves less risk and a larger potential payout.

The Return of the Analyzer

In August of 2008, an Israeli hacker named Ehud Tenenbaum (aka "The Analyzer") was arrested by the police in Calgary under suspicion of breaking into systems at Direct Cash Management, a Canadian firm that deals in prepaid credit and debit cards. Canadian authorities contend that he's stolen somewhere on the order of $1.5 million using stolen prepaid card data.

If that weren't bad enough, as he was about to enter the Canadian justice system, officials from the United States extradited him on grounds of hacking into a string of American financial institutions. The breaches occurred in the first half of 2008 and resulted in losses of roughly $10 million. According to the indictment, Tenebaum used SQL injection as an attack vector to access data from various companies on pre-paid cards.

Tenenbaum made things easy for law enforcement investigators. The Hotmail account that he used to coordinate the attacks was registered under his actual name. Then there was also ATM footage that showed Tenenbaum withdrawing money from an account that he'd cracked. It's surprising that an attacker like this would have such poor operational discipline while having the technical sophistication to breach the companies in the first place. In August of 2009, Tenebaum pleaded guilty in New York.

As in the case of Heartland Payment Systems and RBS WorldPay, poorly designed software played a central role in enabling a $10 million theft to occur. At the same time, we also witness a rare instance of casual attribution, where law enforcement officers catch an offender simply by following the obvious trail that he left.

The Ballad of Max Butler

Back in 2002, a hacker named Max Butler was busy scoring credit card numbers by breaking into computers maintained by other online crooks. That is, he was making a living stealing from those who stole. After several months of sharpening his teeth on poorly secured outlaw sites, he moved up the food chain and started targeting local mom-and-pop banks; the sort of modest regional establishments that couldn't muster a substantial security budget. In his quest for credit card data, Butler would eventually expand his horizons and target retail outlets and payment processing stations.

Butler relied on a man named Christopher Aragon to fence the data he stole. Aragon's area of expertise was in fabricating counterfeit credit cards. He also managed a ring of money mules that used the cards he manufactured to buy high-end goods, items that could easily be sold for cash.

Problems started in the spring of 2004 when Aragon began to get sloppy. In one instance, he was nabbed by police after trying to use a couple of bogus credit cards at a hotel in San Francisco. This made Butler nervous. If Aragon's carelessness became a liability he'd need to find somewhere else to sell his data. In an effort to head off trouble before it struck, Butler began looking for other ways to convert his credit card dumps into cash.

Butler ended up creating his own carding site, CardersMarket, a vast online bazaar for stolen data which boasted some 6,000 members. He fashioned this clearinghouse, arguably the largest on the Internet at the time, by forcefully consolidating the carding sites that belonged to rival administrators. And when we say "forcefully," we mean it. In the summer of 2006, during a hacking marathon that lasted for days, he broke into the web sites managed by his rivals and emptied them out, taking all of their logins and databases with him.

This kind of success tends to get the attention of law enforcement. Slowly but surely, the Feds started to close in on Butler. People got arrested and began to talk. Informants were cultivated and weaseled their way into Butler's inner circle. The day finally came, in September of 2007, when Secret Service agents came busting through his front door to take him into custody.

The banks who owned the card data that Butler stole claimed that approximately $86.4 million of fraudulent charges had been made. Butler received a 13-year sentence in February of 2010 in addition to a court order to pay $27.5 million in restitution.[23]

If Butler's story says anything, it's that prosecuting organized criminal groups will always be a resource-intense process that requires a sustained infusion of good old-fashioned police work. There's no silver bullet when it comes to tracking down skillful intruders.

Operation Trident Breach

Operation Trident Breach began in May of 2009, when FBI agents in Omaha, Nebraska, were alerted to suspicious financial transactions involving 46 different bank accounts. After a substantial amount of digging, they uncovered a group of five Ukrainians who hatched a scheme to use a customized instance of the Zeus Trojan to pillage corporate bank accounts. This tiny cabal of malware developers and hackers disseminated their hand-tailored malware via e-mail to small and mid-sized companies.

The attackers succeeded in penetrating machines at more than 390 U.S. corporations. The Zeus Trojan captured the banking credentials of users as they typed them in and then funneled the credentials back to the Ukrainians. They used the stolen login data to access the victims' accounts and clear them out.

To launder the stolen loot, the crooks maintained a network of some 3,500 money mules:[24] Russian nationals recruited to receive the stolen funds in their own bank accounts and then re-route them back to the Ukrainians. The Ukrainians recruited mules by placing advertisements for students with J-1 visas on Russian language web sites.[25]

In the fall of 2010, Operation Trident Breach came to an end as a coalition of law enforcement officials launched a dragnet against the Ukrainians' crime ring. More than 150 suspects were nabbed in a sweep that spanned from the United States, to the United Kingdom, and then on into Eastern Europe. Losses attributed to the criminal enterprise over 18 months were reported on the order of $70 million.[26]

Though a $70 million loss won't cause the world economy to collapse, this case study still serves to demonstrate a point; cybercrime is not a threat based on apocalyptic nightmares, it's a concrete threat based on documented losses.

From China with Love

On April 26, 2011, the Internet Crime Complaint Center (IC3) published an alert regarding a large-scale hacking campaign emanating from China[27]. Over the 12-month period preceding the alert, the FBI registered 20 incidents in which intruders stole online banking credentials from small-to-medium sized organizations.

According to investigators, the attackers explicitly targeted users who had access to corporate bank accounts. They'd infiltrate the victim's machine using booby-trapped e-mails or by directing the victim to a malicious webpage. The intruders used malware like Zeus Backdoor.bot, and Spybot to pilfer banking credentials. In one specific case, attackers went so far as to cover their tracks by erasing the hard drive of a victim remotely to frustrate investigators.

The attackers used the information they collected to initiate fraudulent money transfers to Chinese companies in port cities of the Heilongjiang province, located near the Russian border. In the 20 incidents investigated by the FBI, the average amount of money moved via wire transfer to China typically exceeded $900,000. Attackers also initiated a number of domestic Automated Clearing House (ACH) transfers within the U.S. that ranged from $222,500 to $1,275,000. Total losses resulting from the intrusions are estimated to be roughly $11 million, though the attackers attempted to steal close to $20 million.

The attackers avoided patterns that would lead to their capture. As things stand now, investigators don't know who's responsible for these transfers, if the bank accounts used in China were the ultimate destination, or if the money was then transferred to yet another account in a different bank. In other words, this very well could have been the work of Russian hackers using China as a launch pad. It's also unknown as to why presumably legitimate businesses received the stolen funds.

This raises questions related to attribution. While this is the first instance presented where the bad guys evaded capture and made off with $11 million, it's hardly an isolated incident. Disciplined and technically capable operatives like King Arthur, the Eastern European hacker who ran a carding site called CarderPlanet, are smart enough to work through multiple proxies, pivot off of compromised machines, conceal their identities, and generally cover their tracks. Recall that Max Butler was caught as the result of traditional meat-and-potatoes police work (e.g. developing informants, chasing the leads they provided, and beating the pavement). Knowing the IP address of the machine involved in an attack may not tell you anything at all. Or, even worse, it may send investigators down the wrong path.

Sony under Siege

In the spring of 2011, various business units of Sony Corporation were beset by a series of attacks that left the company embarrassed and beleaguered. The first sign of trouble appeared on April 20, when Patrick Seybold, the Senior Director of Corporate Communication, posted the following cryptic message on the Sony PlayStation blog:

> We're aware certain functions of PlayStation Network are down. We will report back here as soon as we can with more information.[28]

He didn't mention that the outage was the direct result of Sony intentionally disabling the network when server administrators realized that someone had penetrated their perimeter and made off with a mother-load of data.

Almost a week later, the truth came out. Seybold posted another message indicating that between April 17 and April 19, the PlayStation Network suffered an intrusion that compromised account information.[29] As many as 77 million accounts may have been affected.[30] Sony estimated that the PlayStation breach cost the company $171 million.[31]

The second wave hit servers belonging to Sony Online Entertainment (SOE). The intrusion was announced on May 3 of 2011.[32] Approximately 24.6 million user accounts were compromised. The data snatched by intruders was mostly personal information (e.g. e-mail, birthdate, phone number, login name, hashed password, etc.). An older, outdated, database was also penetrated. It contained 10,700 direct debit records for users in Austria, Germany, the Netherlands, and Spain.

To add insult to injury, a few weeks later in June, the LulzSec hacking collective declared that they'd infiltrated the Sony Pictures Entertainment website (SonyPictures.com) using a SQL injection attack:

> From a single injection, we accessed EVERYTHING. Why do you put such faith in a company that allows itself to become open to these simple attacks?

LulzSec claims that user information was stored as unencrypted data.[33] To prove this, the hacking collective released information on approximately 50,000 users.

Yet again, SQL injection exposes poorly designed software. All attackers need is one little opening and Sony gave it to them. What's even more disappointing is that a large company like Sony could have easily afforded to audit its software for security flaws and re-design the offending code to eliminate SQL injection bugs. For a tiny fraction of the amount of money that it spent dealing with the aftermath of the attacks, Sony could have avoided the incidents entirely.

Citigroup Comes Clean

In May of 2011, hackers penetrated Citigroup's Citi Account Online systems and accessed account information belonging to more than 360,000 customers.[34] The company started sending out notification letters on June 3rd and re-issued credit cards for more than 217,000 customers. Citigroup claims that data required to commit fraudulent transactions (e.g. social security numbers, birth dates, card security codes, etc.) were not stolen. Nevertheless, bogus charges were made on less than 1 percent of the compromised accounts (around 3,400).

A study conducted by the Ponemon Institute and Symantec in 2010 calculates that the average cost of data theft in the United States is $214 per record.[35] Assuming this is correct, Citigroup's losses would have been on the order of $77 million. The actual reported loss from Citigroup is much lower, about $2.7 million.[36]

Citigroup is no stranger to security incidents. Back in 1995, a Russian hacker broke into Citibank's systems and made off with $2.8 million in illicit fund transfers.[37] Later on, in the winter of 2009 the *Wall Street Journal* reported that Citigroup lost tens of millions of dollars as a result of another data breach. Citigroup denied this allegation, stating that "there has been no breach and there have been no associated losses."[38]

Breach or no breach, law enforcement has yet to prosecute anyone in connection with these incidents. The intruder(s) simply vanished into the ether with their stolen data in tow. This goes to show that even highly visible mega-corporations are vulnerable to attacks that can be difficult to investigate

The FIS Breach

Fidelity Information Services (FIS) is a publicly held financial services company that's based out of Jacksonville, Florida. In the company's first quarter earnings statement, released on May 3, 2011, FIS revealed that it had suffered a loss of $13 million as a result of "unauthorized activities involving one client and 22 prepaid card accounts."[39]

FIS called in the FBI. The ensuing investigation turned up 7,170 compromised prepaid debit card accounts. Other details on this incident have been scarce, though journalist Brian Krebs was able to dig up some additional bits of information.[40]

As in the RBS WorldPay attack, the intruders were able to raise the withdrawal limit on the 22 prepaid card accounts they accessed. Then they fabricated counterfeit cards for the compromised accounts and passed them on to a network of "cashers" who were spread out all over Europe. On Saturday, March 5, as business hours in the U.S. drew to a close, the cashers sprang into action. They worked for nearly 24 hours straight withdrawing cash from ATMs in the U.K., Russia, the Ukraine, Spain, and Sweden. As the cards ran low on funds, the hackers would leverage their access to the compromised FIS system to replenish the cards with more money.

As in the previous Citigroup fiasco, no arrests have been made in this case. Even worse, in this instance the crooks walked away with $13 million.

Operation Trident Tribunal

Scareware schemes are based on convincing a victim that their computer is infected with malware. The con artists typically get their feett in the door by using web-based advertisements that warn of a malware infestation and offer a "free" virus scan. Sometimes the ad will even appear as a separate pop-up window that looks a lot like a legitimate anti-virus warning from the user's existing security software.

Accepting the free scan usually downloads an application that performs a mock inspection, warning of non-existent infections. This application is actually malicious. In the background, this fake scanner disables the existing legitimate anti-virus software and then barrages the victim with prompts to purchase bogus anti-virus software. In extreme cases, the targeted machine will freeze up until the user either buys the anti-virus software or rebuilds their machine.

Scareware is big business. For example, Innovative Marketing Ukraine (IMU) made off with roughly $180 million in 2008 through developing and selling faux security software.[41] To deal with customers who wanted their money back and throttle the level of credit chargebacks, the company made getting a refund more difficult by investing in a call center. Shady businesses like IMU survive by operating in locales where laws are vague (even permissive) or the officials charged with enforcement are willing to turn a blind eye.

Operation Trident Tribunal was an international effort by law enforcement to take down two criminal rings that sold more than $74 million worth of phony security software to over a million un-suspecting users. On June 22, 2011, the FBI issued a press release providing specifics on the campaign. The FBI, in conjunction with authorities in other countries, seized more than 40 computers and servers located in the United States, United Kingdom, Germany, France, Sweden, Lithuania, and Latvia. Law enforcement officials also froze five bank accounts. Both of the scareware networks that police disrupted appear to have been based in Latvia. One of the groups used advertising space on the *Minneapolis Star Tribune's* website to launch their scam.

While this story lauds the benefits of international collaboration, it also exposes the limits that law enforcement officials face. Specifically, what can investigators do when faced with attackers operating out of a country that doesn't necessarily wish to cooperate? Local corruption in some foreign countries is pervasive, and this sort of fundamental problem doesn't lend itself to overnight solutions. The very fact that companies like IMU exist, and thrive, is a testimony to this reality.

The Big Picture

Looking back through the previous cases reveals a number of recurring themes. First and foremost, cybercrime is often enabled by buggy software and poor operational decisions. Time after time SQL injection reared its ugly head as intruders deftly fed tiny snippets of SQL code to insecure applications and made off with entire corporate data stores. Then there were businesses that deployed insecure network protocols, as in the TJX Hack, or neglected to properly encrypt sensitive user data. These deficiencies reside at the organizational level, where decision makers have either failed to mandate the establishment of security standards or failed to enforce them.

The elusive criminals who exploit these security holes can be difficult to apprehend. Successful prosecution of an experienced hacker like Max Butler entails heavy application of well-known undercover techniques. There's no quick fix, just the day-after-day grind of following up on an endless stream of seemingly dead-end leads. To make matters worse, the really cagey offenders have been known to utilize the same strategies and technologies used by national intelligence services and likewise evade attribution entirely.

The crooks, who escape capture, end up funneling their stolen data into what could be characterized as a global online commodity market. The DarkMarket Sting should give you a whiff of how extensive it is. The underground scene for pilfered data is teeming with thousands of cyber outlaws who facilitate cybercrime by providing a way for hackers to turn their raw data into cash. The existence of these forums is proof that there's a demand for stolen data and that cybercrime can be very lucrative. The losses are shouldered by individual and institutional investors – and even more frequently, the customers affected.

Loss Statistics

To give you an idea of how widespread cybercrime is, let's step back from the trees to view the forest. Though before we wade into actual loss statistics, wed like to acknowledge an observation that's been made by researchers at Microsoft. Specifically, they contend that estimated losses due to cybercrime are vastly overstated:

> It turns out, however, that such widely circulated cybercrime estimates are generated using absurdly bad statistical methods, making them wholly unreliable.
>
> Most cybercrime estimates are based on surveys of consumers and companies. They borrow credibility from election polls, which we have learned to trust. However, when extrapolating from a surveyed group to the overall population, there is an enormous difference between preference questions (which are used in election polls) and numerical questions (as in cybercrime surveys).[42]

Notice that they're referring to *estimates*. That is, extrapolations based on statistical surveys rather than concrete figures. The textbook example of this pseudo-scientific guessing is McAfee's 2009 *estimate* that cybercrime global losses amounted to $1 trillion, an outlandish estimate which company executives later (after rounding their speculative statistic down to $100 billion in the summer of 2013)[43] regretted.[44]

There are also those who suggest that cybercrime constitutes the *greatest transfer of wealth in history*, similar to hyperbolic claims that we examined at the end of Chapter Two. In an op-ed piece that appeared in the *Providence Journal*, Senators Lindsey Graham and Sheldon Whitehouse stated:

Foreign agents raid companies, stealing plans, formulas and designs. Foreign criminal networks take money out of banks, defraud consumers with scams and sell illicit goods and products, cheating U.S. manufacturers. It may be the greatest illicit transfer of wealth in history.

Reflecting on these ridiculous assertions, we would partially agree with the people at Microsoft. For genuine financial statistics that hover in the range of $1 trillion, which result in documented economic fallout, the public might be better advised to look toward outstanding student loans.[45] We are sure someone feels like they were robbed.

Keeping this in mind we are going to eschew projected figures based on surveys and stick exclusively to figures that correspond to concrete losses. Despite the naysaying of skeptics, the losses are real and categorically nontrivial, such that cybercrime is taking a toll on society. It's just that loss figures are nowhere near at the level that certain groups would like us to believe.

In one recent case, an ATM heist involving re-loadable prepaid debit cards, the perpetrators walked away with $11 million in cash.[46] In another case hackers stole over $1 million out of the payroll account used by a public hospital in Leavenworth, Washington.[47] In May of 2012, federal prosecutors in Brooklyn, New York, charged eight men with stealing $45 million in a hacking scheme that targeted prepaid debit cards.[48] In yet another case an escrow firm in California lost $1.1 million to fraudulent wire transfers.[49]

Let's view the problem at a national level. In 2010 the Identity Theft Resource Center, a nonprofit that compiles data and assists victims, recorded 662 data breaches in the U.S. which exposed more than 16 million database records.[50] A similar report was published in April of 2011 by Verizon, in conjunction with the U.S. Secret Service and the Dutch National High Tech Crime Unit.[51] The report covers a larger set of data breaches (761), which also occurred during 2010. Statistics compiled by DatalossDB.org report an even larger number of incidents, 802, in 2010.[52]

The Verizon report provides some additional insight into how the breaches occurred and the losses associated with them. Specifically, the 2011 Verizon report states that most of the breaches involved external attackers who surreptitiously gained access and installed malware on the victim's system. This report also states that in 2010 the Secret Service apprehended over 1,200 people suspected of being involved in cybercrime and that the ensuing investigations revealed more than $500 million of loss due to fraud.

There you have it: over half a billion dollars lost on behalf of some 761 data breaches. Compare this to "old-fashioned" bank robbery. In 2010, the FBI recorded just over 5,500 incidents of bank robbery where the crooks made off with approximately $43 million.[53] On average, a bank robbery yielded less than ten grand.

Contrast this figure against the crooks that were rounded up in Operation Trident Breach. They made off with something in the neighborhood of $70 million. In 2011 the FBI announced that it was investigating roughly 400 cases of corporate bank account takeover where the criminals stole $85 million.[54] And the numbers just keep growing. A year later, late 2012, the U.S. Department of Justice announced that the FBI, in tandem with security services overseas, arrested ten people running a massive 11 million node botnet that *allegedly* generated losses on the order of $850 million.

To make matters worse, there doesn't seem to be a light at the end of the tunnel. Statistics collected by DatalossDB.org on events involving the loss, theft, or exposure of personally identifiable information (PII) demonstrate that the phenomenon of cybercrime exhibits no signs of abating (see Figure 4-1). Likewise, figures compiled by Verizon detailing the number of confirmed data breaches per year also support this conclusion (see Figure 4-2). Widespread cybercrime is the new normal.

Across the Atlantic, law enforcement officials in Germany have also been collecting statistics on cybercrime. In June of 2011, the German Federal Police announced a 20 percent rise in cybercrime (from approximately 50,000 cybercrime incidents in 2009 to approximately 60,000 incidents in 2010), resulting in a loss of $89 million.[55] Chief Joerg Ziercke observed in particular that phishing attacks related to online banking fraud had risen 82 percent, to a total of 5,300 incidents in 2010. This, taken together

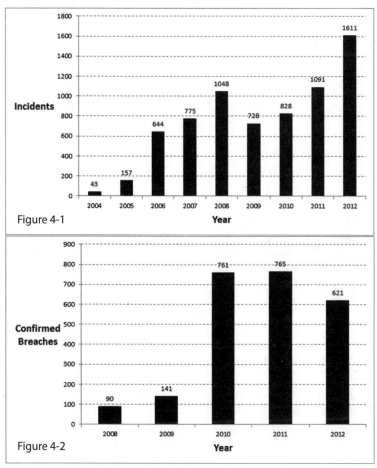

Figure 4-1

Figure 4-2

with the Verizon report, indicates that, at a national level, cybercrime creates losses that normally run into hundreds of millions of dollars.[56]

Let's step back even further from our national vantage point and look at things from a worldwide perspective. The *Nilson Report* is a trade publication for the payment system industry,[57] definitely not something you'd see at your average news stand. A study performed by this publication found that total credit and debit card fraud worldwide was $7.6 billion in 2010, an increase of 10 percent from 2009.[58] To help put this into perspective, the United Nations Office on Drugs and Crime reports that the market for cocaine in the United States is around $37 billion.[59]

The Punch Line

In retrospect, are U.S. citizens going to worry about bombs dropping on their houses or burglars breaking into them? While proponents of cyberwar prefer to fixate on hypothetical visions of Cyber-Armageddon, there is a nontrivial amount of cybercrime taking place. As with the crack cocaine epidemic that hit the United States in the 1980s, it's not necessarily an existential threat. Crime has always been with us and it always will be. Nevertheless, the resulting damage is significant enough to warrant attention.

Endnotes

1) ichard Marosi, "Unraveling Mexico's Sinaloa drug cartel," *Los Angeles Times*, June 24, 2011, http://articles.latimes.com/2011/jul/24/local/la-me-cartel-20110724.

2) "Marijuana Farming Is Lucrative Business in California, but Who's Profiting?" *PBS News Hour*, August 31, 2011, http://www.pbs.org/newshour/bb/social_issues/july-dec11/marijuana_08-31.html.

3) Juan Caballero, Chris Grier, Christian Kreibich, Vern Paxson, "Measuring Pay-per-Install: The Commoditization of Malware Distribution," Proceedings of the 20th USENIX Security Symposium (Security '11), San Francisco, California, August 2011.

4) Gunter Ollmann, "The Botnet Distribution and Helpdesk Services," *The Day Before Zero Blog*, December 18th, 2009, http://blog.damballa.com/?p=454.

5) Jeremy Kirk, "Russian-Armenian botnet suspect raked in €100,000 a month," *IDG News Service*, October 29, 2010, http://www.computerworld.com/s/article/9194019/Russian_Armenian_botnet_suspect_raked_in_140_000_a_month.

6) Kim Zetter, "Cyber Criminals Industrialize to Increase Effectiveness," *Wired*, April 22, 2009, http://www.wired.com/threatlevel/2009/04/cyber-criminals/.

7) Michael Ligh, Steven Adair, Blake Hartstein, Matthew Richard, *Malware Analyst's Cookbook and DVD*, Wiley, 2010.

8) Sergey Golovanov and Igor Soumenkov, *TDL4 – Top Bot*, SecureList, June 27, 2011, http://www.securelist.com/en/analysis/204792180/TDL4_Top_Bot#5.

9) Robert McMillan, "In China, $700 Puts a Spammer in Business," *IDG News Service*, May 8, 2009, http://www.computerworld.com/s/article/9132758/In_China_700_puts_a_spammer_in_business.

10) *Regional Internet Registries (RIRs)*, American Registry for Internet Numbers, https://www.arin.net/knowledge/rirs.html.

11) Brian Krebs, "Shadowy Russian Firm Seen as Conduit for Cybercrime," *Washington Post*, Oct. 13, 2007, http://www.washingtonpost.com/wp-dyn/content/article/2007/10/12/AR2007101202461.html.

12) *U.S. Secret Service's Operation Firewall Nets 28 Arrests*, U.S. Secret Service Press Release, October 28, 2004, http://www.secretservice.gov/press/pub2304.pdf.

13) *The TJX Companies, Inc. Victimized by Computer Systems Intrusion; Provides Information to Help Protect Customers*, TJX Press Release, January 17, 2007, http://www.businesswire.com/news/tjx/20070117005971/en.

14) Denise Lavoie, "Credit cos. watchful after TJX breach," *Associated Press*, January 18, 2007, http://www.washingtonpost.com/wp-dyn/content/article/2007/01/18/AR2007011801361_pf.html.

15) Kim Zetter, "TJX Hacker Was Awash in Cash; His Penniless Coder Faces Prison," *Wired*, June 18, 2009, http://www.wired.com/threatlevel/2009/06/watt/.

16) Joseph Pereira, "Breaking the Code: How Credit-Card Data Went Out Wireless Door," *Wall Street Journal*, May 4, 2007.

17) Kim Zetter, "TJX Hacker Charged With Heartland, Hannaford Breaches," *Wired*, August 17, 2009, http://www.wired.com/threatlevel/2009/08/tjx-hacker-charged-with-heartland/.

18) Open Web Application Security Project, OWASP Top Ten Project, https://www.owasp.org/index.php/Category:OWASP_Top_Ten_Project.

19) Charles Cooper, "To catch a (cyber) thief: It's not easy," *CNET News*, April 22, 2009, http://news.cnet.com/8301-10787_3-10225278-60.html.

20) Maggie Shiels, "Trojan Virus Steals Banking Info," *BBC News*, October 13, 2008, http://news.bbc.co.uk/2/hi/technology/7701227.stm.

21) Brett Stone-Gross, Marco Cova, Lorenzo Cavallaro, Bob Gilbert, Martin Szydlowski, Richard Kemmerer, Chris Kruegel, and Giovanni Vigna, "Your Botnet is My Botnet: Analysis of a Botnet Takeover," in Proceedings of the ACM CCS, Chicago, IL, November 2009.

22) *RBS WorldPay Announces Compromise of Data Security and Outlines Steps to Mitigate Risk*, WorldPay Press Release, December 23, 2008, http://www.worldpay.us/media/news_media25.htm.

23) Kevin Poulsen, "Record 13-Year Sentence for Hacker Max Vision," *Wired*, February 12, 2010, http://www.wired.com/threatlevel/2010/02/max-vision-sentencing/.

24) Brian Krebs "Ukraine Detains 5 Individuals Tied to $70 Million in U.S. eBanking Heists," *krebsonsecurity.com*, October 2010, http://krebsonsecurity.com/2010/10/ukraine-detains-5-individuals-tied-to-70-million-in-ebanking-heists/.

25) Elinor Mills, "Dozens charged in use of Zeus Trojan to steal $3 million," *CNET*, September 30, 2010, http://news.cnet.com/8301-27080_3-20018177-245.html.

26) "Cyber Banking Fraud: Global Partnerships Lead to Major Arrests," Federal Bureau of Investigation, October 1, 2010, http://www.fbi.gov/news/stories/2010/october/cyber-banking-fraud/cyber-banking-fraud.

27) "Fraud Alert Involving Unauthorized Wire Transfers to China," Federal Bureau of Investigation, the Financial Services Information Sharing and Analysis Center (FS-ISAC), and the Internet Crime Complaint Center (IC3), April 26, 2011, http://www.ic3.gov/media/2011/ChinaWireTransferFraudAlert.pdf.

28) Patrick Seybold, "Update on PSN Service Outages," April 20, 2011, *PlayStation Blog*, http://blog.us.playstation.com/2011/04/20/update-on-psn-service-out-ages-2/.

29) Patrick Seybold, "Update on PlayStation Network and Qriocity," April 26, 2011, *PlayStation Blog*, http://blog.us.playstation.com/2011/04/26/update-on-play-station-network-and-qriocity/.

30) Ben Quinn and Charles Arthur, "PlayStation Network hackers access data of 77 million users," *Guardian*, April 26, 2011, http://www.guardian.co.uk/technolo-gy/2011/apr/26/playstation-network-hackers-data.

31) Mark Hachman, "Playstation Hack to Cost Sony $171M," *PCMag.com*, May 23, 2011, http://www.pcmag.com/article2/0,2817,2385790,00.asp.

32) "Sony Online Entertainment Announces Theft Of Data From Its Systems," Sony Press Release, May 3, 2011, http://www.soe.com/securityupdate/pressre-lease.vm.

33) "Sony investigating another hack," *BBC News*, June 3, 2011, http://www.bbc.co.uk/news/business-13636704.

34) "Updated Information on Recent Compromise to Citi Account On-line," *Business Wire*, June 15, 2011, http://online.barrons.com/article/PR-CO-20110615-914373.html.

35) "Cost of a data breach climbs higher," PoneMon Institute, March 8, 2011, http://www.ponemon.org/blog/post/cost-of-a-data-breach-climbs-higher.

36) "Citigroup lost $2.7 million from credit card hack attack in May," *Consumer Reports*, June 27, 2011, http://news.consumerreports.org/money/2011/06/citi-group-lost-27-million-from-credit-card-hack-attack-in-may.html.

37) David Johnson, "Russian Accused of Citibank Computer Fraud," *New York Times*, August 18, 1995, http://www.nytimes.com/1995/08/18/business/rus-sian-accused-of-citibank-computer-fraud.html.

38) "FBI probes cyber attack on Citigroup," *Reuters*, December 22, 2009, http://www.reuters.com/article/2009/12/22/us-citigroup-fbi-idUSTRE5B-L0I320091222.

39) "FIS Announces First Quarter Results," FIS Press Release, May 3, 2011, http://www.fisglobal.com/EMEA/Qatar/NEWSRELEASE-2011-05-03-900.

40) "Coordinated ATM Heist Nets Thieves $13M," Brian Krebs, August 26th, 2011, http://krebsonsecurity.com/2011/08/coordinated-atm-heist-nets-thieves-13m/.

41) Jim Finkle, "Inside a global cybercrime ring," *Reuters*, March 24, 2010, http://www.reuters.com/article/2010/03/24/us-technology-scareware-idUS-TRE62N29T20100324.

42) Dinei Florencio and Cormac Herley, "The Cybercrime Wave That Wasn't," *New York Times*, April 14, 2012, http://www.nytimes.com/2012/04/15/opinion/sun-day/the-cybercrime-wave-that-wasnt.html.

43) Siobhan Gorman, "Annual U.S. Cybercrime Costs Estimated at $100 Billion," *Wall Street Journal*, July 22, 2013, http://online.wsj.com/news/articles/SB100014 24127887324328904578621880966242990.

44) James Hutchinson, "McAfee regrets 'flawed' trillion dollar cybercrime claims," *Australian Financial Review*, August 19, 2013, http://www.afr.com/p/technology/mcafee_regrets_flawed_trillion_dollar_msQ2WFkVLEZKx7Yv7ZCMQI.

45) Josh Mitchell and Maya Jackson-Randall, "Student-Loan Debt Tops $1 Trillion," *Wall Street Journal*, March 22, 2012.

46) Brian Krebs, "Crooks Net Millions in Coordinated ATM Heists," *Krebs On Security*, February 6, 2013, http://krebsonsecurity.com/2013/02/crooks-net-millions-in-coordinated-atm-heists/#more-18348.

47) "Hackers steal more than $1 million from Leavenworth hospital," *Associated Press*, April 26, 2013, http://blogs.seattletimes.com/today/2013/04/hackers-steal-more-than-1-million-from-leavenworth-hospital/.

48) Marc Santora, "In Hours, Thieves Took $45 Million in A.T.M. Scheme," *New York Times*, May 9, 2013, http://www.nytimes.com/2013/05/10/nyregion/eight-charged-in-45-million-global-cyber-bank-thefts.html.

49) Brian Krebs, "$1.5 million Cyberheist Ruins Escrow Firm," *Krebs On Security*, August 13, 2013, http://krebsonsecurity.com/2013/08/1-5-million-cyberheist-ruins-escrow-firm/.

50) *2010 Data Breach Stats*, Identity Theft Resource Center, December 29, 2010, http://www.idtheftcenter.org/ITRC Breach Stats Report 2010.pdf.

51) *2011Data Breach Investigations Report*, Verizon, April 19, 2011, http://www.verizonbusiness.com/resources/reports/rp_data-breach-investigations-report-2011_en_xg.pdf.

52) Data Loss Statistics, Open Security Foundation, http://www.datalossdb.org/statistics.

53) *Bank Crime Statistics (BCS), Federal Insured Financial Institutions*, January 1, 2010 – December 31, 2010, Federal Bureau of Investigation, http://www.fbi.gov/stats-services/publications/bank-crime-statistics-2010/bank-crime-statistics-2010.

54) Gordon Snow. "Cyber security: Threats to the financial sector." Testimony before the House Financial Services Committee, September 2011. http://financialservices.house.gov/UploadedFiles/091411snow.pdf.

55) Associated Press, "Germany sees nearly 20 percent rise in cybercrime," June 30, 2011, http://arabnews.com/lifestyle/science_technology/article464517.ece.

56) Edwin Chan, "Facebook helps FBI bust cybercriminals blamed for $850 million losses," *Reuters*, December 11, 2012, http://www.reuters.com/article/2012/12/12/us-cybercrime-fbi-idUSBRE8BB04B20121212.

57) http://www.nilsonreport.com/.

58) Ross Kerber, "Banks losing ground on card security," *Reuters*, Oct. 4, 2011, http://www.reuters.com/article/2011/10/04/us-banks-security-idUSTRE7935XO20111004.

59) *World Drug Report 2011*, United Nations Office on Drugs and Crime, http://www.unodc.org/documents/data-and-analysis/WDR2011/World_Drug_Report_2011_ebook.pdf.

Chapter 5

Espionage

When the automobile was invented people still moved from point A to point B. Different means, same outcome. As the Internet has matured, information has begun to move online en masse. Although this provides additional means to acquire data, there's nothing conceptually new going on here. For decades world powers have supported sprawling intelligence services that execute targeted, long-term, covert operations. For decades, private corporate interests have looked to gain competitive advantage by collecting intelligence on their rivals and customers. Spying is spying, whether it occurs on the Internet or otherwise.

As mentioned in previous chapters, a common tactic employed in the media is to point to an incident of espionage and refer to it as cyberwar. This is because there are plenty of examples of espionage to draw from. In this chapter we'll examine a series of such cases, instances of alleged cyberwar that have been covered by the mainstream press. In each incident we'll try to identify where the attack emanated from, how the intruders got access, and assess what sort of evidence was left behind. Then we'll step back and use these results to discuss recurring themes that appear.

Moonlight Maze

In March of 1998, a series of intrusions were launched against the U.S. government in a campaign that targeted computers owned by the Department of Energy nuclear weapons and research labs, the Pentagon, NASA, and several academic institutions. The attacks continued for the better part of two years before being discovered.

In response, the FBI led an investigation code-named *Moonlight Maze*. All told, they weren't able to come up with much. Over the course of the inquiry they were unable to determine how many systems were compromised, the identity of the intruders, their underlying motive, or even the attack vector that was employed. People close to the investigation suspect that organized crime groups may be involved.[1]

The extent of the damage resulting from the attack is also unknown. The attackers did not make off with any classified information.[2] According to an executive from iDEFENSE who testified about the incident in front of the Senate Committee on Governmental Affairs in March of 2000:

> The value of this stolen information is in the tens of millions, perhaps hundreds of millions of dollars; there's really no way to tell.[3]

Investigators traced the geographic source intrusions to a mainframe located within 20 miles of Moscow.[4] As you might expect, U.S. officials lodged a formal complaint with the former Soviet Union. Likewise, the Russians denied any connection with the attacks. After all, the evidence was strictly circumstantial. The intruders could very well have "bounced" their attacks off of the mainframe in Moscow and staged things in a manner that led investigators to suspect Russian involvement. For example, the intrusions occurred between the hours of 8 A.M. and 5 P.M. Moscow time. Activity was also discernibly absent during Russian holidays.

This first example is an archetype for all of the incidents that will follow. Though the authorities were aware that something happened, the specifics eluded them. Furthermore they couldn't determine who was responsible or even the extent of the damage. At the same time this didn't prevent people involved in the investigation from passing on conjectures to the media, which gratefully received the speculative information and repackaged it as a tentative version of the truth. This explains why, despite the dearth of substantive evidence, the *Los Angeles Times* referred to this incident with headlines such as: "Russians Seem to be Hacking into Pentagon."

Titan Rain

From 2003 to 2005 a series of organized intrusions, dubbed *Titan Rain* by federal investigators, hit networks belonging to the U.S. government, military, defense contractors, and the World Bank. The intruders worked quickly and efficiently, scanning blocks of IP addresses for vulnerabilities and then executing orchestrated attacks that lasted from 10 to 30 minutes. As a coup de grace, they used rootkit technology to eliminate evidence and facilitate later access.[5]

A freelance security professional who volunteered his services to the FBI, Shawn Carpenter, traced the attacker's network traffic back to routers in the Chinese province of Guandong.[6] In terms of attribution, the director of research for the SANS Institute, Alan Paller, suggested that the Chinese Military was responsible.

> These attacks come from someone with intense discipline. No other organization could do this if they were not a military organization.[7]

As in the case of Moonlight Maze, the media jumped on this statement. For instance, the *Agence France-Presse* report on Titan Rain was entitled "Hacker Attacks in U.S. Linked to Chinese Military: Researchers."

One blogger who's well-versed in these matters, George Smith, offers a glimpse of insight into what's going on:

> The undisputed ruler, the head passer-on of all wisdoms, is Alan Paller of the Sans Institute, a business that sells training and seminars on computer security.
>
> Paller is the go-to purveyor of quote on Chinese cyberattacks, of hackers compromising everything, of cyber-looting everywhere, of the electrical grid going down, on the need for more computer security training courses and of getting a press release in as a footnote in the Obama administration's Cyberspace Policy Review ... [8]

Paller's conjectures are just that. As Navy Rear Admiral Elizabeth Hight, deputy director of the DOD's Joint Task Force for Global Network Operations, cautioned:

> We are seeing attacks that traversed through China. I can't say with any real assurance that that's where they start.[9]

In other words, despite what Paller says, investigators were unable to even determine if this is the work of state sponsored agents, private-sector operatives, or independent hired guns. Damage estimates are equally muddled. According to official reports, no classified U.S. systems were breached during the course of the attacks.[10] This makes sense, as the military's classified networks aren't on the Internet. The people who designed them were prudent enough to implement air-gap security.

Operation Byzantine Hades

Most of what's known about *Byzantine Hades* is based exclusively on U.S. State department diplomatic cables that were leaked into the public domain and subsequently published by WikiLeaks.[11] A diplomatic cable dated December of 2008 offers a concise description:

> Byzantine Hades, a series of related computer-network intrusions with a believed nexus to the PRC, has affected U.S. and foreign government systems as well as those systems belonging to international organizations.

The attacks were so prolific, in fact, that U.S. investigators grouped the intrusion into subsets which exhibited common characteristics. The diplomatic cables used codenames like *Byzantine Anchor*, *Byzantine Candor*, and *Byzantine Foothold* to refer to these subsets.

Related activity appears to have manifested on a global scale. Officials from both France and Germany claimed to have observed attacks that were very similar in nature to Byzantine Hades. A cable from November of 2008 states:

> The GoG [Government of Germany] assesses these efforts are conducted for the purpose of espionage and present a significant threat to German interests. Targets cover a broad range of GoG activities including the military, the economy, science and technology, commercial interests, diplomatic efforts, and research and development. The officials also indicated such espionage focused activity increases before major negotiations involving German and Chinese interests.

In addition to activity similar to the aforementioned GoG infiltrations, the French claimed to have been victims of specific technical monitoring facilitated through computer network operations. The representatives indicated that believed Chinese actors had gained access to the computers of several high-level French officials, activating microphones and Web cameras for the purpose of eavesdropping.

The attack vector common to most incidents is spear-phishing. The intruders would send off bogus e-mail which leveraged malware to exploit buggy software in an effort to establish control over the targeted machines:

> Infiltrations are generally accomplished through the use of socially engineered e-mail messages crafted to appear authentic and specifically targeted to individuals of interest. These messages normally contain an attachment or embedded link which is used to deliver malicious software (malware) onto the victim computer.

As far as attribution is concerned, there are lots of conjectures and very little, if any, solid proof. For example, a State Department cable from April of 2009 points out coincidences that could be interpreted to suggest PLA involvement (the cable sensibly refers to these inferences as "tenuous"):

> Sensitive reports indicate the domains www.indexnews.org, www.indexindian.com, www.lookbytheway.net, and www.macfeeresponse.org were involved in Byzantine Hades (BH) intrusion activity in 2006. All four domains were registered in Chengdu, China. The IP addresses associated with these domains substantiate this as the location. Subsequent analysis of registration information also leads to a tenuous connection between these hostile domains and the People's Liberation Army (PLA) Chengdu Military Region First Technical Reconnaissance Bureau (TRB). When registering the indexnews and indexindian domains, Chen Xingpeng (a.k.a. Richard Chen) listed his postal code as 610041, the precise area of Chengdu associated with the PLA First TRB (a.k.a. Military Unit Cover Designator 78006). There is no official connection

between BH activity and the PLA's First TRB. However, much of the intrusion activity traced to Chengdu is similar in tactics, techniques, and procedures to BH activity attributed to other PLA TRBs.

Never mind that all of this is circumstantial evidence. Even then, not all pieces fit together. Timing and types of target do seem to fit with the PLA hypothesis. But what doesn't fit is why a government backed operation would be so sloppy as to commence an operation from an address in its own country.

GhostNet

In June of 2008, the Office of the Dalia Lama asked investigators to examine office computers that they suspected had been compromised. One of the investigators was the editor of the Information Warfare Monitor (IWM), an independent research lab based in Canada.[12] For the next six months they collected forensic evidence in Brussels, London, New York, and Tibet. This data was then passed on to researchers at the Citizen Lab at the Munk School of Global Affairs, University of Toronto (the public-sector component of the IWM).

The investigators at the Citizen Lab used the evidence to identify four control servers (located in both China and the United States) and six command servers (located in China and Hong Kong). After scanning the four control servers with network probes, they discovered that the control servers were all running a (poorly secured) web application that was used by the attackers to manage infected machines. They co-opted these web-based management consoles to uncover a set of 1,295 compromised machines that were spread across more than 100 countries.

The intruders relied heavily on spear-phishing as an attack vector.[13] Infection was realized through malicious e-mail attachments or by links contained in the email that directed victims to drive-by download websites. Many of the compromised machines were infested with a "gh0st RAT," an open source *Remote Access Tool* (e.g. "RAT") which is readily available in the dark corners of the Internet.

According to the IWM, approximately a third of the infected machines were *high-value targets*. In the context of this investigation, targets were labeled as such because:

> They were either significant to the relationship between China and Tibet, Taiwan or India, or were identified as computers at foreign embassies, diplomatic missions, government ministries, or international organizations.

But does this mean that the information contained in these machines was actually valuable? Researcher Evgeny Morozov points out:

> What may be most remarkable about GhostNet is what did not happen. No computers belonging to the U.S. or U.K. governments – both deeply concerned about cyber-security – were affected; one NATO computer was affected, but had no classified information on it.[14]

While streams of network traffic often led to China, investigators admit that they have no idea who was behind the attacks:

> Who is ultimately in control of the GhostNet system? While our analysis reveals that numerous politically sensitive and high-value computer systems were compromised, we do not know the motivation or the identity of the attacker(s) or how to accurately characterize this network of infections as a whole.

In fact, the investigators at the IWM are sensible enough to acknowledge the possibility of a false-flag operation:

> It is not inconceivable that this network of infected computers could have been targeted by a state other than China, but operated physically within China (and at least one node in the United States) for strategic purposes. Compromised proxy computers on Hainan Island, for example, could have been deployed as staging posts, perhaps in an effort to deliberately mislead observers as to the true operator(s) and purpose of the GhostNet system.

The events surrounding GhostNet have all the hallmarks of a prototypical cyber-espionage campaign: Attackers leverage malicious e-mail as an entry tool in a widespread effort to steal an undetermined amount of sensitive information. Investigators know that something happened, and sometimes can even recover forensic artifacts, but their success in attributing the attacks is strictly limited.

Joint Strike Fighter Breach

On April 21, 2009, the *Wall Street Journal* reported that intruders hacked into computers belonging to the F-35 Lightning II project and absconded with several terabytes of data.[15] They gained entry by penetrating the networks belonging to contractors involved with the $300 billion project. The attackers somehow achieved access to a system used to diagnose maintenance issues during flight.

The intruders, however, were unable to access "the most sensitive material" as high-security systems are normally not connected to the Internet. Again, air-gap security seems to afford some degree of protection. The project's primary contractor, Lockheed Martin, has formally stated that it does not believe that classified information was lost.[16]

Because the intruders used an encrypted covert channel during exfiltration, investigators cannot determine the exact scope of the damage. Also, while the attacks were traced back to IP addresses in China, the actual identity of the intruders is unknown.

Operation Aurora

On January 12, 2010, Google posted a blog message stating:

> In mid-December, we detected a highly sophisticated and targeted attack on our corporate infrastructure originating from China that resulted in the theft of intellectual property from Google.[17]

Within minutes of Google's post, Adobe also released a similar announcement:

Adobe became aware on January 2, 2010 of a computer security incident involving a sophisticated, coordinated attack
against corporate network systems managed by Adobe and
other companies.[18]

Notice how both companies describe the attacks as "sophisticated," or "highly sophisticated." This is because no one likes to admit that they suffered at the hands of commonplace malware. Yet,
as researchers from security vendor Damballa concluded:

> While "Aurora" was a very damaging attack that breached
> some of the most sophisticated networks in the world, it is a
> "garden variety" botnet and can be traced back to July 2009,
> when the criminal operators first began testing ...

HBGary's Greg Hoglund concurred with Damballa's findings:

> The Aurora stuff isn't that complicated. It smells like any other
> criminal malware that's out there.[19]

As you might expect, the intruders used a spear-phishing strategy to gain access. Specifically, they sent out malicious e-mails
containing a web link to a website in Taiwan. The web site, in turn,
would cause the victim's browser to execute a malicious snippet of
JavaScript. This JavaScript contained a zero-day exploit that leveraged a software flaw in Internet Explorer.[20] Having undermined Internet Explorer, this exploit established a foothold on the victim's
machine and linked up with command and control servers in Illinois, Taiwan, and Texas.[21]

By poking around the command and control servers used by
the attackers, investigators were able to identify at least thirty-four
companies that had been targeted.[22] In addition to Adobe and Google, the list included big names like Dow Chemical, Juniper Networks, Northrop Grumman, Symantec, and Yahoo!.

In its initial release, Adobe claimed that it had:

> No evidence to indicate that any sensitive information –
> including customer, financial, employee or any other sensitive
> data – has been compromised." Dow Chemical also stated

that it had "no reason to believe that the safety, security and intellectual property of our operations are in jeopardy.[23]

Most of the other companies have remained silent about the extent of the damage done. Google is one notable exception. It went public about its loss of intellectual property from day one.

Google's intellectual property, its source code (i.e. the engineering blueprints that describe the internal operation of its technology), was located on a series of *software-configuration management* (SCM) systems. SCM systems are basically glorified file servers that can track all of the revisions that get made to the files that they store. Every little change is logged and archived for future reference. In the old days, these servers would be referred to as *source code control* machines. It's almost certain that intruders were able to access Google's SCM repositories.

Dmitri Alperovitch, McAfee's vice president for threat research, explains how these SCM servers were an open invitation to attackers:

> No one ever thought about securing them, yet these were the crown jewels of most of these companies in many ways – much more valuable than any financial or personally identifiable data that they may have and spend so much time and effort protecting.[24]

As an aside, it was McAfee's examination of the offensive payload that led the company to refer to the incident as Operation Aurora:

> Based on our analysis, "Aurora" was part of the filepath on the attacker's machine that was included in two of the malware binaries that we have confirmed are associated with the attack. That filepath is typically inserted by code compilers to indicate where debug symbols and source code are located on the machine of the developer. We believe the name was the internal name the attacker(s) gave to this operation ...[25]

All told, U.S. officials have failed to provide concrete evidence that implicates anyone in particular. This has done little to halt a deluge of innuendo. For example, investigators discovered that the malware they unearthed made use of a cyclic redundancy check (CRC) algorithm designed by a Chinese developer. Researcher Joe Stewart comments:

> Perhaps the most interesting aspect of this source code sample is that it is of Chinese origin, released as part of a Chinese-language paper on optimizing CRC algorithms for use in microcontrollers. The full paper was published in simplified Chinese characters, and all existing references and publications of the sample source code seem to be exclusively on Chinese websites. This CRC-16 implementation seems to be virtually unknown outside of China, as shown by a Google search for one of the key variables, "crc_ta[16]." At the time of this writing, almost every page with meaningful content concerning the algorithm is Chinese.[26]

What this implies directly is that the person who used the CRC implementation was capable of understanding simplified Chinese. But that's it.

Investigators also traced back network traffic to computers at Shanghai Jiaotong University and the Lanxiang Vocational School.[27] Though, this doesn't necessarily say that much because the machines involved could have just as easily been cover for a false-flag operation. According to Guinness World Records, Lanxiang boasts the world's largest computer lab, capable of accommodating 1,135 students.[28]

When Google set up shop in China in 2006, the company agreed to censor its search engine results. This decision was criticized by numerous human-rights groups, as Google's corporate motto is "Don't be evil." In the aftermath of the Aurora attacks, Google openly threatened to disable content filtering and leave China. As the company stated in its initial blog entry:

> We have decided we are no longer willing to continue censoring our results on Google.cn, and so over the next few weeks we will be discussing with the Chinese government the basis on which we could operate an unfiltered search engine within the law, if at all. We recognize that this may well mean

having to shut down Google.cn, and potentially our offices in China.[29]

The State Department also issued a public statement. Secretary of State Hilary Clinton said, "We look to the Chinese government for an explanation." Privately, the accusations were more pointed. A leaked State Department cable suggested that Aurora might have been initiated at the behest of China's Politburo and involved a smattering of freelance operators, outlaws, and government agents.[30]

Over time, Google would continue to suffer additional high-profile attacks, like the Gmail account compromises of Chinese political activists that were reported in June of 2011.[31] The Chinese government, which largely ignored Clinton's statement, eschewed an official public response. Though, a spokesman for China's Ministry of Industry and Information Technology was quoted as saying that the Clinton accusation was "groundless and aims to denigrate China."[32]

Shadows in the Cloud

About half a year after the IWM published its report on Ghost-Net, the researchers at the IWM collaborated with the ShadowServer Foundation[33] to follow up on some of the loose ends that remained from the original investigation. Eight months of detective work ensued, and in April of 2010 the joint venture published their findings online.[34] What they unearthed was an intricate distributed system of computers characterized by noteworthy advances in reliability, availability, and concealment.

While GhostNet self-destructed very shortly after news of its existence went public, there were other attackers involved who left evidence at the scene. One of these other groups created what investigators dubbed the *Shadow Network*. As in the case of Ghost-Net, the intruders relied upon malicious e-mails to compromise end-users. What distinguished these intruders from the GhostNet campaign was their highly advanced command and control infrastructure.

The Shadow Network's command and control scheme was implemented using a novel *tiered* model that used several layers of servers. The first tier of servers used social networking sites to communicate directly with compromised machines. This is clever use of cloud technology, which leverages the underlying redundancy and fault tolerance of services like Twitter, Google groups, and Yahoo! Mail. Not to mention that the bits of data sent and received from these web sites tend to blend in well with typical network traffic.

The first-tier of servers was used to distribute malware payloads and direct infected computers to a second tier of command and control servers. This second phalanx of servers, which relied on machines maintained by free web hosting providers, is how the architects of Shadow Network built disaster recovery features into their system. They knew that investigators would eventually close in on their command and control infrastructure. As second-tier servers were detected and disabled by investigators, the first-tier would then re-direct infected clients to a more stable subset of dedicated command and control servers located in China.

Investigators succeeded in gaining entry to a subset of poorly secured command and control servers. They also re-registered expired domain names used by intruders during the attacks. This allowed them to enumerate a list of compromised computers and acquire a snapshot of pilfered documents. Most of the attacks they analyzed targeted computers in India with an emphasis on networks run by the government and the military. However, computers belonging to the United Nations were also penetrated, in addition to machines owned by the foreign embassies (e.g. India and Pakistan) in the United States.

With regard to attribution, the researchers conclude:

> Although the identity and motivation of the attackers remain unknown, the report is able to determine the location (Chengdu, PRC)

Though they do stipulate:

The most plausible explanation, and the one supported by the evidence, is that the Shadow network is based out of the PRC by one or more individuals with strong connections to the Chinese criminal underground.

Though, at the same time, they also add:

We hypothesize that political espionage networks may be deliberately exploiting criminal kits, techniques and networks both to distance themselves from attribution and strategically cultivate a climate of uncertainty.

The fact that the data targeted belonged to government agencies and that the attacks originated from computers in Chengdu might be seen as implying involvement on behalf of the Chinese Government. But without solid corroborative evidence (i.e. proof beyond a reasonable doubt) from traditional sources, eye witnesses, video footage, or undercover operations, the actual culprit is still unknown.

Night Dragon

In February of 2011 Security Software vendor McAfee published a report about a campaign of attacks that targeted the oil industry.[35] The codename they used to collectively refer to the incidents was *Night Dragon*. According to George Kurtz, McAfee's CTO:

Starting in November 2009, covert cyberattacks were launched against several global oil, energy, and petrochemical companies. The attackers targeted proprietary operations and project-financing information on oil and gas field bids and operations. This information is highly sensitive and can make or break multibillion dollar deals in this extremely competitive industry.[36]

Details on the exact nature of the targets are scarce. McAfee only states that the victims include:

Global oil, gas, and petrochemical companies, as well as individuals and executives in Kazakhstan, Taiwan, Greece, and the United States.

The attackers gained a foothold in targeted corporate LANS using a multipronged strategy. Specifically, the attackers would penetrate outward facing web servers via SQL-injection exploits. These breached servers would then be used to capture user credentials needed to penetrate machines deeper in the network and install remote access tools (RATs). The attackers also used spear-phishing as an alternative mechanism to install RAT malware. Ultimately, the attackers used the embedded RATs to manage the exfiltration of sensitive data.

The attackers used hosting services in the U.S. and compromised machines in the Netherlands to establish a set of command and control servers. McAfee traced traffic from these servers to locations in China.

McAfee admits they don't know who's behind the attack, and that whatever forensic evidence they collected could very well be part of a false-flag operation. However, given the origin of the malware deployed in the attacks, the corresponding origin of the network activity, and the fact that the attacks occurred during business hours in Beijing's time zone, investigators at McAfee suspect that the intruders may be Chinese.

> Although it is possible that all of these indicators are an elaborate red-herring operation designed to pin the blame for the attacks on Chinese hackers, we believe this to be highly unlikely. Further, it is unclear who would have the motivation to go to these extraordinary lengths to place the blame for these attacks on someone else.

In other words, besides circumstantial evidence, the case is enhanced by the claim that no one would have the motivation to blame the Chinese.

RSA and SecurID

RSA is an encryption algorithm that was developed by Ron Rivest, Adi Shamir and Leonard Adleman in the late 1970s. That is, RSA as in Rivest, Shamir, and Adleman. In 1982 they established a software company, named RSA Data Security to capitalize on their technology. The RSA algorithm played a vital role in the emergence of web security protocols like SSL in the mid-1990s. The company is also credited with providing the general public with security software that implemented *strong* encryption, something that did not endear them to the spooks at the NSA (who were probably hoping to limit the public to weak algorithms, ones that they could decipher). RSA is currently a security division of the EMC Corporation.

Anyway, on March 17, 2011, RSA posted an announcement on its web site about "an extremely sophisticated cyber-attack" that had been launched against the company.[37] As with Google and Adobe, no one likes to admit that they were done in by everyday hackers. The announcement didn't provide many details, but it did mention:

> Our investigation has led us to believe that the attack is in the category of an Advanced Persistent Threat (APT). Our investigation also revealed that the attack resulted in certain information being extracted from RSA's systems. Some of that information is specifically related to RSA's SecurID two-factor authentication products. While at this time we are confident that the information extracted does not enable a successful direct attack on any of our RSA SecurID customers, this information could potentially be used to reduce the effectiveness of a current two-factor authentication implementation as part of a broader attack.

For most people, authentication traditionally means providing a computer with a username and password. Two-factor authentication confirms a user's identity by validating not only the password but also a second additional bit of information. This is done to make it harder to impersonate someone. It's not enough to just steal the password.

In the case of RSA's SecurID product, the additional piece of information is a long number that's displayed on a small device called a *token* (often a *key fob*). This pseudo-random number is generated computationally with a new number being generated about once a minute. The basic idea is that only the user's token and the remote server being accessed can reproduce the same stream of random numbers. If you don't have a token, you can't specify the necessary password/random-number combination.

RSA claimed that the intrusion didn't "enable a successful direct attack" against companies using SecurID. But this turned out to be wishful thinking on behalf of corporate leaders running in damage control mode. In May of 2011, defense contractor Lockheed witnessed an attack against its network. As a result, the company disabled most of its remote access facilities (e.g. VPN connections) and hastily distributed new SecurID tokens to its employees.[38]

In a later blog entry, RSA stated:

> On Thursday, June 2, 2011, we were able to confirm that information taken from RSA in March had been used as an element of an attempted broader attack on Lockheed Martin, a major U.S. government defense contractor. Lockheed Martin has stated that this attack was thwarted.[39]

This same announcement mentioned that customers with "concentrated user bases" (whatever that means) could get new SecurID tokens from RSA. So it looks like whatever the attackers stole, the consequences were potentially systemic.

Yet again, the attacks against RSA were initiated via spear-phishing. The corresponding e-mails contained a Microsoft excel file as an attachment. The attached file employed a zero-day exploit targeting Adobe's Flash player.[40] The malicious payload activated by the exploit installed a RAT, allowing the attackers to accumulate credentials and move laterally across the organization until they found what they were after. From there, they would move pilfered data to a staging machine before exfiltrating it to remote servers.

The use of the acronym *APT* (Advanced Persistent Threat) to describe attackers in RSA's initial disclosure would seem to indicate a certain degree of sophistication. Yet, aside from the Adobe zero-day exploit, the intruders used fairly conventional tools. The only thing that truly stands out regarding the attack is that it was probably executed as a stepping stone to get into Lockheed's network. It goes without saying that a company like RSA would prefer not to admit that they were done in by commonplace attackers.

Attribution is sketchy at best. Researchers at Dell traced network traffic back to China.[41] But, as we've explained earlier, this doesn't necessarily mean anything other than the attackers may have routed their attacks through China. Subsequent revelations seem to confirm this. During a conference in the fall of 2011, RSA's executive chairman stated:

> There were two individual groups from one nation state, one supporting the other. One was very visible and one less so... We've not attributed it to a particular nation state although we're very confident that with the skill, sophistication and resources involved it could only have been a nation state.[42]

Operation Shady RAT

In early 2009 an unnamed U.S. defense contractor got in touch with McAfee when it detected potentially malicious activity on its corporate LAN. Investigators unearthed a RAT infestation and traced it back to a spear-phishing campaign directed at key individuals in the organization.

As the investigation progressed, in March of 2011, researchers from McAfee were able to penetrate a poorly secured web-based command and control server used by the intruders in a western country and recover logs which allowed them to identify a tentative list of victims. What they discovered was a large-scale effort that targeted 71 organizations spread out over 14 countries over a span of more than five years.[43] Dmitri Alperovitch, VP in the Threat Research division at McAfee christened this effort as *Operation Shady RAT*.

The attacks recorded by the captured logs began in 2006 and continued onward until 2011. Dmitri suspects that near the end the intruders may have switched to other command and control servers and that this accounts for the eventual decline in attacks. It's interesting to note that around 70 percent of the targets were in the United States and 13 of the 71 attacks involved corporations in the defense industry. Though there was a broad range of targets, including a number of national governments, heavy industry, hi-tech, the press (including the Associated Press), and a couple of think tanks. Individual attacks lasted anywhere from a month to over a year.

Investigators are not certain what type of information the attackers were after. As far as attribution is concerned, McAfee's Hon Lau states:

> Due to the variety of organizations and individuals impacted, there is no clear motive. There has been some discussion of this being a government-sponsored attack. However, the finger can't be pointed at any particular government. Not only are the victims located in various places around the globe, so too are the servers involved in these attacks.[44]

Dmitri Alperovitch also declined to comment on who was behind the attacks.[45]

The Nitro Attacks

In late October of 2011, a reported issued by Symantec[46] described a series of attacks that began in April of 2011 and continued until mid-September. These attacks targeted forty-eight different companies situated in twenty countries. Over half of the targets were private sector interests in the chemical and advanced material industry.

The intruders appeared to be looking for intellectual property, though they often tried to acquire Windows domain administrator credentials to facilitate their search. No details are available as to the specific nature of the data targeted. As usual, they used a malicious e-mail as their primary attack vector. Compromised hosts were sometimes set up as staging servers to receive stolen data before being shipped off to external systems.

With regard to attribution, Symantec claims:

> The attacks were traced back to a computer system that was a virtual private server (VPS) located in the United States. However, the system was owned by a 20-something male located in the Hebei region in China. We internally have given him the pseudonym of Covert Grove based on a literal translation of his name.

Symantec also stipulates:

> We are unable to determine if Covert Grove is the sole attacker or if he has a direct or only indirect role. Nor are we able to

definitively determine if he is hacking these targets on behalf of another party or multiple parties.

Targeting Certificate Authorities

It's often hard to know whom to trust on the Internet. For example, how can you be certain that the web site you're visiting is the real McCoy and not some cheap knock-off trying to steal your credit card number? This fundamental question has driven untold mountains of security R&D. Most web sites currently solve this identity predicament using what's known a *digital certificate*.

Here's some background: a digital certificate is like a formal letter of introduction used back in the 18th century. It tells people who you are, details your credentials, and is signed by a known trusted individual. In situations where people who trusted each other were separated by large distances, letters of introduction were an accepted way to extend trust to a third party.

In the case of digital certificates the known trusted signatory is a *Certificate Authority* (CA), typically a multinational company like VeriSign or Comodo which has gone through the process of independently confirming the identity of a web site so that normal Internet users don't have to.

Having vetted the identity of a web site, a process that can sometimes take days depending on the level of certainty required, a CA will subsequently issue the web site a cryptographically signed digital certificate. The certificate is instantiated as a special sort of computer file which follows a standardized format. Just as in the days of yore when the Duke of Windsor would bestow a letter of introduction to a departing emissary and stamp the letter with his seal, a CA puts its mark on a digital certificate to let the world know that the file is one of theirs.

Web sites use a protocol suite called *Secure Sockets Layer* (SSL) to formally present their digital certificate to web site visitors upon arrival. Likewise, most web browsers have the built-in ability to validate the certificates that they receive. If a web browser comes across a digital certificate that it doesn't recognize it will loudly complain by presenting the user with a highly visible message box.

The cryptographic algorithms used by digital certificates may not be perfect, but they're usually strong enough that attackers often decide that it's easier to undermine the institutions that issue certificates, the CAs, rather than forge certificates head on. In other words, counterfeiting a digital certificate from scratch is difficult enough that it's far easier to simply break into the network of a CA and get their servers to issue a bogus certificate.

There have been people who have publicly voiced concern about this. For example, Julian Assange, the founder of WikiLeaks, claims that intelligence agencies have infiltrated and compromised certificate authorities.[47] In light of Ed Snowden's revelations, Julian's assertion has significant merit.

There are over 600 organizations which act as CAs.[48] Peter Eckersley, the Technology Projects Director for the Electronic Frontier Foundation, has noticed a disturbing trend: up until June of 2011, only fifty-five certificates were revoked because the corresponding CA had been compromised. Since June 2011 approximately 200 certificates, issued by four different CAs, have been revoked for the same reason.[49]

In this section we'll examine two well-known cases in which an intruder found a way inside the perimeter of a CA and used their access to generate rogue digital certificates. Then we'll see how attacking a CA is actually a specific instance of a more general trend: carefully orchestrated *multistage attacks*.

Comodogate

On March 23, 2011, certificate authority Comodo announced[50] that an affiliate in Southern Europe had been compromised and that, as a result, nine fraudulent digital certificates had been issued for the following seven web sites:

- mail.google.com
- login.live.com
- www.google.com
- login.yahoo.com
- login.skype.com
- addons.mozilla.org
- "Global Trustee"

A fraudulent digital certificate is like a fake driver's license, it allows the owner to impersonate the entity associated with the certificate. This, in turn, could be used to redirect users to fake web sites (e.g. a spoofed instance of Gmail) so that the imposter can harvest user credentials. This is particularly attractive to nation-states that wish to monitor people who belong to dissident groups.

According to Comodo, the intruder somehow acquired the credentials (i.e. the user name and password) to a user account owned by the affiliate organization which had the ability to issue digital certificates, and then used these credentials to create a whole series of counterfeit digital certificates. Investigators were able to trace back the origin of the attack:

> The IP address of the initial attack was recorded and has been determined to be assigned to an ISP in Iran. A web survey revealed one of the certificates deployed on another IP address assigned to an Iranian ISP. The server in question stopped responding to requests shortly after the certificate was revoked.

Though they're astute enough to admit that this might not mean very much:

> While the involvement of two IP addresses assigned to Iranian ISPs is suggestive of an origin, this may be the result of an attacker attempting to lay a false trail.

Three days after Comodo came clean about the attack someone using the handle *ComodoHacker* claimed responsibility and posted information related to the incident on pastebin[51]:

> I hacked Comodo from InstantSSL.it, their CEO's e-mail address mfpenco@mfpenco.com
>   Their Comodo username/password was: user: gtadmin password: globaltrust
>   Their DB name was: globaltrust and instantsslcms

The ComodoHacker claimed to be a 21-year-old Iranian, working alone, who happened upon a server at InstantSSL.it in his quest to break the RSA algorithm. In other words, this wasn't the work of a formally tasked APT. However, there's no way to tell if any of this is true.

Comodo stated that the attack was detected within hours of its occurrence. To counter the breach they simply revoked the fraudulent certs and suspended the compromised RA account. The attacker was actually still logged on when they suspended the account.

All told, Comodo survived the ordeal. But was this a function of the incident itself or the size of Comodo's customer base? Peter Gutmann, a security researcher at the University of Auckland, claims that:

> Once you've issued enough (certificates), the browser vendors won't pull your CA cert anymore because it would affect too many people. This is what saved Comodo.[52]

Operation Black Tulip

A few months later, another CA came forward with news of an attack. On August 30, 2011, a CA called DigiNotar (a Dutch subsidiary of VASCO Data Security) posted the following at its website:

> On July 19th 2011, DigiNotar detected an intrusion into its Certificate Authority (CA) infrastructure, which resulted in the fraudulent issuance of public key certificate requests for a number of domains, including Google.com.[53]

A few days later, on September 2, DigiNotar announced that the government was getting involved, not an encouraging sign:

> VASCO Data Security International, Inc. (Nasdaq: VDSI; www.vasco.com) today announced that it has invited the Dutch government to jointly solve the DigiNotar incident. As part of its proposal, VASCO invites the Dutch Government to send staff to work together to jointly assess and remedy the problem.[54]

Security consultants from a Dutch company named Fox-IT were brought in. On September 5th they published a report on the incident, which they referred to as "Operation Black Tulip."

Tulips have a special place in Dutch history as they were at the center of the world's first recorded financial bubble known as "tulip mania."

Anyway, the report states that 531 fraudulent certificates were issued as a result of the attack. The severity of this breach will become obvious once the following list of domain names is perused:

www.update.microsoft.com
www.facebook.com
*.skype.com
*.torproject.org
www.sis.gov.uk
www.mossad.gov.il
www.cia.gov

These are just a few of the domains for which fraudulent SSL certificates were issued.[55]

Security at DigiNotar was another issue raised by the Fox-IT report. Investigators discovered that the administrator password used to manage the certificate servers was simple enough to brute force. They also noticed machines that were missing anti-virus software and public-facing servers that hadn't been patched.

Investigators traced a significant amount of related network activity back to Iran. Most certificate authorities maintain what's called *Online Certificate Status Protocol* (OCSP) servers. These machines can be queried by web browsers to determine if a certificate has been revoked or not. During the attack on DigiNotar, investigators found that 99% of the lookups against DigiNotar's OCSP servers were from computers in Iran.

Right on cue, the ComodoHacker popped up again[56] to take credit:

> Hi again! I strike back again, huh
> You know, I have access to 4 more so HIGH profile CAs, which I can issue certs from them too which I will, I won't name them, I also had access to StartCom CA, I hacked their server too with so sophisticated methods, he was lucky by being sitted in front of HSM for signing, I will name just one more which I still have access: GlobalSign, let me use these accesses and CAs, later I'll talk about them too.

By the way, ask DigiNotar about this username/password combination:

Username: PRODUCTION\Administrator (domain administrator of certificate network)

Password: Pr0d@dm1n

As before, the Comodohacker laced his post with political messages. Again, there's no way to tell if the alleged impetus for the attack is genuine or not.

GlobalSign was, understandably, not very pleased:

> GlobalSign takes this claim very seriously and is currently investigating. As a responsible CA (certificate authority), we have decided to temporarily cease issuance of all Certificates until the investigation is complete. We will post updates as frequently as possible ... [57]

The browser vendors also pulled their DigiNotar certs, a sign of things to come. Within weeks after the original press release, DigiNotar made one final public announcement:

> VASCO Data Security International, Inc. (Nasdaq: VDSI) (www.vasco.com) today announced that a subsidiary, DigiNotar B.V., a company organized and existing in The Netherlands ("DigiNotar") filed a voluntary bankruptcy petition under Article 4 of the Dutch Bankruptcy Act in the Haarlem District Court, The Netherlands (the "Court") on Monday, September 19, 2011 and was declared bankrupt by the Court today.

Multistage Attacks Emerge

Attackers usually aim for the weakest link when they operate. If a target is sufficiently hard, interlopers may find it easier simply to redirect their attention to an outside dependency, like a third-party vendor that provides outsourced security services. For instance, if a bank's security is too much of a challenge, bank robbers may simply opt to undermine the company that responds to the bank's alarm.

As we saw in the case of RSA and SecurID, this sort of multistage attack takes long-term planning and coordination, but the stakes have gotten high enough that in some cases the more sophisticated organizations are willing to make the up-front investment.

This is exactly the strategy used by attackers who broke into the corporate network of Bit9, a high-end security software vendor. Bit9 sells *white listing* software, which is the hi-tech equivalent of a nightclub bouncer. A white listing application stands guard as a computer runs, allowing only "trusted" software to launch. Usually this means that the software's files have been digitally signed by some known CA (Adobe, Microsoft, Oracle, Bit9, etc.). The software presents its digital signature to the White Listing application and, if all is well, the White Listing application lets the software load into memory and execute.

There are two basic ways to keep malware from gaining a foothold. Conventional anti-virus software works by identifying, and disabling, *known bad* software. White-listing is the inverse of this process; it identifies *known good* (trusted) software and prevents anything that's not trusted from running. Only officially approved software is allowed into the nightclub by the bouncer. You've got to be on the guest list, so to speak.

As it turns out, someone at Bit9 neglected to install the company's white listing product on a set of machines inside of Bit9's internal corporate network.[58] These machines were compromised in July of 2012 and the attackers then used them as a base of operations to steal a digital certificate which was used by Bit9 to digitally sign software. Because Bit9's white listing software trusts Bit9's digital certificate by default, the attackers could digitally sign their malware with this digital certificate and use it to attack customers who were using Bit9's product. Bit9 did not provide details about the customers who were targeted, other than they were "three non-critical infrastructure entities."[59] The company has also stated in its corporate blog that it's found 32 different files that were signed by the stolen digital certificate.[60]

Operation Red October

In January of 2013, Russian security software vendor Kaspersky announced that it in October of 2012 it had uncovered an intelligence operation that spanned the continents, targeting diplomatic and government data in Western Europe, Africa, Eastern Europe, several former Soviet republics, Asia, North America, and South America. Investigators believe that the campaign began in 2007 and lasted up until Kaspersky published its findings.

The attackers used spear-phishing to compromise targeted systems, relying heavily on booby-trapped Microsoft Word documents, Excel documents, and PDFs. Once a machine was infected, intruders installed a modular offensive framework that Kaspersky researchers referred to as *Sputnik*.[61]

The Sputnik framework supported over a thousand custom modules. It included modules intended to interface with desktop systems, servers, mobile devices, USB drives, and even network equipment. In other words, this was not the work of rank amateurs. To give you an idea of how meticulous and systematic the attackers were, the people that attackers pursued were literally assigned their own specific ID values, and in some cases the attackers went to the trouble to design and build custom modules, dedicated specifically to collecting information from a certain person.

Researchers at Kaspersky were not able to determine the identity of the attackers. But they were able to make a couple of salient observations:

> As a notable fact, the attackers used exploit code that was made public and originally came from a previously known targeted attack campaign with Chinese origins. The only thing that was changed is the executable which was embedded in the document; the attackers replaced it with their own code...
>
> Basing on registration data of C&C servers and numerous artifacts left in executables of the malware, we strongly believe that the attackers have Russian-speaking origins. Current attackers and executables developed by them have been unknown until recently, they have never related to any other targeted cyberattacks.[62]

Patterns Emerge

Looking back at the previous string of incidents there are features that repeatedly materialize. Specifically, unlike the domain of cybercrime, overall statistics on dollar losses resulting from incidents of espionage aren't available. This is a logical consequence of the fact that investigators frequently aren't even sure what intruders made off with.

This hasn't stopped people from making extravagant proclamations. As noterd, with regard to U.S. losses due to intellectual property theft, CYBERCOM chief Keith Alexander melodramatically stated:

> In my opinion, it's the greatest transfer of wealth in history ... [63]

And it's not just losses due to espionage that are unknown either. When you're up against disciplined attackers, *knowing* the geographic origin of an incident doesn't necessarily amount to much. As Robert McClelland, Australia's Attorney-General, commented on a spate of attacks against resource firms:

> We don't comment on the source of those (attacks). It is often literally hard to identify. They are often re-routed through other countries and other providers.[64]

This hasn't stopped some investigators from attempting to triangulate the true source of an attack. In February of 2013, computer security vendor Mandiant published a detailed report describing an extensive intelligence campaign targeting various American news outlets. Mandiant claims that the campaign, dubbed *APT1*, was directly linked to PLA's Unit 61398. After tracking the APT1 intrusion set over a period of seven years, the report qualifies its findings:

> We believe the totality of the evidence we provide in this document bolsters the claim that APT1 is Unit 61398. However, we admit there is one other unlikely possibility:
> A secret, resourced organization full of mainland Chinese speakers with direct access to Shanghai-based telecommunications infrastructure is engaged in a multi-year, enterprise scale computer espionage campaign right outside of Unit 61398's gates, performing tasks similar to Unit 61398's known mission.[65]

Would it be possible for an organization other than the Chinese government to pull off this kind of attack? Could another foreign government even hope to pull off an intricate multi-year scheme involving thousands of people in near total secrecy?

It's been known to happen. The U.S. government's Manhattan Project, which led to the development of the first nuclear weapon, fits this description perfectly. The Manhattan Project was an enormous undertaking involving over 100,000 people under extremely tight security. Security was so high, and so effective, that *not even Vice President Truman knew about it.* That is, until he assumed the helm as President.[66]

As far as geography and network access are concerned, they're also red herrings. It's been revealed that American spies use an elaborate web of foreign covers to launch cyber-attacks[67] and have developed a real talent for subverting telecom backbones in other countries.[68] What better place to operate out of than the locale of a known intelligence service?

If the United States can accomplish feats like this so can other world powers. Hence, the campaign analyzed by Mandiant could have been the work of some intelligence outfit other than China's.

Having said that, the Chinese government provided a public response to the report:

> It is neither professional nor responsible to make groundless speculations and accusations on hacker attacks for various purposes, which does not help solve the problem.[69]

Shortly after this formal statement was relayed, China's Foreign Minister Yang Jiechi added his two cents:

> Anyone who tries to fabricate or piece together a sensational story to serve a political motive will not be able to blacken the name of others nor whitewash themselves ...[70]

As we discussed at length in the chapter on China, there are a plurality of actors (many of them foreign) operating freely in the country's rather lawless networks. We will spend much the next chapter extending this idea, in addition to addressing the problem of attribution at length later on in the book.

While most of the ink in the press is spilled over who *might be* culpable for particular incidents there are very few where investigators were able to conclusively assign responsibility. While news reports and the blogosphere are rife with juicy innuendo, at the end of the day investigators usually fail to supply *proof beyond a reasonable doubt*. If this level of certainty is good enough for a court of law, shouldn't it be good enough in the court of public opinion?

Granted, there are those rare occasions when it's fairly clear who spied on who and what was stolen. For example, in May of 2013 the Associated Press published a report describing how the U.S. Department of Justice, over a period of two months, secretly collected the telephone records of editors and reporters working for the Associated Press.[71] Though the Department of Justice offered no formal explanation for its surveillance, it's likely that the covert operation may be related to classified information that was leaked in an Associated Press story about a foiled terror plot in Yemen.[72] The CEO of the Associated Press, Gary Pruitt, said the following in a letter sent to Attorney General Eric Holder:

> There can be no possible justification for such an overbroad collection of the telephone communications of The Associated Press and its reporters. These records potentially reveal communications with confidential sources across all of the newsgathering activities undertaken by the AP during a two-month period, provide a road map to AP's newsgathering operations, and disclose information about AP's activities and operations that the government has no conceivable right to know ...

Despite the usual myriad of unknowns, investigators can agree on one fact: with regard to breaching a network, e-mail appears to be the attack vector of choice. The NSA admits as much:

> Malicious email or web-based attacks, called "spear phishing" when tailored for particular targets, remain the most likely front door to DoD networks for globally remote attackers.[73]

Stepping back for a moment, it doesn't help that many details are shrouded under a veil of secrecy. This leads to a question. Is this secrecy implemented to protect national security, as we're told, or are organizations merely using secrecy to *conceal inadequate operational security*?

Several public-sector examples demonstrate that even in the major leagues security can be sloppy. The Comodogate and DigiNotar breaches are case studies in the danger of poorly chosen administrator passwords. There's really no excuse for this sort of incompetence, especially when it comes to a certificate authority. Let's not forget Google, where people are so busy being brilliant that they left the company's source code relatively unprotected.

Even purportedly secured government networks apparently suffer from insufficient day-to-day security. U.S. Army soldier Chelsea Manning was able to successfully smuggle out thousands of diplomatic cables from SIPRNet by burning them to a faux Lady Gaga CD. As Manning observed in an on-line chat session:

> Weak servers, weak logging, weak physical security, weak counter-intelligence, inattentive signal analysis … a perfect storm.[74]

Endnotes

1)Elinor Abreu, "Cyberattack Reveals Cracks in U.S. Defense," *The Industry Standard*, May 9, 2001, http://edition.cnn.com/2001/TECH/internet/05/10/3.year.cyberattack.idg/index.html.

2) Bob Drogin, "Russians Seem to be hacking Into Pentagon," *Los Angeles Times*, October 7, 1999, http://www.sfgate.com/cgi-bin/article.cgi?f=/c/a/1999/10/07/MN58558.DTL&type=printable.

3) Testimony of James Adams, CEO of iDEFENSE, Committee on Governmental Affairs, United States Senate, March 2, 2000, http://www.fas.org/irp/congress/2000_hr/030200_adams.htm.

4) Ibid.

5) Nathan Thornburgh, "The Invasion of the Chinese Cyberspies," *Time*, Aug. 29, 2005, http://www.time.com/time/magazine/article/0,9171,1098961,00.html.

6) Nathan Thornburgh, "The Invasion of the Chinese Cyberspies," *Time*, Aug. 29, 2005, http://www.time.com/time/magazine/article/0,9171,1098961,00.html.

7) "Hacker Attacks In US Linked to Chinese Military: Researchers," *Agence France-Presse*, December 12, 2005, http://www.spacewar.com/news/cyberwar-05zzq.html.

8) George Smith, "Cult Of Cyberwar – Narrow Sourcing And The King Of Quote," *Dick Destiny Blog*, January 19, 2010, http://www.dickdestiny.com/blog/2010/01/cult-of-cyberwar-narrow-sourcing-and.html.

9) Dawn Onley and Patience Wait, "Red Storm Rising," *Government Computing News*, August 21, 2007, http://gcn.com/articles/2006/08/17/red-storm-rising. aspx.

10) Bradley Graham, "Hackers Attack Via Chinese Web Sites," *Washington Post*, August 25, 2005, http://www.washingtonpost.com/wp-dyn/content/article/2005/08/24/AR2005082402318.html.

11) Cablegate Full-Text Search for "Byzantine Hades," WikiLeaks, http://www.cablegatesearch.net/search.php?q=byzantine+hades&qo=0&qc=0&qto=2010-02-28.

12) http://www.infowar-monitor.net.

13) Shishir Nagaraja, Ross Anderson, "The snooping dragon: social-malware surveillance of the Tibetan movement," University of Cambridge Computer Laboratory, Number 746, March 2009, http://www.cl.cam.ac.uk/techreports/UCAM-CL-TR-746.pdf.

14) Evgeny Morozov, "Cyber-Scare: The exaggerated fears over digital warfare," *Boston Review*, July/August 2009, http://bostonreview.net/BR34.4/morozov.php.

15) Siobhan Gorman, August Cole And Yochi Dreazen, "Computer Spies Breach Fighter-Jet Project," *Wall Street Journal*, April 21, 2009, http://online.wsj.com/article/SB124027491029837401.html.

16) Simon Cullen, "Jet maker denies F-35 security breach," *ABC News*, April 22, 2009, http://www.abc.net.au/news/2009-04-22/jet-maker-denies-f-35-security-breach/1658970.

17) *A New Approach to China*, Google Blog, January 12, 2010, http://googleblog.blogspot.com/2010/01/new-approach-to-china.html.

18) Pooja Prasad, *Adobe Investigates Corporate Network Security Issue*, Adobe Featured Blogs, January 12, 2010, http://blogs.adobe.com/conversations/2010/01/adobe_investigates_corporate_n.html.

19) Robert McMillan, "HBGary Releases Aurora Detection Tool," *PC World*, February 10, 2010, http://www.networkworld.com/news/2010/021010-hbgary-releases-aurora-detection.html.

20) *Protecting Your Critical Assets: Lessons Learned from "Operation Aurora,"* McAfee, 2010, http://www.mcafee.com/us/resources/white-papers/wp-protecting-critical-assets.pdf.

21) Kim Zetter, "Google Hack Attack Was Ultra Sophisticated, New Details Show," *Wired*, January 14, 2010, http://www.wired.com/threatlevel/2010/01/operation-aurora/.

22) Kim Zetter, "Google Hackers Targeted Source Code of More Than 30 Companies," *Wired*, January 13, 2010, http://www.wired.com/threatlevel/2010/01/google-hack-attack/.

23) Ariana Eunjung Cha and Ellen Nakashima, "Google China cyberattack part of vast espionage campaign, experts say," *Washington Post*, January 14, 2010, http://www.washingtonpost.com/wp-dyn/content/article/2010/01/13/AR2010011300359.html?hpid=topnews.

24) Kim Zetter, "'Google' Hackers Had Ability to Alter Source Code," *Wired*, March 3, 2010, http://www.wired.com/threatlevel/2010/03/source-code-hacks/.

25) George Kurtz, *Operation "Aurora" Hit Google, Others*, McAfee Blog Central, January 14, 2010, http://blogs.mcafee.com/corporate/cto/operation-%E2%80%-9Caurora%E2%80%9D-hit-google-others.

26) Joe Stewart, *Operation Aurora: Clues in the Code*, Dell SecureWorks, January 19, 2010, http://www.secureworks.com/research/blog/research/20913/.

27) John Markoff And David Barboza, "2 China Schools Said to Be Tied to Online Attacks ," *New York Times*, February 19, 2010, http://www.nytimes.com/2010/02/19/technology/19china.html.

28) "U.S. pinpoints code writer behind Google attack: report," *Reuters*, February 22, 2010, http://www.reuters.com/article/2010/02/22/us-china-internet-idUS-TRE61L0OG20100222.

29) *A New Approach to China*, Google Blog, January 12, 2010, http://googleblog.blogspot.com/2010/01/new-approach-to-china.html.

30) Scott Shane And Andrew W. Lehren, "Leaked Cables Offer Raw Look at U.S. Diplomacy," *New York Times*, November 28, 2010, http://www.nytimes.com/2010/11/29/world/29cables.html?pagewanted=all.

31) Amir Efrati and Siobhan Gorman, "Google Mail Hacked Blames on China," *Wall Street Journal*, June 2, 2011, http://online.wsj.com/article/SB100014240527 02303657404576359770243517568.html.

32) Michael Joseph Gross, "Enter the Cyber-dragon," *Vanity Fair*, September 2011, http://www.vanityfair.com/culture/features/2011/09/chinese-hacking-201109.

33) http://www.shadowserver.org/wiki/pmwiki.php/Shadowserver/Mission.

34) *Shadows In The Cloud: Investigating Cyber Espionage 2.0*, JR03-2010, Information Warfare Monitor, Shadowserver Foundation, April 6, 2010, http://www.infowar-monitor.net/2010/04/shadows-in-the-cloud-an-investigation-into-cyber-espionage-2-0/.

35) *Global Energy Cyberattacks: "Night Dragon,"* McAfee, February 20, 2011, http://www.mcafee.com/us/resources/white-papers/wp-global-energy-cyber-attacks-night-dragon.pdf.

36) Goerge Kurtz, *Global Energy Industry Hit In Night Dragon Attacks*, McAfee, February 9, 2011, http://blogs.mcafee.com/corporate/cto/global-energy-industry-hit-in-night-dragon-attacks.

37) Arthur W. Coviello, Jr., *Open Letter to RSA Customers*, RSA, http://www.rsa.com/node.aspx?id=3872.

38) Christopher Drew And John Markoff, "Data Breach at Security Firm Linked to Attack on Lockheed," *New York Times*, May 27, 2011, http://www.nytimes.com/2011/05/28/business/28hack.html.

39) Arthur W. Coviello, Jr., *Open Letter to RSA SecureiD Customers*, RSA, http://www.rsa.com/node.aspx?id=3891.

40) Riva Richmond, "The RSA Hack: How They Did It," *New York Times*, April 2, 2011, http://bits.blogs.nytimes.com/2011/04/02/the-rsa-hack-how-they-did-it/.

41) Ellen Messmer, "RSA SecurID hack originated in China, says researcher," *Network World*, August 4, 2011, http://news.techworld.com/security/3295222/rsa-securid-hack-originated-in-china-says-researcher/.

42) Graham Cluley, "Security firm RSA blames nation state for attack on its servers," *Sophos Naked Security*, October 11, 2011, http://nakedsecurity.sophos.com/2011/10/11/rsa-blames-nation-state-attack/.

43) Dmitri Alperovitch, *Revealed: Operation Shady RAT*, McAfee, August 2011, http://www.mcafee.com/us/resources/white-papers/wp-operation-shady-rat.pdf.

44) Hon Lau, *The Truth Behind the Shady RAT*, Symantec, August 4, 2011, http://www.symantec.com/connect/blogs/truth-behind-shady-rat.

45) Michael Joseph Gross, "Operation Shady rat: Unprecedented Cyber-espionage Campaign and Intellectual-Property Bonanza," *Vanity Fair*, August 2, 2011, http://www.vanityfair.com/culture/features/2011/09/operation-shady-rat-201109.

46) Eric Chien and Gavin O'Gorman, *The Nitro Attacks: Stealing Secrets from the Chemical Industry*, Symantec, http://www.symantec.com/content/en/us/enterprise/media/security_response/whitepapers/the_nitro_attacks.pdf.

47) Jeremy Kirk, "WikiLeaks working on new whistle-blowing platform," *IDG News*, December 1, 2011, http://www.computerworld.com/s/article/9222308/WikiLeaks_working_on_new_whistle_blowing_platform.

48) The EFF SSL Observatory, Electronic Frontier Foundation, https://www.eff.org/observatory.

49) Peter Eckersley, *How secure is HTTPS today? How often is it attacked?* Electronic Frontier Foundation, October 25, 2011, https://www.eff.org/deeplinks/2011/10/how-secure-https-today.

50) Phillip Hallam-Baker, *The Recent RA Compromise*, Comodo, March 23, 2011, http://blogs.comodo.com/it-security/data-security/the-recent-ra-compromise/.

51) COMODOHACKER, *A message from Comodo Hacker*, PasteBin, March 26, 2011, http://pastebin.com/74KXCaEZ.

52) Robert Lemos, "Are Some Certificate Authorities Too Big To Fail?" *Threat Post*, September 7, 2011, http://threatpost.com/en_us/blogs/are-some-certificate-authorities-too-big-fail-090711.

53) *DigiNotar reports security incident*, VASCO, August 30, 2011, http://www.vasco.com/company/press_room/news_archive/2011/news_diginotar_reports_security_incident.aspx.

54) *VASCO offers Dutch Government Joint Approach of Diginotar Incident*, VASCO, September 2, 2011, http://www.vasco.com/company/press_room/news_archive/2011/news_vasco_offers_dutch_government_joint_approach_of_diginotar_incident.aspx.

55) List of Rogue Certificates, Tor Project, https://blog.torproject.org/files/rogue-certs-2011-09-04.csv.

56) COMODOHACKER, Striking Back... , PasteBin, September 5, 2011, http://pastebin.com/1AxH30em.

57) Elinor Mills, "Second firm stops issuing digital certificates," *CNET*, September 7, 2011, http://news.cnet.com/8301-27080_3-20102818-245/second-firm-stops-issuing-digital-certificates/.

58) Jim Finkle, "Hackers breached security firm Bit9, then attacked its customers," *Reuters*, February 8, 2013, http://www.reuters.com/article/2013/02/08/us-cybersecurity-attacks-idUSBRE91710H20130208.

59) Brian Krebs, "Malware Found Matches Code Used Vs. Defense Contractors in 2012," *Krebs On Security*, February 20, 2013, http://krebsonsecurity.com/2013/02/bit9-breach-began-in-july-2012/.

60) Harry Sverdlove, "Bit9 Security Incident Update," *Bit9 Blog*, February 25, 2013, https://blog.bit9.com/2013/02/25/bit9-security-incident-update/.

61) Mathew J. Schwartz, "Operation Red October Attackers Wielded Spear Phishing," *InformationWeek*, January 18, 2013, http://www.informationweek.com/security/attacks/operation-red-october-attackers-wielded/240146621.

62) Kaspersky Lab's Global Research & Analysis Team (GReAT), "'Red October' Diplomatic Cyber Attacks Investigation," *SecureList*, January 14, 2013, http://www.securelist.com/en/analysis/204792262/Red_October_Diplomatic_Cyber_Attacks_Investigation.

63) Tabassum Zakaria and David Alexander, "U.S. spy agencies say won't read Americans' email for cybersecurity," *Reuters*, July 9, 2012, http://mobile.reuters.com/article/idUSBRE86901620120710?irpc=932.

64) Rob Taylor, "Australia warns on cyber attacks on resource firms," *Reuters*, May 30, 2011, http://www.reuters.com/article/2011/05/30/us-australia-cyber-idUSTRE74T0KH20110530.

65) *APT1: Exposing One of China's Cyber Espionage Units*, Mandiant, http://www.mandiant.com/apt1.

66) *The Manhattan Project*, American History: From Pre-Columbian to the New Millennium, http://www.ushistory.org/us/51f.asp.

67) Matthew Aid, "The NSA's New Code Breakers," *Foreign Policy*, October 15, 2013, http://www.foreignpolicy.com/articles/2013/10/15/the_nsa_s_new_codebreakers?print=yes&hidecomments=yes&page=full.

68) Lana Lam, "Edward Snowden: US government has been hacking Hong Kong and China for years," *South China Morning Post*, June 13, 2013, http://www.scmp.com/news/hong-kong/article/1259508/edward-snowden-us-government-has-been-hacking-hong-kong-and-china.

69) Foreign Ministry Spokesperson Hong Lei's Regular Press Conference on February 20, 2013, http://www.fmprc.gov.cn/eng/xwfw/s2510/2511/t1015425.shtml.

70) David Barboza, "In Wake of Cyberattacks, China Seeks New Rules," *New York Times*, March 10, 2013, http://www.nytimes.com/2013/03/11/world/asia/china-calls-for-global-hacking-rules.html.

71) Mark Sherman, "Govt obtains wide AP phone records in probe," *Associated Press*, May 13, 2013, http://cryptome.org/2013/05/ap-13-0507.htm.

72) Adam Goldman and Matt Apuzzo, "US: CIA thwarts new al-Qaida underwear bomb plot," *Associated Press*, May 7, 2012, http://cryptome.org/2013/05/ap-13-0507.htm.

73) *New Smartphones and the Risk Picture*, The Information Assurance Mission at NSA, April 2012, http://cryptome.org/2012/05/nsa-mobile-risks.pdf.

74) Kevin Poulsen and Kim Zetter, "'I Can't Believe What I'm Confessing to You': The Wikileaks Chats," *Wired*, June 10, 2010, http://www.wired.com/threatlevel/2010/06/wikileaks-chat/.

Chapter 6

The Scope of U.S. Espionage

The United States government has been very vocally running around for years accusing China of engaging in espionage and surveillance for economic advantage and industrial advantage. And these revelations prove that the United States is doing exactly the same thing.

– Glenn Greenwald[1]

There's been spying for years, there's been surveillance for years, and so forth, I'm not going to pass judgment on that, it's the nature of our society ...

– Eric Schmidt, CEO of Google[2]

While the press seems to focus on the intelligence gathering of other countries (e.g. China, Russia, Eastern Europe), the truth is that the United States stands out with regard to stealing other people's secrets. Just ask the career officers over in the NSA's *Signals-Intelligence Directorate* or the agents in the CIA's *Special Activities Division*. Michael Hayden, former director of the NSA and CIA[3] admitted:

Now look, I'm going to be very candid, alright? We steal secrets. We steal other nations' secrets. One cannot do that above board and be very successful for a very long period of time.

As noted earlier, the NSA's Office of Tailored Access Operations has compromised more than 80,000 systems over the years.[4] Let's look at some specific examples.

In early June of 2013, the *South China Morning* Post revealed that the NSA had been compromising backbone networks in Hong Kong since 2009 to eavesdrop on communications en masse. One of the targets was Chinese University, which hosts a backbone network known as the Hong Kong Internet Exchange.[5]

A few weeks later, *Der Spiegel* reported that the United States had executed cyber-attacks against offices of the European Union in Washington and New York.[6] In later articles *Der Spiegel* would divulge that U.S. intelligence agencies had also targeted offices at the International Atomic Energy Agency (IAEA) in addition to the United Nations video conferencing system.[7]

French newspaper *Le Monde* disclosed that in a single month, from December 10, 2012 to January 8, 2013, the NSA collected over 70 million metadata records on telephone calls in France.[8] The journalists who reported this story observed that targets included people involved in business, the state bureaucracy, and politicians. In one internal NSA memo described by *Le Monde*, then American ambassador to the United Nations, Susan Rice, was quoted as saying that the NSA's surveillance of French diplomats allowed the United States to gain the upper hand during negotiations.[9]

An Italian news outlet, *L'Espresso*, reports that the NSA and the UK's Government Communications Headquarters GCHQ monitored Italian corporations in addition to the Italian government using three fiber optic cables with landings in Italy. This surveillance took place under the auspices of an information sharing-agreement with Italian intelligence services.[10]

Then the press in Spain got wind of a similar development in their country. *El Mundo* published a report which stated that in a single 30-day period that the NSA monitored approximately 60 million phone calls in Spain.[11]

In a deliberate effort to diffuse responsibility, General Keith Alexander stated that all of this monitoring wasn't the sole work of the NSA, that allied intelligence services also played a part:

> This is not information we collected on European citizens.... It represents information that we and our NATO allies have collected in defense of our countries and in support of military operations.[12]

Let's step back from the trees for a moment and look at the entire forest. Based on leaked documents and media reports, the web site *Cryptome* published an analysis which calculates that the NSA collected approximately 124.8 billion telephone metadata records in a single 30-day period. The breakdown for the 30 days leading up to January 8, 2013 follows:

Pakistan: 12.76 Billion
Afghanistan: 21.98 Billion
India: 6.28 Billion
Iraq: 7.8 Billion? (blurry image)
Saudi Arabia: 7.8 Billion? (blurry image)
United States: 3 Billion? (blurry image)
Egypt: 1.9 Billion? (blurry image)
Iran: 1.73 Billion
Jordan: 1.6 Billion
Germany: 361 Million
France: 70.2 Million
Spain: 61 Million
Italy: 46 Million
Netherlands: 1.8 Million[13]

High ranking politicians seem to be attractive targets. A TV news program broadcast in Brazil, *Fantastico*, revealed that both the presidents of Brazil and Mexico had been targets of NSA surveillance.[14] This was corroborated in more detail by a later report in *Der Spiegel*.[15] A leaked internal document boasted:

TAO successfully exploited a key mail server in the Mexican Presidencia domain within the Mexican Presidential network to gain first-ever access to President Felipe Calderon's public email account.

In October of 2013, the Chancellor of Germany, Angela Merkel, called up U.S. President Barack Obama and angrily demanded explanations regarding reports that the NSA had been monitoring her mobile phone. Shortly afterwards the White House's National Security Council spokeswoman, Caitlin Hayden, offered a public statement:

The United States is not monitoring and will not monitor the communications of Chancellor Merkel. Beyond that, I'm not

173

in a position to comment publicly on every specific alleged intelligence activity.[16]

Notice how any reference to past monitoring is absent. A leaked NSA memo from 2006 indicates that several U.S. officials handed over their contact lists to the NSA, allowing the agency to monitor 35 world leaders.[17] Furthermore the memo admits that such monitoring produced "little reportable intelligence."

Once more consider this: these are heads of state being watched, people who ostensibly have countermeasures in place being configured and operated by full-time professional security services. Despite these defenses they were successfully monitored over long periods of time.

The U.S. is very good at collection, and its efforts are pervasive. In August of 2010, former NSA director Michael Hayden made the following self-congratulatory statement on the *PBS News Hour* television show:

> There was a survey done not too many months ago. They asked the citizens of some cyber-savvy nations around the world, who do you fear most in the cyber-domain? And, quite interestingly, we were number one.
>
> The Chinese were a close second, but we were number one, which I think is simply a reflection that we are a technologically agile country, and we have very good intelligence services, and the rest of the world is kind of responding to that reality.

This message was driven home by the current director of the NSA, General Keith Alexander, at a hearing before the House Subcommittee on Intelligence in March of 2013:

> We believe our offense is the best in the world. Cyber offense requires a deep, persistent and pervasive presence on adversary networks in order to precisely deliver effects. We maintain that access, gain deep understanding of the adversary, and develop offensive capabilities through the advanced skills and tradecraft of our analysts, operators and developers. When authorized to deliver offensive cyber effects, our technological and operational superiority delivers unparalleled effects against our adversaries systems.[18]

As an aside, you may wonder who these adversaries are. A leaked intelligence budget document plainly states:

> We are investing in target surveillance and offensive CI [confidential informant] against key targets, such as China, Russia, Iran, Israel, Pakistan, and Cuba.[19]

Who tops this list? In March of 2013 top-secret NSA documents indicate that Iran and Pakistan garnered the most attention from the NSA.[20]

So while Israel is listed as an adversary, the United States government also has a secret deal in place with Israel to pass on raw signal intelligence data to Israel with very few strings attached. The duality of this relationship is spelled out by an NSA official in leaked top-secret documents:

> On the one hand, the Israelis are extraordinarily good Sigint partners for us, but on the other, they target us to learn our positions on Middle East problems... A NIE [National Intelligence Estimate] ranked them as the third most aggressive intelligence service against the U.S.
>
> One of NSA's biggest threats is actually from friendly intelligence services, like Israel. There are parameters on what NSA shares with them, but the exchange is so robust, we sometimes share more than we intended.[21]

Israel is a *frenemy*. And though it's probably expected that intelligence services occasionally share information, this is kind of raw data sharing agreement is different. Alex Adbo, a staff attorney at the ACLU, spells out what's particularly disturbing:

> Information about innocent Americans that hasn't been taken out of the data that's being shared with our intelligence partners. And it's troubling for a couple of reasons, the first of which, we haven't known about this, and this may have been going on for years, and the second of which, there's no avenue for Americans, innocent Americans who are swept up into these dragnets and have their information handed over to our intelligence partners, to stop that flow of information, to assert their rights and prevent it.[22]

Anyway, it goes without saying that Michael Hayden and Keith Alexander are probably correct. The United States is the Internet's *number one offender*. This only makes sense, as the United States feeds a mountain of resources into its intelligence apparatus. In 2010 the U.S. government spent $80.1 billion on intelligence.[23] This is more than the U.K.'s entire 2012 defense budget.[24]

The $80 billion figure from 2010 can be broken down into two parts. Roughly $53 billion was allocated to non-military agencies, and $27 billion was devoted to military operations. In 2011, the non-military portion of intelligence appropriations was increased to $54 billion.[25] In 2013 this figure was roughly consistent at $53 billion.[26]

Of the 16 intelligence agencies under the DNI that make up the U.S. intelligence Community, the CIA currently receives by far the largest share of this budgetary pie ($14.7 billion in 2013, which is almost 50 percent more than the NSA).[27]

Booby-Trapped Chips

Officials declare that this heavy public investment is indispensable because we live in a dangerous world where foreign powers secretly plot our undoing. Former security service directors like Mike McConnell assert:

> Because we are the most developed technologically – we have the most bandwidth running through our society and are more dependent on that bandwidth – we are the most vulnerable. [28]

One thing that officials seem to be particularly worried about is the threat of foreign entities selling us hardware that's been modified with hidden "backdoors" and self-destruct functionality. This fear is not necessarily unfounded. As respected security researcher Joanna Rutkowska observes:

> It's funny how various people, e.g. European government institutions, are afraid of using closed source software, e.g. Windows, because they are afraid of Microsoft putting backdoors there. Yet, they are not concerned about using processors made by some other U.S. companies. It is significantly more risky for Microsoft to put a backdoor into its software, where

even a skilled teenager equipped with IDA Pro can find it, than it is for Intel or AMD, where effectively nobody can find it. [29]

In other words, software-level backdoors may be a threat but at least you can identify them. Hardware-level subversion is much more insidious because it's very difficult to detect, as public research on hardware-level rootkits has verified.[30] Concerns of this nature were voiced in May 2009, by the Obama administration's Cyberspace Policy Review:

> The emergence of new centers for manufacturing, design, and research across the globe raises concerns about the potential for easier subversion of computers and networks through subtle hardware or software manipulations.[31]

A few months later, former Secretary of Homeland Security Michael Chertoff echoed this message:

> Increasingly when you buy computers they have components that originate from places all around the world. We need to look at the question of how we assure that people are not embedding in very small components or things that go into computers that can be triggered remotely and then become the basis of ways to [steal] information ... [32]

On November 17, 2011, the House Intelligence Committee announced it was launching an investigation to examine the threats that Chinese telecom interests posed to national security.[33] According to Representative Dutch Ruppersberger:

> The same way hacking can be a threat, vulnerabilities can derive from compromised hardware on which our telecommunications industry rely. The purpose of this investigation is to determine to what extent Chinese communications companies are exploiting the global supply chain and how we can mitigate this threat to our national and economic security.

Rigged computer chips are obviously something that our intelligence agencies are extremely worried about. Chinese telecom giant Huawei, in particular, has developed a real talent for raising the hackles of bureaucrats in the U.S. and U.K.

In 2008 a merger between 3Com and Huawei was blocked after members of the U.S. intelligence community voiced opposition to the deal on the grounds of national security.[34] Similar protest arose from spies in the U.K. when British Telecom agreed to use equipment from Huawei in a massive £10 billion network overhaul.[35] In March of 2012, despite significant diplomatic outcry, the Australian federal government out-and-out banned Huawei from tendering offers in multibillion-dollar deals to supply equipment for the country's national broadband network.[36]

At the same time something similar happened in the United States. Buried deep in a spending bill (H.R. 933) were two paragraphs (i.e. see Section 516) which stipulate that technology acquired by the Department of Commerce, the Department of Justice, NASA, and the National Science Foundation must be vetted by the government if they're "being produced, manufactured, or assembled by one or more entities that are owned, directed, or subsidized by the People's Republic of China."[37]

Is there any real substance to these claims? Perhaps, but it's all classified. In July of 2013, news leaked of secret government reports contending that PC maker Lenovo, which is headquartered in Beijing, was selling machines that contained hardware-level backdoors. Though this is a fairly recent story, the security services have known about it for a while. For the past ten years or so intelligence services in the U.S., UK, Canada, Australia, and New Zealand have banned computers manufactured by Lenovo.[38]

U.S. Subversion Programs

In light of all the apparent caution and finger pointing at other nations, would it surprise you to know that *the U.S. is neck deep in this kind of subversion ourselves, and has been for some time?*

For example, in a 1995 article published by the *Baltimore Sun*, reporters divulged that the NSA had secretly worked with a Swiss company named Crypto AG during the Cold War to rig the company's encryption hardware so that the NSA could easily decipher coded messages generated by the hardware.[39] Crypto AG, which sold its products to over 120 different countries, had repeatedly and vehemently denied such collaboration.

This sort of hardware subversion is still ongoing. According to an article that appeared in *Time*:

> The CIA has a clandestine program that would insert booby-trapped computer chips into weapons systems that a foreign arms manufacturer might ship to a potentially hostile country – a technique called "chipping."[40]

Intel, in particular, sells processors that have features which are implemented in reprogrammable logic embedded within the chips themselves (aka *microcode*). Microcode update packages released by Intel include payloads that are encrypted and adhere to a proprietary specification, making them an ideal mechanism for intelligence services to insert backdoors.

Some Intel processor families, like the Intel Core vPro, already have autonomous remote access features built-in. This kind embedded *Out-of-Band* (OOB) access is based on a miniature operating system and network stack that's packaged onto the chips. Intel calls this *Active Management Technology*. It offers full, unadulterated, access to a computer *even if the machine is turned off*. Heck, the machine doesn't even have to be plugged into a wired network as the remote technology supports wireless connectivity.[41] Having a special back door into technology like this would yield a gratis rootkit that should make even the most skilled security professional squeamish. Perhaps this explains why, in the wake of Ed Snowden's leaks about offensive U.S. operations, the Kremlin has fallen back on electric typewriters?[42]

But the government isn't just into hardware-level subversion; it's also involved in more pedestrian software-level tricks. *Der Spiegel* has reported that intelligence services can easily compromise smart phones sold by Apple, BlackBerry, and Google. As you might expect they're a treasure trove of data. The NSA literally formed teams to attack each mobile platform:

> According to the documents, it [the NSA] set up task forces for the leading smartphone manufacturers and operating systems.

Specialized teams began intensively studying Apple's iPhone and its iOS operating system, as well as Google's Android mobile operating system. Another team worked on ways to attack BlackBerry, which had been seen as an impregnable fortress until then.[43]

How the NSA actually implements subversion can vary. Sometimes it's something as simple as a plain-old bribe.[44]

> The agency [the CIA] is looking at how independent contractors hired by arms makers to write software for weapons systems could be bribed to slip in viruses. "You get into the arms manufacturer's supply network, take the stuff off-line briefly, insert the bug, then let it go to the country," explained a CIA source who specializes in information technology. "When the weapons system goes into a hostile situation, everything about it seems to work, but the warhead doesn't explode."

In other instances, the intelligence services don't have to bribe anyone because they're able to get software vendors to cooperate using export controls. A former senior intelligence official says that in the late 1990s a bargain was struck between the NSA and hi-tech companies over the use of strong cryptography (i.e. encryption tools that are difficult to crack). The gist of the deal between the government and the private sector was this: vendors were allowed to export high-grade cryptographic components in return for allowing the NSA to "review" it (peek at the internal workings) and, if deemed necessary, establish back doors.[45]

Bruce Schneier describes how the NSA sent a man named Lew Giles around to cryptography companies:

> The deal went something like this: Giles offered you preferential treatment for export if you would add a back door. The back door could be subtle enough that it wouldn't show up in the design, and only be obvious if someone analyzed the binary code. It could be something that would easily be viewed as a mistake if someone learned about it. Maybe you could weaken your random number generator, or leak a few key bits in a header. Anything that would let the NSA decrypt the ciphertext without it looking like the crypto was broken.[46]

In one particular case, the NSA required MasterCard International to dumb down the Secure Electronic Transaction (SET) protocol, a widespread credit-card encryption standard.[47]

Though public knowledge is scarce, this sort of cryptographic subversion is part of an industry-wide campaign. The NSA spends over $250 million each year on what called the *Sigint Enabling Project* (Sigint as in Signal Intelligence). According to top-secret documents the NSA "actively engages the U.S. and foreign IT industries to covertly influence and/or leverage their commercial product designs" so that their commercial products are "exploitable."[48]

A leaked budget related to this project document plainly states that corporate partnerships are used to:

> Insert vulnerabilities into commercial encryption systems, IT systems, networks, and endpoint communications devices used by targets ... [49]

In addition to weakening the security of individual products, the NSA also applies itself to weaken the underlying international encryption standards that commercial products are based on. This campaign against encryption is known internally as Project BULLRUN:

> Project Bullrun deals with NSA's abilities to defeat the encryption used in specific network communication technologies. Bullrun involves multiple sources, all of which are extremely sensitive.[50]

For example, when a couple of in-house cryptographers at Microsoft discovered a serious flaw in a standard that had been adopted by the National Institute of Standards and Technology (NIST) in 2006, a classified government memo confirmed that the flaw was intentionally introduced by the NSA, which had hounded the NIST to accept the standard.[51]

The NSA has also been known to use the direct approach and outright seize encryption keys. In July of 2013 an anonymous source told journalists from *CNET* that the government was asking Internet service providers to hand over the encryption keys used to secure web-based communication (i.e. the keys used to facilitate SSL-based sessions).[52]

In September of 2013, the *New York Times* further revealed that the NSA maintains what's known as the *Key Recovery Service*, a special unit which is tasked with acquiring encryption keys, though the specifics of how they acquire them (e.g. theft, bribery) is sketchy.[53] Having these keys allows intelligence services to decrypt connections en masse so that thousands of otherwise secure sessions can be analyzed.

When all else fails, the spooks send in members of the *Special Collection Service* (SCS). The SCS is a covert program that leverages expertise from both the CIA and NSA to intercept communication in circumstances where U.S. spies need to direct access to targets in order to plant and operate eavesdropping equipment (e.g. think breaking and entering, close surveillance).[54] There are 74 staffed SCS sites worldwide.[55]

It's ironic that the apparatchik of our political machinery go into hysterics about China sabotaging exported hi-tech components when, as we saw in the first chapter of this book, the United States is actively doing just that very thing across the board.

U.S. Economic Espionage

As we mentioned earlier, the United States government spends a tremendous amount of money collecting intelligence. In 2012 the military's "black" budget was roughly $51 billion,[56] and the non-military budget for intelligence services was approximately $54 billion.[57]

There's little doubt that the United States spies, primarily on other national governments. But at the same time there are people who claim that it all stops there. For example, in an op-ed that appeared in the Washington Post, James Lewis of the think tank the Center for Strategic and International Studies (CSIS) asserts unequivocally:

> The United States, by contrast, does not engage in economic espionage.[58]

Likewise an NSA spokesman, in a strongly worded message, told the *Washington Times*:

The department does ***not*** engage in economic espionage in any domain, including cyber.[59]

Keep in mind that this statement includes the NSA, as it is a part of the Department of Defense.

This basic message has been repeated all the way up the political ladder. Appearing on an episode of Charlie Rose, President Barack Obama singled out the Chinese as the exclusive perpetrators of industrial espionage:

> Every country in the world, large and small, engages in intelligence gathering, and that is an occasional source of tensions, but is generally practiced within bounds. There is a big difference between China wanting to figure out how can they find out what my talking points are when I'm meeting with the Japanese which is standard fare…. There's a big difference between that and a hacker directly connected with the Chinese government or the Chinese military breaking into Apple's software systems to see if they can obtain the designs for the latest Apple product. That's theft. And we can't tolerate that.[60]

The reality is, however, that the narrative which Mr. Lewis and President Obama are trying so hard to establish, that China is hitting below the belt by resorting to economic espionage and the United States doesn't do that sort of thing, is incorrect.

The United States does indeed steal secrets from foreign businesses. Back in 1995 former CIA officer Philip Agee stated during a television interview that the CIA has been involved in economic espionage since its inception, particularly with regard to developing negotiating positions on trade agreements.[61] In fact, he went further, claiming that the practice of state intervention abroad in this manner, on behalf of multinational businesses, is something that predates World War II.

According to statements made by former CIA Director James Woolsey at a press conference held in the State Department's Foreign Press Center in D.C., the United States regularly spies on foreign corporate interests to track dual-use technology, detect the violation of economic sanctions, as well as unearth political cor-ruption.[62] But that's not all.

James Bamford, a well-known NSA historian, adds that the U.S. government also uses its intelligence services to gain the upper hand during trade negotiations:

> On trade issues, we know what others are thinking before the multilateral meetings, how to play poker by knowing which cards everyone has at the table ...[63]

Whistleblower Ed Snowden, the Booz Allen server admin who came in from the cold, corroborated this during an interview with the *South China Morning Post* in June of 2013:

> We [the NSA] hack network backbones – like huge Internet routers, basically – that give us access to the communications of hundreds of thousands of computers without having to hack every single one ...
>
> The hypocrisy of the U.S. government when it claims that it does not target civilian infrastructure, unlike its adversaries ...
>
> Not only does it do so, but it is so afraid of this being known that it is willing to use any means, such as diplomatic intimida-tion, to prevent this information from becoming public.[64]

Snowden also told journalist Glenn Greenwald that the goal of stopping terrorist attacks is merely a cover story, and that the *ultimate aim of U.S. spying is to acquire a strategic economic advantage*:

> The tactics of the U.S. government since September 11 is to say that everything is justified by terrorism. Scaring people to accept these measures as necessary. But most of the spying they do does not have anything to do with national security, it is to obtain an unfair advantage over other nations in their industrial and commerce economic agreements.[65]

The government's own records support this view. In a 2009 letter to written to the NSA by Thomas Shannon, then the Assistant Secretary of State, he lauded the NSA for information it passed on before the Fifth Summit of the Americas, a conference where the heads of state of the continent deliberated over commercial issues:

More than 100 reports we received from the agency gave us a deep understanding of the plans and intentions of other summit participants and allowed our diplomats to be well prepared to advise President Obama on how to deal with controversial issues.[66]

An article in *Der Spiegel* describes an operation in Mexico known as *WhiteTamale*.[67]

> In August 2009, according to internal documents, the agency gained access to the emails of various high-ranking officials in Mexico's Public Security Secretariat that combats the drug trade and human trafficking. This hacking operation allowed the NSA not only to obtain information on several drug cartels, but also to gain access to "diplomatic talking-points." In the space of a single year, according to the internal documents, this operation produced 260 classified reports that allowed U.S. politicians to conduct successful talks on political issues and to plan international investments.

According to documents disclosed by Snowden to a Brazilian news outlet, United States intelligence has a lengthy history of targeting foreign commercial interests, like the oil industry in Venezuela and Mexico's energy sector.[68]

Within weeks of this information becoming public knowledge, the Globo news outlet published a story detailing how the NSA targeted a Brazilian oil giant named Petrobras, a company partially run by the state which sports annual profits on the order of $120 billion.[69] So it would seem that, at a bare minimum, the NSA engages in economic espionage in Latin America.

Globo also reported that the NSA was spying on the Society for Worldwide Interbank Financial Telecommunication (SWIFT), the cooperative network of over 10,000 banks in 212 countries which handles the transmission of almost every financial payment order that crosses international borders. This is interesting because the U.S. Treasury already has access to SWIFT data through the *Terrorist Finance Tracking Program* (TFTP). TFTP was launched in the wake of 9/11 in the name of counterterrorism. Supposedly officials implemented various controls and safeguards to ensure that data subpoenaed by the U.S. Treasury is used strictly for that purpose. Globo's disclosure implies that perhaps the NSA has been secretly acquiring SWIFT data for reasons not related to counterterrorism. This raises a lot of questions.

After the Globo revelations, *Der Spiegel* revealed that the NSA was tracking the transactions of credit card customers in Africa, Europe, and the Middle East:

> The information from the American foreign intelligence agency, acquired by former NSA contractor and whistleblower Edward Snowden, show that the spying is conducted by a branch called "Follow the Money" (FTM). The collected information then flows into the NSA's own financial databank, called "Tracfin," which in 2011 contained 180 million records. Some 84 percent of the data is from credit card transactions.[70]

When confronted with these documented facts, a group of unnamed U.S. officials stated:

> We have been clear that the United States does gather foreign intelligence of the type gathered by all nations.[71]

DNI James Clapper also responded by saying:

> It is not a secret that the Intelligence Community collects information about economic and financial matters, and terrorist financing.[72]

From the standpoint of officials this is a good thing because spying is viewed as an essential part of maintaining national interests. But at the same time do you suppose this robs the United States of its moral authority?

Of course, the United States isn't alone in spying on foreign companies. The 2013 National Intelligence Estimate, which represents a consensus opinion of the U.S. Intelligence Community, claims that China, France, Israel, and Russia are also involved in stealing economic secrets.[73] The difference is that the U.S. government pours a whole lot more resources into it. As we'll see in Chapter Ten the sheer scale of the U.S. surveillance apparatus dwarfs that of other countries.

Apologists and Opposing Views

Researchers who study political game theory have been known to theorize that spying is inevitable. They'd argue, using logical models like the *Prisoner's Dilemma*, that national governments are forced to spy. This stance concludes that decision makers don't have a choice, they either spy or they lose (because if they don't spy, their opponents may spy and in doing so gain the edge). So, governments choose to spy. Often under the guise of intentionally vague, self-serving, generalities like the *national interest*. Former officials have warned that the United States would be put at a severe disadvantage if it limited engagement in cyber espionage.[74]

As Raytheon's Scott Chase has surmised:

Everyone is hacking everyone.[75]

Indeed, this is the justification that DNI James Clapper and General Keith Alexander have used to explain why the decade-spanning habit of spying on foreign leaders is not only acceptable but necessary:

It is one of the first things I learned in intelligence school in 1963…. It's a fundamental given.[76]

Reading the subtext: everyone spies, and the officials who complain about it are just jealous that they can't do it as well as the NSA.

Journalist Kevin Gosztola illuminates the dangers of this argument:

The idea that everyone is doing it and others would do it if they could except we're better so they hate us for our capabilities is a race to the bottom argument. It could be used to excuse just about any intrusive and objectionable conduct, such as flying surveillance drones in any country's airspace or building secret prisons for interrogating prisoners in any country's land.[77]

With regard to U.S. dragnet surveillance, it's a matter of scale. There are people who believe that there's a huge difference between watching specific individuals, based on carefully acquired grounds for suspicion, versus simply watching everyone en masse. The President of Brazil, Dilma Rousseff, for example, refuses to buy into the dragnet surveillance apologia:

> The privacy of citizens and the sovereignty of countries cannot be infringed in the name of security ... [78]

As does the editor of the *Guardian*, Alan Rusbridger:

> I think Americans haven't quite understood the anger of other states, of people living in Germany, you say, that Americans feel free to spy on anybody else in the world, and you just have to, sort of, reverse that and think how would Americans feel if Germans were spying on them, or the Chinese. Well, we know how people feel about the Chinese.... I mean, again, put it the other way around, if we discovered that Brazil was trying to listen to President Obama's phone calls or emails, there would be outrage. So, you can understand why other states just are offended by this kind of behavior. [79]

This is an astute point. Would you want to live in a country where everything you do is aggressively monitored, without any legal restrictions, by a largely unaccountable entity?

And while the NSA siphons up data all over the world, U.S. officials ironically laud the virtues of Internet freedom. Recall Hilary Clinton, then Secretary of State, prattling on about human rights at The Hague:

> As people increasingly turn to the Internet to conduct important aspects of their lives, we have to make sure that human rights are as respected online as offline... we all have a responsibility to support human rights and fundamental freedoms everywhere ... [80]

It's clear that unbridled mass interception tramples on fundamental human rights, the very same rights which safeguard against the emergence of police states. It would seem that the purveyors of Orwell's nightmare are willing to pay for their alleged "national security" using individual privacy at home and abroad as currency.

American Exceptionalism

This sense of entitlement is a defining aspect of the Deep State. It's rooted in our history. An early example of this mindset was noted by Mark Twain on September 7, 1906, during a speech at the Ends of the Earth Club. An indignant Twain remarked that he had recently witnessed a Union General make the following statement:

> We are of the Anglo-Saxon race, and when the Anglo-Saxon wants a thing he just takes it.[81]

Native Americans can attest to the veracity of this statement.

A century later, in 2006, journalist John Pilger interviewed Duane "Dewey" Clarridge, the man who directed CIA operations in Latin America during the 1980s. When Pilger asked Clarridge what gave the CIA the right to overthrow other governments, Clarridge responded:

> Like it or lump it, we'll do what we like. So just get used to it, world.[82]

During a speech at the United Nations General Assembly, President Obama echoed this sympathy with regard to American foreign policy in the Middle East:

> The United States of America is prepared to use all elements of our power, including military force, to secure these core interests in the region.[83]

Journalist Jeremy Scahill responds:

> He basically came out and said the United States is an imperialist nation and we are going to do whatever we need to conquer areas to take resources from around the world. I mean, it was a really naked sort of declaration of imperialism, and I don't use that word lightly, but it really is.

Our leaders certainly don't make much of a fuss when other countries get hacked. When the Chinese complain of "massive and shocking" intrusions, its disclosures are met with silence.[84] At

189

the same time many U.S. officials seem to erupt in fits of righteous indignation when other countries steal our secrets.[85]

According to top-secret documents acquired by the *Washington Post*, U.S. intelligence services launched 231 separate offensive cyber operations in 2011.[86] Roughly three-quarters of these operations targeted high-priority assets in the networks of countries like Iran, Russia, China and North Korea. NSA Whistleblower Ed Snowden told reporters in Hong Kong that the United States has conducted more than 61,000 hacking operations globally.[87]

The basic narrative that officials seem to stick to is that it's acceptable for the United States to break into foreign networks but everyone else should be strongly reprimanded when they follow our example because, well, U.S. cyber-attacks are executed by the good guys.

Glenn Greenwald points out the problem with this sort of exceptionalism:

> This self-affirming belief – I can do X because I'm Good and you are barred from X because you are Bad – is the universally invoked justification for all aggression. It's the crux of hypocrisy. And most significantly of all, it is the violent enemy of law: the idea that everyone is bound by the same set of rules and restraints ... [88]

Exerting soft power and attracting other people to follow your lead means steering clear of double standards. If you knew someone who feverishly went around breaking windows in other people's houses day after day, you'd probably be hard pressed to offer any sympathy when someone finally turned around and broke a window in his house. Not only that, but you'd probably be mystified that someone so versed and experienced at breaking windows would even be so thoughtless as to even have windows to begin with. In fact, you might even be tempted to conclude that they had it coming.

Perhaps the outcry of our officials isn't intended to shame other countries? Do decision makers genuinely believe that formal remonstrations would actually pressure other nations to suddenly halt their intelligence collection? This is highly unlikely.

In 2010 the nations of France and the United States tried to broker a written agreement where they agreed not to spy on each other. It was a more formal attempt of the long-standing gentleman's agreement that exists between the U.S. and the UK. The deal with France fell through because there were high-level officials on both sides that wanted to keep spying.[89]

Look at it this way, if the U.S. was confronted by Chinese leaders over an intelligence campaign inside China's borders, would the CIA suspend its efforts or simply push them deeper undercover? Would, under any circumstances, the CIA truly cease to spy? Not if the Deep State has any say in things (espionage is a growth sector).

The Malware-Industrial Complex

In the realm of cyber-espionage there's a burgeoning industry devoted to selling offensive software and surveillance tools. This little-known industry caters to an audience that includes governments, corporate interests, organized crime, and independent operators. Furthermore, increased demand has commoditized these products such that anyone with the requisite funding can enter the game.

Mass Surveillance Systems

The private sector is a significant source of cyber-tools for U.S. intelligence agencies. If you doubt this, check out the WikiLeaks *Spy Files* submission site,[90] or the *Wall Street Journal's Surveillance Catalogue.*[91] There's a flourishing market that services repressive regimes, like Tunisia, that want to spy on their citizenry.[92] As Julian Assange stated as a press conference in December of 2011:

> Who here has an iPhone? Who here has a BlackBerry? Who here uses Gmail? Well you are all screwed. The reality is intelligence contractors are selling right now to countries across the world mass surveillance systems for all of those products.

Much of the surveillance trade's activity takes place at ISS World conferences organized by TeleStrategies, a company based out of McLean, Virginia. The sponsor list for ISS World provides a veritable who's-who of the industry.[93] This invitation-only setting allows vendors to meet spies from all over the world and sell them high-end interception solutions.

For example, there's one vendor from northern California called Glimmerglass which sells fiber optic technology. Glimmerglass sells a product called CyberSweep which can be deployed at "submarine landing stations" to "extract actionable information" from fiber optic cables.[94]

ISS stands for *Intelligence Support Systems*, and the gatherings ostensibly are directed towards law enforcement types, telecom providers, and government employees. Nevertheless, the technology is inherently dual-use. There's really nothing to stop this equipment from being used by organizations to monitor political dissidents, human rights advocates, journalists, and alleged enemies of the state. Kaspersky researcher Sergey Golovanov remarks:

> The problem with so-called -legal- spy tools is that any government can purchase them, including governments from countries with poor human rights records. Additionally, one government can purchase these tools and use them against another country. … The lack of regulation, the widespread trading of such dangerous technologies to pretty much anyone who has the money and the fact that they've already been in many dubious cases raises a big question about who will be held liable … [95]

In March of 2011, protestors in Egypt raided the headquarters of the State Security Services. They found what looks like a $353,000 invoice for a surveillance software framework called FinFisher that's sold by a software company called the Gamma International.[96] There's no evidence if the transaction was executed or not.

A few months later, in August of 2011, the *Wall Street Journal* published an article revealing that a French vendor named Amesys had developed a mass interception product for the Libyan regime of Moammar Gadhafi. The monitoring package was implemented for Libya after it signed a contract with Amesys in 2007, and it was wielded for several years to collect the e-mails, social media posts, and online chat messages of anyone perceived to be a threat. Data interception fizzled out sometime during the Libyan revolution.

Amesys defended its deal with the dictator's government:

> The contract was concluded at a time when the international community was in the process of diplomatic rapprochement with Libya, which was looking to fight against terrorism and acts perpetrated by al Qaeda ...[97]

Amesys wasn't the only business interest assisting Libya. A Chinese company, ZTE Corp., as it happens, also had agreements with Libyan security services[98] and it appears that the company may have ties with other repressive governments. In March of 2012, it came to light that ZTE had sold a mass interception system to Iran as part of a $130 million contract. The system, which utilizes what's known as *deep packet inspection*, allows operators to dig into the contents of e-mails, web browser traffic, and video chat sessions.[99]

It's no surprise that there's a thriving market for surveillance technology in China. The central party leadership sees it as a necessary tool for maintaining control, and leading hi-tech companies have been there to assist towards this end. For example, a leaked internal Cisco document, written back in 2002, shows that Cisco viewed China's Golden Shield censorship system as a money-making opportunity.[100]

Contrary to popular perception, the censors in China don't erase every criticism that they intercept. According to Gary King, a professor from Harvard who has researched Chinese censorship in depth:

> Negative posts do not accidentally slip through a leaky or imperfect system. The evidence indicates that the censors have no intention of stopping them. Instead, they are focused on removing posts that have collective action potential, regardless of whether or not they cast the Chinese leadership and their policies in a favorable light.[101]

So it's not that Chinese officials are concerned about criticism per se. In fact, giving the *impression* of tolerating dissent may provide the Chinese government with a certain amount of credibility. Its content that *incites people to mobilize* that really scares them.

In addition to spying on ordinary citizens, it's well known that Chinese leaders frequently spy on each other. In a development that's reminiscent of Nixon's Watergate scandal, Bo Xilai, the former Communist Party Chief of the city of Chongqing, was found to have been monitoring central party leaders.[102] The level of intrigue among Chinese leaders is so deep that important information is usually conveyed only in person or in writing. The police state in China is eating itself. Though this is not a phenomenon limited to China. Anyone who witnessed the fall of CIA Director David Petraeus may observe similar developments in the United States.[103]

Roughly a year after *Wall Street Journal*'s initial report on Amesys, Bahraini political activists started to receive rather blatant phishing e-mails. Researchers at the University of Toronto's Citizen Lab volunteered to analyze the malware payloads mailed to the activists and concluded that they were dealing with a component of the FinFisher framework known as FinSpy.[104] To follow up on this discovery, Citizen Lab conducted a network scan for FinFisher command and control (C&C) servers and identified suspected servers in countries like Bahrain, Brunei, Turkmenistan, and the United Arab Emirates (UAE).[105] All told, researchers identified 25 governments with dubious human rights records using FinSpy.[106]

One tactic used by vendors is to disguise their malware as legitimate software. In a report published by the Citizen Lab in May of 2013, researchers disclosed that they had identified samples of FinSpy that masqueraded as Mozilla's Firefox browser.[107] Mozilla responded by sending the vendor, Gamma International, a cease and desist letter.[108]

These kinds of events are hardly isolated. Within months of the FinSpy disclosure, one of the investigators involved in the Citizen Lab publication on the incident, a researcher named Morgan Marquis-Boire, came across yet another surveillance tool, one sold by Italian vendor Hacking Team, while investigating a cyber-attack on group of citizen journalists in Morocco. Furthermore, Marquis-Boire found that this same tool also happened to be used against a political dissident in the United Arab Emirates, who received a spear-phishing e-mail that installed Hacking Team's malware.[109]

It's not just foreign companies that are assisting the United Arab Emirates. U.S. defense contractor Booz Allen Hamilton, with the consent of U.S. intelligence, helped the sheikdom create its own signal intelligence processing infrastructure, largely based on the architecture used by the NSA.[110] The implications fleshed out by *Salon's* David Sirota are worth considering:

> American politicians who are financed by Booz and other firms with a similar multinational business model not only have a vested campaign-contribution interest in shilling for the domestic surveillance state that their donors profit from. They also have a similar interest in denigrating the democratic protest movements that challenge Mideast surveillance states that make those donors big money, too.[111]

This is how the Deep State helps to "spread democracy" to other countries.

Exploits and Arms Dealers

But it's not just surveillance equipment. There's also a burgeoning market for offensive software, commonly known as *weaponized malware* or *cyberweapons*. Malware that's been weaponized is specially engineered so that it's easy to delivery, remains stable and manageable in hostile environments, and reliably contaminates the target. These are also the very same qualities that distinguish a military-grade bioweapon from naturally occurring pestilence.

A cyberweapon can be likened to a drink that's been spiked. The average cyberweapon is concealed inside of legitimate input that's fed to a software application. This input could be a web page, a Microsoft Office document, an Adobe PDF, etc. Having ingested the malicious payload, which is stashed inside the input data, the software application becomes sick. It enters a trancelike state where it will accept arbitrary commands dictated by the voodoo priest. It's like something that you'd see in the 1932 Bela Lugosi movie *White Zombie*.

Weaponized malware (see Figure 6-1) relies on a series of software components that fit together into a chain of sorts. This chain of components is delivered as an encapsulated package of data, a poison pill made up of digital ones and zeros.

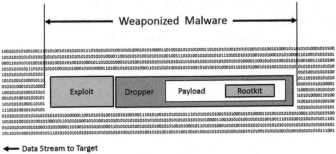

Figure 6-1

The first component in the chain is the most crucial: *the exploit*. An exploit is a tiny series of instructions that takes advantage of an unpatched flaw (i.e. a bug) in targeted software. For example, if the cyberweapon is delivered by means of a web page, the exploit may be a malformed snippet of JavaScript which the web browser is unable to process correctly. The exploit leverages the software bug to sidestep existing defenses and gain entry. It's like a burglar who finds a hole in the side of a vault and uses it to climb inside.

Once inside the perimeter, the exploit launches the second stage of the cyberweapon. Typically this is what's known as a *dropper*. A dropper is a kind of installer that sets up a base camp inside the infected computer for the cyberweapon's third stage: the *payload*. The dropper unwraps the payload, perhaps downloading additional components from the Internet, sticks the payload somewhere, and then configures the target machine so that the payload can run. The payload can be anything: a monitoring module to capture passwords, a logic bomb that destroys data, a routing component that re-directs network traffic to help conceal an attack, or a combination of all of these.

Payloads often contain something called a *rootkit*. A rootkit is essentially a stealth module, it's a collection of special tools that allow the payload to run silently so that no one knows that it's there.[112] Many cyberweapons don't explicitly try to conceal themselves. There are literally hundreds of moving pieces in the average operating system, so many that it's pretty easy for a cyberweapon to hide in plain sight. So the presence of a rootkit is usually the hallmark of an advanced weapon.

Of all of the cyberweapon elements in the chain of components, the exploit is the most valuable. This is because it takes specialized skills to identify new software bugs, bugs that the vendor often isn't aware of, and after doing so determine a way to capitalize on them. An unpatched bug provides a way to attack computers that's nearly impossible to defend against.

U.S. agencies shell out big bucks for zero-day exploits in the black market.[113] Intelligence services, in particular, are one of the most active buyers.[114] The market thrives because of the U.S. government's patronage. For example, though the NSA designs and builds the bulk of its own malware, in 2013 it allocated over $25 million to purchase exploits in the private sector.[115]

The price for a single weaponized exploit can range from several thousand dollars to a quarter of a million.[116] There's word from the *New York Times* that a single exploit for Apple's iOS operating system was sold for half a million.[117]

Demand is so great that there are literally middlemen, like a South African fellow known only as "the Grugq," who earns a good living funneling zero-day exploits from independent developers to U.S. intelligence services. The Grugq claims that he makes roughly 80 percent of his income selling to the U.S. government.[118]

The government also buys exploits directly from outfits like Endgame Systems, which sells exploits that typically fetch between $100,000 and $200,000.[119] Well-heeled organizations can purchase a combo-pack from Endgame Systems of 25 exploits for about $2.5 million.[120] To help them locate computers to use these exploits on, Endgame sells a product called *Bonesaw* which maps out devices connected to the Internet (e.g. routers, servers, desktop PCs). *Wired* magazine offers the following description of how Bonesaw might be used in practice:

> The client locates a region on the password-protected web-based map, then picks a country and city – say, Beijing, China. Next the client types in the name of the target organization, such as the Ministry of Public Security's No. 3 Research Institute, which is responsible for computer security – or simply enters

its address, 6 Zhengyi Road. The map will then display what software is running on the computers inside the facility, what types of malware some may contain, and a menu of custom-designed exploits that can be used to secretly gain entry.[121]

Other U.S. firms like Immunity, KEYW, Netragard, and Exodus Intelligence also sell offensive technology, though they tend to be tight-lipped about the specifics.

It goes without saying that the traditional stalwarts of the defense industry like Northrop Grumman, Raytheon, and General Dynamics have begun to establish a foothold in this market.[122] As in the case of mass interception gear, many of the American vendors who sell offensive software are listed as sponsors at ISS World conferences.

To leverage these exploits the government (with ample help from the private sector) sometimes builds its own malware payloads.[123] We've already discussed canonical examples, like Stuxnet and Flame, which have been deployed oversees. But there are also offensive payloads that have been used by the security services domestically.

For example, an offensive tracking application referred to as a *Computer and Internet Protocol Address Verifier* (CIPAV) has been deployed by the feds on multiple occasions via drive-by-download or a malicious e-mail.[124] It's particularly useful as a way to locate targets who are trying to hide behind proxy servers.

The FBI has also, in what may be the ultimate eavesdropping tactic, been known to deploy malware that remotely enables the microphones on laptop computers and smart phones so that law enforcement can surreptitiously listen in on conversations that occur in the vicinity of the compromised devices.[125]

The market for cyberweapons in the United States reflects a larger reality. The United States dwarfs the rest of the world in terms of arms sales. Despite the fact that civilian manufacturing has all but vanished and cities like Detroit have become ghost towns, in terms of exporting weapons that kill people and break stuff, this is one area where the United States stands head and shoulders above everyone else. As the *New York Times* reports:

Overseas weapons sales by the United States totaled $66.3 billion last year, or more than three-quarters of the global arms market, valued at $85.3 billion in 2011. Russia was a distant second, with $4.8 billion in deals.[126]

Here's something else to consider: it's not just U.S.-based companies getting into this domain. Business interests in other countries have also begun to ply their wares in the cyber arms bazaar, as the Russian, British, Middle Eastern, and Asian governments are also active buyers.[127]

For instance, Gamma International sells an attack platform call FinIntrusion. According to the product's brochure:

> The FinIntrusion Kit is an up-to-date and covert operational Kit that can be used for the most common IT Intrusion Operations in defensive and offensive areas. Current customers include Military Cyberwar Departments, Intelligence Agencies, Police Intelligence and other Law Enforcement Agencies.

VUPEN Security, a vendor that operates out of France, sells packs of zero day exploits to law enforcement agencies in NATO member countries. As a result of a Freedom of Information Act request submitted by MuckRock it's now part of the public record that this includes the U.S. government.[128]

The marketing literature for this product states:

> Law enforcement agencies need the most advanced IT intrusion research and the most reliable attack tools to covertly and remotely gain access to computer systems. Using previously unknown software vulnerabilities and exploits which bypass Antivirus products and modern operating system protections such as Data Execution Prevention (DEP) and Address Space Layout Randomization (ASLR) could help investigators to successfully achieve this task.

It's alleged that VUPEN clients pay around $100,000 per year merely for the opportunity to buy their tools.[129] Like a fickle mistress, VUPEN will pit customers from different countries against each other as new exploits are unearthed. Not surprisingly the technique is effective and profitable.

The Italian firm HackingTeam sells a Remote Control System product which is essentially a multiplatform botnet kit (e.g. command and control console, agent software, attack vectors) with some rootkit functionality thrown in for good measure.

The list goes on and on. For example, Appin Technologies is a New Delhi company that offers custom exploit development.[130] ERA IT Solutions is a Swiss company that developed a Trojan application designed to intercept VoIP-conversations. In short, vendors have cropped up all over the world.

There are even purveyors like Ntrepid that offers a service that provides "operational non-attribution" for people performing open source intelligence (OSINT) collection on the Internet. According to their marketing brochure, their Internet Operations Network (ION) ensures that:

> All client traffic is funneled through the ION network allowing the analyst in the U.S. to research and target enemy sites while appearing to originate from a foreign point of presence, in this case Cairo. The target website will never have reason to be suspicious of analyst visits, as all identifying HTTP information (location, operating system, language, etc.) will be appropriate and non-attributable to any U.S. entity.

Go back and reread the previous paragraph. Now perhaps you'll understand why knowing the origin of an attack doesn't necessarily tell you who's behind it.

There are commercial services available to undermine attribution.

Attribution is a quagmire because there's a lucrative market patronized by organizations that spy.

Falling Barriers to Entry

What the previous section demonstrates, at least indirectly, is that developing malware doesn't require anywhere near as much overhead investment as conventional high-yield ordnance. Early work on intercontinental ballistic missiles in the late 1940s, for example, was so resource intensive that it necessitated the full backing of the federal government and thousands of specialists.

At the SOURCE Boston 2010 conference, H.D. Moore announced that the source code base of the Metasploit Framework had surpassed the 100,000 line mark. This may seem like a lot of code but it's actually a fairly manageable amount of logic (enterprise middleware suites often grow to be millions of lines of code in size). Also keep in mind that Moore's brainchild started as an after-hours pet project.[131] If a random collection of volunteers can produce a tool like Metasploit, imagine what a formally tasked squad of well-funded, full-time, veteran engineers could crank out.

Expertise is pervasive and available, for a price. This is only logical. If you recall the dynamics of the revolving door that we discussed earlier, the private sector pays better and has the funds to buy the latest tools, leading to a steady exodus of talent from the public sector.

Charlie Miller, a well-known expert in the field of exploit development, spent five years with the NSA before leaving for the corporate sector. Jamie Butler, another well-known specialist in the area of rootkits, also got his start at the NSA. What this demonstrates is that the private sector has the advantage of scooping up talent that has already climbed the learning curve, and gleans the benefit of this experience, thanks to taxpayer revenue.

Independent Operators

Moxie Marlinspike once queried:

> Who knows more about the citizens in their own country, Kim Jong-Il or Google?[132]

Given that the talent needed to build and deploy spy gear exists in abundance outside of the government, it isn't much of a jump to presume that an autonomous group would be able to acquire the resources to execute their own black-bag operations. With enough money, you can recruit the people and purchase the tools needed to set up your own shop. This is the purview of the independent operator.

The demand for private sector intelligence presents lucrative options for experienced intelligence officers looking for opportunities outside of the government. As mentioned earlier, private sector operations are not driven by love of country. They exist to benefit the bottom line, even if it means undermining democratic governments, trampling on civil rights, or supporting oligarchs. The same covert tactics are brought into action.

Only in this case the inner workings of the outfits are even more opaque because there's no need to provide the impression of legislative oversight. CNBC correspondent Eamon Javers explains:

> The corporate espionage industry is deliberately hidden in a thicket of complex relationships designed to obscure just who is working for whom. Often, these firms are hired as subcontractors for corporate law firms and they argue that everything they do is covered by attorney-client privilege. Thus, their operations do not surface to the public.[133]

There's at least one well-known example of a law firm enlisting hired guns. In October of 2009, WikiLeaks founder Julian Assange claimed to have acquired a trove of incriminating information from a hard drive belonging to an executive at Bank of America.[134] The executives at Bank of America, fearing that this data would be released to the public, decided to act preemptively and, at the recommendation of the Department of Justice, went to an international law firm Hunton & Williams.

The attorneys at Hunton & Williams, in turn, sought out hired guns. Specifically, they entertained a proposal submitted to them by Palantir Technologies, HBGary Federal, and Berico Technologies.[135] The proposal described a collection of what could only be called strong-arm tactics. Specifically, it advised that WikiLeaks supporters in the press like Glenn Greenwald "if pushed will choose professional preservation over cause." The proposal also recommended an expansive campaign of disinformation as well as head on cyber-attacks against the WikiLeaks infrastructure.

As you might expect, when these plans were exposed, the Bank of America denied everything. Glenn Greenwald commented:

> The very idea of trying to threaten the careers of journalists and activists to punish and deter their advocacy is self-evident-

ly pernicious; that it's being so freely and casually proposed to groups as powerful as the Bank of America, the Chamber of Commerce, and the DOJ-recommended Hunton & Williams demonstrates how common this is. These highly experienced firms included such proposals because they assumed those deep-pocket organizations would approve and it would make their hiring more likely.[136]

This blueprint for corporate-sponsored coercion came to light in February of 2011 when the chief executive of HBGary Federal, Aaron Barr, threatened to reveal the identities of the Anonymous hacking collective. Anonymous retaliated by hacking into HBGary and stealing Barr's e-mail, in addition to laying waste to the company's website and backup data. For good measure, in a move that's reminiscent of a professional wrestler's choke slam, they wiped Barr's iPad remotely.

The sad part of all this, as blogger Josh Glasstetter observes, is that the companies involved with the proposed schemes largely walked away unscathed:

> Two years later, there have been no consequences for the contractors. Berico recently won a contract with Special Operations Command, HBGary Federal's parent company was purchased by a larger contractor, Mantech, and Palantir is rumored to be worth $8 billion – your tax dollars at work.[137]

History Repeats Itself

Using the corporate checking account to hire mercenaries isn't necessarily a new idea. In 1850 Allen Pinkerton saw a business opportunity and formed the North-Western Police Agency. It grew into a veritable private army called the Pinkerton National Detective Agency that catered to business interests by infiltrating unions and breaking strikes. When normal groups of people tried to organize, protest, and assert their rights, the Pinkertons were there to enforce the status quo on behalf of the corporate interests that paid their substantial fee.

In 1871 Congress set aside $50,000 on behalf of the Department of Justice to create an organization dedicated to "the detection and prosecution of those guilty of violating federal law." [138] This could have very well been the moment of inception for the FBI, but it wasn't. In a move that should seem eerily familiar, political leaders at the time found it more expedient to outsource this work to the Pinkertons.[139]

It's interesting to note that the tactics used by the Pinkerton agents were eventually seen as so disruptive that the *Anti-Pinkerton Act* of 1893 (5 USC Sec. 3108) was passed in an effort to ensure that:

> An individual employed by the Pinkerton Detective Agency, or similar organization, may not be employed by the Government of the United States or the government of the District of Columbia.

The public-private entanglement continued on into the next century. For example, the Office of Strategic Services (OSS), was a core component of the United States intelligence apparatus during World War II. It was disbanded in 1945 by President Harry Truman. Its successor, the CIA, didn't formally come into existence until President Truman signed the National Security Act of 1947. In the interim, OSS veterans like Allen Dulles and William Donovan were involved in the formation of a private spy organization that functioned under the auspices of a company called the *World Commerce Corporation*.[140]

In February of 2007, a holding company led by Erik Prince, the founder of Xe Services (the company formerly known as Blackwater USA), launched a private intelligence service out of Arlington, Virginia, and called it *Total Intelligence Solutions* (TIS).[141] The company claimed to offer "the skills traditionally honed by CIA operatives directly to the board room."[142] At the time of its launch the company was chaired by Cofer Black. Included in its portfolio of services were "surveillance and counter surveillance, deployed intelligence collection, and rapid safeguarding of employees or other key assets."[143] In May of 2010, TIS apparently discontinued its corporate security information services.[144]

In February of 2011 the *Guardian* published a report that detailed how large corporate interests in Britain's energy industry hired a "business risk management" firm named Vericola to secretly monitor environmental activists.[145] Agents of Vericola attended campaign meetings, subscribed to mailing lists, and generally tried to ingratiate themselves with group members. Police have voiced concern that such private-sector actors are completely unregulated.

According to the *Washington Post*'s Top Secret America project, there are over three hundred private sector companies that perform intelligence analysis, over a hundred companies capable of executing cyber operations, and at least fifty firms that handle human intelligence collection, raking in billions of dollars each year.[146]

Spies Abound ...

There are consequences associated with the rise of the private sector in this arena. As the GhostNet trackers from the Information Warfare Monitor explained:

> Cyberspace has empowered individuals and small groups of non-state actors to do many things, including executing sophisticated computer network operations that were previously only the domain of state intelligence agencies. We have entered the era of do-it-yourself (DIY) signals intelligence.[147]

With a couple of million dollars, the right equipment, and a handful of the right people, any group can launch an intelligence operation. Furthermore, information is a form of currency. Such groups may very well be driven by profit rather than an inherent sense of patriotism, making it difficult to depict cyber-espionage as a contest strictly driven by national interests.

Spies exist to unearth sensitive information, often breaking laws in the process. That's what they do: steal secrets. This is scarcely a domain where national governments have some sort of absolute monopoly, they just happen to employ agents who tend to be better funded and better organized. There's no doubt that national governments have the resources to support extended campaigns. Yet, as the Russians can readily testify, sometimes criminals can effectively run their own long-running intelligence operations, especially when they're using former government operatives.[148]

This will only serve to make attribution more problematic in the domain of cyber-attacks. When an incident takes place on a classified network, investigators cannot simply assume that it is the work of their opposite numbers on the other continent. The playing field is becoming more crowded. The usual state-sponsored teams are being joined by a broad spectrum of non-state actors, who are just as sophisticated, have access to the same technology, and possess their own peculiar motives for pilfering secrets.

But Some Groups Spy More Than Others

While most national entities steal secrets under the rubric of national security, this doesn't imply that they're all equally culpable. As mentioned earlier, it's a matter of scale. There's a big difference between monitoring a tiny fraction of a population and monitoring the entire population. Given the sheer amount of resources that the U.S. government channels to its intelligence apparatus, it should not come as a surprise that the scale of U.S. espionage dwarfs all other efforts.

Author and journalist James Bamford, who's covered the NSA for decades, explains how the United States, more so than other nations, is in the position of being able to spy rapaciously:

> The U.S. spies with the eavesdropping equivalent of a nuclear weapon because of the money, the power, the technological capability of the U.S.. The NSA is the largest intelligence agency in the world. Other countries spy with the equivalent of a canon. One of the benefits the U.S. has is that the major Internet companies are located in the U.S. so they can put pressure on them to turn over information.
>
> If you look at the worldwide telecommunications net, almost all of it goes through the United States. 80 percent of telephone communications go through the United States. So the U.S. is in the unique position of being able to eavesdrop on the world without much difficulty.[149]

He's right, roughly *90 percent* of the world's Internet communication flows through the United States.[150] This gives U.S. intelligence a home field advantage that other countries can't dream of duplicating.

Bamford's assertions are also supported by an article that appeared in the *Washington Post* in early July of 2013. The report described elements of the NSA's FAIRVIEW program,[151] where the U.S. government got large foreign telecom providers (the companies that run fiber-optic cables across the oceans) into providing special access to U.S. intelligence.

The *Post* provides details of one such instance that took place in 2003, when Tier 1 provider Global Crossing was slated for takeover by foreign investors:

> The security agreement for Global Crossing, whose fiber-optic network connected 27 nations and four continents, required the company to have a "Network Operations Center" on U.S. soil that could be visited by government officials with 30 minutes of warning. Surveillance requests, meanwhile, had to be handled by U.S. citizens screened by the government and sworn to secrecy – in many cases prohibiting information from being shared even with the company's executives and directors.[152]

In light of evidence that the United States is vacuuming up data en masse from countries like Germany and Brazil, often with the cooperation of foreign Internet providers,[153] Glenn Greenwald comments on the relative scope of the U.S. mass interception program:

> There are many more populations of non-adversarial countries which have been subjected to the same type of mass surveillance net by the NSA: indeed, the list of those which haven't been are shorter than those which have. The claim that any other nation is engaging in anything remotely approaching indiscriminate worldwide surveillance of this sort is baseless.[154]

Recall Hilary Clinton's speech at The Hague. There is clearly dissonance between our leaders' stated values and their actions. Politicians depict our political system to us as "a shining city on a hill" that's devoted to making the world "safe for democracy." What people in other countries see is a different face: a face that is clearly visible to those attending Pashtun wedding parties in Pakistan.

Endnotes

1) "Glenn Greenwald: U.S. Spying on Allies Shows "Institutional Obsession" with Surveillance," *Democracy Now!* October 28, 2013, http://www.democracynow.org/2013/10/28/glenn_greenwald_us_spying_on_allies#.

2) Amanda Holpuch, "Google's Eric Schmidt says government spying is 'the nature of our society'," *Guardian*, September 13, 2013, http://www.theguardian.com/world/2013/sep/13/eric-schmidt-google-nsa-surveillance/print.

3) "Julian Assange on Meeting with Google, Responds to Anti-WikiLeaks Attacks from New Film to Finances," *Democracy Now!*, May 29, 2013, http://www.democracynow.org/2013/5/29/julian_assange_on_meeting_with_google#.

4) Matthew Aid, "The NSA's New Code Breakers," *Foreign Policy*, October 15, 2013, http://www.foreignpolicy.com/articles/2013/10/15/the_nsa_s_new_code-breakers?print=yes&hidecomments=yes&page=full.

5) Lana Lam, "Edward Snowden: US government has been hacking Hong Kong and China for years," *South China Morning Post*, June 13, 2013, http://www.scmp.com/news/hong-kong/article/1259508/edward-snowden-us-government-has-been-hacking-hong-kong-and-china?page=all.

6) Laura Poitras, Marcel Rosenbach, Fidelius Schmid and Holger Stark, "NSA Spied on European Union Offices," *Der Spiegel*, June 29, 2013, http://www.spiegel.de/international/europe/nsa-spied-on-european-union-offices-a-908590-druck.html.

7) Madeline Chambers, "U.S. spy agency bugged U.N. headquarters: Germany's Spiegel," *Reuters*, August 25, 2013, http://www.reuters.com/article/2013/08/25/us-usa-security-nsa-un-idUSBRE97O0DD20130825.

8) Jacques Follorou and Glenn Greenwald, "France in the NSA's crosshair : phone networks under surveillance," *Le Monde*, October 21, 2013, http://www.lemonde.fr/technologies/article/2013/10/21/france-in-the-nsa-s-crosshair-phone-networks-under-surveillance_3499741_651865.html.

9) Jacques Follorou, "The NSA wiretapped French diplomats in the US," *Le Monde*, October 22, 2013, http://www.lemonde.fr/technologies/article/2013/10/22/the-nsa-wiretapped-french-diplomats-in-the-us_3500733_651865.html.

10) "Britain and US 'spied on Italy'," *Reuters*, October 25, 2013, http://www.telegraph.co.uk/news/worldnews/europe/italy/10404329/Britain-and-US-spied-on-Italy.html.

11) Glenn Greenwald and Germán Aranda, "La NSA espió 60 millones de llamadas en España en sólo un mes," *El Mundo*, October 28, 2013, http://www.elmundo.es/espana/2013/10/28/526dcbad61fd3d07678b456b.html.

12) Michael S. Schmidt, "N.S.A. Head Says European Data Was Collected by Allies," *New York Times*, October 30, 2013, http://www.nytimes.com/2013/10/30/

us/politics/u-s-intelligence-officials-defend-surveillance-operations-on-capitol-hill.html.

13) "NSA Spied 124.8 Billion Phone Calls in a Month," *Cryptome*, October 23, 2013, http://cryptome.org/2013/10/nsa-125b-calls.htm.

14) Joshua Goodman, "U.S. Spied on Presidents of Brazil and Mexico, Globo Reports," *Bloomberg*, September 2, 2013, http://www.bloomberg.com/news/2013-09-02/nsa-intercepted-calls-of-brazil-mexico-presidents-globo-says.html.

15) Jens Glüsing, Laura Poitras, Marcel Rosenbach and Holger Stark, "Fresh Leak on US Spying: NSA Accessed Mexican President's Email," *Der Spiegel*, October 20, 2013, http://www.spiegel.de/international/world/nsa-hacked-email-account-of-mexican-president-a-928817.html.

16) Ian Traynor, Philip Oltermann, and Paul Lewis, "Angela Merkel's call to Obama: are you bugging my mobile phone?," *Guardian*, October 23, 2013, http://www.theguardian.com/world/2013/oct/23/us-monitored-angela-merkel-german/print.

17) James Ball, "NSA monitored calls of 35 world leaders after US official handed over contacts," *Guardian*, October 24, 2013, http://www.theguardian.com/world/2013/oct/24/nsa-surveillance-world-leaders-calls/print.

18) *Information Technology and Cyber Operations: Modernization and Policy Issues to Support the Future Force*, Hearing Before the Subcommittee on Intelligence, Emerging Threats and Capabilities, March 13, 2013, http://www.fas.org/irp/congress/2013_hr/cyber.pdf, page 87.

19) "Inside the 2013 U.S. intelligence 'black budget'," *Washington Post*, August 29, 2013, http://apps.washingtonpost.com/g/page/national/inside-the-2013-us-intelligence-black-budget/420/.

20) Glenn Greenwald and Ewen MacAskill, "Boundless Informant: the NSA's secret tool to track global surveillance data," *Guardian*, June 11, 2013, http://www.theguardian.com/world/2013/jun/08/nsa-boundless-informant-global-data-mining.

21) Glenn Greenwald, Laura Poitras and Ewen MacAskill, "NSA shares raw intelligence including Americans' data with Israel," *Guardian*, September 11, 2013, http://www.theguardian.com/world/2013/sep/11/nsa-americans-personal-data-israel-documents/print.

22) "Snowden Documents Reveal NSA Gave Israeli Spies Raw Emails, Texts, Calls of Innocent Americans," *Democracy Now!*, September 12, 2013, http://www.democracynow.org/2013/9/12/snowden_documents_reveal_nsa_gave_israeli#

23) Ken Dilanian, "Overall U.S. intelligence budget tops $80 billion," *LA Times*, October 28, 2010, http://articles.latimes.com/2010/oct/28/nation/la-na-intel-budget-20101029.

24) Christopher Chantrill, "Public Spending in the United Kingdom," http://www.ukpublicspending.co.uk/uk_defence_spending_30.html#ukgs302.

25) "DNI Releases Fy 2011 Appropriated Budget Figure For The National Intelligence Program," ODNI News Release No. 29-11, October 28, 2011, http://www.dni.gov/press_releases/20111028_release_budget.pdf.

26) "DNI Releases Budget Figure for 2013 National Intelligence Program," Office of DNI, October 30, 2013, http://www.dni.gov/index.php/newsroom/press-releases/191-press-releases-2013/957-dni-releases-budget-figure-for-2013-national-intelligence-program.

27) Barton Gellman and Greg Miller, "U.S. spy network's successes, failures and objectives detailed in 'black budget' summary," *Washington Post*, August 29, 2013, http://www.washingtonpost.com/world/national-security/black-budget-summary-details-us-spy-networks-successes-failures-and-objectives/2013/08/29/7e57bb78-10ab-11e3-8cdd-bcdc09410972_print.html.

28) *Mike McConnell: An American Cyber Expert On Cyberwar*, Booz Allen, July 14, 2009, http://www.boozallen.com/media-center/press-highlights/48399871/42400037.

29) Joanna Rutkowska, *Trusting Hardware*, The Invisible Things Lab's blog, March 25, 2009, http://theinvisiblethings.blogspot.com/2009/03/trusting-hardware.html.

30) Francis M. David, Ellick M. Chan, Jeffrey C. Carlyle, and Roy H. Campbell, "Cloaker: Hardware Supported Rootkit Concealment," *Proceedings of the 2008 IEEE Symposium on Security and Privacy*, Pages 296-310, IEEE Computer Society.

31) *Cyberspace Policy Review: Assuring a Trusted and Resilient Information and Communications Infrastructure*, White House, May 29, 2009, http://www.whitehouse.gov/assets/documents/Cyberspace_Policy_Review_final.pdf.

32) Glenn Dereene and Joe Pappalardo, "Counterfeit Chips Raise Big Hacking, Terror Threats, Experts Say," *Popular Mechanics*, October 1, 2009, http://www.popularmechanics.com/technology/gadgets/news/4253628.

33) *House Intelligence Committee Launches Investigation into National Security Threats Posed by Chinese Telecom Companies Working in the U.S.*, Permanent Select Committee on Intelligence, November 17, 2011, http://intelligence.house.gov/sites/intelligence.house.gov/files/documents/111711ChineseTelecom.pdf.

34) Bruce Einhorn, "Huawei's 3Com Deal Flops," *BusinessWeek*, February 21, 2008, http://www.businessweek.com/blogs/eyeonasia/archives/2008/02/huaweis_3com_de.html.

35) Michael Smith, "Spy chiefs fear Chinese cyber attack," *Sunday Times*, March 29, 2009.

36) Geoffrey Barker and David Ramli, "China's Huawei banned from NBN," *Financial Review*, March 24, 2012, http://www.afr.com/p/technology/china_giant_banned_from_nbn_9U9zi1oc3FXBF3BZdRD9mJ.

37) H.R. 933, "An Act making appropriations for the Department of Defense, the Department of Veterans Affairs, and other departments and agencies for the fiscal year ending September 30, 2013, and for other purposes." March 20, 2013, http://docs.house.gov/billsthisweek/20130318/BILLS-113hr933eas.pdf.

38) Christopher Joye, Paul Smith and John Kerin, "Spy agencies ban Lenovo PCs on security concerns," *Australian Financial Review*, July 27, 2013, http://www.afr.com/p/technology/spy_agencies_ban_lenovo_pcs_on_security_HVgcKTHp-4bIA4uICPqC7SL.

39) Scott Shane and Tom Bowman, "No Such Agency Part Four, Rigging the Game," *Baltimore Sun*, December 4, 1995, http://cryptome.org/jya/nsa-sun.htm.

40) Douglas Waller, "Onward Cyber Soldiers," *Time*, August 21, 1995, http://www.time.com/time/magazine/article/0,9171,983318,00.html.

41) "The All New 2010 Intel® Core™ vPro™ Processor Family: Intelligence that Adapts to Your Needs," Intel Corporation, http://www.intel.com/content/dam/www/public/us/en/documents/white-papers/remote-support-vpro-intelligence-that-adapts-to-your-needs-paper.pdf, see pages 9-10.

42) Chris Irvine and Tom Parfitt, "Kremlin returns to typewriters to avoid computer leaks," *Telegraph*, July 11, 2013, http://www.telegraph.co.uk/news/worldnews/europe/russia/10173645/Kremlin-returns-to-typewriters-to-avoid-computer-leaks.html.

43) Marcel Rosenbach, Laura Poitras and Holger Stark, "iSpy: How the NSA Accesses Smartphone Data," *Der Spiegel*, September 9, 2013, http://www.spiegel.de/international/world/how-the-nsa-spies-on-smartphones-including-the-blackberry-a-921161.html.

44) Douglas Waller, "Onward Cyber Soldiers," *Time*, August 21, 1995, http://www.time.com/time/magazine/article/0,9171,983318,00.html.

45) Michael Hirsh, "How America's Top Tech Companies Created the Surveillance State," *National Journal*, July 25, 2013, http://www.nationaljournal.com/magazine/how-america-s-top-tech-companies-created-the-surveillance-state-20130725.

46) Bruce Schneier, "Back Doors, Export, and the NSA," *CRYPTO-GRAM*, February 15, 1999.

47) Ellen Messmer, "Charge it to the NSA," *NetworkWorld*, July 20, 1998, http://www.networkworld.com/news/0720nsa1.html.

48) Nicole Perlroth, Jeff Larson And Scott Shane, "N.S.A. Able to Foil Basic Safeguards of Privacy on Web," *New York Times*, September 5, 2013, http://www.nytimes.com/2013/09/06/us/nsa-foils-much-internet-encryption.html.

49) Computer Network Operations, SIGINT Enabling, Project Description, http://cryptome.org/2013/09/nsa-sigint-enabling-propublica-13-0905.pdf.

50) James Ball, Julian Borger and Glenn Greenwald, "Revealed: how US and UK spy agencies defeat internet privacy and security," *Guardian*, September 5, 2013, http://www.theguardian.com/world/2013/sep/05/nsa-gchq-encryption-codes-security/print.

51) Nicole Perlroth, Jeff Larson And Scott Shane, "N.S.A. Able to Foil Basic Safeguards of Privacy on Web," *New York Times*, September 5, 2013, http://www.nytimes.com/2013/09/06/us/nsa-foils-much-internet-encryption.html.

52) Declan McCullagh, "Feds put heat on Web firms for master encryption keys," *CNET*, July 24, 2013, http://news.cnet.com/8301-13578_3-57595202-38/feds-put-heat-on-web-firms-for-master-encryption-keys/.

53) Nicole Perlroth, Jeff Larson And Scott Shane, "N.S.A. Able to Foil Basic Safeguards of Privacy on Web," *New York Times*, September 5, 2013, http://www.nytimes.com/2013/09/06/us/nsa-foils-much-internet-encryption.html.

54) Jason Vest and Wayne Madsen, "A Most Unusual Collection Agency," *Village Voice*, February 24-March 2, 1999.

55) "CIA/NSA Special Collection Service," *Cryptome*, October 28, 2013, http://cryptome.org/2013/10/cia-nsa-scs.htm.

56) Robert Beckhusen and Noah Shachtman, "See for Yourself: The Pentagon's $51 Billion 'Black' Budget," *Wired*, February 15, 2012, http://www.wired.com/dangerroom/2012/02/pentagons-black-budget/.

57) "DNI Releases FY 2012 Appropriated Budget Figure For The National Intelligence Program," ODNI News Release No. 13-12, October 30, 2012, http://www.dni.gov/index.php/newsroom/press-releases/96-press-releases-2012/756-dni-releases-fy-2012-appropriated-budget-figure?tmpl=component&format=pdf.

58) James Lewis, "Five myths about Chinese hackers," *Washington Post*, March 22, 2013, http://www.washingtonpost.com/opinions/five-myths-about-chinese-hackers/2013/03/22/4aa07a7e-7f95-11e2-8074-b26a871b165a_story.html.

59) Barton Gellman and Ellen Nakashima, "U.S. spy agencies mounted 231 offensive cyber-operations in 2011, documents show," *Washington Post*, August 30, 2013, http://articles.washingtonpost.com/2013-08-30/world/41620705_1_computer-worm-former-u-s-officials-obama-administration.

60) Jacob Davidson, "China Accuses U.S. of Hypocrisy on Cyberattacks," *Time*, July 1, 2013, http://world.time.com/2013/07/01/china-accuses-u-s-of-hypocrisy-on-cyberattacks/print/.

61) "The Company and The Country: A Conversation with Philip Agee, Part I" *Alternative View TV*, December 1995, https://www.youtube.com/watch?v=nvZQa0hkfgw.

62) James Woolsey, News Briefing, March 7, 2000, http://cryptome.org/echelon-cia.htm.

63) "Spying documents reveal U.S. agency spied Dilma," *Globo*, September 1, 2013, http://cryptome.org/2013/09/nsa-spying-brazil.htm.

64) Lana Lam, "Edward Snowden: US government has been hacking Hong Kong and China for years," *South China Morning Post*, June 13, 2013, http://www.scmp.com/news/hong-kong/article/1259508/edward-snowden-us-government-has-been-hacking-hong-kong-and-china.

65) "Spying documents reveal U.S. agency spied Dilma," *Globo*, September 1, 2013, http://cryptome.org/2013/09/nsa-spying-brazil.htm.

66) Ibid..

67) Jens Glüsing, Laura Poitras, Marcel Rosenbach and Holger Stark, "Fresh Leak on US Spying: NSA Accessed Mexican President's Email," *Der Spiegel*, October 20, 2013, http://www.spiegel.de/international/world/nsa-hacked-email-account-of-mexican-president-a-928817.html.

68) Glenn Greenwald, Roberto Kaz e José Casado, "Espionagem dos EUA se espalhou pela América Latina," *O Globo*, July 9, 2013, http://oglobo.globo.com/mundo/espionagem-dos-eua-se-espalhou-pela-america-latina-8966619.

69) "NSA Documents Show United States Spied Brazilian Oil Giant," *Globo*, September 9, 2013, http://g1.globo.com/fantastico/noticia/2013/09/nsa-documents-show-united-states-spied-brazilian-oil-giant.html.

70) "'Follow the Money': NSA Spies on International Payments," *Der Spiegel*, September 15, 2013, http://www.spiegel.de/international/world/spiegel-exclusive-nsa-spies-on-international-bank-transactions-a-922276.html.

71) Juan Forero, "Paper reveals NSA ops in Latin America," *Washington Post*, July 9, 2013, http://www.washingtonpost.com/world/the_americas/paper-reveals-nsa-ops-in-latin-america/2013/07/09/eff0cc7e-e8e3-11e2-818e-aa29e-855f3ab_print.html.

72) James Clapper, *Statement by Director of National Intelligence James R. Clapper on Allegations of Economic Espionage,* September 8, 2013, Office of the Director of National Intelligence, http://www.dni.gov/index.php/newsroom/press-releases/191-press-releases-2013/926-statement-by-director-of-national-intelligence-james-r-clapper-on-allegations-of-economic-espionage.

73) Ellen Nakashima, "U.S. said to be target of massive cyber-espionage campaign," *Washington Post*, February 10, 2013, http://www.washingtonpost.com/world/national-security/us-said-to-be-target-of-massive-cyber-espionage-campaign/2013/02/10/7b4687d8-6fc1-11e2-aa58-243de81040ba_print.html.

74) Richard A. Clark and Robert K. Knake, *Cyber War: The Next Threat to National Security and What to Do About It*, Ecco, 2010, page 230.

75) Christopher Drew and John Markoff, "Cyberwar Contractors Vie for Plum Work, Hacking for U.S.," *New York Times*, May 31, 2009, http://www.nytimes.com/2009/05/31/us/31cyber.html?pagewanted=all.

76) Michael S. Schmidt, "N.S.A. Head Says European Data Was Collected by Allies," *New York Times*, October 30, 2013, http://www.nytimes.com/2013/10/30/us/politics/u-s-intelligence-officials-defend-surveillance-operations-on-capitol-hill.html.

77) Kevin Gosztola, "The Banal Justification for Directing the US Surveillance State at World Leaders," *Fire Dog Lake*, October 25, 2013, http://dissenter.firedoglake.com/2013/10/25/the-banal-justification-for-directing-the-us-surveillance-state-at-world-leaders/.

78) "Biden calls Brazil's Rousseff over NSA spying tensions," *Reuters*, July 19, 2013, http://www.reuters.com/article/2013/07/20/us-usa-security-snowden-brazil-idUSBRE96J00Q20130720.

79) "Spilling the NSA's Secrets: *Guardian* Editor Alan Rusbridger on the Inside Story of Snowden Leaks," *Democracy Now!* September 23, 2013, http://www.democracynow.org/2013/9/23/spilling_the_nsas_secrets_guardian_editor#.

80) Remarks by Hillary Rodham Clinton, Secretary of State, Conference on Internet Freedom, Fokker Terminal, The Hague, Netherlands, December 8, 2011, http://www.state.gov/secretary/rm/2011/12/178511.htm.

81) Mark Twain, Ends of the Earth Club Dictation, http://cryptome.org/2013/10/mark-twain-takes-it.pdf.

82) John Pilger, "In an Age of 'Realists' and Vigilantes," *Counterpunch*, September 19, 2013, http://www.counterpunch.org/2013/09/19/in-an-age-of-realists-and-vigilantes/.

83) Barack Obama, "Text of Obama's Speech at the U.N.," *New York Times*, September 24, 2013, http://www.nytimes.com/2013/09/25/us/politics/text-of-obamas-speech-at-the-un.html.

84) Edward Cody, "Chinese Official Accuses Nations of Hacking," *Washington Post*, September 13, 2007, http://www.washingtonpost.com/wp-dyn/content/article/2007/09/12/AR2007091200791.html.

85) "U.S. Calls Out China and Russia for Cyber Espionage Costing Billions," *Fox-News.com*, November 3, 2011, http://www.foxnews.com/politics/2011/11/03/us-calls-out-china-and-russia-for-cyber-espionage-costing-billions/.

86) Barton Gellman and Ellen Nakashima, "U.S. spy agencies mounted 231 offensive cyber-operations in 2011, documents show," *Washington Post*, August 30, 2013, http://www.washingtonpost.com/world/national-security/us-spy-agencies-mounted-231-offensive-cyber-operations-in-2011-documents-show/2013/08/30/d090a6ae-119e-11e3-b4cb-fd7ce041d814_print.html.

87) Lana Lam, "Edward Snowden: US government has been hacking Hong Kong and China for years," *South China Morning Post*, June 13, 2013, http://www.scmp.com/news/hong-kong/article/1259508/edward-snowden-us-government-has-been-hacking-hong-kong-and-china.

88) Glenn Greenwald, "The premises and purposes of American exceptionalism," *Guardian*, February 18, 2013, http://www.guardian.co.uk/commentisfree/2013/feb/18/american-exceptionalism-north-korea-nukes/print.

89) Mark Mazzetti, "Dispute Over France a Factor in Intelligence Rift," *New York Times*, May 21, 2010, http://www.nytimes.com/2010/05/22/us/politics/22intel.html.

90) WikiLeaks: The Spy Files, http://wikileaks.org/the-spyfiles.html.

91) "The Surveillance Catalog," The *Wall Street Journal*, November 19, 2011, http://projects.wsj.com/surveillance-catalog/.

92) Vernon Silver, "Post-Revolt Tunisia Can Alter E-Mail With `Big Brother' Software," *Bloomberg*, December 12, 2011, http://www.bloomberg.com/news/2011-12-12/tunisia-after-revolt-can-alter-e-mails-with-big-brother-software.html.

93) 2013 Intelligence Support Systems World Program, http://www.issworldtraining.com/ISS_MEA/sponsors2.html.

94) WikiLeaks, *The Spy Files*, Glimmerglass CyberSweep, December 1, 2011, http://www.wikileaks.org/spyfiles/docs/glimmerglass/55_glimmerglass-cyber-sweep.html.

95) Sergey Golovanov, "Adobe Flash Player 0-day and HackingTeam's Remote Control System," *SecureList*, February 12, 2013, http://www.securelist.com/en/blog/208194112/Adobe_Flash_Player_0_day_and_HackingTeam_s_Remote_C.

96) Mikko Hypponen, "Egypt, FinFisher Intrusion Tools and Ethics," *News from the Lab*, March 8, 2011, https://www.f-secure.com/weblog/archives/00002114.html.

97) Paul Sonne and Margaret Coker, "Spy-Gear Business to Be Sold," *Wall Street Journal*, March 9, 2012, http://online.wsj.com/article/SB10001424052970203961204577269391401776590.html.

98) Paul Sonne and Margaret Coker, "Firms Aided Libyan Spies," *Wall Street Journal*, August 30, 2011, http://online.wsj.com/article/SB1000142405311190419940457653872126016 6388.html.

99) Steve Stecklow, "Special Report: Chinese firm helps Iran spy on citizens," *Reuters*, March 22, 2012, http://www.reuters.com/assets/print?aid=US-BRE82L0B820120322.

100) Sarah Lai Stirland, "Cisco Leak: 'Great Firewall' of China Was a Chance to Sell More Routers," *Wired*, May 20, 2008, http://www.wired.com/threatlevel/2008/05/leaked-cisco-do/.

101) Mark McDonald, "Taking It to the Street in China," *New York Times*, July 29, 2012, http://rendezvous.blogs.nytimes.com/2012/07/29/taking-it-to-the-street-in-china/?pagewanted=print.

102) Jonathan Ansfield And Ian Johnson, "Ousted Chinese Leader Is Said to Have Spied on Other Top Officials," *New York Times*, April 25, 2012, http://www.nytimes.com/2012/04/26/world/asia/bo-xilai-said-to-have-spied-on-top-china-officials.html.

103) Amy Davidson, "Questions About the Petraeus Resignation," *New Yorker*, November 9, 2012, http://www.newyorker.com/online/blogs/closeread/2012/11/questions-about-the-petraeus-resignation.html.

104) Morgan Marquis-Boire, "From Bahrain with Love: FinFisher's Spy Kit Exposed?" The Citizen Lab, Munk School of Global Affairs, Research Brief Number 09, July 2012, https://citizenlab.org/wp-content/uploads/2012/08/09-2012-from-bahrainwithlove.pdf.

105) Morgan Marquis-Boire, Bill Marczak and Claudio Guarnieri, "The Smart-Phone Who Loved Me: FinFisher Goes Mobile?," The Citizen Lab, Munk School of Global Affairs, Research Brief Number 11, August 2012, https://citizenlab.org/wp-content/uploads/2012/08/11-2012-thesmartphonewholovedme.pdf.

106) Nicole Perloth, "Researchers Find 25 Countries Using Surveillance Software," *New York Times*, March 13, 2013, http://bits.blogs.nytimes.com/2013/03/13/researchers-find-25-countries-using-surveillance-software/.

107) Morgan Marquis-Boire, Bill Marczak, Claudio Guarnieri, and John Scott-Railton, "For Their Eyes Only: The Commercialization of Digital Spying," University of Toronto Citizen's Lab, May 1, 2013, https://citizenlab.org/storage/finfisher/final/fortheireyesonly.pdf.

108) Alex Fowler, "Protecting our brand from a global spyware provider," *The Mozilla Blog*, April 30, 2013, http://blog.mozilla.org/blog/2013/04/30/protecting-our-brand-from-a-global-spyware-provider/.

109) Nicole Perloth, "Ahead of Spyware Conference, More Evidence of Abuse," *New York Times*, October 10, 2012, http://bits.blogs.nytimes.com/2012/10/10/ahead-of-spyware-conference-more-evidence-of-abuse/.

110) David Sanger and Nicole Perlroth, "After Profits, Defense Contractor Faces the Pitfalls of Cybersecurity," *New York Times*, June 15, 2013, http://www.nytimes.com/2013/06/16/us/after-profits-defense-contractor-faces-the-pitfalls-of-cybersecurity.html.

111) David Sirota, "How cash secretly rules surveillance policy," *Salon*, June 18, 2013, http://www.salon.com/2013/06/18/how_cash_secretly_rules_surveillance_policy/.

112) Bill Blunden, *The Rootkit Arsenal*, Second Edition, Jones & Bartlett Learning, 2012, ISBN-10: 144962636X.

113) Jordan Robertson, "Google attack highlights 'zero-day' black market," *Associated Press*, January 29, 2010, http://www.newsmax.com/SciTech/US-TEC-China-Google/2010/01/28/id/348348.

114) "The digital arms trade,The market for software that helps hackers penetrate computer systems," *The Economist*, March 30th 2013, http://www.economist.com/news/business/21574478-market-software-helps-hackers-penetrate-computer-systems-digital-arms-trade.

115) Barton Gellman and Ellen Nakashima, "U.S. spy agencies mounted 231 offensive cyber-operations in 2011, documents show," *Washington Post*, August 30, 2013, http://www.washingtonpost.com/world/national-security/us-spy-agencies-mounted-231-offensive-cyber-operations-in-2011-documents-show/2013/08/30/d090a6ae-119e-11e3-b4cb-fd7ce041d814_print.html.

116) Andy Greenberg, "Shopping For Zero-Days: A Price List For Hackers' Secret Software Exploits," *Forbes*, March 23, 2012, http://www.forbes.com/sites/andygreenberg/2012/03/23/shopping-for-zero-days-an-price-list-for-hackers-secret-software-exploits/print/.

117) Nicole Perlroth and David Sanger, "Nations Buying as Hackers Sell Flaws in Computer Code," *New York Times*, July 13, 2013, http://www.nytimes.com/2013/07/14/world/europe/nations-buying-as-hackers-sell-computer-flaws.html.

118) Nicole Perlroth and David Sanger,"Nations Buying as Hackers Sell Flaws in Computer Code," *New York Times*, July 13, 2013, http://www.nytimes.com/2013/07/14/world/europe/nations-buying-as-hackers-sell-computer-flaws.html.

119) "The digital arms trade,The market for software that helps hackers penetrate computer systems," *The Economist*, March 30th 2013, http://www.economist.com/news/business/21574478-market-software-helps-hackers-penetrate-computer-systems-digital-arms-trade.

120) Michael Riley and Ashlee Vance,"Cyber Weapons: The New Arms Race," *BusinessWeek*, July 20, 2011, http://www.businessweek.com/magazine/cyber-weapons-the-new-arms-race-07212011.html.

121) James Bamford, "The Secret War," *Wired*, June 12, 2013, http://www.wired.com/threatlevel/2013/06/general-keith-alexander-cyberwar/all/.

122) Christopher Drew and John Markoff, "Cyberwar Contractors Vie for Plum Work, Hacking for U.S.," *New York Times*, May 31, 2009, http://www.nytimes.com/2009/05/31/us/31cyber.html?pagewanted=all.

123) Jennifer Valentino-Devries And Danny Yadron, "FBI Taps Hacker Tactics to Spy on Suspects," *Wall Street Journal*, August 1, 2013.

124) Kevin Poulsen, "Documents: FBI Spyware Has Been Snaring Extortionists, Hackers for Years," *Wired*, April 16, 2009, http://www.wired.com/threatlevel/2009/04/fbi-spyware-pro/.

125) Jennifer Valentino-Devries And Danny Yadron, "FBI Taps Hacker Tactics to Spy on Suspects," *Wall Street Journal*, August 1, 2013.

126) Thom Shanker, "U.S. Arms Sales Make Up Most of Global Market," *New York Times*, August 26, 2012, http://www.nytimes.com/2012/08/27/world/middlee-ast/us-foreign-arms-sales-reach-66-3-billion-in-2011.html?pagewanted=print.

127) Nicole Perlroth and David Sanger, "Nations Buying as Hackers Sell Flaws in Computer Code," *New York Times*, July 13, 2013, http://www.nytimes.com/2013/07/14/world/europe/nations-buying-as-hackers-sell-computer-flaws.html.

128) FOI request, Vupen Contracts with NSA, Filed September 11, 2013, Muck-Rock, https://www.muckrock.com/foi/united-states-of-america-10/vupen-con-tracts-with-nsa-6593/#787524-cover-letter.

129) Andy Greenberg, "Meet The Hackers Who Sell Spies The Tools To Crack Your PC (And Get Paid Six-Figure Fees)," *Forbes*, march 21, 2012, http://www.forbes.com/sites/andygreenberg/2012/03/21/meet-the-hackers-who-sell-spies-the-tools-to-crack-your-pc-and-get-paid-six-figure-fees/.

130) http://www.labs.appinonline.com/.

131) HD Moore, *Metasploit and Money*, Black Hat DC 2010, http://www.black-hat.com/presentations/bh-dc-10/Moore_HD/BlackHat-DC-2010-Moore-Metasploit-and-Money-wp.pdf.

132) Moxie Marlinspike, *Changing Threats To Privacy*, SOURCE Boston 2010, http://www.sourceconference.com/publications/bos10pubs/Moxie.pdf.

133) Eamon Javers, *Secrets and Lies: The Rise of Corporate Espionage in a Global Economy*, Georgetown Journal of International Affairs, Winter/Spring 2011, http://journal.georgetown.edu/wp-content/uploads/53-60-FORUM-Javers.pdf.

134) Dan Nystedt, "WikiLeaks plans to make the web a leakier place," *Computerworld*, October 9, 2009, http://www.computerworld.com/s/article/9139180/Wikileaks_plans_to_make_the_Web_a_leakier_place.

135) *The WikiLeaks Threat*, An Overview by Palantir Technologies, HBGary Federal, and Berico Technologies, http://wikileaks.org/IMG/pdf/WikiLeaks_Response_v6.pdf.

136) Glenn Greenwald, "The leaked campaign to attack WikiLeaks and its supporters," *Salon*, February 11, 2011.

137) Josh Glasstetter, "Few Consequences When Cybersecurity Contractors Go Bad," *TechPresident*, June 27, 2013, http://techpresident.com/news/24101/back-channel-few-consequences-when-cybersecurity-contractors-go-bad.

138) U.S. Congress, Appropriations to the Budget of the United States of America, 1872, section 7, United States Department of Justice, http://www.salon.com/2011/02/11/campaigns_4/.

139) Max Lowenthal, *The Federal Bureau of Investigation*, William Sloan Assoc., 1950.

140) Peter Dale Scott, *Drugs, Oil, and War: The United States in Afghanistan, Colombia, and Indochina*, Rowman & Littlefield Publishers, 2003.

141) http://www.totalintel.com/index.php.

142) Dana Hedgpeth, "Blackwater's Owner Has Spies for Hire," *Washington Post*, November 3, 2007, http://www.washingtonpost.com/wp-dyn/content/article/2007/11/02/AR2007110202165.html.

143) Jeremy Scahill, "Blackwater's Private Spies," *The Nation*, June 5, 2008, http://www.thenation.com/article/blackwaters-private-spies.

144) Jeff Stein, "Blackwater subsidiary's corporate work appears to fade," *Washington Post*, September 17, 2010, http://voices.washingtonpost.com/spy-talk/2010/09/blackwater_subsidiarys_corporate_work_fades.html.

145) Rob Evans and Paul Lewis, "Revealed: how energy firms spy on environmental activists," *Guardian*, February 14, 2011, http://www.guardian.co.uk/environment/2011/feb/14/energy-firms-activists-intelligence-gathering/print.

146) Top Secret America, *Washington Post*, http://projects.washingtonpost.com/top-secret-america/articles/functions/.

147) *Tracking GhostNet: Investigating a Cyber Espionage Network*, Information Warfare Monitor, March 29, 2009, http://www.scribd.com/doc/13731776/Tracking-GhostNet-Investigating-a-Cyber-Espionage-Network.

148) "The rise and rise of the Russian mafia," *BBC News*, November 21, 1998, http://news.bbc.co.uk/2/hi/special_report/1998/03/98/russian_mafia/70095.stm.

149) "NSA Scandal: 'The Agency is Out of Control,'" *DW*, July 3, 2013, http://www.dw.de/the-agency-is-out-of-control/a-16926086.

150) James Ball, "NSA stores metadata of millions of web users for up to a year, secret files show," *Guardian*, September 30, 2013, http://www.theguardian.com/world/2013/sep/30/nsa-americans-metadata-year-documents/print.

151) Glenn Greenwald, "The NSA's mass and indiscriminate spying on Brazilians," *Guardian*, July 6, 2013, http://www.guardian.co.uk/commentisfree/2013/jul/07/nsa-brazilians-globo-spying/print.

152) Craig Timberg and Ellen Nakashima, "Agreements with private companies protect U.S. access to cables' data for surveillance," *Washington Post*, July 6, 2013, http://www.washingtonpost.com/business/technology/agreements-with-private-companies-protect-us-access-to-cables-data-for-surveillance/2013/07/06/aa5d017a-df77-11e2-b2d4-ea6d8f477a01_print.html.

153) Siobhan Gorman And Jennifer Valentino-Devries, "New Details Show Broader NSA Surveillance Reach," *Wall Street Journal*, August 20, 2013.

154) Glenn Greenwald, "The NSA's mass and indiscriminate spying on Brazilians," *Guardian*, July 6, 2013, http://www.guardian.co.uk/commentisfree/2013/jul/07/nsa-brazilians-globo-spying/print.

Chapter 7

The Infrastructure

If you think about what's possible, you spend too much time on low-probability events.

–Jon Callas[1]

As discussed earlier, the infrastructure is the topic of choice among doomsayers. For example, in 1997 a journalist by the name of John Carlin wrote a piece in *Wired* where he quoted the director of Darpa's Information Technology Office about the spate of power outages on the West Coast:

> Each time I hear about one of these things, I say to myself, "OK, it's started!" And when I find out it really didn't, I just think we've bought some additional time. But it will start.[2]

In a cover letter to the Clinton-era strategy document, then National Security Coordinator Richard Clarke repeated similar mantras:

> Attacks upon our cyberspace could crash electrical power grids, telephone networks, transportation systems, and financial institutions.[3]

Again, in April of 2012 the Chairman of the Joint Chiefs of Staff, General Martin Dempsey, stood up in front of the Kennedy School of Government at Harvard University and solemnly announced:

> A cyber attack could stop our society in its tracks.[4]

Such is the effect of dramatic predictions. Anxiety is a powerful tool because worried people can be encouraged to accept all kinds of solutions without critically scrutinizing their effectiveness or cost. But while the apocalypse appears at the edge of the event horizon and lurks as a constant threat, history tells a markedly different story of the threats we face and the degree of risk that they represent.

In this chapter we're going to look at high profile cyber incidents which have involved infrastructure components, with an initial emphasis on the United States. Given the nature of these events, we could have simply relegated them to Chapters 4 and 5. Instead we decided to group them into their own chapter because they're a great lead-in to the concept of threat inflation.

What we'll see is that there really haven't been any earthshaking infrastructure attacks. In fact, more often than not, the outcomes have been drastically overstated and misdiagnosed, in some instances farcically.

For example, On August 14 of 2013, the *New York Times* web site went offline. *Fox Business* published a story which claimed that the incident was the result of a cyber-attack.[5] The *New York Times* apologized to readers later that day, explaining that the lapse in service was merely the result of a scheduled maintenance update on the company's servers.[6] In response to the outage, the satire mavens at the *Onion* posted the following message on Twitter:

> BREAKING: @nytimes Receives Pulitzer For Coverage Of "Http/1.1 Service Unavailable" Story 9:40 AM – 14 Aug 2013

The Financial System

You may recall Mike McConnell's opinion that there are ominous threats to our financial system. The gist of his argument goes something like this:

Our money supply is backed by "the full faith and credit" of the United States government. It's been this way since 1971 when Nixon withdrew the United States from the Bretton Woods system and got us off the gold standard. Consequently, most people's financial assets and debts are nothing more than bytes stored in high-end mainframes. If an attacker were somehow able to challenge the underlying trust that people have in the financial markets, or the banking system, by subverting the integrity of these bytes, people would lose faith and the global economy would face trouble.

For example, in June of 2010 at a debate sponsored by Intelligence Squared, former DNI Mike McConnell stated:

The United States economy is $14 trillion a year. Two banks in New York City move $7 trillion a day. On a good day, they do eight trillion. Now think about that. Our economy is $14 trillion. Two banks are moving $7 trillion to $8 trillion a day. There is no gold; they're not even printed dollar bills. All of those transactions, all those transactions are massive reconciliation and accounting. If those who wish us ill, if someone with a different world view was successful in attacking that information and destroying the data, it could have a devastating impact, not only on the nation, but the globe.

So, how does this scenario stack up against what's been observed?

The Stock Exchanges
In late 2010 the company that runs the NASDAQ stock exchange, NASDAQ OMX Group, discovered "suspicious files" on servers that run a web-based application called *Directors Desk*, a platform designed to allow NASDAQ clients to share non-public information. Initially the incident was handled by the Secret Service. Later on the FBI took over as the lead investigative agency, and eventually the NSA also became involved.[7]

NASDAQ claims the exchange's trading platforms were not breached[8] and that no data was compromised by the intrusion.[9] According to an unnamed person involved with the investigation, "So far, [the perpetrators] appear to have just been looking around."[10]

Specifics about the attackers are nonexistent. Spokeswomen from the NSA and FBI both declined to comment. One thing that did come to light as a result of the inquiry was sub-standard security. According to a story broken by Reuters:

> Investigators were surprised to find some computers with out-of-date software, misconfigured firewalls and uninstalled security patches that could have fixed known "bugs" that hackers could exploit. Versions of Microsoft Corp's Windows 2003 Server operating system, for example, had not been properly updated.[11]

Unpatched servers and misconfigured firewalls: from a company that spends close to $1 billion annually on security?[12] Hello?

Web servers seem to be a popular attack vector because they're publicly accessible. In 1999 NASDAQ's website was defaced by vandals, with little or no effect on trading systems.[13] This is not something that's limited to the United States either. On August 5, 2011, the Zimbabwe Stock Exchange was forced to shut down its website after it was breached by intruders. Note that this did not hamper trading systems.[14] On August 10, 2011, the news web site maintained by Hong Kong Exchanges & Clearing Ltd. was attacked. Again, the impact on trading was strictly limited. The company suspended afternoon trading for seven companies that had published price-sensitive news releases during the exchange's lunch break.[15]

All told, earth-shaking incidents are nowhere to be found. The cyber-attacks that took place made the headlines because they targeted highly visible public-facing web servers. Nevertheless, relatively speaking these were peripheral computers, not meat-and-potatoes trading systems.

This doesn't mean that the core systems that run exchanges haven't gone down. It's just that in the past when they've gone offline it's not been the result of cyber-attacks. For example, in late August of 2013 the NASDAQ exchange went down for three hours as a result of an unspecified issue with the data feed from which stock prices are derived. One unnamed chief executive provided the following comment:

> We didn't lose any money on the shutdown, but we also made
> very little money today ... [16]

The Federal Reserve

If there's one segment of the financial infrastructure that invests in contingency planning and disaster recovery it's our central bank: the U.S. Federal Reserve. For example, on April 8, 1991, the Minneapolis Federal Reserve got a chance to put its disaster recovery plan to the test. In the wee hours of the morning a water pipe burst, flooding the building in the vicinity of its mainframe.

Within minutes, in a move which has no known historical rival, disaster recovery procedures were initiated. By 3:00 A.M. employees re-grouped, suitcases in hand, for deployment via charter flight to the backup site in Virginia. By noon electronic wire transfer service was restored, ten hours ahead of the disaster plan.[17]

These are obviously folks who plan ahead. Hot backups, redundant network links, and split operational models (where workloads can be absorbed by distinct production systems in the event of failure) are par for the course. History seems to reflect this emphasis on security and availability as there have been very few recorded penetrations.

In October of 2010, a 32-year-old Malaysian national named Lin Mun Poo was taken into custody by Secret Service Agents as he arrived at JFK International Airport in New York. Among other crimes, he was charged with breaching a network of ten computers run by the Cleveland Federal Reserve. Prosecutors claimed the attack did thousands of dollars of damage. According to a report by NBC News:

> June Gates, a spokeswoman for the Federal Reserve in Cleveland, said the penetration was restricted to a network of "test" computers used for checking out new software and applications and did not contain sensitive Federal Reserve data about banks in the region. She declined, however, to respond to questions about whether Federal Reserve officials were aware of the hacking attack when it occurred in June – or only learned about it last month after Secret Service agents seized Poo's computer.[18]

Again, this is more of a fizzle than a bang. The attacker merely succeeded in accessing a set of disposable test computers. No data loss here. No fear and loathing. Not to mention that the intrusion was obviously mitigated before anything serious happened.

Serious Threats

Ostensibly credible authorities on National Security matters have publicly and vocally warned that our economy will nosedive if hackers undermine our financial infrastructure. That's a mighty big *if*, given that most of the hacking incidents involving the stock exchanges or the Federal Reserve have generated little if any long-term economic disruption.

In fact, viewing these incidents from the vantage point of the 2008 mortgage crisis, which led the Federal Reserve to commit around $7.7 trillion[19] to rescue our financial system (more than half of our entire annual GDP), it's probably more accurate to conclude that a handful of prominent U.S. banking interests represent far greater systemic risk to our financial system than any outside agents have.[20] Federal investigators admit as much:

> We do place special responsibility with the public leaders charged with protecting our financial system, those entrusted to run our regulatory agencies, and the chief executives of companies whose failures drove us to crisis.[21]

Yet Secretary of Defense Leon Panetta would direct your attention to cyber-attacks:

> The reality is that there is the cyber capability to basically bring down our power grid to create ... to paralyze our financial system in this country to virtually paralyze our country.[22]

George Smith, senior fellow at GlobalSecurity.org, provides a response to Panetta's proclamations:

> Nobody in the great mass that is not the 1 percent or in the service of the same cares about attacks on the American financial system. They do, on the other hand, wish our financial system would stop attacking them.[23]

With regard to existential threats, which endanger society as a whole, the United States faces far greater peril from financial crises driven by the greed and venality of the bankers.

The Power Grid

After the banks, the power grid is another popular target for hypothetical attacks. In April of 2008, the *Wall Street Journal* published an article where an anonymous intelligence official claimed that other nations have navigated their way through our grid, leaving malicious software which could be activated in the event of hostilities.[24] The unnamed official claimed:

If we go to war with them, they will try to turn them on.

To give you an idea just how weak the evidence is behind this threat, in early 2012 the Government Accountability Office (GAO) published a report entitled *CYBERSECURITY: Challenges in Securing the Modernized Electricity Grid.*[25] The report, which is 19 pages in length, strikes a very grim tone. Or, at least, it attempts to. There's only one problem, which George Smith points out:

> When it gets to delivering examples of blackouts caused by cyberattack it has none.
>
> Since the report can offer no examples it cites a couple instances of malware at energy facilities, not particularly remarkable news.
>
> The first is Stuxnet, which was used to attack Iran's uranium-enrichment program and which is thought to be a joint creation of U.S. and Israeli intelligence. Stuxnet did not turn off the power in Iran. And most reasonable minds have now concluded that Iran has purged Stuxnet from the targeted systems.
>
> Another example offered by GAO is the Slammer worm, a widespread malware infection that was also found disabling a "safety monitoring system" at Davis-Besse, an idled nuclear power plant in 2003.[26]

That's right: the GAO is at such a loss for actual examples that it has to borrow incidents from another domain that don't really even qualify.

It's as if people believe that somewhere in a cramped, windowless, government office there's a big red switch that shuts everything off. Nothing could be further from the truth. Our national power grid is a labyrinth of local subsystems. Roughly 1,600 providers in the United States generate bulk electricity at, or higher than, the 100 kilovolt level.[27] How difficult would it be to put all of these providers out of business in one fell swoop?

We've already seen a number of examples where people conclude that the threat of foreign governments disabling our grid is severe.[28] *Wired* columnist Michael Tanji, responds to these concerns with a question:

If it's so easy to turn off the lights using your laptop, how come it doesn't happen more often?[29]

Likewise, a power grid study from MIT remarks:

Despite alarmist rhetoric, there is no crisis here.[30]

Actual documented incidents of hackers disabling power en masse are pretty rare, and the stories that get reported often turn out to be based on bad information.

For instance, in November of 2009, the television news show *60 Minutes* broadcast a story entitled "Cyber War: Sabotaging the System." In this episode, *60 Minutes* reported that "prominent" unnamed members of the intelligence community blamed cyber-attacks for a power outage in Brazil that occurred in 2007. The power outage in question, which took place in the state of Espirito Santo on September 26, lasted for two days and impacted over 3 million people.

Yet, according to Furnas Centrais Elétricas, the region's utility company, the outage was the result of high-voltage insulators on a 345-kilovolt line being covered with soot as nearby farmers burned their fields. This conclusion was later confirmed by the Brazilian independent systems operator group.[31]

On November 10, 2009, just two days after the *60 Minutes* story aired, there was yet another blackout in Brazil. This time, it affected 18 out of 26 states, leaving broad segments of the nation's population without power for several hours.

According to a diplomatic cable published by WikiLeaks, officials from Brazil's Operator of the National Electricity System (ONS) doubt that it was the work of hackers and then go on to explain their conclusion:

> Oliveira and Geraldes further ruled out the possibility of hackers because, following some acknowledged interferences in past years, GOB has closed the system to only a small group of authorized operators, separated the transmission control system from other systems, and installed filters. Coimbra confirmed that the ONS system is a CLAN network using its own wires carried above the electricity wires. Oliveira pointed out

that even if someone had managed to gain access to the system, a voice command is required to disrupt transmission.

Coimbra said that while sabotage could have caused the outages, this type of disruption would have been deadly, and investigators would have found physical evidence, including the body of the perpetrator. He also noted that any internal attempts by system employees to disrupt the system would have been easily traceable, a fact known to anyone with access to the system.[32]

You may notice, right in the beginning, there's mention of "acknowledged interferences in past years." According to *Wired*, back around 2006 some Eastern European hackers breached a machine at a government agency in Brazil that was configured with a default password.[33] The intruders copied some files, deleted the originals, and then demanded ransom for the data's return.

The ransom demand (which the victim originally interpreted as a practical joke) was ignored and the lost files were retrieved from a backup. To prevent future incidents like this, the government adopted a stronger password policy.

In June of 2000, California suffered from a series of rolling blackouts. In the winter and spring of 2001 more rolling blackouts hit California. These outages, which impacted millions of people, were not the result of hacking. The blackouts were a result of California's deregulation of its electric utility industry in 1996 and subsequent market manipulation by companies like Enron.[34] According to Bill Richardson, the Secretary of Energy from 1998 to 2001:

> I believe that the deregulation plan was botched. Did the power marketeers take advantage of the situation? Yes. To make more money? Yes. But the rules of the game were created badly by those that passed that flawed deregulation plan in 1996.[35]

As in the financial sector, which engaged in a self-inflicted meltdown in October 2008, when it comes to power grid outages *we may be our own worst enemies.*

For the engineers at the NSA, no doubt, this remark cuts close to home. The agency's new $1.4 billion, 65-megawatt, datacenter in Bluffdale, Utah, suffered a series of 10 show-stopping electrical meltdowns over a 13 month period.[36] These meltdowns have delayed the datacenter's opening for a year as investigators scrambled for months to isolate their origin. Each incident is reported to have destroyed as much as $100,000 in equipment.

The Telecoms

In the aftermath of the Iraq invasion the U.S. Department of Commerce stated that more than half of the telephone lines in Baghdad were out of service.[37] Re-reading this sentence you could just as easily see the glass as half full and gain an appreciation for just how much effort would be required to silence all the phones.

A shock and awe assault by the most powerful military on the planet, and yet half of the phones still work. Could software, which military leaders view as being nowhere near as reliable as conventional ordnance, be counted on to do a job that tons of smart bombs couldn't?

Despite the warnings that officials make about the Chinese company Huawei, with its alleged ties to the PLA, there aren't that many documented instances (outside of direct military action) where aggressors have incapacitated a telecom network. There have, however, been recorded incidents of vandalism. For example, in April of 2009, someone cut a bunch of fiber optic cables in the California cities of San Jose and San Carlos. Service for tens of thousands of customers was offline for roughly 12 hours.[38] But even then the shock and awe was lacking, so to speak. As a Verizon spokeswoman remarked:

> Fiber cuts happen more often than people realize. It happens by accident all the time when someone is drilling or digging up a street. Or they're doing regular maintenance.[39]

Aerospace

In October of 2011, *Wired* ran a story about a virus infestation that afflicted the U.S. drone fleet.[40] According to the report, ground control station (GCS) computers at a secluded outpost in

Creech, Nevada were compromised by malware that logged pilot keystrokes as they remotely flew drone missions in the Middle East.

The knee-jerk response for many people was to assume the worst-case scenario: foreign spies had succeeded in penetrating our drone program to subvert its missions. Conversely, other security researchers postulated that it might be a legitimate monitoring package quietly deployed by the Defense Department to keep tabs on the rank and file.

It turns out that the virus in question was garden-variety malware originally built to target the credentials of users who play online games.[41] As such, it had no real impact on drone-related software. It found its way on to the GCS machines via a portable hard drive used to transfer data between systems.

Other, more serious, allegations of compromise have been made. In its 2011 annual report to Congress, the U.S.-China Economic Review Commission stated:

> In recent years, two U.S. government satellites have experienced interference apparently consistent with the cyber exploitation of their control facility.
>
> • On October 20, 2007, Landsat-7, a U.S. earth observation satellite jointly managed by the National Aeronautics and Space Administration and the U.S. Geological Survey, experienced 12 or more minutes of interference. This interference was only discovered following a similar event in July 2008 (see below).
> • On June 20, 2008, Terra EOS [earth observation system] AM–1, a National Aeronautics and Space Administration-managed program for earth observation, experienced two or more minutes of interference.‡ The responsible party achieved all steps required to command the satellite but did not issue commands.
> • On July 23, 2008, Landsat-7 experienced 12 or more minutes of interference. The responsible party did not achieve all steps required to command the satellite.
> • On October 22, 2008, Terra EOS AM–1 experienced nine or more minutes of interference. The responsible

party achieved all steps required to command the satellite but did not issue commands.[42]

Was the interference the result of actions taken on behalf of hostile foreign powers? Perhaps it was user error or a software glitch? Maybe this was actually just the handiwork of a third-party integrator on vacation with his family in Russia? The report leans towards China as the culprit, asserting that the events are in line with Chinese military papers that promote the subversion of satellite control facilities.

The Internet: Denial of Service Attacks

Some cyber-attacks get attention because the target is prominent and the stories are conveyed using the vernacular of war. But the truth is that *Distributed Denial of Service* (aka DDoS) attacks, which attempt to overwhelm Internet servers with torrents of network traffic, are some of the most popular and simplest attacks. The end result of a DDoS attack is the suspension of network-based services for a period of time, often for a few hours or days. While time sensitive businesses (e.g. online betting) are the most vulnerable to this kind of attack, other targets don't necessarily suffer catastrophic losses. Let's look at a couple of the more recent examples.

Estonia

In late April and early May of 2007, a series of DDoS attacks flooded the country of Estonia after it moved a statue dedicated to Russian soldiers who died fighting the Nazis. Estonians see this statue as a reminder of the authoritarian government which took over after kicking the Germans out. The BBC covered this story with a title that read *Estonia hit by "Moscow cyber war."*[43]

Accusations flew in the wake of the Estonia attacks. The country's Prime Minister, Andrus Ansip, claimed that the Russian government was directly responsible. There was even talk among Estonian decision makers of invoking Article V of the North Atlantic Treaty to drag other NATO countries into the fray.[44]

The whole affair ended with a whimper. In January of 2008, the Estonians tracked the attacks to an ethnic Russian living in Estonia, a man named Dmitri Galushkevich. The courts fined the 20-year-old the equivalent of $1,620 dollars and let him walk away. Almost a year later, in November of 2009, a Kremlin-backed youth group called Nashe took responsibility for the attacks.[45]

Georgia

In August of 2008, Georgia came under DDoS attacks during military engagement with Russian troops. The *New York Times* published an article about this entitled *Georgia Takes a Beating in the Cyberwar with Russia*.[46] More than 50 web sites were kicked to the sidelines by a flood of network traffic. The attackers, who were using a modified tool from Microsoft that's normally used to stress-test web servers, targeted government and media sites initially and then expanded their scope to include financial institutions. The disruption was effective enough that the National Bank of Georgia was offline for 10 days.[47]

The U.S. Cyber Consequences Unit,[48] a non-profit research institute, looked into this.[49] They concluded that the attack was orchestrated by civilians who recruited participants and exchanged logistical information using social networking tools like Twitter and Facebook. Because the DDoS attacks appear to have been closely timed with operations on the ground, investigators suspect that there may have been coordination between the cyber attackers and the Russian military.

The inquiry also examined botnet activity involved in the DDoS attack and traced back the corresponding command and control traffic to web sites registered in Turkey and Russia. These sites were set up using stolen American identification. The servers that hosted the command and control web sites had previously been used by criminal elements. According to the report issued by the Cyber Consequences Unit:

> It appears that Russian criminal organizations made no effort to conceal their involvement in the cyber campaign against Georgia because they wanted to claim credit for it.

Kyrgyzstan

On January 18, 2009, the two largest ISPs in Kyrgyzstan, which handle more than 80% of the nation's Internet bandwidth, came under a massive DDoS attack that lasted for approximately 10 days. The *Wall Street Journal* mentioned this incident in a report titled "Winning a Cyber War." Again the war meme permeates the media's coverage. There were several theories put forward as to the motivation for the attacks, which were allegedly executed by a Russian cyber-militia. For example, reporters suspected that the attack was intended to stymie political opposition that relied heavily on the Internet to reach the public.[50]

South Korea and the United States

On the Fourth of July, 2009, a DDoS attack hit U.S. and South Korean networks. Researchers from Bkis Security in Hanoi discovered that the attack involved over 166,000 machines spread across 74 different countries. The master command and control server that coordinated these compromised machines was originally traced to the UK.[51] In a press release, the British company that owns this server, Global Digital Broadcast, stated that:

> Our engineers quickly discounted it as coming from a North Korean Government site, as suggested and was tracked back to the source which was on a VPN circuit in Miami.
>
> As a global delivery platform taking South American content, ingested in Miami and streaming it globally, GDBTV have to take anything like this seriously. Our head of development was contacted by Serious Organised Crime Agency who were also expressing the gravitas of the situation.[52]

How about that? Miami, of all places? Naturally there's really no way to tell who was in control of the machine in Miami...

Though hard evidence as to the source of the attacks was lacking,[53] this didn't stop Peter Hoekstra, the lead Republican on the House Intelligence Committee, from demanding that the United States conduct a "show of force" against North Korea.[54]

> Whether it is a counterattack on cyber, whether it is, you know, more international sanctions ... but it is time for America and South Korea, Japan and others to stand up to North Korea or the next time ... they will go in and shut down a banking sys-

tem or they will manipulate financial data or they will manipulate the electrical grid, either here or in South Korea.

To an extent, Hoekstra's saber rattling is a predictable. A series of research studies at San Francisco State University after 9/11 demonstrated that participants who externalized blame for an attack were more likely to support a military response, while those participants more inclined towards introspection were less likely.[55]

South Korea, Again

Twenty months later, on March 4, 2011, South Korea once again came under a DDoS attack. The incident was investigated by McAfee,[56] which dubbed the attack "10 Days of Rain." As in the earlier 2009 episode, the DDoS attack targeted web sites run by South Korea and the United States. In fact, over a third of the sites attacked this time around were also targeted in the previous 2009 campaign.

The attack was executed using a botnet based in South Korea. The malware that infected individual hosts was heavily armored to discourage static forensic analysis. Investigators view this as a gambit to buy time and allow the DDoS attack to run its course. The malware supported dynamic updates and was programmed to self-destruct after ten days, taking down the host computer with it by overwriting the host's master boot record (MBR).

Botnet members communicated with over 40 command and control servers spread out over 19 countries. The topology they implemented exposed a certain degree of architectural sophistication. Command and control servers were organized using a multi-tier architecture to facilitate scalability and make the botnet more difficult to decapitate.

Despite the conspicuous nature of the attack, attribution wasn't achieved. McAfee investigators speculate that the relatively high level of technical expertise exhibited by the developers coupled with the hard-coded self-destruct mechanism indicates that the attacks may have been a test run that was intended to evaluate South Korea's ability to defend itself. McAfee's VP of threat research, Dmitri Alperovitch, suggested that North Korea might be the culprit.[57] However, as usual, hard evidence is lacking.

McAfee

If DDoS attacks are indeed interpreted as acts of war, then McAfee has got some explaining to do. In April of 2010 McAfee distributed a buggy update to its antivirus suite, causing tens of thousands of computers running Windows XP Service pack 3 to treat the service host process (i.e. SVCHOST.EXE) as malware and quarantine/ delete it. This file, it just so happens, is required for Windows to operate normally. Machines all over the Internet blue-screened, shut down, and generally acted out.[58]

As George Smith of GlobalSecurity.org observed:

> It's nearly the biggest mistake you can make as an anti-virus software developer. And in one fell swoop, it bricked machines nationwide, allowing McAfee to easily surpass North Korea as a cyberpower to be feared.[59]

Commercial Bank Attacks

In September of 2012 a number of U.S. commercial banks were hit with a salvo of DDoS attacks. The banks targeted included big names like Bank of America, Citigroup, HSBC, and Wells Fargo. James Lewis of the CSIS, acting as if he were some sort of emissary, was quoted in the *New York Times* as claiming that the U.S. government believed that Iran was behind the attacks.[60] Though no substantial proof has been provided that backs up this accusation.

As you might expect, the attacks were often characterized as "unprecedented" in terms of their sophistication. Other experts have disputed this, as the attackers used plain old commodity malware to compromise datacenters, using cloud-based platforms to create large volumes of traffic.[61] All told, the attacks generated media buzz but that's about it. No accounts were compromised, no customers lost their money, and nobody was killed. If this was payback for Stuxnet, we're not that impressed. Freelance journalist Constantine von Hoffman remarked:

> What did the Iranians fire back with? A series of massive, on-going and ineffective DDoS attacks on American banks. This is a disproportionate response but not in the way military

experts usually mean that phrase. It's the equivalent of some-one stealing your car and you throwing an ever-increasing number of eggs at his house in response.[62]

Iran is a country with a nuclear program. Is this the best the Ira-nian intelligence agencies can do? Or maybe Iran isn't responsible. Strictly speaking, a troupe of hackers called "Izz ad-Din al-Qassam Cyber Fighters" claimed responsibility for the attack. The group declared that the DDoS attacks were executed in protest of the an-ti-Islam movie *The Innocence of Muslims*. The *Times* reported that American intelligence officials believed this group to be a front or-ganization created by the Iranian government.[63]

Spamhaus

A recent high-profile DDoS attack took place in late March of 2013, when a non-profit organization called Spamhaus was hit by what might have been the largest publicly known DDoS attack (some-where on the order of 300 gigabits per second).[64] Spamhaus, as its name suggests, tracks organizations on the Internet that send junk emails en masse (i.e. spam). The DDoS attack began after Spamhaus observed a Dutch company, CyberBunker, hosting spammers and subsequently put CyberBunker on its e-mail blacklist. This black-list is widely distributed to email providers so that they can screen out spam before it reaches user mailboxes. This means that email emanating from CyberBunker's network will, in most cases, never reach its intended destination, as it will be intercepted as spam.

CyberBunker is a bullet-proof hosting site in the Netherlands which resides inside of a refurbished nuclear bunker. According to CyberBunker's officially stated policy:

> Customers are allowed to host any content they like, except child porn and anything related to terrorism. Everything else is fine.[65]

It would appear that someone was retaliating against Spamhaus for marking CyberBunker as a purveyor of spam.

Let's look at some technical aspects of the DDoS attack. A key ingredient was the misuse of DNS servers. DNS servers perform name resolution, so that computers hooked up to the Internet can locate resources online. For example, when you type www.google.com into a browser, it's a DNS server that takes the string www.google.com and locates the physical servers hosting Google's web site.

Normally when you initiate a DNS query the response returns to your machine which originally made the query (see Figure 7-1).

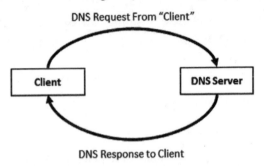

DNS Request From "Client"

DNS Response to Client

Figure 7-1

It's one thing to place a take-out pizza order and have them send the pizza to your home address. It's another to place a few million bogus orders to someone else's address. In a nutshell, this is what the attackers did. They made millions of requests to DNS servers all over the Internet and had the response to those requests (i.e. the pizza, so to speak) sent to Spamhaus. By analogy, attackers found a way to re-route the response of a DNS query so that it was forwarded to the target. To direct the response of a DNS query to the victim of a DDoS attack, the attacker spoofs their IP address so that the initial request appears to be originating from the victim (see Figure 7-2).

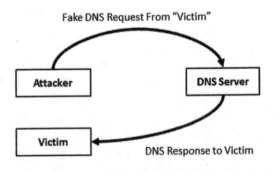

Fake DNS Request From "Victim"

DNS Response to Victim

Figure 7-2

Get an entire botnet to make this kind of request and the targeted network is flooded with a torrent of phony DNS responses. To add insult to injury, the Spamhaus DDoS attack relied on what's known as *DNS amplification*, where the attacker sends a small query to a DNS server which then responds with a much larger response. This effectively amplifies the amount of data in transit.

The Spamhaus DDoS worked because there are DNS servers on the Internet that are configured to respond to any client that makes a query (as opposed to a much smaller set of authorized computers). Such DNS servers are known as *open DNS resolvers*.

One way to stifle DNS amplification DDoS would be to shut down all of the open DNS resolvers on the Internet. Another, less drastic solution, would be to configure these DNS servers so that they didn't respond to requests originating from a spoofed IP address. The steps needed to do so were spelled out years ago in a document known as Best Current Practice #38 (BCP38).[66] Many companies simply decided not spend the resources to implement these steps.

So, here it is, allegedly one of the most prolific DDoS attacks of all time. Granted it did cause some temporary congestion among a handful of Internet exchanges,[67] but it didn't force the Internet to a grinding halt. In fact, a spokesperson from NTT, one of the backbone providers on the Internet, placidly stated:

> I'm sure you read the same 300gbps figure that I did, and while that's a massive amount of bandwidth to a single enterprise or service provider, data on global capacities from sources like TeleGeography show lit capacities in the tbps range in most all regions of the world.[68]

Sure, there were a couple of minor traffic jams in Western Europe but it was business as usual for everyone else. CNET journalist Zack Whittaker summed up this state of affairs:

> While the Internet got punched in the kidneys, it turns out the Internet is the technological equivalent of Chuck Norris.[69]

This didn't stop people from suggesting that the entire Internet was at risk. In particular, the CEO of CloudFlare, the company that

Spamhaus hired to help defend itself during the incident, equated DDoS attacks to nuclear bombs.[70] He also wrote about the attacks in a blog entry entitled "The DDoS That Almost Broke the Internet."

Guardian journalist Heather Brooke provides a much needed dose of skepticism:

> In whose interest is it to hype up the collapse of the Internet from a DDoS attack? Why, the people who provide cyber-security services of course. And looking at the reporting, almost all the sources are directly involved and have a vested interest.[71]

A Nuisance at Best

Recall earlier in the book we discussed Thomas Rid's criteria for acts of war: they must be violent, instrumental, and political. While many of the DDoS attacks we've surveyed may have been politically motivated and were instrumental to reach certain goals, the damage incurred does not measure up to the violence in traditional warfare nor the capabilities of other cyber-attack methods.

Despite the media's annoying tendency to print headlines that label these incidents as acts of war, the absence of real violence is palpable. Compare, if you will, the Estonia DDoS attacks against the fire-bombing of Dresden in World War II. DDoS attacks, as a rule, result in a negligible amount of physical damage; though they definitely generate news coverage. The bombing of Dresden leveled the city and killed over 20,000 people.

In terms of dollars lost, some of the most damaging DDoS attacks occur in the online gambling industry.[72] Can you imagine how much money bookies would lose if they were unable to function during the Super Bowl or the World Cup? Once more, because online gambling is a legally sticky issue in the United States, operations are often forced to defend themselves and may be incline to simply pay for "protection" rather than hire the talent necessary to fend off DDoS attacks. In that sense, we are talking about cybercrime rather than cyberwar.

With the right equipment and skillset, however, it's entirely viable to sustain network operations and mitigate a DDoS attack. This is exactly what the online gambling operations do; they hire specialists and invest in the necessary technology. Once more, there are well-known name brand companies like CloudFlare and Pro-lexic which openly sell protection against DDoS attacks as a core business service. CloudFlare, in particular, allegedly pumps 5 percent of all Internet traffic through its network.[73]

The NSA has even published a series of measures[74] that can be used to mitigate the threat of a DDoS attack, though the emphasis appears to be on proactive measures, as reactive measures can take too long. These measures, verbatim, are as follows:

2. (U) Proactive DDoS Protections
   a. (U) Establish connections with multiple Internet Service Providers (ISPs) for redundancy.
   b. (U) Ensure Service Level Agreements with ISPs contain provisions for DDoS prevention (eg: through IP address rotation).
   c. (U) Design network with redundant systems and sufficient excess capacity.
   d. (U) Conduct rate-limiting of traffic at the network perimeter.
      (U) Note: Quality of Service for Legitimate Traffic may also be adversely affected.
   e. (U) Creation of backup, remote-site network infra-structure utilizing multiple addressing schemes
   f. (U) Content Delivery Network (CDN) providers which host geographically or logically separated services can limit the impact of DDoS attacks.

3. (U) Reactive DDoS Protections:
   a. (U) Execute Internet Service Provider address rotation.
   b. (U) Blocking of source IP addresses generating DDoS traffic at enterprise boundary or within ISP infrastructure
      (U) Note: Adversary capabilities will make blocking of individual addresses (or even blocks of addresses) very difficult to implement.
   c. (U) Acquire increased bandwidth capability from ISP.

DDoS attacks aren't the breathless military assaults that the press makes them out to be. DDoS attacks are an unimaginative form of sabotage. As security industry luminary Bruce Schneier succinctly commented:

> Enough of the hype and the bluster. The news isn't the attacks, but that some networks had security lousy enough to be vulnerable to them.[75]

The Internet: Manipulating Traffic

In its 2010 report to Congress, the U.S.-China Economic and Security Review Commission described an incident where the Great Firewall of China started to affect users in Chile and the United States. The report states:

> Starting on March 24, 2010, when certain Internet users in the United States and Chile attempted to connect to popular social networking websites, their computers requested routine Internet Protocol information, and a Beijing-based Domain Name Server (a clone-like iteration of a Swedish root server) replied with faulty responses. As a result, these users were directed to incorrect servers, as if the users were trying to access restricted content from behind China's Great Firewall. These conditions persisted in some cases for several days before the administrators of the Sweden based root server temporarily disabled requests to their Beijing server "clone."

The report mentions that this probably wasn't intentional:

> These incidents do not appear to be a deliberate act of cross-border censorship from China. Rather, because of vulnerabilities in the Internet's architecture, the faulty information likely resulted from an accidental "leak" of conditions intended only for a Chinese audience.

In another incident, described by the report, a Chinese ISP rerouted a nontrivial amount of Internet traffic:

> For about 18 minutes on April 8, 2010, China Telecom advertised erroneous network traffic routes that instructed U.S. and other foreign Internet traffic to travel through Chinese servers. Other servers around the world quickly adopted these paths,

routing all traffic to about 15 percent of the Internet's destinations through servers located in China. This incident affected traffic to and from U.S. government (".gov") and military (".mil") sites, including those for the Senate, the army, the navy, the marine corps, the air force, the office of secretary of Defense, the National Aeronautics and Space Administration, the Department of Commerce, the National Oceanic and Atmospheric Administration, and many others. Certain commercial websites were also affected, such as those for Dell, Yahoo!, Microsoft, and IBM.[76]

The Chinese engineers involved stated that this was an accident. The Commission's 2010 report doesn't come to any definitive conclusions:

> Evidence related to this incident does not clearly indicate whether it was perpetrated intentionally and, if so, to what ends. However, computer security researchers have noted that the capability could enable severe malicious activities.

In other words, they're not sure if it was an accident or not, but it doesn't matter because it *could* be a really dangerous weapon. Right on cue, the report launches straight into a hypothetical scenario:

> This level of access could enable surveillance of specific users or sites. It could disrupt a data transaction and prevent a user from establishing a connection with a site. It could even allow a diversion of data to somewhere that the user did not intend (for example, to a "spoofed" site). Arbor Networks Chief Security Officer Danny McPherson has explained that the volume of affected data here could have been intended to conceal one targeted attack. Perhaps most disconcertingly, as a result of the diffusion of Internet security certification authorities, control over diverted data could possibly allow a telecommunications firm to compromise the integrity of supposedly secure encrypted sessions.

Of course, if traffic capture on this order of magnitude was performed intentionally, it would be difficult to conceal, and even harder to deny involvement. Attribution would be relatively straightforward.

Endnotes

1) Jon Callas, "Reply to Zooko," *Silent Circle*, August 17, 2013, http://silentcircle. wordpress.com/2013/08/17/reply-to-zooko/.

2) John Carlin, "A Farewell to Arms," *Wired*, May 1997, http://www.wired.com/ wired/archive/5.05/netizen.html.

3) *National Plan For Information Systems Protection*, Executive Summary, January 2000, http://clinton4.nara.gov/media/pdf/npisp-execsummary-000105.pdf.

4) Bryan Bender, "World more dangerous, top general says," *Boston Globe*, April 13, 2012, http://articles.boston.com/2012-04-13/nation/31330084_1_top-military-officer-warfare-cyber-attack.

5) Matt Egan and Jennifer Booton, "Source: New York Times Website Hit by Cyber Attack," *Fox Business*, August 14, 2013, http://www.foxbusiness.com/technology/2013/08/14/new-york-times-site-experiences-major-outage/.

6) "To Our Customers," *New York Times*, August 14, 2013, http://www.nytimes. com/2013/08/14/business/media/to-our-customers.html.

7) Michael Riley, "U.S. Spy Agency Is Said to Investigate Nasdaq Hacker Attack," Bloomberg, March 30, 2011, http://www.bloomberg.com/news/2011-03-30/u-s-spy-agency-said-to-focus-its-decrypting-skills-on-nasdaq-cyber-attack.html.

8) Graham Bowley, "Hackers Gained Access to Nasdaq Systems, but Not Trades," *New York Times*, February 5, 2011, http://www.nytimes.com/2011/02/06/business/06nasdaq.html.

9) Andrea Shalal-Esa and Jim Finkle, "Lax security at Nasdaq helped hackers," *Reuters*, November 18, 2011, http://www.reuters.com/article/2011/11/18/us-nasdaq-cyber-idUSTRE7AG2NU20111118.

10) Devlin Barrett, "Hackers Penetrate Nasdaq Computers ," *Wall Street Journal*, February 5, 2011, http://online.wsj.com/article/SB1000142405274870470930457 6124502351634690.html.

11) Andrea Shalal-Esa and Jim Finkle, "Lax security at Nasdaq helped hackers," *Reuters*, November 18, 2011, http://www.reuters.com/article/2011/11/18/us-nasdaq-cyber-idUSTRE7AG2NU20111118.

12) Don Reisinger, "Nasdaq hackers spied on company directors, report says," *CNET*, October 21, 2011, http://news.cnet.com/8301-13506_3-20123854-17/nasdaq-hackers-spied-on-company-directors-report-says/.

13) Devlin Barrett, "Hackers Penetrate Nasdaq Computers ," *Wall Street Journal*, February 5, 2011, http://online.wsj.com/article/SB1000142405274870470930457 6124502351634690.html.

14) "Zimbabwe stock exchange shuts down hacked site," *Associated Press*, August 5th, 2011, http://news.yahoo.com/zimbabwe-stock-exchange-shuts-down-hacked-110551055.html.

15) Kate O'Keeffe and Jeffry Ng, "Hong Kong Exchange Website Hacked," *Wall Street Journal*, August 10, 2011, http://online.wsj.com/article/SB100014240531 1190391810457649948326911492.html.

16) Nathaniel Popper, "Pricing Problem Suspends Nasdaq for Three Hours," *New York Times*, August 22, 2013, http://dealbook.nytimes.com/2013/08/22/nasdaq-market-halts-trading/?ref=todayspaper&_r=0&pagewanted=print.

17) David Fettig, "Small Leak Teaches Big Lessons," *The Region*, June 1, 1991, http://www.minneapolisfed.org/publications_papers/pub_display.cfm?id=3772.

18) Michael Isikoff, "'Scary Stuff': Cyberattack arrests highlight risk," *NBC News*, November 11, 2010, http://www.msnbc.msn.com/id/40306517/ns/us_news-security/t/scary-stuff-cyberattack-arrest-highlights-risk/#.TxnjqYE5Bpg.

19) Bob Ivry, Bradley Keoun and Phil Kuntz, "Secret Fed Loans Gave Banks $13 Billion Undisclosed to Congress," *Bloomberg Markets*, November 27, 2011, http://www.bloomberg.com/news/2011-11-28/secret-fed-loans-undisclosed-to-congress-gave-banks-13-billion-in-income.html.

20) Matt Taibbi, *Griftopia: Bubble Machines, Vampire Squids, and the Long Con That Is Breaking America*, Spiegel & Grau, November 2010.

21) Financial Crisis Inquiry Commission, *The Financial Crisis Inquiry Report*, U.S. Government Printing office, January 2011, http://www.gpo.gov/fdsys/pkg/GPO-FCIC/pdf/GPO-FCIC.pdf.

22) Scott Pelley, "Panetta: Cyber warfare could paralyze U.S.," *CBS News*, January 5, 2012, http://www.cbsnews.com/8301-18563_162-57353420/panetta-cyber-warfare-could-paralyze-u.s/.

23) George Smith, "The Joker," *Dick Destiny Blog*, January 6, 2012, http://dickdestiny.com/blog1/2012/01/06/the-joker/.

24) Siobhan Gorman, "Electrical Grid in U.S. Penetrated by Spies," *Wall Street Journal*, April 8, 2009, http://online.wsj.com/article/SB123914805204099085.html.

25) *CYBERSECURITY: Challenges in Securing the Modernized Electricity Grid*, GAO-12-507T, February 28, 2012, http://cryptome.org/2012/01/gao-12-507t.pdf.

26) George Smith, "Lights out mythology finds its way into GAO report," *Dick Destiny Blog*, March 5th, 2012, http://dickdestiny.com/blog1/2012/03/05/lights-out-mythology-finds-its-way-into-gao-report/.

27) Kim Zetter, "Efforts to Secure Nation's Power Grid's Ineffective," *Wired*, February 1, 2011. http://www.wired.com/threatlevel/2011/02/doe-power-grid-report/.

28) Siobhan Gorman, "Electricity Grid in U.S. Penetrated By Spies," *Wall Street Journal*, April 8, 2009, http://online.wsj.com/article/SB123914805204099085.html.

29) Michael Tanji, "Hacking the Electric Grid? You and What Army?" *Wired*, July 13, 2010, http://www.wired.com/dangerroom/2010/07/hacking-the-electric-grid-you-and-what-army/.

30) *The Future of the Electric Grid*, MIT Energy Initiative, Massachusetts Institute of Technology, 2011, http://web.mit.edu/mitei/research/studies/documents/electric-grid-2011/Electric_Grid_Full_Report.pdf.

31) Marcelo Soares, "Brazilian Blackout Traced to Sooty Insulators, Not Hackers," *Wired*, November 9, 2009, http://www.wired.com/threatlevel/2009/11/brazil_blackout/.

32) *Brazil: Blackout -causes And Implications*, Diplomatic Cable, Reference ID 09BRASILIA1383, WikiLeaks, December 2, 2010, http://www.cablegatesearch.net/cable.php?id=09BRASILIA1383&q=plinio%20president.

33) Marcelo Soares, "WikiLeaked Cable Says 2009 Brazilian Blackout Wasn't Hackers, Either," *Wired*, November 6, 2010, http://www.wired.com/threatlevel/2010/12/brazil-blackout/.

34) Timothy Egan, "Tapes Show Enron Arranged Plant Shutdown," *New York Times*, February 4, 2005, http://www.nytimes.com/2005/02/04/national/04energy.html.

35) *Blackout*, Interview with Bill Richardson, Fronline, June 5, 2001, http://www.pbs.org/wgbh/pages/frontline/shows/blackout/interviews/richardson.html.

36) Siobhan Gorman, "NSA Utah Data Center Hobbled," *Wall Street Journal*, October 8, 2013, http://cryptome.org/2013/10/nsa-utah-hobbled.htm.

37) Linda Astor, "Post-War Telecommunications Developments in Iraq," Office of Technology and Electronic Commerce, http://web.ita.doc.gov/ITI/itiHome.nsf/6502bd9adeb499b285256cdb00685f77/e781b255ae7a4f9a85256d-9c0068abd9?OpenDocument.

38) Peter Svensson and Jason Dearen, "Low-tech tools take out phones in Silicon Valley," *Associated Press*, April 10, 2009, http://www.technologyreview.com/wire/22431/page1/.

39) Marguerite Reardon, "How secure is the U.S. communications network?" *CNET*, April 13, 2009, http://news.cnet.com/8301-1035_3-10217550-94.html.

40) Noah Shachtman, "Computer Virus Hits U.S. Drone Fleet," *Wired*, October 7, 2011, http://www.wired.com/dangerroom/2011/10/virus-hits-drone-fleet/.

41) Lolita c. Baldor, "Military: Computer virus wasn't directed at drones," *Associated Press*, October 12, 2011, http://news.yahoo.com/military-computer-virus-wasnt-directed-drones-233425448.html.

42) *2011Report To Congress Of The U.S.-China Economic And Security Review Commission*, One Hundred Twelfth Congress, November 2011 http://www.uscc.gov/annual_report/2011/annual_report_full_11.pdf.

43) "Estonia hit by 'Moscow cyber war'," *BBC News*, May 17, 2007, http://news.bbc.co.uk/2/hi/europe/6665145.stm.

44) Ian Traynor, "Russia accused of unleashing cyberwar to disable Estonia," *The Guardian*, May 16, 2007, http://www.guardian.co.uk/world/2007/may/17/topstories3.russia.

45) Marge Tubalkain-Trell, "Kremlin-backed group behind Estonia cyber blitz," *Baltic Business News*, November 3, 2009, http://www.bbn.ee/Default.aspx?PublicationId=b737410e-e519-4a36-885f-85b183cc3478&comments=1&page=1.

46) John Markoff, "Georgia Takes a Beating in the Cyberwar With Russia," *New York Times*, August 11, 2008, http://bits.blogs.nytimes.com/2008/08/11/georgia-takes-a-beating-in-the-cyberwar-with-russia/.

47) Jeremy Kirk, "Georgia Cyberattacks Linked to Russian Organized Crime," *IDG News Service*, August 17, 2009, http://www.computerworld.com/s/article/9136719/Georgia_cyberattacks_linked_to_Russian_organized_crime.

48) The U.S. Cyber Consequences Unit, http://www.usccu.us/.

49) Siobhan Gorman, "Hackers Stole IDs for Attack," *Wall Street Journal*, August 17, 2009, http://online.wsj.com/article/SB125046431841935299.html.

50) Nathan Hodge, "Russian 'Cyber Militia' Takes Kyrgyzstan Offline?" *Wired*, January 28, 2009, http://www.wired.com/dangerroom/2009/01/cyber-militia-t/.

51) "Korea and US DDoS attacks: The attacking source located in United Kingdom," *Bkis Global Task Force Blog*, July 14, 2009, http://blog.bkis.com/en/korea-and-us-ddos-attacks-the-attacking-source-located-in-united-kingdom/.

52) *DDoS on US and South Korea*, Global Digital Broadcast, July 14, 2009, http://www.globaldigitalbroadcast.com/newspage.php?newsId=123.

53) Siobhan Gorman and Evan Ramstad, "Cyber Blitz Hits U.S., Korea," *Wall Street Journal*, July 9, 2009, http://online.wsj.com/article/SB124701806176209691.html.

54) Kim Zetter, "Lawmaker Wants 'Show of Force' Against North Korea for Website Attacks," *Wired*, July 10, 2009, http://www.wired.com/threatlevel/2009/07/show-of-force/.

55) Violet Cheung-Blunden, "Paving the Road to War with Group Membership, Appraisal Antecedents, and Anger," *Aggressive Behavior*, Volume 34 Issue 2, Pages 175 – 189.

56) Georg Wicherski, *10 Days of Rain in Korea*, McAfee Labs, July 5, 2011, http://blogs.mcafee.com/mcafee-labs/10-days-of-rain-in-korea.

57) Martyn Williams, "DDoS attack in March likely N. Korean work, says McAfee," *IDG News*, July 6, 2011, http://www.pcworld.com/businesscenter/article/235098/ddos_attack_in_march_likely_nkorean_work_says_mcafee.html.

58) *Microsoft Knowledge Base Article (2025695), McAfee delivers a false-positive detection of the W32/wecorl.a virus when version 5958 of the DAT file is used*, Microsoft Corp., June 15, 2010, http://support.microsoft.com/kb/2025695.

59) George Smith, "Cult of Cyberwar: McAfee surpasses North Korea as cyberattack power," *Dick Destiny Blog*, April 22, 2010, http://dickdestiny.com/blog1/2010/04/22/cult-of-cyberwar-mcafee-surpasses-north-korea-as-cyberattack-power/.

60) Nicole Perlroth and Quentin Hardy, "Bank Hacking Was the Work of Iranians, Officials Say," *New York Times*, January 8, 2013, http://www.nytimes.com/2013/01/09/technology/online-banking-attacks-were-work-of-iran-us-officials-say.html.

61) Michael Mimoso, "Automated Toolkits Named in Massive DDoS Attacks Against U.S. Banks," *ThreatPost*, October 2, 2012, http://threatpost.com/en_us/blogs/automated-toolkits-named-massive-ddos-attacks-against-us-banks-100212.

62) Constantine von Hoffman, "Cyber War is Upon Us-But Only One Side is Attacking," *CIO Blogs*, January 23, 2013, http://blogs.cio.com/print/17722.

63) Nicole Perlroth and Quentin Hardy, "Bank Hacking Was the Work of Iranians, Officials Say," *New York Times*, January 8, 2013, http://www.nytimes.com/2013/01/09/technology/online-banking-attacks-were-work-of-iran-us-officials-say.html.

64) John Markoff And Nicole Perlroth, "Firm Is Accused of Sending Spam, and Fight Jams Internet," *New York Times*, March 26, 2013, http://www.nytimes.com/2013/03/27/technology/internet/online-dispute-becomes-internet-snarling-attack.html.

65) CyberBunker Stay Online Policy, http://cyberbunker.com/web/stay-online-policy.php.

66) Ferguson and Senie, *Network Ingress Filtering: Defeating Denial of Service Attacks which employ IP Source Address Spoofing*, Internet Engineering Task Force (IETF), May 2000, http://tools.ietf.org/html/bcp38.

67) Matthew Prince, "The DDoS That Almost Broke the Internet," *CloudFlare Blog*, March 27, 2013, http://blog.cloudflare.com/the-ddos-that-almost-broke-the-internet.

68) Sam Biddle, "That Internet War Apocalypse Is a Lie," *Gizmodo*, March 27, 2013, http://gizmodo.com/5992652.

69) Donna Tam, "Did the spam cyber fight really slow down the Internet?" *CNET*, March 27, 2014, http://news.cnet.com/8301-1009_3-57576699-83/did-the-spam-cyber-fight-really-slow-down-the-internet/.

70) John Markoff And Nicole Perlroth, "Firm Is Accused of Sending Spam, and Fight Jams Internet," *New York Times*, March 26, 2013, http://www.nytimes.com/2013/03/27/technology/internet/online-dispute-becomes-internet-snarling-attack.html.

71) Heather Brooke, "How a cyberwar was spun by shoddy journalism," *Guardian*, March 29, 2013, http://www.guardian.co.uk/commentisfree/2013/mar/29/cyberwar-spun-shoddy-journalism/print.

72) Mark Ward, "Bookies suffer online onslaught," *BBC News*, March 19, 2004, http://news.bbc.co.uk/2/hi/technology/3549883.stm.

73) Gerry Shih, "Selling flak jackets in the cyberwars," *Reuters*, Dec 13, 2012, http://www.reuters.com/article/2012/12/13/net-us-usa-cyberwar-cloudflare-idUSBRE8BC0OB20121213.

74) Information Assurance Directorate, *NSA Mitigations Guidance for Distributed Denial of Service Attacks*, National Security Agency, http://publicintelligence.net/nsa-iad-ddos/.

75) Bruce Schneier, "So-Called Cyberattack was Overblown," *MPR News*, July 13, 2009, http://minnesota.publicradio.org/display/web/2009/07/10/schneier/.

76) *2010 Report To Congress Of The U.S.-China Economic And Security Review Commission*, One Hundred Eleventh Congress, November 2010, http://www.uscc.gov/annual_report/2010/annual_report_full_10.pdf.

Chapter 8

Threat Inflation

The whole aim of practical politics is to keep the populace alarmed (and hence clamorous to be led to safety) by an endless series of hobgoblins, most of them imaginary.

– H.L. Mencken[1]

In the 1980s, it wasn't unusual to see physicist Edward Teller at press conferences warning of an existential threat: a large meteor hitting the earth and wiping out humanity. This worst-case scenario (which was later explored by a number of Hollywood blockbusters) was a sales pitch for a nuclear-powered energy weapon he had developed called the *x-ray laser*. Teller had earlier tried to promote his invention as a way to combat the Soviet threat in space, but with the dissolution of the Soviet Union in the late 1980s he needed a new use for it.

Meteor strikes that precipitate mass extinction are exceedingly rare. They are prototypical black swan events. Yet witness a respected, world-renowned, scientist blatantly exaggerating the danger in an effort to produce a sense of alarm which any insurance actuary would laugh at. There's a name for this phenomenon, it is called *threat inflation*.[2]

We saw threat inflation back in the 1950s when elites clamored over the imaginary Missile Gap, and we saw it again before our invasion of Iraq. After reading through Chapter Seven you may recognize the fingerprints of threat inflation once more.

Threat inflation works because humans are irrational. As Charles Mackay documented in his book *Extraordinary Popular Delusions and the Madness of Crowds*, humans are fundamentally emotional creatures who succumb to primitive irrational impulses. When confronted with doomsday scenarios the average person rarely stops to perform a careful assessment or to consider the presence of ulterior motives. Most people tacitly accept the speakers' authority (given that most of them are former high-ranking officials) and take the story at somewhere near face value.

According to Mencken, the goal is to generate anxiety, to instill a profound sense of apprehension, *so that the public is receptive to preconceived solutions.* Psychological research has shown that anxious people will choose to be safe rather than sorry. In the throes of an alleged crisis, anxious people aren't particular about the solution as long as it is presented as a preventative measure; they don't care much about the cost, as they are willing to pay a steep price to feel safe again.

The Clarion of Threat Inflation
Figure 8-1

Conflicts of Interest

Basically, what we have is an intelligence ruling class, public and private, that hold the secrets.

–Tim Shorrock[3]

Cyberwar proponents often have long-standing relationships with the corporate entities that serve the defense industry. Mike McConnell is a classic example of this. He served as the director of the National Security Agency (NSA) from 1992 to 1996. After retiring from the NSA in 1996, McConnell took a job with a company called Booz Allen Hamilton, where he rose to the level of senior vice president. According to an article in *The New Yorker*, he was making about $2 million a year.[4]

In early 2007, after a decade or so with Booz Allen, President Bush appointed McConnell to succeed John Negroponte as the Director of National Intelligence (DNI). McConnell held this position for a couple of years before going right back through Washington's revolving door to Booz Allen.

The executive ranks at Booz Allen sport a long list of government officials, like James Clapper our current Director of National Intelligence, and former CIA director James Woolsey.[5]

Booz Allen is majority owned by the Carlyle Group. It should come as no surprise, then, that Booz is heavily involved in classified military projects. A quick glance through its annual report reinforces this fact.[6]

According to the Top Secret America project, spearheaded by the likes of Dana Priest and Bill Arkin, Booz maintains a head count of over 23,000 employees and reports annual revenue is in excess of $5 billion.[7] It boasts more than 1,000 former intelligence officials among its ranks and employs more than 10,000 TS/SCI (Top-Secret/Sensitive Compartmented Information) cleared personnel.[8] With resources like this at its disposal, Booz Allen maintains relationships with 26 different three-letter clients in the government (e.g. the CIA, NSA, DHS, DIA, NRO, etc.).

Booz Allen made more the $3 billion in defense contracts from 1998 to 2003, where the contracts awarded increased on average by about $100 million each year.[9] Almost $800 million of these proceeds were from no-bid contracts, over half of which were related to national security. Given Booz Allen's role in the creation of CYBERCOM,[10] it's obvious that this close level of involvement with the military has continued. In March of 2013 Booz Allen, which is ranked 436 on the Fortune 500, reported annual revenues of $5.76 billion, with the government providing 98 percent of these proceeds.[11]

Contractors like Booz Allen can make a lot of money if the United States government decides that massive retaliation or Big Brother is the way to realize cyber-security. Do you suppose there may be a conflict of interest? Even if McConnell comes from the most patriotic orientation and harbors the most genuine intent to protect the nation that he loves, a human mind is not the best equipment to separate all that from the vested interest that would benefit him and his employer.

The author of the book *Spies for Hire*, Tim Shorrock, repeats this concern:

> We have no way of knowing how people like Mr. McConnell formed their business relationships, and what agreements or compromises they might have made to get their private-sector jobs (and vice versa). They may be honorable men, but as recent history has shown us, there's no reason to take them at their word. And the current one-year ban on lobbying for former officials does little to prevent conflicts of interest.[12]

McConnell's not alone. Senator Barbara Mikulski of Maryland has publicly echoed McConnell's message of cyberwar:

> We are at war ... we are being attacked, and we are being hacked.[13]

Would it surprise you to discover that Mikulski sits on the Senate Select Committee on Intelligence, as well as the Appropriations Committee? According to OpenSecrets.org, her top campaign contributors during the period 2007-2012 include names like Northrop Grumman, Mantech International, SAIC, and Raytheon. This is only logical, as Maryland hosts several big military contractors. For instance, Lockheed Martin is headquartered in Bethesda. According to Maryland's Department of Business and Economic Development, the state ranks second with regard to federal research and development spending ($13.3 billion).[14] Could Senator Mikulski have reasons, outside of raw patriotism, for depicting current developments as acts of war?

Stepping back, do you suppose that this raises questions about the role that for-profit business interests play in the U.S. intelligence apparatus? Does the potential for a conflict of interest exist when approximately 70 percent of the national intelligence budget is spent on what's essentially a "Digital Blackwater"?[15]

Is it wise for the decision making process to be so deeply intertwined with corporate entities that are primarily driven by the fiduciary requirement to maximize revenues? Does the requirement to cater to the bottom line interfere with other obligations?

The potential for waste and graft are substantial. A number of contracting firms were involved in what's known as the *Trailblazer project*. Trailblazer was an initiative originally formulated in 2001 by the NSA to allow analysts to sift through the tidal wave of phone calls and e-mails that they collected every day. The goal was to allow end-users to identify useful patterns (as opposed to capturing everything, which isn't feasible anymore).

While NSA leadership pushed for Trailblazer, they could have opted for an equivalent, not to mention functioning, million-dollar project called ThinThread that was developed in house. According to Bill Binney, one of the creators of ThinThread:

> [ThinThread] was small, cost-effective, easy to understand, and protected the identity of Americans. But it wasn't what the higher-ups wanted. They wanted a big machine that could make Martinis, too.[16]

Thomas Drake, an NSA employee who was eventually prosecuted for leaking details of Trailblazer's mismanagement, added that in the NSA:

> Careers are built on projects and programs. The bigger, the better their career.[17]

Under the leadership of General Michael Hayden, the Trailblazer project lasted several years and consumed $1.2 billion in funding. The NSA, however, was unable to deploy an operational system and the project was declared a complete failure by the NSA's inspector general. Though the contractors involved in the project would probably beg to differ, for them it was a welcome payday. Congress was so appalled by what happened that they took away the NSA's authority to handle major contracts.[18]

In addition to waste, there's also the risk that national security policies, ones which impact our civil liberties, could be driven from boardrooms in the private sector. *Salon* columnist David Sirota describes how such influence is exerted and by whom:

> There are huge corporate forces with a vested financial interest in making sure the debate over security is tilted toward the surveillance state and against critics of that surveillance state. In practice, that means when those corporations spend big money on campaign contributions, they aren't just buying votes for specific private contracts. They are also implicitly pressuring politicians to rhetorically push the discourse in a pro-surveillance, anti-civil liberties direction – that is, in a direction that preserves the larger political assumptions on which the profits of the entire surveillance-industrial complex are based.[19]

Whistleblower Ed Snowden, himself a former NSA contractor employed by Booz Allen, described the result of this dynamic:

> You end up in a situation where government policies are being influenced by private corporations who have interests that are completely divorced from the public good in mind.[20]

A man named Chris Pyle can also offer a degree of insight into the quagmire of public-private entanglement, from a slightly different angle. Pyle is an old-school whistleblower from the 1970s who exposed an extensive surveillance program run by the CIA and Army Intelligence while working as an instructor for the Army. Pyle revealed a massive effort to track Americans who were involved in lawful political activity. Pyle recalls:

> There were about 1,500 Army agents in plain clothes watching every demonstration in the United States of 20 people or more. There was also a records system in a giant warehouse on about six million people. I disclosed the existence of that surveillance and then recruited 125 of the Army's counterintelligence agents to tell what they knew about the spying to Congress, the courts and the press. As a result of those disclosures and the congressional hearings, the entire U.S. Army Intelligence Command was abolished.[21]

His disclosures helped to launch the Church Committee, an investigation led by Senator Frank Church which aimed to curb abuses of authority and impose greater oversight.

Pyle warns what can happen when an intelligence organization blindly follows the necessity to validate its existence:

> Many people believe that they have nothing to fear from government/corporate surveillance because they have nothing to hide. But every bureaucracy is a solution in search of a problem, and if it can't find a problem to fit its solution, they will redefine the problem. In the 1960s, the surveillance bureaucracies redefined anti-war and civil rights protests as communist enterprises; today the same bureaucracies redefine anti-war Quakers, environmentalists, and animal rights activists as "terrorists." So political activists, no matter how benign, have good reasons to fear these bureaucracies.[22]

When genuine threats are in short supply, faced with financial pressure certain elements in U.S. security services will create new ones. This is a documented phenomenon that's part of the public record; the tendency for citizens engaged in political activity to end up as targets of monitoring. This kind of repression has taken place in the 1960s (e.g. the FBI's COINTELPRO and the CIA's Operation CHAOS), during the Invasion of Iraq,[23] and during the Occupy Wall Street protests.[24]

Moving Towards Cyber-Security

By taking an apocalyptic event and treating it as if was "imminent," society enters a logic-free zone dominated by emotion that clouds our ability to reason. This puts the economic and political imperatives of special interests before our own. As we mentioned earlier, an existential threat like Cybergeddon can justify any cost in the throes of a crisis mentality. It's a dangerous mindset, one that can be extremely wasteful because it draws us away from logical risk assessment.

There are many kinds of insurance (e.g. health, house, car, hurricane, earth quake, life, disability), but this doesn't mean you should go out and buy all of them. That would be a huge waste of money. *A savvy consumer buys insurance strategically; there are prices that clear-headed people won't pay.*

If society is going to consider Cybergeddon, however remote the possibility, why not do so in a manner that's focused primarily on safeguarding us from immediate and tangible threats? *Society needs to consider solutions that will mitigate direct threats (i.e. cybercrime, espionage, etc.) without completely dismissing the hypothetical ones.* To this end, one must be willing to sift through a myriad of details in order to pinpoint the origins of cyber insecurity and explore constructive solutions. We'll do this in Part IV of this book.

Endnotes

1) H.L. Mencken, *In Defense of Women*, Dover Publications, March 2004.

2) Trevor Thrall and Jane Cramer, *American Foreign Policy and the Politics of Fear*, Routledge, 2009.

3) "Digital Blackwater: How the NSA Gives Private Contractors Control of the Surveillance State," *Democracy Now!* June 11, 2013, http://www.democracynow.org/2013/6/11/digital_blackwater_how_the_nsa_gives#.

4) Lawrence Wright, "The Spymaster, Can Mike McConnell fix America's intelligence community?" *The New Yorker*, January 21, 2008, http://www.newyorker.com/reporting/2008/01/21/080121fa_fact_wright.

5) Julian Borger, "Booz Allen Hamilton: Edward Snowden's US contracting firm," *Guardian*, June 9, 2013, http://www.guardian.co.uk/world/2013/jun/09/booz-allen-hamilton-edward-snowden/print.

6) *Fiscal Year 2011 Annual Report*, Booz Allen Hamilton, http://www.boozallen.com/investors/annual-report/annual-report-fy2011.

7) Dana Priest and Bill Arkin, "Top Secret America," *Washington Post*, http://projects.washingtonpost.com/top-secret-america/.

8) Tim Shorrock, "The spy who came in from the board room," *Salon*, January 8, 2007, http://www.salon.com/2007/01/08/mcconnell_5/.

9) "Booz Allen Not An Independent Check On SWIFT Surveillance," A Memo by the American Civil Liberties Union and Privacy International, September 14, 2006 , http://www.aclu.org/pdfs/safefree/boozallen20060914.pdf.

10) Ryan Singel, "Cyberwar Doomsayer Lands $34 Million in Government Cyberwar Contracts," *Wired*, April 13, 2010, http://www.wired.com/threatlevel/2010/04/booz-allen/.

11) Binyamin Appelbaum and Eric Lipton, "Leaker's Employer Is Paid to Maintain Government Secrets," *New York Times*, June 9, 2013, http://www.nytimes.com/2013/06/10/us/booz-allen-grew-rich-on-government-contracts.html.

12) Tim Shorrock, "Put the Spies Back Under One Roof," *New York Times*, June 17, 2013, http://www.nytimes.com/2013/06/18/opinion/put-the-spies-back-under-one-roof.html?_r=0&pagewanted=print.

13) Gus G. Sentementes, "Governor points to proximity of defense contractors, size of state's technology work force," *Baltimore Sun*, January 12, 2010.

14) *Choose Maryland > Facts & Stats: Rankings*, Maryland Department of Business and Economic Development, http://www.choosemaryland.org/factsstats/Pages/Rankings.aspx#research.

15) "Digital Blackwater: How the NSA Gives Private Contractors Control of the Surveillance State," *Democracy Now!* June 11, 2013, http://www.democracynow.org/2013/6/11/digital_blackwater_how_the_nsa_gives#.

16) Jane Mayer, "The Secret Sharer, Is Thomas Drake an enemy of the state?" *The New Yorker*, May 23, 2011, http://www.newyorker.com/reporting/2011/05/23/110523fa_fact_mayer.

17) "The Espionage Act: Why Tom Drake was indicted," *60 Minutes*, May 22, 2011, http://www.cbsnews.com/stories/2011/08/21/60minutes/main20093660.shtml.

18) Ellen Nakashima, "Former NSA executive Thomas A. Drake may pay high price for media leak," *Washington Post*, July 14, 2010, http://www.washingtonpost.com/wp-dyn/content/article/2010/07/13/AR2010071305992.html.

19) David Sirota, "How cash secretly rules surveillance policy," *Salon*, June 18, 2013, http://www.salon.com/2013/06/18/how_cash_secretly_rules_surveillance_policy/.

20) Government Accountability Project, "GAP Client Edward Snowden Speaks to German Press," *Whistleblogger*, February 03, 2014, http://www.whistleblower.org/blog/48-2014/3160-full-transcript-of-12614-snowden-television-interview-with-german-journalist-hubert-seifel.

21) *Democracy Now!*, "Chris Pyle, Whistleblower on Domestic Spying in 70s, Says Be Wary of Attacks on NSA's Critics," June 13, 2013, http://www.democracynow.org/2013/6/13/chris_pyle_whistleblower_on_cia_domestic.

22) Christopher H. Pyle, "Will We Pay Attention? Edward Snowden and the Real Issues," *Counterpunch*, June 13, 2013, http://www.counterpunch.org/2013/06/13/edward-snowden-and-the-real-issues/print.

23) Eric Lichtblau, "Large Volume of F.B.I. Files Alarms U.S. Activist Groups," *New York Times*, July 18, 2005, http://www.nytimes.com/2005/07/18/politics/18protest.html.

24) Matt Sledge, "Homeland Security Tracked Occupy Wall Street 'Peaceful Activist Demonstrations,'" *Huffington Post*, April 2, 2013, http://www.huffingtonpost.com/2013/04/02/homeland-security-occupy-wall-street_n_3002445.html.

Part III – The Futility of Offensive Solutions

Chapter 9
The Quandary of Attribution

Chapter 10
Shades of Orwell

Chapter 9

The Quandary of Attribution

Once an incident is detected in the wild, investigators turn to the discipline of computer forensics to determine how events unfolded. In doing so, forensic analysts will pose questions like: When did the attack occur? How was the attack executed? Were assets compromised? Who was behind the attack? It's this last question, the quest to assign attribution that we will focus on in this chapter.

In an attempt to identify perpetrators, investigators will consider the nature of the data that the intruders were targeting and the organization that owns it. They'll inspect the time-frame of the attacks to see if there's a correlation with other major events. Investigators will also try to recognize attack signatures by inspecting the tools that attackers used (e.g. exploits, payloads, and the delivery mechanism), the actions that attackers took once they gained a foothold inside the internal network, and the evidence that the attackers left behind.

But most important of all, they'll be keenly interested in the source of the attacker's network traffic. The Internet Protocol (IP) addresses used in an attack (e.g. used by staging machines, C2 servers, zombie hosts, etc.) are universally acknowledged pieces of investigative data.

The problem with IP addresses is that they're not necessarily a useful identifier as far as human actors are concerned. An IP address designates a device, not a person. It's bad enough just trying to associate a person with a device, sometimes it's not even possible to associate a given IP address with a specific device. The incidental admissions published in government reports and offhand remarks made by security professionals in the press reflect this state of affairs.

Recall the October 2011 report by the Office of the National Counterintelligence Executive cited earlier. It mentions attacks that originate in China but at the same time concedes:

> The IC [Intelligence Community] cannot confirm who was responsible.

So while they know where the traffic is coming from, they cannot assign attribution.

The Department of Defense says as much in its 2010 annual report on Military and Security Developments Involving the People's Republic of China:

> In 2009, numerous computer systems around the world, including those owned by the U.S. Government, continued to be the target of intrusions that appear to have originated within the PRC. These intrusions focused on exfiltrating information, some of which could be of strategic or military utility. The accesses and skills required for these intrusions are similar to those necessary to conduct computer network attacks. It remains unclear if these intrusions were conducted by, or with the endorsement of, the PLA or other elements of the PRC government.[1]

Tim McKnight is the chief information security officer at Northrop Grumman. He echoes the basic message conveyed by the aforementioned reports:

> Attribution is probably one of the biggest problems for our nation, both from a defensive and an offensive posture as a country. Obviously we know that the likes of China and Russia have the greatest capabilities, like the U.S., from an espionage perspective. But we are starting to see quite a capability in the organized crime, criminal aspect.[2]

Achieving Anonymity Online

If an attacker wants to evade attribution it's not necessarily a difficult task. With the right tools maintaining anonymity is well within the reach of non-state actors, criminal organizations, and even resourceful independent operators. Even worse, it's also entirely feasible for an attacker to utilize anti-forensic strategies to mislead investigators and frame a third party.

Do-It-Yourself Anonymity

Contrary to what some people might tell you,[3] simply going to a coffee shop with a dedicated laptop/tablet and using the free wireless access will not provide reliable anonymity. For an attacker it will more likely result in jail time. Not only will investigators be able to trace back the network traffic to a distinct geographic location, but they may very well be able to use existing close circuit camera footage to literally catch the intruder in the act. Starbucks franchises tend to be located in high traffic business zones were cameras are prevalent. Once more, if the attacker gets comfortable and makes a habit of using the same coffee shop access point they also risk establishing a pattern that can eventually be leveraged against them.

One way to foil geographic attribution is to piggyback on a poorly secured wireless network from a distance. RadioLabs sells a number of high-gain omni-directional antennas, like the WaveRV Marine XL,[4] which fit the bill. On a busy street it's likely that there will be at least one unsecured wireless router that an attacker can use as a gateway. Or, there may be access points that are secured with older protocols, like WEP or LEAP, which can be compromised with automated tools.

This technique has been so successful that it's not unheard of for police to repeatedly raid the wrong house in pursuing a criminal case because the suspect is using someone else's wireless router to get on the Internet.[5]

Nota Bene: shrewd operators recognize the all-too-real hazards of data correlation. They work clean. During a job they pay for everything in cash (to avoid leaving a credit card paper trail) and leave all other electronic devices at home. Cell phones and other wireless gadgets are essentially tracking devices.

Another way attackers subvert attribution is to rely on what's known as a *highly anonymous* proxy server. A proxy is just a computer somewhere out on the Internet that receives network requests and forwards them in such a way that they appear to originate from the proxy rather than the original computer. As an extra measure, it's not unheard of for security-conscious users to set up an encrypted Secure Shell (SSH) connection between their client computer and the proxy in an effort to protect traffic that they send to the proxy.

Though, we should also note, someone using a highly anonymous proxy is putting an incredible amount of trust in whoever is hosting the proxy machine. Blackmail anyone? Caveat emptor, a proxy server could very well be a sting operation run by law enforcement to track and entrap.

This may explain why attackers have been known to build their own ad-hoc proxy servers. When attackers gain entry to an internal network, they'll sometimes use the initially compromised machine as a proxy of sorts from which they can scan and attack other systems. The motivating idea behind this is that it allows the attacker to pick the low-hanging fruit, perhaps a desktop system used by the receptionist, and then move laterally towards more attractive targets, which themselves may also become proxies. This practice is known as *pivoting* and it is a feature supported by penetration testing frameworks like CORE IMPACT and Metasploit.

Criminals have proven that they can utilize this tactic effectively. For instance, in December of 2012 the Japanese National Police Agency (Japan's version of the FBI) announced a reward of $36,000 for information leading to the arrest of a miscreant who was posting gruesome warnings at popular Japanese bulletin board about mass killings at an elementary school. The perpetrator used compromised machines to post these messages, and police mistakenly arrested four innocent people before they realized what was going on.[6]

As mentioned earlier, using a botnet software like TDSS to create an anonymity service is merely an extension of the proxy server concept. Instead of forwarding traffic through a single proxy server, network traffic is pin-balled through hundreds of proxies before exiting to its final destination.

The general strategy, of blindly forwarding traffic through several intermediary machines, has been technically refined into a process known as *onion routing*. With a single proxy server there's always the threat that an investigator will subpoena log data from the ISP and use it to home in on an attacker's geographic location. By onion routing through a cloud of zombies, spread out over several continents, the probability of geo-location is significantly diminished. We'll explore onion routing again in the section on government-funded efforts.

Browser Profiling

Another thing that attackers are mindful of, especially during initial reconnaissance, is that the configuration of his computer can be used to construct a profile that uniquely identifies him. Web browsers, in particular, are susceptible to being fingerprinted by inspecting the meta-data they transmit to web servers during a HTTP conversation.[7] This includes stuff like the fonts that are installed, the host operating system, language settings, plug-ins, and so forth.

To minimize the amount of information revealed, an attacker will stick to a widely available browser without installing any plug-ins, add-ons, or extensions. An attacker might completely disable Javascript, disable automatic image loading (e.g. JPGs, GIFs, etc), and configure the browser not to maintain extraneous information (e.g. browsing history, cache data, cookies, etc.). Many of the popular browsers, like Firefox, offer privacy browsing modes that limit how much data they persist.

An attacker can test their browser configuration to see how it ranks. The Electronic Frontier Foundation hosts a site called Panopticlick which examines a browser's meta-data to calculate how unique its configuration is.[8] As an experiment, perform a series of runs with this web-based tool, gradually disabling browser functionality to see what sort of gains can be achieved. When it comes to anonymity, less is more.

Then there's the matter of forensic artifacts left behind on an attacker's computer (e.g. cached temporary files, browser cookies). If the computer is seized, all of these traces can be fairly damning evidence. Manually scrubbing with secure file deletion tools and disk wiping utilities is one approach. But this requires consistent operational discipline. Why take chances?

To hedge a bet, an attacker can launch their online session from an operating system that's loaded from a bootable CD. This way the OS files are guaranteed to be pristine with every system restart. The idea is to prevent forensic data from surviving the session. Any artifacts created will vanish once the machine shuts down, as most live CDs execute from an artificial system drive that's carved out of memory. There are live distributions that are specially tailored to enhance anonymity, like The Amnesiac Incognito Live System (TAILS).

Defense in Depth

An effective approach is one that relies on defense in depth. That is, combine tactics for better security. For example, an attacker can launch a network session from a laptop that boots from a TAILS CD and employs a high-gain antenna to communicate with an open wireless access point, which then routes traffic to a proxy server in another country which is linked to a command and control server managing a botnet that's providing an anonymity service. Even a veteran network security engineer would be hard-pressed to track a person using this sort of multi-tiered strategy.

Retail Products

For users with an actual budget, there are all-in-one commercial subscription-based services like Ntrepid's Internet Operations Network (ION). ION offers what they refer to as *operational non-attribution* (i.e. a sexed-up way of saying anonymity). The company maintains a veritable cloud of rotating IP addresses which utilizes multiple levels of indirection to conceal the identity of its subscribers, most of whom are likely government agents involved in open source intelligence collection.

This brings to light an important point: the government doesn't necessarily want dependable attribution to be a reality because that would make it harder for them to spy on people and execute covert operations. The following story highlights this fact.

Ntrepid has already put its technology to use on behalf of the U.S. Central Command. As part of the military's Operation Earnest Voice (OEV), a PSYOP campaign initially launched during the invasion of Iraq, Ntrepid was awarded a $2.76 million contract to develop software that would allow the Pentagon to disseminate propaganda via social media web sites.[9] The so-called "online persona management service," known as MetalGear,[10] would enable up to 50 military servicemen to control up to 10 fictitious online identities each. These fake online personas would come complete with background details and would generate network requests that appear to originate from within other countries.

For mere mortals who lack a federal budget, there's a company called Anonymizer, Inc. that offers a subscription-based non-attribution service. For about $80 a year, customers can establish an encrypted VPN session with a proxy server. This proxy then assigns the user an "untraceable" public IP address.[11] The company claims that logs are not archived or even monitored.

As I mentioned earlier, users are putting a significant amount of trust in a vendor like this. Perhaps that's why criminals prefer to take matters into their own hands and create their own anonymity networks. There's definitely something to be said for *aspiring to autonomy*.

Government-Funded Efforts

If an attacker has a large enough budget, he or she could marshal the resources necessary to design and build a custom anonymity service from the ground up, cryptographic primitives and all. *The Onion Router* (aka Tor) project was originally based on one such effort.

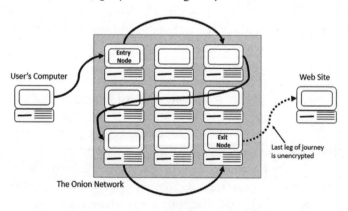

Figure 9-1

The Tor network (see Figure 9-1) is a massive collection of geo-distributed computers, or nodes. The scheme used by Tor to ensure anonymity is similar to the botnet approach. A computer running the Tor client software establishes an encrypted session with an entry node in the Tor network, and the encrypted data sent from the client is bounced around through a bunch of intermediary nodes, at random, until the corresponding network traffic hits an exit node and is sent off to the originally intended destination.

Tor is effective enough at what it does that law enforcement is often at a loss to identify attackers that use the service. For instance, the National Police Agency in Japan found the process of tracking down cyber criminals so work-intensive that in April of 2013 they asked ISPs across the country to block Tor traffic altogether.[12]

In May of 2013 *The New Yorker* launched a platform called Strong Box to receive information anonymously from whistleblowers. The site's main page (www.newyorker.com/strongbox/) includes the following statement:

> To help protect your anonymity, Strongbox is only accessible using the Tor network (https://www.torproject.org). When using Strongbox, The New Yorker will not record your I.P. address or information about your browser, computer, or operating system, nor will we embed third-party content or deliver cookies to your browser.

So it would seem that *The New Yorker* is asking users to trust Tor and offers assurances that identifying information will not be tracked. The operators of the website Cryptome offer a disclaimer regarding this service:

> StrongBox is at best only moderately secure due to its use of insecure-by-design Tor and .onion. At worst it is highly insecure due to excessive and misleading promotion of Tor and .onion, both easily spied upon services by officials, their contractors and individuals who have the same hacking and cracking skills ...
>
> Security experts claim that undisclosed weaknesses are far more valuable than strengths because promoting widespread use of a trusted but faulty system facilitates covert hacking and cracking.[13]

The NSA is leveraging Tor's gaining popularity. While a top-secret internal document admits that the NSA will never be able to undermine the privacy of *all Tor users all of the time*, the document also states:

> [A] critical mass of targets use tor. Scaring them away from Tor might be counterproductive ... [14]

The *Washington Post* reports:

> One document provided by Snowden included an internal exchange among NSA hackers in which one of them said the agency's Remote Operations Center was capable of targeting anyone who visited an al-Qaeda Web site using Tor.[15]

It seems that the NSA *wants* people to keep using Tor because it will keep targets of interest in a domain where the NSA can use a growing collection of tools to spy on them.

This underscores Cryptome's cautionary statement. What better way to spy on people than to get them to use a technology that they mistakenly believe will protect their privacy? Though Tor is open source and uses a technique that looks great on paper, it's not entirely without risks.

For example, it's possible for Tor nodes to become subverted by malware (or unscrupulous node operators) and subsequently be used to determine who's talking to whom. It's been shown that if someone using Tor also happens to be using an inherently insecure peer-to-peer file sharing application (e.g. BitTorrent) they face the risk of exposing their position.[16]

Then there's the fact that older versions of Tor server software (i.e. prior to version 2.4) use weak encryption that many people believe the NSA can easily crack using arrays of custom-built hardware. Security researcher Rob Graham describes the results of an experiment involving over 22,000 Tor connections:

> Recently, I ran a "hostile" exit node and recorded the encryption negotiated by incoming connections (the external link encryption, not the internal circuits). This tells me whether

they are using the newer or older software. Only about 24% of incoming connections were using the newer software.[17]

In what's known as a *traffic confirmation attack* (also known as *end-to-end correlation*), an opponent watching both the network traffic going into a circuit of Tor nodes and the traffic exiting the circuit can wield statistical tools to identify a specific communication path. This attack works primarily because Tor is a low-latency service which aims to get network traffic to its destination with minimal delay. Given that roughly 90 percent of the world's Internet communication flows through the United States,[18] there are those who argue that an organization like the NSA could wield this technique successfully.[19]

There may be other, less public, state-sponsored anonymity frameworks that have tackled this issue by injecting random cover traffic to generate signal noise and frustrate traffic confirmation.

Staining documents with watermarks, or other less flagrant identifiers, is an age-old technique used by intelligence services to track down moles. In an attack which leverages this concept, the NSA has been known to stain network traffic by purchasing ad space from online companies like Google.[20] The NSA advertisements incite a user's web browser to create a cookie which identifies the user viewing the ad. The NSA uses this cookie as a stain of sorts so that they can spot a particular user even if their IP address changes.

It's also possible for client machines using Tor to be purposefully infected by drive-by malware so that they can be identified. In early August of 2013 a report appeared in *Wired* magazine about one such incident. Researchers discovered malware that leveraged a software flaw in Mozilla's Firefox web browser to identify users trying to disguise their location via anonymity services like Tor.[21] It turned out that the FBI was behind the subversion campaign.[22]

Attribution via malware is used heavily by the NSA.[23] According to leaked documents, the NSA performs what's known as a *man-in-the-middle* (MITM) attack to impersonate legitimate web sites and then infect Tor users who visit these doppelganger web sites.

Looking at the NSA's approach in more detail, the MITM attack is implemented by a series of servers (codenamed QUANTUM) which have been placed at strategic points on the high-speed cables that make up the Internet's backbone. This placement is crucial, and depends heavily on cooperation with major Telecom providers. QUANTUM servers have to be is a position where they can respond more quickly than the legitimate web sites, so that the QUANTUM servers can beat them to the punch line, so to speak. It's sort of a *High-Frequency Trading* effect, where servers gain an inside edge because their privileged geographic placement offers faster access.

Once QUANTUM servers have acquired the undivided attention of the Tor user's web browser, they execute a packet injection attack that directs the Tor user to a second set of servers, codenamed FOXACID. FOXACID servers are *exploit orchestrators* that can use a variety of specially-tailored attacks to infect a visiting computer. Once infected, a compromised machine establishes a covert communication channel, known as a *callback*, with FOX-ACID servers to funnel user data to the NSA and install additional malware if needed to ensure long-term infestation. In essence, FOXACID servers are command and control machines.

To get an idea of the scale of this program, in 2008 the volume of callback traffic became so great that the NSA had to develop a dedicated system just to handle it. In retrospect it would appear that the NSA is building its own botnets and is following the basic operational strategies and multi-tiered architectural schemes presented in Chapter Four.

The Origins of Tor

Weaknesses aside, the Tor project was originally funded by the U.S. Naval Research Laboratory,[24] and it still receives a significant amount of money from the government.[25] The Tor project's 2012 financial report states the Department of Defense (via SRI) provided $876,099 in funds.[26] This is roughly 40 percent of the project's $2 million budget.

According to Michael Reed, one of the founding fathers of Tor:

> The original *QUESTION* posed that led to the invention
> of Onion Routing was, "Can we build a system that allows

for bi-directional communications over the Internet where the source and destination cannot be determined by a mid-point?" The *PURPOSE* was for DoD/Intelligence usage (open source intelligence gathering, covering of forward deployed assets, whatever). Not helping dissidents in repressive countries. Not assisting criminals in covering their electronic tracks. Not helping bit-torrent users avoid MPAA/RIAA prosecution. Not giving a 10 year old a way to bypass an anti-porn filter. Of course, we knew those would be other unavoidable uses for the technology, but that was immaterial to the problem at hand we were trying to solve (and if those uses were going to give us more cover traffic to better hide what we wanted to use the network for, all the better ... I once told a flag officer that much to his chagrin). I should know, I was the recipient of that question from David, and Paul was brought into the mix a few days later after I had sketched out a basic (flawed) design for the original Onion Routing.

The short answer to your question of "Why would the government do this?" is because it is in the best interests of some parts of the government to have this capability ... [27]

Why would a government need to develop anonymous communication technology? As Reed states, onion routing was invented because the U.S. government wanted to collect intelligence.

Attribution for Everyone ... But The Inner Party

Mr. Reed's candid e-mail raises issues. There's a sort of cognitive dissonance at play. Officials publicly announce that they want "to make attribution, geolocation, intelligence analysis and impact assessment – who did it, from where, why and what was the result – more manageable."[28] In other words, they want to drive anonymity out of the Internet. Yet, oddly, at the same time the Department of Defense forged ahead to investigate technology that helped create the Tor project.

Such is the apparent double standard. In a world of stark transparency the invisible man is king. The U.S. government is completely trustworthy a priori, and so it's assumed that it should be the sole beneficiary of truly high-security technology. Everyone else, outside of the government's circle of trust, must surrender their privacy and make do with intentionally hobbled software.

The Folly of Attribution

As far as espionage is concerned the absence of attribution appears to be the rule rather than the exception. In fact, there have been instances in the past where when investigators thought that a nation-state was involved and strongly believed that they knew who was responsible, and were completely wrong.

A DDoS attack noted earlier in Chapter Seven is an example: early in July of 2009, the *Wall Street Journal* published an article about DDoS attacks that simultaneously hit government networks belonging to the United States and South Korea.[29] The article intimated that North Korea might be responsible, given that the attacks began following the United Nations decision to impose new sanctions on the country.

Right on cue, Peter Hoekstra, the lead Republican on the House Intelligence Committee, made a public appearance on a conservative radio show calling for a "show of force" against North Korea:

> It is time for America and South Korea, Japan and others to stand up to North Korea or the next time … they will go in and shut down a banking system or they will manipulate financial data or they will manipulate the electrical grid, either here or in South Korea.[30]

Investigators eventually traced the attacks to a server in Great Britain. The company that owned this server, Global Digital Broadcast, published a press release a few days after Hoekstra's call to arms:

> Global Digital Broadcast Limited were aware of the circumstance in the middle of Monday night and due to the nature and potential location it was coming from, have treated it with utmost severity. Our engineers quickly discounted it as coming from a North Korean Government site, as suggested and was tracked back to the source which was on a VPN circuit in Miami.[31]

For all of the bombast about North Korea, the attacks were tracked back to an ambiguous dead end in Miami, which could have been anyone or perhaps another relay in a longer circuit. Can you imagine how our leaders would look if they had followed Hoekstra's suggestion? This episode should be a lesson to anyone who feels the urge to entertain the sabre rattling of politicians in the wake of a cyber-attack.

History repeated itself years later in March of 2013, when two South Korean broadcasters and three South Korean banks suffered cyber-attacks that affected some 32,000 computers. The attackers, a group calling itself the "Whois Team," executed their attack using relatively unsophisticated commodity malware which wipes the hard drive of the computers it compromises.[32]

Investigators initially traced the attacks to what they believed was the IP address of a server in China,[33] and commentators were quick to direct blame towards North Korea which had been making threats in response to a new round of economic sanctions by the United Nations.[34] Shortly afterwards, the Korea Communications Commission discovered that the IP address that they thought belonged to a Chinese server was actually the virtual IP address of a computer within one of the attacked banks.[35] One of the officers involved in the investigation lamented that it could take longer than a murder investigation to determine responsibility.[36]

In early April of 2013, South Korean investigators revealed some of their findings.[37] Specifically they announced that of the more than 1,000 IP addresses used in the attack (which were spread over 40 countries) only 13 were linked to locations in North Korea. Investigators also noted that of the 76 malicious software applications used in the attack, 30 were used in previous attacks where North Korea was suspect. Based on what we've seen so far, in addition to the material presented in the following section, these artifacts hardly assign culpability. Though the South Korean Internet and Security Agency (KISA) thinks that they do.

Anti-Forensics

The techniques surveyed in this chapter, which conceal the origin of network traffic, are just one subset of tools in a much larger black bag of tools. There are countless types of evidence that can be rigged, overwritten, manufactured, and distorted. In fact, over the years an entire discipline has evolved that's dedicated to turning the whole process of computer investigation on its ear: we are referring to anti-forensics.[38]

As the Grugq has noted, the goal of anti-forensics is to significantly reduce both the *quantity* of useful evidence that's left behind and the *quality* of this evidence.[39] This goal can be expressed in terms of five core strategies:

Data destruction	Destroy artifacts that have been created.
Data source elimination	Prevent artifacts from being created to begin with.
Data concealment	Hide artifacts in unexpected places.
Data transformation	Encode artifacts that cannot be destroyed.
Data fabrication	Create false artifacts that appear genuine.

Restating the original definition, anti-forensics seeks to defeat the process of forensic investigation by minimizing the number of forensic artifacts (data source elimination and data destruction). The artifacts that do remain will be tough to identify (data concealment) and difficult to interpret (data transformation). To add insult to injury, an attacker can leave behind misinformation that lures the incidence response to incorrect conclusions (data fabrication).

In 1992 an article appeared in the *Los Angeles Times* about "nearly perfect" counterfeit U.S. $100 bills that had found their way into circulation.[40] A congressional report placed the blame on Iran. The Secret Service, on the other hand, declined to comment on this report or its allegations. Nevertheless, there's a relevant point here: if it's possible to create "nearly perfect" forgeries of American currency, then creating forged cyber-attacks is also completely plausible. People who develop anti-forensic tools can testify that the technology has attained a level of sophistication where an attacker can tell whatever story they want … and it will entirely convince more credulous members of the public.

False-Flag Operations

Anti-forensics enables false-flag operations, a stratagem as old as espionage and a time-honored approach for justifying wars. From the standpoint of an offensive operation, it's usually in an attacker's best interests to muddy the water as much as possible. Should people expect anything less from national intelligence services or organized criminal enterprises?

It's only logical that an operator running a spy shop, as a matter of standard procedure, would go to great lengths to obfuscate any trail and stage operations in such a way as to implicate a third-party. Using internationalized tools, a different language, foreign computing algorithms, planted artifacts, and pivot points in other countries are all par for the course. Any spies worth their salt will use these techniques.

Intelligence officials describe measures taken by the NSA's Office of Tailored Access Operations (TAO):

> TAO increasingly depends on clandestine techniques, such as commercial cover, to hide its activities. TAO uses an array of commercial business entities, some of them proprietary companies established specifically for this purpose, to try to hide its global computer-hacking activities from computer security experts in a maze of interlocking computer servers and command-and-control systems located in the United States and overseas that have no discernible link to the NSA or the U.S. government. [41]

The companies that sell security services appear to discount this reality. For instance, during an interview on the *PBS News Hour*, a representative from one vendor described how his company allegedly tracked down a series of cyber-attacks to China.

> We have got some proprietary methods. But I would probably – there's a corollary to the physical world, to a real-life burglary.
>
> A detective will look for the M.O. of a particular thief. And they will look at the tools they use, the techniques they use, the time of day they break in, and what approach they take to casing out a particular site.
>
> And we do much the same thing in the cyber-world. We look at hundreds, if not thousands, of indicators. We group those into particular groups of threat actors. And when we see those tools and techniques used again, we can usually pinpoint it with pretty good accuracy.[42]

But indicators and signatures need to be interpreted, and this means they can be manipulated to manufacture different perceptions.

Despite what security vendors may want us to accept, with coy references to proprietary methods (forensic "special sauce"), attribution is meaningless when squaring off against a disciplined opponent.

It's meaningless because *governments and private sector outfits in several nations have developed, and invested heavily in, anti-forensic technology which ensures that this is the case.* The bottom line: there are high-level actors stealing secrets, and foiling attribution is a necessary prerequisite. Welcome, dear reader, to the wilderness of mirrors.

Ultimately, most forensic artifacts are primarily just a sequence of bytes. These bytes can be manipulated by an attacker to create the desired perception of culpability. To compound matters, everyone has good reasons to fabricate evidence. A post at the website Cryptome describes a few such reasons[43]:

> Security experts plant malware, genuine and spoofed, as poison pills or APTs to trace, combat and counterattack attackers, to deceive and scare downloaders and to muddle publicity about attacks. Competitors plant malware to disparage products and services. AV firms plant malware to boost the market. Governments plant malware to increase fear, doubt and dependency on national security. Hackers plant malware for lulz and braggardy. Malware – and reports of malware – can be an attention-getting hoax as with any form of fear-driven security.

Given the ease with which a funded operation could stage a cyber-attack and make it appear to emanate from a particular foreign country, it's risky to put one's faith in the clues that attackers leave behind. In fact, *you should be particularly suspicious of government officials like Peter Hoekstra who fail to question the veracity of digital forensic artifacts and then hastily overreact.*

Deterrence

In the quest for better security, former DNI Mike McConnell advises us to look back to the Cold War, where the United States used to threat of massive retaliation to keep enemies in check. He's not alone, former DHS Secretary Michael Chertoff has said that countries should have the capability to respond "with overwhelming force" to cyber-attacks.[44]

This mindset has been spelled out formally in official documents. For example, The Defense Science Board (DSB)'s Task Force on *Resilient Military Systems and the Advanced Cyber Threat* is the product of an 18-month study and outlines what it refers to as an "overall risk reduction strategy."[45] That strategy projects a future of cyber warfare in which the U.S. will deter attacks in part by ensuring a nuclear strike capability in the face of "existential cyber attack" and developing "*world* class cyber offensive capabilities" and an expanded legion of "cyber warriors."

What this entails is investing heavily in cyber arms and, as a direct consequence, providing a healthy infusion of tax dollars to the defense industry. The problem with leveraging a stockpile of pricey cyber weapons to discourage attackers is that the government needs to know where to aim them once attacked. If you can't determine who's behind an attack, how do you retaliate? Martin Libicki, a senior researcher at Rand, warns:

> If you can't execute it [massive retaliation], you're bluffing. It's possible to believe people will call our bluff. If it turns out we can't do what we say, we not only look embarrassed for ourselves, but we end up calling all of our other deterrents into question.[46]

During the Cold War, it was easy to pinpoint where intercontinental ballistic missiles were launched from. As we have clearly shown, the same dynamic doesn't hold on the Internet. Operational anonymity is well within the reach of a funded group, whether the attackers are part of a campaign run by an intelligence agency, sponsored by rogue corporate interests, or bankrolled by criminal organizations. To be effective, deterrence depends on attribution. But attribution is a scarce commodity at best.

There are those who would take the convenient shortcut of equating attribution with origin. Pay no heed to who's actually behind an attack, all they care about is where it came from. Former NSA director Michael Hayden proposes:

Since the price of entry is so low, and ... it's difficult to prove state sponsorship, one of the thoughts ... is to just be uninterested in that distinction and to actually hold states responsible for that activity emanating from their cyberspace.[47]

Would this approach simply make it easier for one country to incriminate another and instigate conflict? This mindset effectively lowers the bar with respect to assessing culpability, raising the effectiveness of false-flag ops to a whole new level.

Arms Control Treaties

Back in 1972, when Richard Nixon was President, the United States joined in an international treaty with the United Kingdom and the Soviet Union to ban research on and the production of bioweapons. What the United States didn't realize is that the Soviets interpreted the 1972 Biological Weapons Convention as a green light to aggressively race ahead with its own program that scaled up into hundreds of tons. Perhaps the Soviets thought that they could gain a strategic advantage while everyone else was dismantling their own programs? According to Kanatjan Alibekov, the First Deputy Director of Biopreparat (the Soviet's biological weapons program):

In the '70s and beginning of '80s the Soviet Union started developing new biological weapons – Marburg infection biological weapon, Ebola infection biological weapon, Machupo infection, [or] Bolivian hemorrhagic biological weapon, and some others.[48]

In 1979, somewhere in the neighborhood of 100 people died suddenly from anthrax in the city of Sverdlovsk, Russia. At the time the Soviets claimed the deaths were caused by tainted meat. Over a decade later, President Boris Yeltsin admitted that the deaths were a result of military activity.

For years, the Soviets were secretly running the world's most sophisticated bioweapons program while claiming publicly that they were adhering to the 1972 treaty. Keep in mind that manufacturing bioweapons on an industrial scale entails a nontrivial footprint that involves dozens of locations and thousands of people. This kind of program was something that was not easy to disguise, especially with CIA specialists engaged heavily in "all source analysis" to ferret out indicators.

The same dynamic doesn't apply to cyber weapons. Software engineers don't need fermenting vats that are a story and a half high. Cyber weapons tend to be small and easy to conceal. Engineers can develop cyber weapons anywhere, with little or no footprint, using tightly compartmentalized cells of developers hidden away in unremarkable office spaces. All that's needed is computers, development tools, and access to the Internet (none of which will raise any eyebrows). In the end, all of the documentation and finished binaries can be zipped up and archived in an encrypted file that takes up a less than 100 megabytes. Try hunting that down with a spy satellite!

Even if a country signed a treaty that bound them not to develop certain types of cyber weapons, there would be no way to verify such an agreement. Once more, if a country actually breaks its promise and deploys offensive cyber ordnance, it will no doubt also utilize anonymity technology in conjunction with anti-forensics to throw off investigators. In other words, the notion that we could use arms control to limit the development of cyber weaponry is probably not practical.

Endnotes

1) *Military and Security Developments Involving the People's Republic of China 2010*, Office of the Secretary of Defense, Office http://www.defense.gov/pubs/pdfs/2010_CMPR_Final.pdf.

2) "Under Cyberthreat: Defense Contractors," *Bloomberg Businessweek*, July 6, 2009, http://www.businessweek.com/technology/content/jul2009/tc2009076_873512.htm.

3) Nicholas Weaver, "Hear Ye, Future Deep Throats: This Is How to Leak to the Press," *Wired*, May 14, 2013, http://www.wired.com/opinion/2013/05/listen-up-future-deep-throats-this-is-how-to-leak-to-the-press-today/.

4) WaveRV Marine XL – Ultra Long Range Marine Wifi Antenna, RadioLabs, http://www.radiolabs.com/products/wireless/marine-wifi-antenna.php.

5) John Emshwiller, "So Many Local Crimes, So Few Cybercops to Help," *Wall Street Journal*, October 7, 2009, http://online.wsj.com/article/SB125487044221969127.html.

6) Jay Alabaster, "Japan police offers first-ever reward for wanted hacker," *IDG News*, December 13, 2012, http://www.networkworld.com/news/2012/121312-japan-police-offers-first-ever-reward-265060.html.

7) Peter Eckersley, "How Unique Is Your Web Browser," *Proceedings of the Privacy Enhancing Technologies Symposium (PETS 2010)*, Springer Lecture Notes in Computer Science, http://panopticlick.eff.org/browser-uniqueness.pdf.

8) Panopticlick: How Unique – and Trackable – Is Your Broswer, Electronic Frontier Foundation, http://panopticlick.eff.org/.

9) Nick Fielding and Ian Cobain, "Revealed: US spy operation that manipulates social media," *Guardian*, March 17, 2011, http://www.guardian.co.uk/technology/2011/mar/17/us-spy-operation-social-networks.

10) Steve Ragan, "Representative Johnson refuses to sweep Team Themis under the rug," *thetechherald.com*, April 8, 2011, http://www.thetechherald.com/articles/Representative-Johnson-refuses-to-sweep-Team-Themis-under-the-rug.

11) Anonymizer, Inc., "How it Works," http://www.anonymizer.com/homeuser/universal#howitworks.

12) Ravi Mandalia, "Japanese Police Urge ISPs to Block Tor," *Parity News*, April 22, 2013, http://paritynews.com/government/item/1000-japanese-police-urge-isps-to-block-tor?tmpl=component&print=1.

13) "The New Yorker StrongBox," May 16, 2013, http://cryptome.org/2013/05/newyorker-strongbox.htm.

14) *Tor Stinks*, National Security Agency, January 8, 2007, http://s3.documentcloud.org/documents/801434/doc2.pdf.

15) Barton Gellman, Craig Timberg, and Steven Rich, "Secret NSA documents show campaign against Tor encrypted network," *Washington Post*, October 4, 2013, http://www.washingtonpost.com/world/national-security/secret-nsa-documents-show-campaign-against-tor-encrypted-network/2013/10/04/610f08b6-2d05-11e3-8ade-a1f23cda135e_print.html.

16) *One Bad Apple Spoils the Bunch*, Stevens Le Blond Pere Manils Abdelberi Chaabane Mohamed Ali Kaafar Claude Castelluccia Arnaud Legout Walid Dabbous, LEET 2011, 4th USENIX Workshop on Large-Scale Exploits and Emergent Threats, March 29, 2011, http://static.usenix.org/event/leet11/tech/slides/leblond.pdf.

17) Robert Graham, "Tor is still DHE 1024 (NSA crackable)," *Errata Security*, September 6, 2013, http://blog.erratasec.com/2013/09/tor-is-still-dhe-1024-nsa-crackable.html.

18) James Ball, "NSA stores metadata of millions of web users for up to a year, secret files show," *Guardian*, September 30, 2013, http://www.theguardian.com/world/2013/sep/30/nsa-americans-metadata-year-documents/print.

19) Maxim Kammerer, *[tor-talk] End-to-end correlation for fun and profit*, August 20, 2007, https://lists.torproject.org/pipermail/tor-talk/2012-August/025254.html.

20) Seth Rosenblatt, "NSA tracks Google ads to find Tor users," *CNET*, October 4, 2013, http://news.cnet.com/8301-1009_3-57606178-83/nsa-tracks-google-ads-to-find-tor-users/.

21) Kevin Poulsen, "Feds are Suspects in New Malware That Attacks Tor Anonymity," *Wired*, August 5, 2013, http://www.wired.com/threatlevel/2013/08/freedom-hosting/.

22) Kevin Poulsen, "FBI Admits It Controlled Tor Servers Behind Mass Malware Attack," *Wired*, September 13, 2013, http://www.wired.com/threatlevel/2013/09/freedom-hosting-fbi/.

23) Bruce Schneier, "Attacking Tor: how the NSA targets users' online anonymity," *Guardian*, October 4, 2013, http://www.theguardian.com/world/2013/oct/04/tor-attacks-nsa-users-online-anonymity/print.

24) David M. Goldschlag, Michael G. Reed, and Paul F. Syverson. "Hiding Routing Information," *Workshop on Information Hiding*, Cambridge, UK, May, 1996, http://www.onion-router.net/Publications/IH-1996.pdf.

25) Alan Taylor, "Tor Funding Smoke Screen," *PGPBOARD*, December 7, 2011, https://eta.securesslhost.net/~pgpboar/viewtopic.php?t=573&p=755.

26) The Tor Project, Inc. and Affiliate Consolidated Financial Statements And Reports Required For Audits In Accordance With Government Auditing Standards And Omb Circular A-133, December 31, 2012 And 2011, https://www.torproject.org/about/findoc/2012-TorProject-FinancialStatements.pdf.

27) Michael Reed, "Re: [tor-talk] Iran cracks down on web dissident technology," tor-talk mailing list, March 22, 2011, http://cryptome.org/0003/tor-spy.htm.

28) Mike McConnell, "Mike McConnell on how to win the cyberwar we're losing," *Washington Post*, February 28, 2010, http://www.washingtonpost.com/wp-dyn/content/article/2010/02/25/AR2010022502493.html.

29) Siobhan Gorman and Evan Ramstad, "Cyber Blitz Hits U.S., Korea," *Wall Street Journal*, July 9, 2009, http://online.wsj.com/article/SB124701806176209691.html.

30) Kim Zetter, "Lawmaker Wants 'Show of Force' Against North Korea for Website Attacks," *Wired*, July 10, 2009, http://www.wired.com/threatlevel/2009/07/show-of-force/.

31) *DDoS on US and South Korea*, Global Digital Broadcast Press Release, July 14, 2009, http://www.globaldigitalbroadcast.com/newspage.php?newsId=123.

32) Mathew J. Schwartz, "South Korea Bank Hacks: 7 Key Facts," *InformationWeek*, March 21, 2013, http://www.informationweek.com/security/attacks/south-korea-bank-hacks-7-key-facts/240151355.

33) Ju-min Park, "UPDATE 3-Hacking highlights dangers to Seoul of North's cyber-warriors," *Reuters*, March 21, 2013, http://www.reuters.com/article/2013/03/21/korea-cyber-idUSL3N0CD0SF20130321.

34) Tania Branigan in Beijing and Ewen MacAskill, "UN backs expansion of North Korea sanctions after nuclear threat," *Guardian*, March 7, 2013, http://www.guardian.co.uk/world/2013/mar/07/north-korea-threat-un-sanctions.

35) Jack Kim and Ju-min Park, "Cyber-attack on South Korea may not have come from China after all: regulator," *Reuters*, March 22, 2013, http://www.reuters.com/article/2013/03/22/us-cyber-korea-idUSBRE92L07120130322.

36) Se Young Lee, "South Korea raises alert after hackers attack broadcasters, banks," *Reuters*, March 20, 2013, http://www.reuters.com/article/2013/03/20/net-us-korea-cyber-outage-idUSBRE92J06F20130320.

37) Youkyung Lee, "SKorea says NKorea behind computer crash in March," *Associated Press*, April 10, 2013.

38) Bill Blunden, *The Rootkit Arsenal*, Jones and Bartlett, 2013, ISBN-13: 9781449626365.

39) The Grugq, *The Art of Defiling: Defeating Forensic Analysis on Unix File Systems*, Black Hat Asia 2003, http://www.blackhat.com/presentations/bh-asia-03/bh-asia-03-grugq/bh-asia-03-grugq.pdf.

40) Sara Fritz, "Iran Accused of Printing Fake U.S. Bills: Counterfeiting: Report by House Republicans says billions in bogus money is circulating with Syria's help," *Los Angeles Times*, July 2, 1992. http://articles.latimes.com/print/1992-07-02/news/mn-1906_1_counterfeit-bills.

41) Matthew Aid, "The NSA's New Code Breakers," *Foreign Policy*, October 15, 2013, http://www.foreignpolicy.com/articles/2013/10/15/the_nsa_s_new_codebreakers?print=yes&hidecomments=yes&page=full.

42) Ray Suarez, Nicole Perlroth and Grady Summers, "*New York Times* Computer System Target of Lengthy Chinese Hacking Attack," *PBS News Hour*, January 31, 2013, http://www.pbs.org/newshour/bb/media/jan-june13/hacked_01-31.html.

43) "Malware Reported in Bank of America Files," *Cryptome*, March 1, 2013, http://cryptome.org/2013/03/boa-malware.htm.

44) Tom Espiner, "Chertoff advocates cyber Cold war," ZDNet UK, October 14, 2010, http://www.zdnet.co.uk/news/security-threats/2010/10/14/chertoff-advocates-cyber-cold-war-40090538/.

45) Defense Science Board, "Task Force Report: Resilient Military Systems and the Advanced Cyber Threat," Office of the Under Secretary of Defense for Acquisition, Technology, and Logistics, January 2013, http://www.acq.osd.mil/dsb/reports/ResilientMilitarySystems.CyberThreat.pdf.

46) Grant Goss, "U.S. cyber war policy needs new focus," *IDG News*, October 29, 2009, http://www.computerworld.com/s/article/9140131/U.S._cyber_war_policy_needs_new_focus_experts_say.

47) Kim Zetter, "Former NSA Director: Countries Spewing Cyberattacks Should Be Held Responsible," *Wired*, July 29, 2010, http://www.wired.com/threatlevel/2010/07/hayden-at-blackhat/.

48) *Plague War*, Frontline, October 13, 1998, http://www.pbs.org/wgbh/pages/frontline/shows/plague/.

Chapter 10

Shades of Orwell

It is really very nearly within our grasp to be able to compute on all human generated information.

– Ira Hunt, CIA Chief Technology Officer[1]

The Internet is being transformed into a military-occupied state.

– Julian Assange[2]

We managed to survive greater threats in our history ... than a few disorganized terrorist groups and rogue states without resorting to these sorts of programs.

– Ed Snowden[3]

I believe there are more instances of the abridgement of the freedom of the people by gradual and silent encroachments of those in power than by violent and sudden usurpations.

– President James Madison[4]

Despite the prevalence of anti-forensic technology, there are still those who believe that they can solve the quandary of attribution by instituting measures which are reminiscent of China's old Hukou and Liangpiao systems. In other words, they believe that if they simply capture, archive, track, and analyze enough data they can achieve the Holy Grail of determining precisely who did what, and to whom, out on the Internet.

Ronald Noble is the current Secretary General of Interpol. In an effort to combat terror he wants to be able to track everything that flies over the Internet.

> One of the things I want to do ... is to create a cyber-fusion centre, where police around the world can go to one place quickly and find out the source of any kind of message or communication that's come across the Internet.[5]

The desire to safeguard national security appears to be a standard pretext. In a letter sent to the Undersecretary of Homeland Security, congressional representatives Jackie Speier and Patrick Meehan stated:

> It would be advantageous for DHS and the broader Intelligence Community to carefully parse the massive streams of data from various social media outlets to identify current or emerging threats to our homeland security.[6]

Few of these proponents seem to question whether this sort of approach will even provide tangible benefits, and if the few morsels of intelligence actually captured will be worth the price of our civil liberties. Back in 2006, a report published by the *Washington Post* put the number of people being watched without court authority at around 5,000. According to this same article, less than 10 of these people succeeded in rousing enough suspicion to justify the interception of their communications.[7]

The Golden Age of Surveillance

That the Internet is a gigantic spying machine has been known since its invention.

– Cryptome

In light of recent technical advances and legal developments it's plausible to argue that society is already in the process of entering a golden age of surveillance.[8] The burgeoning market for mass interception tools that we discussed earlier is an indicator of this trend.

The sheer demand for monitoring technology is reflected by the fact that between 2001 and 2011 the number of instances where the Department of Justice used warrantless surveillance methods increased six-fold: from 5,683 to 37,616.[9] AT&T likewise reports that in 2011 it received in excess of 700 monitoring requests *every day* from various law enforcement agents, of which approximately 230 sidestepped the normal warrant process. This is triple the number of daily requests fielded by AT&T in 2007.[10]

In the second half of 2012, Microsoft received somewhere between 6,000 and 7,000 legal requests for user data (covering some 31,000 to 32,000 accounts). Facebook received somewhere between 9,000 and 10,000 legal requests (covering some 18,000 to 19,000 accounts).[11]

Contrary to the claims of law enforcement officials that they're "going dark," with regard to their inability to monitor the public as technology progresses,[12] the tools available to our security services allow them to do things that they could only have dreamed of back in the 1980s. Then there's also the fact that, in this day and age, most people voluntarily carry a tracking device (i.e. a smart phone) which can be used to pinpoint their geographic locations, past movements, as well as harvesting a wealth of meta-data.[13]

The end result is that people's daily interactions generate a rich trail of digital evidence that investigators can use to map out social relationships and create individual dossiers in ways that were unthinkable in J. Edgar Hoover's era. As Cryptome has claimed for years, the Internet is a massive tool for surveillance.[14] There are sprawling databases of information being maintained about us, and intelligence officers are just itching to find new ways to leverage them.

Warrantless Wiretapping

High-ranking officials have been less than forthcoming about all of this. If anything, they've tried to downplay it, lie about it, or simply keep it under wraps. The program of warrantless wiretapping that took place during the tenure of George W. Bush, known inside the NSA by the code name *Stellar Wind*, was secretly authorized by the executive branch in 2002. It allowed the NSA to tap into the fiber optic cables which connect the United States to other countries using special fiber optic signal splitters.[15]

If you're curious, the website Cryptome has maps that detail the fiber optic cable landings on both the Atlantic and Pacific coasts:

Transatlantic   http://cryptome.org/eyeball/cable/cable-eyeball.htm
Transpacific   http://cryptome.org/eyeball/cablew/cablew-eyeball.htm

In 2005, based on information provided by a whistleblower in the Department of Justice named Thomas Tamm,[16] the *New York Times* broke the story about the Stellar Wind[17] and public outcry was strong enough that the program was presumably halted in early 2007.[18] On the other hand, based on leaked documents, the NSA still accesses these backbone fiber optic cables under a secret program known as UPSTREAM.[19]

It's interesting how the Bush administration attempted to frame this illegal collection by referring to it as the *Terrorist Surveillance Program.*

Years later, in March of 2010, a federal judge ruled that the surveillance program was illegal and awarded damages to an Islamic charity named Al Haramain that had been under scrutiny. The case succeeded because the plaintiffs were able to prove they were the subject of surveillance. The government, it turns out, enabled this lawsuit by accidentally released a classified document proving that the plaintiffs were being monitored.[20]

FISA Amendments Act of 2008

The end of the Terrorist Surveillance Program was not the end of warrantless wiretapping. Lawmakers responded to the suspension of the program by spearheading amendments to the *Foreign Intelligence Surveillance Act* (FISA) of 1978. This was a shot across the bow as far as civil liberties are concerned.

To see why, let's rewind to the Nixon era. The FISA of 1978 is a law that was enacted specifically to outlaw warrantless wiretaps. It was a direct result of the Church Committee investigations of the 1970s, a series of congressional hearings and reports that were conducted to probe abuse of authority by U.S. security services (the FBI, CIA, and NSA) in the wake of the Watergate scandal.

Lawmakers were eager to loosen restrictions established by FISA. The resulting *Protect America Act of 2007* in effect moved the goal posts to legalize aspects of the warrantless wiretapping program that were originally prohibited, in addition to providing complete legal immunity to telecom carriers that had cooperated with the government. When the Protect America Act of 2007 hit its built-in expiration date, the subsequent *FISA Amendments Act of 2008* was enacted to instantiate many of the provisions of the 2007 act.[21]

Specifically, *section 702* of the FISA Amendments Act of 2008 allows the government to monitor communications (email, text messages, phone calls) to acquire "foreign intelligence" on a non-citizen without a probable-cause warrant if that non-citizen is "reasonably believed to be located outside the United States." David Kris, a former attorney for the Department of Justice claims that the government has construed the law in a manner where purely domestic communication can also be captured and analyzed as long as the parties involved are believed to be members of al-Qaeda.[22]

Hence, if you're a suspected terrorist or talking to a targeted non-citizen outside of the United States, you can be monitored without a probable cause warrant.

But even then there are caveats that increase your chances of being watched. For instance, the *Washington Post* reported that analysts only needed to be 51 percent sure that a target was foreign in order to collect information.[23] According to government documents that were leaked by the *Guardian*, it turns out:

> In the absence of specific information regarding whether a target is a United States person ... a person reasonably believed to be located outside the United States or whose location is not known will be presumed to be a non-United States person unless such person can be positively identified as a United States person.[24]

If they can't figure out if a given target is an American or not, they can just keep on spying. This means that anyone using Tor could potentially have communications captured and archived.

And it gets worse. The NSA is doing more than just capturing the exchanges of citizens directly communicating with foreign people targeted outside of the U.S. According to a report published by the *New York Times* in August of 2013, an unnamed senior intelligence official claimed that the NSA is also searching all of the e-mail and other text-based digital communications that cross the U.S. border for anyone who merely references information about a foreign target of interest (e.g. a name, e-mail address, IP address, telephone number, etc.).[25]

In other words, all you have to do is to mention the name of a suspected "terrorist" in a message that crosses the border, perhaps to an e-mail provider that resides outside the U.S.

The NSA somehow doesn't see this as "bulk collection." According to the official that spoke with the *Times*:

> "Bulk collection" is when we collect and retain for some period of time that lets us do retrospective analysis …. In this case, we do not do that, so we do not consider this "bulk collection." [26]

The Electronic Frontier Foundation offers a response to the NSA's semantic acrobatics:

> In other words, because the NSA does some sort of initial content searches of the bulk communications that they collect, perhaps using very fast computers, then only keep some unknown subset of that greater bulk for a later date, no "bulk collection" occurs. This is ridiculous. No matter how you slice it, the NSA is mass collecting and searching millions of American communications without a warrant.[27]

Additionally, in classified briefings the NSA has admitted that it doesn't necessarily require a warrant to eavesdrop on domestic phone calls. According to Representative Jerrold Nadler, all it requires is an *analyst's decision* that it was necessary to do so.[28]

Finally, there's the fact that the NSA could get around domestic restrictions entirely by having an intelligence service in another country, like the UK's GCHQ, do that dirty work on the NSA's behalf. An article in the *Guardian* notes:

> The suspicion is that individual states within the agreement can produce material for partners that might be illegal to gather in the other collaborating states, including the U.S.[29]

This is exactly how the NSA skirts FISA restrictions, by monitoring data from access points outside of U.S. territory. Through secret arrangements with allied intelligence services and foreign telecom providers, the NSA collects contact lists associated with e-mail and instant messaging clients at a rate of over 250 million per year. The assumption is that people using such communication channels aren't U.S. citizens, though there's no guarantee by any means. The *Washington Post* reports:

> In practice, data from Americans is collected in large volumes – in part because they live and work overseas, but also because data crosses international boundaries even when its American owners stay at home. Large technology companies, including Google and Facebook, maintain data centers around the world to balance loads on their servers and work around outages.[30]

We'll see this technique again later in the chapter.

Violations Occur

Legal provisions don't seem to provide much protection against domestic surveillance in practice. In April of 2009, well after the passage of the FISA Amendments Act in 2008, U.S. intelligence officials admitted that the NSA engaged in "significant and system" "overcollection" of domestic communication.[31] A couple of months later, in June of 2009, the chairman of the House Select Intelligence Oversight Panel, Representative Rush Holt, asserted:

> Some actions [overcollection] are so flagrant that they can't be accidental.[32]

In August of 2013, the *Washington Post* released a leaked top-secret internal audit which indicated that the NSA consistently violated surveillance laws thousands of times each year, and that the number of violations per year has been steadily increasing over time despite the quadrupling of oversight staff. In the 12 months leading up to May 2012 alone, auditors found 2,776 incidents where monitoring rules were broken.[33] And these were just the violations that occurred at NSA headquarters in Fort Meade. The NSA has regional outposts worldwide.

Furthermore, in October of 2011 the *Foreign Intelligence Surveillance Court* (FISC), the federal court created by the FISA to issue surveillance warrants, issued an 86-page opinion which concluded that NSA collection guidelines were unconstitutional.[34] For over a year this opinion remained secret at the urging of the Department of Justice.[35] It was finally released in August of 2013, offering conclusive evidence that the NSA indeed had links into backbone networks across the country. According to a staff attorney at the Electronic Frontier Foundation:

> The opinion basically found that the government's FISA Amendments Act surveillance that it was conducting by sitting on the wires of providers was unconstitutional.[36]

Despite all of this our lawmakers extended the FISA Amendments Act of 2008 for another five years via the *FISA Amendments Act Reauthorization Act* of 2012 (H.R. 5949).

Mass Interception

As far as total data collection is concerned, with or without a probable cause-warrant, the current extent of the government's data dragnet has been a point of contention. For example, high-level U.S. intelligence officials repeatedly claim the U.S. is not involved in mass interception.

In March of 2012 the Director of NSA, General Keith Alexander, stood up in front of the House Armed Services subcommittee and explicitly denied that the NSA was intercepting American citizens' communications.[37] The following transcript records an exchange between Congressman Hank Johnson and General Alexander.

> **Hank Johnson:** Does the NSA routinely intercept American citizens' emails?
>
> **Keith Alexander:** No.
>
> **Hank Johnson:** Does the NSA intercept Americans' cellphone conversations?
>
> **Keith Alexander:** No.
>
> **Hank Johnson:** Google searches?

Keith Alexander: No.

Hank Johnson: Text messages?

Keith Alexander: No.

Hank Johnson: Amazon.com orders?

Keith Alexander: No.

Hank Johnson: Bank records?

Keith Alexander: No.

Of course, there was a subtle form of deception at work. General Alexander was using the word *intercept* in a particular way. In NSA parlance, data is only intercepted after it has been specially processed for human perusal. By all means, data can still be collected without being inspected.[38] So if congressional representatives had re-phrased their questions (e.g. "are you storing e-mails"), his answers would have been different.

Roughly a year later, in March of 2013, the Director of National Intelligence James Clapper had a similar exchange with Senator Ron Wyden during a hearing of the Senate Intelligence Committee:

> **Sen. Ron Wyden (D-Ore.):** Does the NSA collect any type of data at all on millions or hundreds of millions of Americans?
>
> **James Clapper:** No, sir.
>
> **Sen. Wyden:** It does not?
>
> **James Clapper:** Not wittingly. There are cases where they could inadvertently perhaps collect, but not wittingly.[39]

According to William Binney, an engineer who served in the trenches at the NSA for over three decades, the NSA is actually collecting all of the information that both Alexander and Clapper denied intercepting. During an interview on *Democracy Now!* Binney explained how this could be implemented:

> **Amy Goodman:** Do you believe all emails, the government has copies of, in the United States?
>
> **William Binney:** I would think – I believe they have most of them, yes.

Amy Goodman: And you're speaking from a position where you would know, considering your position in the National Security Agency.

William Binney: Right. All they would have to do is put various Narus devices at various points along the network, at choke points or convergent points, where the network converges, and they could basically take down and have copies of most everything on the network.[40]

Narus is subsidiary of defense contractor Boeing, and is an ISS World Conference regular. It sells products geared towards managing and analyzing network traffic. According to a former technician at AT&T, Mark Klein, Narus developed equipment used by AT&T to capture and re-route network traffic in San Francisco, Seattle, San Jose, Los Angeles, and San Diego.[41] This data ends up in out-of-the-way places like Bluffdale, Utah, where the NSA is building a massive complex to remotely store and analyze harvested information.[42]

An Aside: Files on Everyone

With all of this data at their disposal, it's only natural to wonder if U.S. security services are building dossiers on everyone. The scary part: certain entities now have the ability to do so.

In a secret arrangement that was established in the absence of legislative approval, U.S. attorney general Eric Holder granted the National Counterterrorism Center (NCTC) the authority to collect and store files on American citizens, from any government database, *regardless of whether they're actually suspected of committing a crime.*[43]

The NCTC, it would seem, is hoping to pinpoint future crimes by tracking everyone. The NCTC can hang on to the data that it digs up on innocent citizens for five years in an effort to identify patterns of criminal behavior. All other data it can store indefinitely.

Verizon FISC Order

It turns out Binney was right on the money: mass interception (warrantless or otherwise) is a reality. In other words, the testimony that presumably trustworthy officials like General Alexander and DNI Clapper gave was false. Glenn Greenwald comments:

James Clapper not been prosecuted, he hasn't even lost his job. He's still the director of national intelligence many months after his lie was revealed, because there is no accountability for the top-level people in Washington.[44]

Confirmation came in early June of 2013 when Ed Snowden, a Booz Allen contractor working for the NSA, leaked a series of top-secret documents to Glenn Greenwald at the *Guardian*.

The first document to come to light was a secret Foreign Intelligence Surveillance Court (FISC) order.[45] FISC is a secret U.S. Federal court set up by the 1978 FISA to issue secret surveillance warrants. This secrecy, by the way, makes it hard to judge the effectiveness of the court as a tool of oversight.

The aforementioned FISC order disclosed by Snowden compelled telecom provider Verizon to hand over metadata on all of the calls routed through its systems for a period of three months, *regardless of whether the customers were within the U.S. or making a call between the U.S. and another country*. In other words, the court order mandated dragnet surveillance of a telecom provider. Everything but the raw content of the calls themselves was handed over.

The Electronic Frontier Foundation announced that this proved that the litany of assurances about monitoring only foreign targets was just a smoke screen:

> Despite the rhetoric surrounding the Patriot Act and the FISA Amendments Act, the government was still vacuuming up the records of the purely domestic communications of millions of Americans. And yesterday, of course, with the Verizon order, we got solid proof.[46]

The Verizon order is allowed by the "business records" provision in the Patriot Act (i.e. U.S. Code, Title 50, Chapter 36, Subchapter IV, section 1861). As a matter of pedagogy, the aforementioned legal provision (section 1861) was inserted into U.S. legal code by Section 215 of the Patriot Act (i.e. the section entitled *Access to Records and Other Items under The Foreign Intelligence Surveillance Act*). So, many writers simply refer to Section 215 of the Patriot Act when referring to record collection provisions.

In October of 2013 the FISC published a six-page legal opinion that explicitly reauthorized the collection of phone metadata.[47]

There are those who would argue that Section 215, as it's being employed by the NSA, violates the letter and the spirit of the law. Christopher Sprigman, a professor at the University of Virginia School of Law, and Jennifer Granick, the director of civil liberties at the Stanford Center for Internet and Society argue:

> Representative F. James Sensenbrenner Jr., a Wisconsin Republican and one of the architects of the Patriot Act, and a man not known as a civil libertarian, has said that "Congress intended to allow the intelligence communities to access targeted information for specific investigations" The N.S.A.'s demand for information about every American's phone calls isn't "targeted" at all – it's a dragnet. "How can every call that every American makes or receives be relevant to a specific investigation?" Mr. Sensenbrenner has asked. The answer is simple: It's not.[48]

Legality aside, NSA whistleblowers contend that the leaked court order is just a drop in the bucket. During an interview on *Democracy Now!* William Binney commented on the Verizon disclosure, claiming that it was probably the tip of the iceberg:

> NSA has been doing all this stuff all along, and it's been all the companies, not just one. And I basically looked at that and said, well, if Verizon got one, so did everybody else, which means that, you know, they're just continuing the collection of this kind of information on all U.S. citizens.[49]

Thomas Drake, another former NSA employee turned whistleblower, reinforced Binney's message:

> There's no need now to call this the Foreign Intelligence Surveillance Court. Let's just call it the surveillance court. It's no longer about foreign intelligence. It's simply about harvesting millions and millions and millions of phone call records and beyond.

It would seem that Binney and Drake were correct. In November of 2010, on behalf of a government mandate known as *Sigint*

Management Directive 424, NSA analysts were secretly granted the authority to track the communication metadata (phone logs, e-mail, etc.) of anyone if they could justify the monitoring in terms of foreign intelligence.[50] This sort of monitoring doesn't require a warrant and is used to create a *contact chain* that maps out the target's social connections. The NSA has vast repositories to store this information. For example the *Marina* database which can store an entire year's worth of computer-based metadata (e.g. web browsing history, e-mail activity, search engine queries).[51] Telephone-based metadata is stored in other classified NSA repositories.

Regarding this sort of metadata collection, General Keith Alexander told Senator Mark Udall where he stood during a meeting of the Senate Intelligence Committee in September of 2013:

> I believe it is in the nation's best interests to put all the phone records into a lockbox that we could search when the nation needs to do it ...[52]

While this lockbox may appeal to General Alexander, it does provide irrefutable proof that the NSA is archiving mountains of data on ordinary Internet users.

PRISM

Shortly after the Verizon court order became public knowledge, additional disclosures followed. The *Guardian* released four slides from a top-secret 41-slide PowerPoint presentation that described a data collection program called PRISM.[53] It's also known as US-984XN, which is the program's *Signals Intelligence Activity Designator* (SIGAD).

The program involves remotely collecting both stored data and real-time data from online service providers located inside the United States to acquire emails, chats, search queries, photos, videos, VoIP data, stored files, etc. The PRISM program doesn't rely on individual warrants to collect data. Instead, the entire initiative collectively is authorized once a year by the FISC.[54]

According to the slides, nine prominent hi-tech corporations have become involved in the collection program over the past several years:

Microsoft	joined in 2007
Yahoo!	joined in 2008
Google	joined in 2009
Facebook	joined in 2009
PalTalk	joined in 2009
YouTube	joined in 2010
Skype	joined in 2011
AOL	joined in 2011
Apple	joined in 2012

The leaked document indicates that the NSA is also planning to add Dropbox as a PRISM provider.

It appears that one of the goals of the PRISM program was to establish a technical solution to expedite the process of providing secretly requested data so that complying companies could both automate the process of responding to secret requests and transfer data in a more standard format.[55] To help participating companies cover the cost of compliance, the NSA has paid out millions of dollars.[56]

As you might expect, in light of FISA secrecy restrictions, when queried about this program corporate executives denied any knowledge of PRISM.[57] In addition, in its initial coverage of the story, the *Guardian* quoted an unnamed senior White House official who asserted that PRISM was entirely legal and followed the restrictions specified in Section 702 of the FISA Amendments Act:

> The *Guardian* and *Washington Post* articles refer to collection of communications pursuant to Section 702 of the Foreign Intelligence Surveillance Act. This law does not allow the targeting of any U.S. citizen or of any person located within the United States.
>
> The program is subject to oversight by the Foreign Intelligence Surveillance Court, the Executive Branch, and Congress. It involves extensive procedures, specifically approved by the court, to ensure that only non-U.S. persons outside the U.S. are targeted, and that minimize the acquisition, retention and dissemination of incidentally acquired information about U.S. persons.[58]

Shortly after the PRISM story broke, President Obama appeared on *Charlie Rose* in an effort to reassure the public:

> What I can say unequivocally is that if you are a U.S. person, the NSA cannot listen to your telephone calls, and the NSA cannot target your emails ... and – unless they – and usually it wouldn't be "they," it would be the FBI – go to a court and obtain a warrant and seek probable cause, the same way it's always been, the same way, when we were growing up and were watching movies, you know, you want to go set up a wiretap, you've got to go to a judge, show probable cause.

Of course, based on the earlier discussion of Section 702 of the 2008 FISA Amendments Act, his appraisal is incorrect. If an American citizen is communicating with a target outside of the United States who's not a U.S. citizen, then the communication can be captured without a warrant. And even then there's really no clear-cut way to ensure that U.S. citizens are not being caught in the surveillance dragnet.

Another thing to remember is that PRISM is a single program. It's just one small part of a much larger and more pervasive effort. Bruce Schneier observes:

> The agency has been playing all sorts of games with names, dividing their efforts up and using many different code names in an attempt to disguise what they're doing. It allows them to deny that a specific program is doing something, while conveniently omitting the fact that another program is doing the thing and the two programs are talking to each other.[59]

This is what happens when information is compartmentalized on a "need to know" basis. It allows for secrets within secrets. Recall how the DHS created a lab to dissect and analyze the Stuxnet worm, not realizing that it was actually a creation of the NSA.

The NSA's MUSCULAR project

While the NSA goes directly to companies, under court-approval, to procure data under PRISM, that doesn't mean that it's the only program for corporate collection or that the NSA even needs court approval to collect the network traffic of Americans. Under project MUSCU-LAR, the NSA, with the involvement of the UK's GCHQ, are tapping fiber-optic links used specifically by Google and Yahoo! datacenters.

The subverted network gateways lie outside of the United States. This fact allows the NSA to conduct bulk collection without running into FISA restrictions, as the NSA is free to assume that anyone using a foreign network is a foreigner. This shows just how fragile FISA rules are, and how nimble the NSA is in bypassing alleged legal limits.

Access to these crucial fiber junctions allows intelligence services to duplicate entire streams of unencrypted network traffic. It's as if they have real-time free reign to internal networks, and the data they collect piles up to the ceiling. The *Washington Post* reports:

> According to a top-secret accounting dated Jan. 9, 2013, the NSA's acquisitions directorate sends millions of records every day from internal Yahoo! and Google networks to data warehouses at the agency's headquarters at Fort Meade, Md. In the preceding 30 days, the report said, field collectors had processed and sent back 181,280,466 new records – including "metadata," which would indicate who sent or received e-mails and when, as well as content such as text, audio and video.[60]

Keep in mind that a company like Google can afford to spend lots of money on high-grade security. Yet the spooks at the NSA casually walk right through whatever defenses Google can muster. Did Google simply turn a blind eye in exchange for plausible deniability? Did the NSA have cooperation from a third party? Or maybe they just cracked the SSL encryption outright?

Opting Into Surveillance

Decades ago, cyber-activists worried that the security services would invade our privacy by restricting the availability of *strong* cryptographic components. That is, tools that could encrypt data in a manner that was difficult to decrypt, even by the government.

As the "Clipper Chip" fiasco in the early 1990s demonstrated, this fear was not unfounded. The government, concerned that emerging encryption technology would hamper intelligence collection, tried to force the private sector to use a special "watered down" encryption hardware platform (Clipper Chip) which provided a built-in back door, by design, for the government. Ultimately cyber-activists foiled the Clipper Chip initiative by globally disseminating high-grade encryption tools.

While the Clipper Chip battle was lost, the larger war quietly raged onward. While strong encryption technology is arguably available to anyone who knows where to look,[61] the security services have responded with a couple of novel counter-maneuvers. As we saw in Chapter Six, the intelligence services went around convincing the big name vendors to insert back doors and intentional flaws into their products. Government spies also worked to weaken cryptographic standards, and (when all else failed) they acquired private encryption keys directly.

But that's not all. The government also decided to leverage the appeal of social media. Rather than sneaking onto people's computers and decrypting their data, data collectors are relying on the fact that in the age of social media, people willfully volunteer their personal information online. The trick eliciting participation is to add a measure of convenience. Security expert Bruce Schneier astutely observes:

> If the government demanded that we all carry tracking devices 24/7, we would rebel. Yet we all carry cell phones. If the government demanded that we deposit copies of all of our messages to each other with the police, we'd declare their actions unconstitutional. Yet we all use Gmail and Facebook messaging and SMS. If the government demanded that we give them access to all the photographs we take, and that we identify all of the people in them and tag them with locations, we'd refuse. Yet we do exactly that on Flickr and other sites ...[62]

It's not your imagination. People are literally opting into surveillance. All intelligence agencies need to do is drag their trawl net through social media web sites.

Vengeful Librarians

The CIA has a team referred to as the *vengeful librarians* that does just that. This open source intelligence effort relies heavily on data collected from Internet-based social media.[63] For example, they followed Twitter after Osama bin Laden was assassinated in order to assess the public's response worldwide. The vengeful librarians also compare the conclusions of their social media analyses with those of polling companies to determine which mechanism produces more accurate results.

We can't help but wonder if the results obtained by the CIA's vengeful librarians have ever experienced signal interference, so to speak, from competing programs over in the Pentagon (e.g. something like Operation Earnest Voice) that are intended to disseminate propaganda via social media? After all, it would be difficult to acquire a clear snapshot of reality when the waters have already been muddied by a military psyop.

As usual, the private sector sees a need it can fill and is looking for a piece of the action. Both the CIA (via its In-Q-Tel venture arm) and Google have invested in a company named Recorded Future which scours the web for data in real-time, to establish relationships between people and events, and then uses this data to make predictions about the future.[64]

Likewise, Raytheon has developed a proof-of-concept tool called *Riot*, which stands for Rapid Information Overlay Technology. Riot uses "extreme-scale analytics" to harvest social media sites like Facebook and Twitter and distill a profile of people's entire lives: their acquaintances, where they've traveled to, details about their daily routines, with the implied potential of being able to extrapolate future behavior.[65]

Then there are companies that don't limit themselves to just social media. Relationship Science is a company that eschews user-generated content in favor of processing raw online data en mass to map out personal relationships. For $3,000 a year, customers can access the company's site and find out exactly who's acquainted with whom, and with what degree of familiarity.[66] It's a "Six Degrees of Separation" sort of tool. Ostensibly, this could be used by an entrepreneur who'd like to pitch his idea to a venture capitalist whom he doesn't personally know.

For instance, he could use the company's relationship database to identify someone who could possibly provide a social introduction. On the other hand, a tool like this could just as easily be used by a spy who'd like to leverage a misplaced sense of trust to acquire information.

The DHS Monitors Social Media

The CIA and the Pentagon aren't the only players in this field. The Department of Homeland Security (with a little help from General Dynamics) has also been mining the Internet for intelligence. In a document dated in June of 2010, the DHS described its activities:

> The Office of Operations Coordination and Planning (OPS), National Operations Center (NOC), will launch and lead the Publicly Available Social Media Monitoring and Situational Awareness (Initiative) to assist the Department of Homeland Security (DHS) and its components involved in fulfilling OPS statutory responsibility (Section 515 of the Homeland Security Act (6 U.S.C. § 321d(b)(1)) to provide situational awareness and establish a common operating picture for the federal government, and for those state, local, and tribal governments, as appropriate.[67]

This DHS document also presented a representative list of over 100 sites being monitored by General Dynamics on behalf of the DHS. To this end, General Dynamics was awarded an $11.3 million contract with the DHS that started in 2010 and came with a four-year renewal option.[68]

So what exactly are they looking for? The Electronic Privacy and Information Center (EPIC) filed Freedom of Information Act (FOIA) requests in search of details about this program back in April of 2011. In December of 2011 EPIC filed a lawsuit against the DHS to compel disclosure of documents. In the following month, as 2012 rolled in, the DHS started to cough up documents (i.e. 285 pages). What EPIC discovered was that the DHS hired General Dynamic to watch for:

> [Media] reports that reflect adversely on the U.S. Government, DHS, or prevent, protect, respond government activities.

And to create:

> Reports on DHS, Components, and other Federal Agencies: positive and negative reports on FEMA, CIA, CBP, ICE, etc. as well as organizations outside the DHS.

As part of an effort to:

> Capture public reaction to major government proposals.

EPIC contends that watching the Internet for "positive and negative reports" on the U.S. government is outside the department's mission to "secure the nation." The director of EPIC's open government program, Ginger McCall, explains:

> This is entirely outside of the bounds of the agency's statutory duties, and it could have a substantial chilling effect on legitimate dissent and freedom of speech.[69]

Corporate Compliance

The Google guys would have gotten rich from the search code without having to create the private spying agency

— Jaron Lanier[70]

The only difference is that the N.S.A. does it for intelligence, and Silicon Valley does it to make money.

— James Risen and Nick Wingfield[71]

The government collects veritable mountains of information about us. Every time you renew a license, pay your taxes, go to court, purchase property, or get pulled over by a police officer, there are entries created in a database somewhere. There are, however, some types of information that the government can't directly accumulate. This is what's driving the idea of *information sharing* between the government and corporate America.

As the NSA's PRISM program illustrated earlier, what the security apparatus can't get through open sources, or their own sprawling databases, they'll get by mandating the cooperation of the private sector. Former DNI Mike McConnell urged:

> The private sector needs to be able to share network information – on a controlled basis – without inviting lawsuits from shareholders and others.[72]

A number of big names in the social network market have proactively published what they call *compliance handbooks* directed specifically towards government officials. These manuals describe what sort of data is archived, how it can be requested, and the services available to access it. Some providers even provide access in real-time for emergency situations related to National Security. A number of these compliance handbooks have been acquired by leak website Cryptome. You can view them at:

http://cryptome.org/isp-spy/online-spying.htm

Here is a sample list of some of these documents:

http://cryptome.org/isp-spy/aol-spy3.pdf
http://cryptome.org/isp-spy/facebook-spy3.pdf
http://cryptome.org/isp-spy/gmail-spy2.pdf
http://cryptome.org/isp-spy/myspace-spy3.pdf
http://cryptome.org//isp-spy/microsoft-spy.zip
http://cryptome.org/isp-spy/twitter-spy.pdf
http://cryptome.org/isp-spy/yahoo-preserve.pdf

As you can see, the major players in social media, like Facebook, Twitter, and MySpace have published guides. Some organizations have gone a step further and have created dedicated interfaces so that security services can access allegedly secure communications. According to a report published by *Moscow News*, this is exactly the path taken by Microsoft:

> Since its acquisition of Skype in May 2011, Microsoft has added a legitimate monitoring technology to Skype, says Maksim Emm, Executive Director of Peak Systems. Now any user can be switched to a special mode in which encryption keys will be generated on a server rather than the user's phone or computer.

Access to the server allows Skype calls or conversations to be tapped. Microsoft has been providing this technology to security services across the world, including Russia.[73]

Not only are lawful interception technologies ripe for abuse by the authorities, there's the very real threat that outlaws and spies will subvert them for their own purposes.

For example, back in early 2005 technicians at Vodafone Greece, a major cellular service provider, discovered that intruders had commandeered lawful interception functionality on a series of telephone switches to eavesdrop on over 100 high-level officials for the better part of a year. The list of people who were monitored included the prime minister of Greece, the mayor of Athens, and an employee of the U.S. embassy.[74]

In September of 2011 the Greek political magazine *Epikaira* leaked the conclusions of a public inquiry incriminating the United States Embassy as the culprit.[75]

In the event that an organization shows any sign of resistance, the government can legally demand information. Using what's known as a "National Security Letter" (NSL), intelligence agencies (e.g. the CIA, FBI, Department of Defense, etc.) can compel organizations to submit information on specific individuals (e-mail and telephone logs, financial records, and credit information) without offering probable cause. Furthermore, the NSL legislation contains provisions for a gag order that prevents recipients from disclosing that they've received an NSL.

To give you a glimpse of the scope of NSLs, an unclassified review released by the inspector general of the Department of Justice reported that the FBI issued 192,499 NSLs between 2003 and 2006.[76] The recipients of these letters, with very few exceptions, have remained silent about it.

One exception is Nicholas Merrill, the owner a New York ISP named Calyx Internet Access. In February of 2004 he received an NSL from the FBI and responded by mounting a legal challenge against it. For years, as the trial dragged on, Merrill was known in official courts documents only as "John Doe." The FBI would eventually drop its demand for records and in July of 2010 the courts released Merrill from the gag order that prevented him from even discussing the case. Looking back over his court battle, Merrill commented:

> I kind of felt at the beginning, so few people challenge this thing, I couldn't just stand by and see, in my opinion, the basic underpinnings of our government undermined ... I was taught about how sophisticated our system of checks and balances is ... and if you really believe in that, then the idea of one branch of government just demanding records without being checked and balanced by the judicial just is so obviously wrong on the surface.[77]

In March of 2013, Google disclosed that in the four-year span covering 2009 to 2012, it received somewhere in the range of zero to 999 National Security Letters per year.[78] In other words, they're certifying that each year they received less than a thousand NSLs.

Shortly after the Google disclosure, Microsoft came forward and released figures that hinted at the number of NSLs the company has received. For example, in both 2010 and 2011 Microsoft received between 1,000 and 1,999 NSLs. So we know with certainty that the companies received at least a thousand NSLs.[79]

The ACLU issued a statement in the wake of Google's release:

> Secrecy is the name of the game. Secret government surveillance is difficult to hold to account. Unless we as Americans insist that the government release basic information about what its surveillance powers authorize and how it is using those powers, there is little reason to believe that the surveillance abuses of the past will not be repeated.[80]

Such is the significance of the NSL's gag order. In lawsuits that questioned the legality of the FISA Amendments Act of 2008 (e.g. *Clapper vs. Amnesty International*), the cases were frequently dismissed because the plaintiffs were unable to demonstrate that they were under surveillance. Gag orders ensure that this state of affairs persists. It's only in rare circumstances, like *Al-Haramain vs. Obama*, where the government accidentally releases classified information and tips its hat to those being monitored.

How can you legally protest the fact that you're being watched if the government won't admit to watching you?

The secretive nature of NSLs may be their undoing. In March of 2013 a federal judge in Northern California, in response to a legal challenge filed by the Electronic Frontier Foundation on behalf of an unnamed telecom, took this issue head on. U.S. District Judge Susan Illston ruled that NSLs were unconstitutional and barred the government from issuing them.[81] Judge Illston stayed her order for 90 days in the event that the government wanted the opportunity to appeal her decision.

CISPA

The Cyber Intelligence Sharing and Protection Act (CISPA, aka H.R. 624) is a bill that was written by Congressman Mike Rogers, a Republican from Michigan who chairs the House Select Committee on Intelligence, and Dutch Ruppersberger, a Democrat from Maryland who also sits on the House Select Committee on Intelligence. Proponents claim that the bill is aimed at allowing the government and the private sector to expediently share threat information in an effort to ward off cyber-attacks.

Yet there are troubling measures buried in the fine print. For example, reading through the text of CISPA, the following provisions appear (certain items have been put in bold font for emphasis):

> **Notwithstanding** any other provision of law, a self-protected entity **may**, for cybersecurity purposes –
> '(i) use cybersecurity systems to identify and obtain cyber threat information to protect the rights and property of such self-protected entity; and
> '(ii) share such cyber threat information with any other entity, including the entities of the Department of Homeland Security and the Department of Justice designated under paragraphs (1) and (2) of section 2(b) of the Cyber Intelligence Sharing and Protection Act.

The presence of the word "notwithstanding" means that CISPA would supersede all existing federal and state laws. The presence of the word "may" means that information sharing is voluntary.

In other words, the above CISPA excerpt provides broad legal immunity to companies that decide to cooperate with warrantless seizure of information, and furthermore exempts them from disclosure rules. CISPA will allow the security apparatus of the U.S. government to hoover up data behind the scenes as long as the private sector actors consent, leaving the general public largely oblivious to when they're being watched. History has shown that companies like AT&T have readily acquiesced when asked to break existing federal wiretap laws.

Then there's the vague wording of using "cybersecurity systems" to acquire "cyber threat information" for the sake of "cybersecurity." This could potentially give companies new rights to monitor users as long as they could find a way to justify the monitoring in terms of a perceived threat to their networks or systems.

On April 18, 2013, the bill was passed in the House of Representatives by a 288-127 vote. At the time of this book's writing it had yet to be passed by the Senate.

The Hemisphere Project

The very fact that the government issues warrants and NSLs implies that it's not just the government that's collecting data. Corporations are also active in the field of mining the Internet and building databases on people.

For example, AT&T maintains a massive phone call database that goes all the way back to 1987, providing details on every single call that has ever passed through the company's telephone switches. To give you an idea of the scale involved, approximately 4 billion calls are added to this database every day. Since 2007 AT&T has been providing metadata on phone calls to the DEA and local law enforcement drug units in a counter-narcotics program called the "Hemisphere Project."[82] Phone metadata is released in response to administrative subpoenas issued by the DEA and the individual requests are handled by AT&T technicians who've been embedded in local crime groups all over the country.

Documents related to the Hemisphere were disclosed by a peace activist in Washington named Drew Hendricks.[83] Other than that, little is known about the program. There is virtually no mention of it in congressional reports or hearings. Secrecy is pretty tight. People involved in the program have been advised:

> All requestors are instructed to never refer to Hemisphere in any official document. If there is no alternative to referencing a Hemisphere request, then the results should be referenced as information obtained from an AT&T subpoena.

Spying as a Business Model

Google is another classic example of a private sector data aggregator. In a *New York Times* op-ed, former FTC member Pamela Jones Harbour remarked that though Google dominates the web search market, the company is actually much more than just a web search provider:

> We need to look at Google's market role – and behavior – through a different prism. Google is not just a "search engine company," or an "online services company," or a publisher, or an advertising platform. At its core, it's a data collection company.[84]

Google exists in a market where it sells its product (user data) to buyers (the advertisers). The company's hallmark web search engine technology, though impressive, is not how Google supports itself. The company's truly valuable commodity, what it charges its customers for, is information on the people who use Google services.

Business is booming. According to Google CEO Eric Schmidt, every day the company generates a couple of exabytes of data.[85] To give you a frame of reference for this figure, the amount of data that mankind had created from its inception up until 2003 is on the order of five exabytes. Google doesn't hesitate to capitalize on this tidal wave of data. For example, it's a well-known fact that Google regularly scans Gmail messages for keywords. In July of 2010 during a hearing before the Senate Committee on Commerce, Science, and Transportation, the privacy engineering lead at Google, Dr. Alma Whitten, said:

> What Gmail has always done, from the very beginning, was to take the same systems that scan an email in order to identi-

fy, for example, whether it's spam and should go in the spam folder and the user shouldn't be bothered with it, to have those very same systems trigger off of keywords to show an ad that might be relevant.[86]

Even worse, online service providers like Apple, Yahoo!, Facebook, and Google see privacy rules as a cost sink and are working to undermine laws that safeguard privacy in an effort to maximize their profits. A *New York Times* article reports:

> Companies have already begun aggressive lobbying campaigns to stop or dilute tighter privacy rules, which they say would interfere with their business models and decrease profits and growth. The companies' efforts are, in turn, supported by countries like England and Ireland that fear that such restrictions would hamper economic recovery.[87]

To evade this kind of data collection you could eschew online services and social networks altogether. For the moment, it's still a tenable alternative. Yet seemingly small decisions can morph into momentous decisions over time. Back in the late 1990s owning a cellphone was still something you could take or leave. Fast forward to 2013 and it became difficult to participate in society if you don't own a cellphone.

While Google is a company that focuses primarily on selling information to other companies, there are some private sector entities out there, known as *information resellers* or *data brokers,* that collect data with the expressed intention of selling it to the government.

Information resellers thrive because they've developed cost-effective ways to aggregate information from a variety of sources,

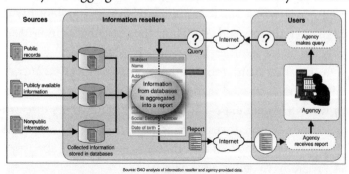

Figure 10-1

correlate it, repackage it, and then provide access to government agencies for a fee (see Figure 10-1). Credit reporting agencies like Equifax, Experian, and Trans Union are well-known information resellers. LexisNexis, a company that opened up the field of electronically accessible legal documents in the 1970s, is another prominent data broker. The vast majority of the information that's purchased on behalf of the government is used by U.S. security services (tracking fugitives, performing background checks, border screening, researching asset ownership, etc.).[88]

The Public-Private Partnership

Many service providers claimed that they were coerced, that they only provided data to the government grudgingly and only under the implied threat that if they didn't obey the law, corporate executives would end up serving jail time.[89]

There is actually one instance of a telecom CEO going to Jail. That would be Joseph Nacchio, the former chief executive of Qwest Communications International. He was convicted on 19 counts of insider trading.[90] Nacchio alleges that in February of 2001, six months before the attacks of 9/11, the NSA approached him about spying on customers and he flat out refused. Nacchio claims that the government then retaliated by canceling a number of unrelated contracts with Qwest and initiating a politically motivated criminal case against him.[91]

Google, Microsoft, Yahoo!, and Facebook all made gestures of legal protest by petitioning the U.S. Foreign Intelligence Surveillance Court to allow them to disclose more detailed statistics on government information requests.[92] Once more, service providers voiced concern that collaborating with the government has damaged their credibility and could hurt their revenue as Internet users flocked en masse to other, less intrusive, platforms.[93]

On the other hand, most of these protests occurred *after* cookie cutter denials proved inadequate,[94] *after* lies about cooperating with the NSA were exposed. Up until Ed Snowden's disclosures, most corporate executives were acting as if nothing was wrong at all, publicly declaring that they didn't know anything about special NSA programs to collect user data.

The FISA Court admits that *none* of the telecommunications companies ever raised a stink when receiving orders for bulk phone records under the Patriot Act:

> No recipient of any Section 215 Order has challenged the legality of such an order, despite the mechanism for doing so.[95]

The public record shows that corporate America has a history of cooperating with U.S. intelligence services. For instance, in the late 1940s the CIA launched a program called "Operation Mockingbird" in an effort to influence the corporate media. The program took place under the supervision of Frank Wisner, the director of the CIA's covert operation branch. Deborah Davis, a *Village Voice* reporter who investigated the CIA's campaign in a 1979 book wrote:

> By the early 1950s, Wisner "owned" respected members of the *New York Times*, Newsweek, CBS and other communications vehicles. Wisner referred to this apparatus as a "Mighty Wurlitzer," referencing the theater organ capable of controlling diverse pipes, instruments, and sound effects from a central console.[96]

This program was eventually publicized by the Church Committee. In its 1976 report the Committee found that:

> The CIA maintained ... a network of several hundred foreign individuals around the world who provide intelligence for the CIA and at times attempt to influence foreign opinion through the use of covert propaganda. These individuals provide the CIA with direct access to a large number of foreign newspapers and periodicals, scores of press services and news agencies, radio and television stations, commercial book publishers, and other foreign media outlets ...[97]

The CIA's influence wasn't limited to foreign news sources. In 1977, one of the journalists who exposed the Watergate Scandal, Carl Bernstein, published a lengthy exposé which revealed that more than 400 American journalists were secretly carrying out assignments on behalf of the CIA. Bernstein noted:

In the field, journalists were used to help recruit and handle foreigners as agents; to acquire and evaluate information, and to plant false information with officials of foreign governments.[98]

These sort of public-private arrangements haven't gone away. In an interview that appeared in the documentary *Mediastan*, former *New York Times* executive editor Bill Keller made no secret of his regular interactions with the U.S. government, implying a relationship with intelligence services.[99]

But it's not just the media. Julian Assange, the founder of WikiLeaks, describes the close-knit relationship between Google and the State Department:

> Documents published last year by WikiLeaks obtained from the U.S. intelligence contractor Stratfor, show that in 2011 Jared Cohen, then (as he is now) Director of Google Ideas, was off running secret missions to the edge of Iran in Azerbaijan. In these internal emails, Fred Burton, Stratfor's Vice President for Intelligence and a former senior State Department official, describes Google as follows:
>
> Google is getting WH [White House] and State Dept support and air cover. In reality they are doing things the CIA cannot do... [Cohen] is going to get himself kidnapped or killed. Might be the best thing to happen to expose Google's covert role in foaming up-risings, to be blunt. The U.S. Gov't can then disavow knowledge and Google is left holding the shit-bag ...[100]

Former CIA case officer Robert Steele has asserted that the CIA provided Google with seed money when it was getting started:

> I think Google took money from the CIA when it was poor and it was starting up and unfortunately our system right now floods money into spying and other illegal and largely unethical activities, and it doesn't fund what I call the open source world ...[101]

Once more Google is now the eighth-largest lobbying engine in D.C., spending more than Microsoft and Lockheed Martin.[102] Julian Assange comments:

In the Google book it even states that what Lockheed Martin was to the 20th century, hi-tech companies will be to the 21st. It's a really quite strong form of neo-imperialism. And I don't want to use that phrase as some sort of hackneyed Marxist expression, but that's what it's about – jacking in the entire world into the U.S. economic and informational system.[103]

What all of this demonstrates is that various components of the private and public sector are tightly interleaved on several different levels, such that with regard to data collection they may as well be a single entity. Heidi Boghosian, the executive director of the National Lawyers Guild, states that it's a matter of projecting elite power:

> For all intents and purposes, the distinction right now between government and the corporate world is virtually nil. They are hand-in-hand working to gather information about Americans as well as people across the globe, to really be in a race to collect more information than any other country can, because I think in their eyes, having this information, storing it, and being able to access it for years on end is a symbol of power and control. So that you can't really make that distinction anymore between big business and government.[104]

While cooperation probably carried risks in the minds of corporate officers (especially if someone found out), the pluses ultimately outweighed the minuses. For example, as demonstrated in the previous section, a number of these companies (some of whom have gone to court in order to publicly disclose government surveillance requests)[105] have been lobbying the government to weaken privacy laws. Remember, spying on consumers is often a fundamental part of the corporate business model.

Government contracts also represent a significant stream of income for hi-tech vendors. For example, in May of 2012 the U.S. Department of the Interior awarded a 7-year $35 million dollar contract to Google to provide e-mail services.[106] Also, in December of 2012 Microsoft signed a three-year $617 million enterprise license agreement with the Department of Defense.[107] The more mature vendors, which have relationships with the federal government that span decades, tend to do very well. Over the course of 2012 IBM won approximately 1.5 billion dollars in contracts with the federal government.[108]

Glenn Greenwald comments on the nature of the relationship between the Pentagon and U.S. telecom providers:

> The Federal Government has its hands dug deeply into the entire ostensibly "private" telecommunications infrastructure and, in return, the nation's telecoms are recipients of enormous amounts of revenues by virtue of turning themselves into branches of the Federal Government ... [109]

Think of it this way, someone has to sell the NSA the acres of supercomputers and networking equipment that it deploys to archive and decipher digital communications. The NSA's new $1.2 billion datacenter in Bluffdale, Utah, is 15 times the size of the MetLife Stadium that hosts the New York Giants.[110] It's bigger than Google's largest data center.[111] Then there's also the NSA's $3.2 billion expansion into Site M, which represents an even larger deployment.[112] Site M will host the U.S. Cyber Command Joint Operations Center (USCYBERCOM JOC). Its High Performance Computer Center (HPCC) is slated as being roughly three times as large as the one in Utah.

This vantage point may seem cynical: that these mega-corporations are driven by profit and abide by government spying because corporate surveillance is easily just as prolific. Detractors of this pessimistic standpoint may insist that it's not as bad as the headlines are implying.

But if Snowden's leaks prove anything, it's that the cynical view has merit. If you had claimed circa 2012 that the government, with the support of every big name in hi-tech, had secretly joined forces to globally defeat both network security and privacy, most people would have laughed and called you a tinfoil-hat-wearing nut job.

Yet top-secret files prove that's exactly what happened.[113]

Hi-tech vendors like Microsoft (sitting on a war chest of over 60 billion in cash reserves)[114] or Apple (whose $147 billion cash hoard represents almost 10% of all corporate money not held by financial institutions[115]) aren't exactly defenseless. Hi-tech giants chose to acquiesce because the benefits outweighed the negative consequences.

So there's a convergence of interests at work. Both the government and corporate America are spying on the public. Both the government and corporate America are leveraging each other to get what they want. It's almost unheard of to encounter a company like Lavabit that takes a firm ideological stance against government surveillance, to the extent that the owner of the company would rather shutter his service than continue to collaborate. You see, dear reader, for large service providers there's too much money at stake.

A Global Panopticon

As we saw earlier, there's a severe dissonance between what our leaders are saying and what whistleblowers like Thomas Tamm, William Binney, and Thomas Drake are saying. The basic narrative that officials have tried to convey is that PRISM and other programs like it are part of a lawful surveillance apparatus that, per the Patriot Act and the FISA Amendments Act of 2008, collects data on specific people rather than hoovering up everything.

An article published by the *Associated Press* implies that this may not be the case:

> Interviews with more than a dozen current and former government and technology officials and outside experts show that, while Prism has attracted the recent attention, the program actually is a relatively small part of a much more expansive and intrusive eavesdropping effort.[116]

Whistleblower Ed Snowden claims, as do the other whistleblowers, that U.S. security services have fallen back on dragnet surveillance as the collection mechanism of choice. What makes Ed Snowden's claims so damning is that he had possession of the classified documents to sufficiently corroborate his assertions. During an interview with journalist Glenn Greenwald he stated:

The NSA specifically targets the communications of everyone. It ingests them by default. It collects them in its system, and it filters them, and it analyzes them, and it measures them, and it stores them for periods of time, simply because that's the easiest, most efficient and most valuable way to achieve these ends. So while they may be intending to target someone associated with a foreign government or someone that they suspect of terrorism, they're collecting your communications to do so. Any analyst at any time can target anyone, any selector anywhere. Where those communications will be picked up depends on the range of the sensor networks and the authorities that that analyst is empowered with. Not all analysts have the ability to target everything. But I, sitting at my desk, certainly had the authorities to wiretap anyone, from you or your accountant to a federal judge, to even the president, if I had a personal email.[117]

From a technical perspective it's more convenient to simply capture everything and then drill down into the details when you need information on a specific target.

Officials like Representative Mike Rogers, chairman of the House Committee on Intelligence, dismissed Snowden's claims as bombast. Rogers said:

He's lying. It's impossible for him to do what he was saying he could do.[118]

Within weeks the *Guardian* disclosed a top-secret document[119] that described a data mining tool used by the NSA, a program called XKeyscore, which allows users to do exactly that. Glenn Greenwald noted:

Training materials for XKeyscore detail how analysts can use it and other systems to mine enormous agency databases by filling in a simple on-screen form giving only a broad justification for the search. The request is not reviewed by a court or any NSA personnel before it is processed ...

One presentation claims the program covers "nearly everything a typical user does on the Internet," including the content of emails, websites visited and searches, as well as their metadata.[120]

Many people will, no doubt, simply shrug their shoulders, claiming that they have nothing to hide. Accept invasive dragnet surveillance as a fact of life, accept that privacy isn't a vital human right, and calmly move on. Google CEO Eric Schmidt encapsulates this mindset:

> If you have something that you don't want anyone to know, maybe you shouldn't be doing it in the first place … [121]

New York Times columnist Joe Nocera responds to Schmidt's comment:

> That is the thought-process that could someday cost us our last shred of privacy … [122]

Once leaders start chipping away at civil liberties, it's a slippery slope. If people aren't bothered by mass interception because they feel they haven't done anything wrong, why not just give the authorities the ability to search anyone's home or digital communication for no particular reason? You've got nothing to hide, right? After all, this might allow our security services to catch more terrorists.

But why stop there? Why dicker with trials and evidence? Why not let the security services lock up anyone they want for as long as they want? Like they say, this is a matter of national security…

Travel down this road long enough and you'll see that eroding basic constitutional rights has nothing to do with national security and everything to do with *control*.

The disquieting fact is that the tools of an Orwellian society, the ability to capture, collect, and analyze every digital communication on the planet, have been put into place with nothing more than secretly interpreted policy directives to prevent abuse by those in power. To assume that this safeguards society is the height of recklessness.

Ed Snowden explains why this is a tenuous position for American society to be in:

> It's [surveillance] only going to get worse, until eventually there will be a time where policies will change, because the

only thing that restricts the activities of the surveillance state are policy.... And because of that, a new leader will be elected, they'll flip the switch, say that because of the crisis, because of the dangers that we face in the world, you know, some new and unpredicted threat, we need more authority, we need more power, and there will be nothing the people can do at that point to oppose it, and it'll be turnkey tyranny.[123]

In the wake of Snowden's many disclosures, President Barack Obama confidently offered assurances:

The American people don't have a Big Brother who is snooping into their business ... [124]

Then, again, in early August of 2013, Obama appeared on Jay Leno to convey the following message:

We don't have a domestic spying program ... what we do have is some mechanisms that can track a phone number or an email address that is connected to a terrorist attack.[125]

This long series of half-truths seriously damages the government's credibility with regard to offering an honest public appraisal of its own surveillance programs. Why should anyone trust what officials have to say when their picture of reality contrasts so sharply against leaked government documents?

President Barack Obama has told us that:

The main thing I want to emphasize is that I don't have an interest and the people at the NSA don't have an interest in doing anything other than making sure that ... we can prevent a terrorist attack ... [126]

But the material presented in Chapter Six, which details U.S. spying on institutions like the U.N. and the International Atomic Energy Agency, shows that mass interception often has nothing to do with counter-terrorism.

General Keith Alexander has publicly stated:

No one has willfully or knowingly disobeyed the law or tried to invade your civil liberties or privacy.[127]

Again, this is false. The *Washington Post* has reported on an internal NSA audit dated May of 2012 which noted 2,776 legal violations in the preceding 12 months.[128] Furthermore it turns out that, according to the NSA's inspector general, approximately a dozen violations over the past ten years were indeed willfully committed.[129] Details on some of these incidents, where analysts abused their monitoring tools, have been released by the NSA and are a part of the public record.[130]

The FISC itself admits that its ability to check whether violations are unintentional or not is fairly limited. The FISA Court's chief judge, Reggie B. Walton, has qualified:

> The FISC is forced to rely upon the accuracy of the information that is provided to the Court…. The FISC does not have the capacity to investigate issues of noncompliance … [131]

In a parallel world driven by secret laws, established by secret courts, which enable a myriad of secret programs, our lawmakers have failed us.

The *Wall Street Journal* has reported that the NSA's surveillance apparatus can encompass up to 75% of all U.S. Internet traffic.[132] Other estimates aren't this optimistic. During a program segment on *Democracy Now!*, the owner of an e-mail provider named Lavabit came on the air to comment on why he shuttered his service. Lavabit gained public notoriety when it was disclosed that the company was the e-mail provider of choice for NSA whistleblower Ed Snowden. In the wake of Snowden's revelations, Lavabit closed its doors to protest legal coercion by U.S. security services. The owner, Ladar Levison, in the presence of his attorney, made the following statement:

> I think you should assume any communication that is electronic is being monitored.[133]

This sort of mass interception undermines constitutionally based freedoms and grants a dangerous amount of control to a small group of people. Imagine the power of an organization that can monitor, archive, and correlate everything that travels through global networks. This power is bolstered by a body of secret laws that has been established to justify the emerging surveillance state and is clearly antithetical to democracy.

Cryptome's John Young elaborates on why this is so:

> Secrecy poses the greatest threat to the United States because it divides the population into two groups, those with access to secret information and those without. This asymmetrical access to information vital to the United States as a democracy will eventually turn it into an autocracy run by those with access to secret information, protected by laws written to legitimate this privileged access and to punish those who violate these laws.
>
> Those with access to secret information cannot honestly partake in public discourse due to the requirement to lie and dissimulate about what is secret information. They can only speak to one another, never in public. Similarly those without access to secret information cannot fully debate the issues which affect the nation, including alleged threats promulgated by secret keepers who are forbidden by law to disclose what they know.[134]

Young's message is substantiated by Alan Grayson, a Democratic representative from Florida who sits on the House Committee on Foreign Affairs:

> We have reached the point where the classified information system prevents even trusted members of Congress, who have security clearances, from learning essential facts, and then inhibits them from discussing and debating what they do know. And this extends to matters of war and peace, money and blood. The "security state" is drowning in its own phlegm.[135]

Given the sheer volume of distortions and lies that authority figures are feeding to the public, you'd be well advised to assume that the government is collecting everything and move on from there. Our republic faces an existential threat from secrecy and surveillance.

Questioning the Official Narrative

As news of the leaked PRISM documents spread, during an interview with the press DNI James Clapper indicated that the resulting damage would be substantial:

> For me, it is literally – not figuratively – literally gut-wrenching to see this happen because of the huge, grave damage it does to our intelligence capabilities ... [136]

Clapper went on to explain why the disclosures would be so damaging:

> Our adversaries, whether nation state adversaries or nefarious groups, benefit from that same transparency. So, as we speak, they are going to school and learning how we do this. And so, that's why it potentially has – can render great damage to our intelligence capabilities.

Across the ocean the director of MI5, Andrew Parker, has expressed a similar opinion:

> It causes enormous damage to make public the reach and limits of GCHQ techniques. Such information hands the advantage to the terrorists. It is the gift they need to evade us and strike at will. Unfashionable as it might seem, that is why we must keep secrets secret, and why not doing so causes such harm.[137]

From this vantage point, these leaks reveal operational details, details that would allow our enemies to evade detection.

Yet it's common knowledge that, in the aftermath of 9/11, the Bush administration ordered sweeping warrantless wiretaps. Is it reasonable to assume that proficient terrorists would really be careless enough to use a well-known major service provider like Google or Yahoo!?

A number of prominent experts doubt this. For example, Bruce Schneier made the following statement in a *New York Times* op-ed:

> The argument that exposing these documents helps the terror-ists doesn't even pass the laugh test; there's nothing here that changes anything any potential terrorist would do or not do.[138]

NSA whistleblower William Binney echoed this sentiment during an interview on *Democracy Now!*:

> The terrorists have already known that we've been doing this for years, so there's no surprise there. They're not going to change the way they operate just because it comes out in the U.S. press ... [139]

Any RPG-slinging terrorist with a modicum of operational dis-cipline and tactical acumen would be inclined to gravitate towards more covert channels.

Foreign intelligence services also concur. For instance, in Jan-uary of 2012 the Dutch General Intelligence and Security Service (the FBI of the Netherlands) published a report titled "Jihadism on the Web: A Breeding Ground for Jihad in the Modern Age."[140] This report describes a "Deep Web," a set of obscure forums that are largely invisible to modern search engines. These sites reside in the uncharted back alleys of the Internet, and constitute the online meeting spots where terrorists actually congregate:

> The AIVD estimates that approximately 25,000 jihadists orig-inating from over 100 countries belong to this group of core Internet forums. Most of them operate on the so-called in-visible Web, a part of the World Wide Web that has not (yet) been indexed and cannot be found by readily accessible search engines. The core forums hidden inside this invisible Web are constructed and maintained by fanatical jihadists. Within the confines of these virtual gathering places, all members can participate in interactive group discussions that lay the foun-dation for radical discourse, paving the way for legitimized violence against the enemies of "true" Islam. Jihadist organiza-

tions, such as Al-Qaeda, do not "own" core forums, but simply make convenient use of their infrastructure and followers.

Organized criminal gangs with comparable levels of sophistication take similar precautions. For example, the criminal gang Mara Salvatrucha has been known to use Sony Playstation and Microsoft Xbox 360 game consoles to establish covert channels of communication. The devices, designed explicitly towards multi-user online gaming, offer voice over IP (VoIP), text chat, and video teleconferencing features which give gang members the ability to interact with associates in other countries.[141]

The Mexican drug cartels take this out-of-band approach to a whole new level. They spent millions of dollars to create their own encrypted radio network from the ground up, an extensible series of antenna and repeaters that constitute a shadow communications system that reaches throughout most of Mexico's thirty-one states.[142]

Watching America's Adversaries

Given the lengths that murky criminal organizations go to, there's no doubt that competent terrorists are far too cautious to use something as mainstream as Yahoo!, or Google, or AOL to run their clandestine ops. But if all of this secrecy isn't about tipping off the jihadists, what's it about?

Whistleblower William Binney indicates where he thinks this is headed:

> The government here is not trying to protect it from the terrorists; it's trying to protect it, that knowledge of that program, from the citizens of the United States. That's where I see it.[143]

As does Ladar Levison, the founder of e-mail provider Lavabit who chose to shutter his business rather than cooperate with the NSA:

> I am wholly opposed, and find it contrary to our way of life, for the government to keep the methods that they use to conduct that surveillance a national secret. What they are really

doing is using that secrecy to hide un-American actions from the general public ... [144]

In light of these statements, an even more disturbing question emerges: why are intelligence services so interested in ordinary people who use service providers like Google and Yahoo!?

As quoted earlier in the book, Chris Pyle concluded that our security services, in an effort to reinforce their budgets, sometimes go out in search of enemies. Former *New York Times* editor Max Frankel, the man who played a vital role in the release of the Pentagon Papers, adds:

> There is money to be made in the mass [interception] approach. We are learning that much of the snooping is farmed out to profit-seeking corporations that have great appetites for government contracts, secured through executives who enrich themselves by shuttling between agency jobs and the contractors' board rooms.[145]

History may also offer some additional insight. In 1974 journalist Seymour Hersh wrote an article that appeared on the front page of the *New York Times* about a CIA program that directly violated the agency's charter.

The article detailed an illegal domestic surveillance program run by a special unit within the CIA which targeted over 10,000 U.S. citizens involved in the antiwar movement and other dissident groups. Inside the CIA this initiative was known as "Operation CHAOS" and was geared towards unearthing "foreign influence" (i.e. communists).[146] Operation CHAOS was launched under the auspices of Lyndon Johnson's administration and, as you might expect, it gained even more traction under President Nixon.

CHAOS wasn't an isolated incident. A group of journalists and scholars at a non-profit called "The National Security Archive" have unearthed an NSA program called "Minaret." Like Operation CHAOS, Minaret was a Vietnam-era watch list operation initiated under President Lyndon Johnson and continued by President Nixon. The program was supposedly launched to track suspected terrorists and drug traffickers. However, as the operation evolved, the White House requested surveillance of high-profile figures like Martin Luther King, *New*

York Times journalist Tom Wicker, and Muhammad Ali, in addition to Senators Frank Church and Howard Baker. Reports derived from this monitoring were sent directly to the office of the President. Documents show that the NSA itself saw Minaret as "disreputable if not outright illegal" due to the complete absence of judicial oversight.[147]

In the 1976 report submitted by the Church Committee, the FBI's former director of intelligence operations, William C. Sullivan, testified that the Bureau conducted an extensive monitoring program against Martin Luther King:

> No holds were barred. We have used [similar] techniques against Soviet agents. [The same methods were] brought home against any organization against which we were targeted. We did not differentiate. This is a rough, tough business.

There are indications that history may be repeating itself. Internal classified documents show that there are elements within U.S. intelligence agencies that view the average citizen as the enemy. With regard to its industry-wide program of technology subversion a leaked document states:

> These design changes make the systems in question exploitable through Sigint collection … To the consumer and other adversaries, however, the systems' security remains intact.[148]

Author John Dvorak offers a take on this:

> Because we know that these recent documents were never expected to see the light of day, you have to know that honesty prevails throughout. There is no good reason to sugarcoat the comments. This is what they really think. They didn't have to be coy about it. The NSA considers the American people to be its adversary, thus its use of the word adversary.[149]

By The Numbers

Our political and military leaders tell us that domestic programs like PRISM are focused on protecting us from the threat of terrorism. In an October 2013 interview with the *New York Times* an unabashed General Alexander said that he saw no effective alternative to dragnet surveillance and that monitoring programs would actually need to be *expanded* for the sake of *national security.*[150]

But, as shown in this chapter, the very nature of domestic mass interception program contradicts this. There's a lot of effort being spent to monitor ordinary people.

Investigative journalists at *Mother Jones* and UC Berkeley reviewed the prosecutions of 508 defendants in cases related to terrorism over the past decade. Of all the cases they came across, only *three* were not FBI stings:

> The exceptions are Najibullah Zazi, who came close to bombing the New York City subway system in September 2009; Hesham Mohamed Hadayet, an Egyptian who opened fire on the El-Al ticket counter at the Los Angeles airport; and failed Times Square bomber Faisal Shahzad.[151]

The journalists also found:

> Sting operations resulted in prosecutions against 158 defendants. Of that total, 49 defendants participated in plots led by an agent provocateur – an FBI operative instigating terrorist action.

Officials steadfastly contend that, given the billions of dollars they receive, their methods yield results. On July 24, 2013, Representative Mike Rogers made the following statement speaking on the House floor:

> Fifty-four times this and the other program stopped and thwarted terrorist attacks both here and in Europe – saving real lives. This isn't a game. This is real.[152]

In a speech on Jun 25, 2013, General Keith Alexander claimed:

> On 21 June we provided over 50 cases to both the House and Senate Intelligence Committees that show the specific contribution of these programs to our understanding and, in many cases, disruption of terrorist plots in the United States and over 20 countries throughout the world.[153]

But Alexander's narrative has been brought into question by his own people. In a hearing that took place on July 31st, the NSA's own Deputy Director John Inglis admitted that the NSA's mass collection of phone metadata under Section 215 of the USA PATRIOT Act had been pivotal in stopping only a single terror plot.

Journalist Spencer Ackerman observed:

> In open session, directly, they can't even say that seven years' worth of phone records collection, basically a network of everyone's social interactions conducted over the telephone, which is very easy to tell from metadata, for seven years, from all Americans, has maybe stopped one terrorist plot.[154]

General Alexander would eventually acknowledge this truth under questioning during an oversight hearing.[155]

Of the 54 instances mentioned earlier by Mike Rogers, the NSA has declassified information on only four instances.[156] In all four cases the news outlet *ProPublica* presented evidence which casts doubt on the actual utility of dragnet surveillance.[157]

The same sort of dynamic is at work on a local level. In the hunt for radical Islamists after 9/11, the New York Police Department went so far as to re-create its intelligence division from scratch. The police Commissioner went out and recruited a former high-ranking CIA officer named David Cohen to show him how to do it.[158] The division launched an operation that was known as the NYPD's *demographics unit* and sent a wave of undercover informants all over the city looking for terrorists. The operation, after years of building and maintaining files on Muslim-Americans, *failed to produce as much as a single lead.*[159]

In a direct rebuttal to high-level officials like James Clapper and Andrew Parker, NSA whistleblower Ed Snowden stated:

> The secret continuance of these [mass interception] programs represents a far greater danger than their disclosure ... [160]

James Carroll, a writer for the *Boston Globe* who spent three summers as a college student working for the FBI's Cryptanalysis-Translation Section, explains why this is the case:

Absolute data collection, however justified, leads to the mass destruction of personal autonomy, whether the collectors intend it or not.... The NSA aims to protect us from the enemy, but who outside the agency's cyber-priesthood can grasp the implications of that "protection"? When does the protector become the enemy?[161]

Coda: Extorting Privacy

You can't have your privacy violated if you don't know your privacy is violated.

— Rep. Mike Rogers, Chairman of the Permanent Select Committee on Intelligence[162]

Based on what we've presented, it's clear that both the government and the private sector are wielding high-powered surveillance tools to extract data from the Internet. Furthermore, though there is plenty of overt data collection, there is also interception (e.g. NSLs) that's shielded by official secrecy.

There are proponents at the outlier of the spectrum who seek to completely drive anonymity from the Internet. They want us to sacrifice our privacy on the altar of security. Stewart Baker, a fellow at the CSIS, believes:

Anonymity is the fundamental problem we face in cyberspace.[163]

Disclaimer:
CSIS has ample individual connections to the defense industry through its advisors and trustees, including CSIS Senior Advisor Margaret Sidney Ashworth, Corporate Vice President for Government Relations at Northrop Grumman, and CSIS Advisor Thomas Culligan, Senior Vice President at Raytheon. CSIS President and CEO John Hamre is a director for defense contractor SAIC.[164]

Likewise, Dan Greer, the chief information security officer at In-Q-Tel, has concluded:

If the tariff of security is paid, it will be paid in the coin of privacy.[165]

Disclaimer:

For more than a decade the CIA has run its own venture capital fund called In-Q-Tel. It was founded in the late 1990s when the CIA was drowning in data and didn't have the tools to connect the dots.[166]

When asked what's wrong with the Internet, Eugene Kaspersky has stated:

There's anonymity. Everyone should and must have an identification, or Internet passport.[167]

Disclaimer:

At 16 he [Kaspersky] was accepted to a five-year program at the KGB-backed Institute of Cryptography, Telecommunications, and Computer Science. After graduating in 1987, he was commissioned as an intelligence officer in the Soviet army.[168]

Do you see a pattern emerging? We see a lot of people with ties to intelligence services telling people that we should yield privacy in the name of security.

Donald Kerr, the Principal Deputy Director of National Intelligence from 2007 to 2009, asserted:

This careful balance we need to strike, however, is nothing new. With the advent of telephones, we entered a new frontier that required careful balancing between safety and privacy.[169]

Figure 10-2

Society is being blackmailed on the grounds of a false dichotomy: give up privacy or leaders can't protect the public from the awful things that are going to happen. The essence of surveillance is control, and the more privacy that we yield the more control society hands over to the small group of people wielding the telescreens.

This mindset is probably best expressed by General Keith Alexander, who solemnly warned:

> If we give up a capability that is critical to the defense of this nation, people will die … [170]

Referring to the Kenya's Westgate Mall Massacre, Alexander repeated the same message:

> If you take those [surveillance powers] away, think about the last week and what will happen in the future…. If you think it's bad now, wait until you get some of those things that happened in Nairobi.[171]

Like General Alexander, *New York Times* columnist Thomas Friedman also refines this technique to a high art form. He claims that he's willing to "reluctantly" trade privacy for security because:

> If there is one more 9/11 – or worse, an attack involving nuclear material – it could lead to the end of the open society as we know it. If there were another 9/11, I fear that 99 percent of Americans would tell their members of Congress: "Do whatever you need to do to, privacy be damned, just make sure this does not happen again." That is what I fear most.[172]

In other words, we must undermine constitutional liberty because a future terror attack might occur, one which might involve *nuclear weapons*. And if an attack like that occured it would surely mean the end of the Constitution. Using absurd logic, Friedman claims that we should *undermine the Constitution in order to save it.*

Friedman intentionally neglects to acknowledge that the true threat to the U.S. constitution isn't a terrorist attack, it's how our leaders respond to an attack. During World War II the British Government produced a poster exhorting people, in the aftermath of German air strikes, to "keep calm and carry on." Instead of clamping down on constitutional freedoms, decision makers could follow this maxim. With homage to Bruce Schneier, leaders could *refuse to be terrorized.*

This basic strategy, ceding civil liberties for alleged gains in security, was put into practice by several governments during World War II. It almost always didn't turn out very well.

> Germans have experienced firsthand what happens when the government knows too much about someone. In the past 80 years, Germans have felt the betrayal of neighbors who informed for the Gestapo and the fear that best friends might be potential informants for the Stasi. Homes were tapped. Millions were monitored.[173]

The fundamental threat to security isn't privacy. Furthermore, you don't have to give up privacy to improve security. *You can have both.* Bruce Schneier eloquently spells this out:

> Security and privacy are not two sides of an equation. This association is simplistic and largely fallacious. The best ways to increase security are not at the expense of privacy and liberty. Giving airline pilots firearms, reinforcing cockpit doors, better authentication of airport maintenance workers, armed air marshals travelling on flights and teaching flight attendants karate are all examples of suggested security measures that have no effect on individual privacy or liberties.
>
> People are willing to give up liberties for vague promises of security because they think they have no choice. What they're not being told is that they can have both. It would require us to discard the easy answers.[174]

Hunting down criminals on the Internet will always be an expensive, resource intensive proposition. Hunting down spies will be even harder than that, if not impossible, because national governments tend to make the necessary investments in anti-forensic technology. The examples that we surveyed in the second part of this book underscore these realities.

As long as officials chase their tails trying to drive anonymity out of the Internet, the struggle to improve security will resemble the fight against bootleggers during prohibition. The victories that are achieved will be short-lived and have little impact in the underlying problem of poor cyber-security. If they succeed at anything it will be setting the stage for a police state.

Endnotes

1)Ira Hunt, *Beyond Big Data: Riding the Technology Wave*, Central Intelligence Agency, March 2012, http://info.publicintelligence.net/CIA-BigData-1.pdf.

2) Bridie Jabour, "PRISM-style surveillance is global, Julian Assange says," *Guardian*, June 14, 2013, http://m.guardian.co.uk/world/2013/jun/14/wikileaks-australia-surveillance-google-julian-assange?CMP=twt_gu.

3) Barton Gellman, "Code name 'Verax': Snowden, in exchanges with Post reporter, made clear he knew risks," *Washington Post*, June 9, 2013, http://www.washingtonpost.com/world/national-security/code-name-verax-snowden-in-exchanges-with-post-reporter-made-clear-he-knew-risks/2013/06/09/c9a25b54-d14c-11e2-9f1a-1a7cdee20287_print.html.

4) *History of the Virginia Federal Convention of 1788*, vol. 1, H.B. Grigsby ed. 1890, p. 130.

5) Rob Hastings, "Ronald Noble: 'Terrorists plan on email. And we can't track them,'" *The Independent*, December 30, 2011. http://www.independent.co.uk/news/people/profiles/ronald-noble-terrorists-plan-on-email-and-we-cant-track-them-6282996.html.

6) Mark Hosenball, "Lawmakers press Homeland Security on Internet monitoring," *Reuters*, January 12, 2012, http://www.reuters.com/article/2012/01/13/us-usa-security-internet-idUSTRE80C06T20120113.

7) Barton Gellman, Dafna Linzer and Carol D. Leonnig, "Surveillance Net Yields Few Suspects," *Washington Post*, February 5, 2006, http://www.washingtonpost.com/wp-dyn/content/article/2006/02/04/AR2006020401373.html.

8) Peter Swire, Kenesa Ahmad, "'Going Dark' Versus a 'Golden Age for Surveillance,'" *Center for Democracy and Technology*, November 28, 2011. http://www.cdt.org/blogs/2811going-dark-versus-golden-age-surveillance.

9) David Kravets, "Justice Department's Warrantless Spying Increased 600 Percent in Decade," *Wired*, September 27, 2012, http://www.wired.com/threatlevel/2012/09/warrantless-surveillance-stats/.

10) Eric Lichtblau, "More Demands on Cell Carriers in Surveillance," *New York Times*, July 8, 2012, http://www.nytimes.com/2012/07/09/us/cell-carriers-see-uptick-in-requests-to-aid-surveillance.html.

11) "NSA snooping: Facebook reveals details of data requests," *BBC News*, June 14, 2013, http://www.bbc.co.uk/news/world-22916329?print=true.

12) *Going Dark: Law Enforcement Problems in Lawful Surveillance*, Federal Bureau Of Investigation Situational Information Report, Cyber Activity Alert, Albany Division, June 29, 2011, http://www.wikileaks.org/gifiles/attach/10/10490_FBI%20Going%20Dark.pdf.

13) Brian Fung, "How stores use your phone's WiFi to track your shopping habits," *Washington Post*, October 19, 2013, http://www.washingtonpost.com/blogs/

the-switch/wp/2013/10/19/how-stores-use-your-phones-wifi-to-track-your-shopping-habits/.

14) Federico Rampini, Cryptome Interview by La Repubblica, October 30, 2013, http://cryptome.org/2013/11/cryptome-la-repubblica.htm.

15) "AT&T Whistle-Blower's Evidence," Wired, May 17, 2007, http://www.wired.com/science/discoveries/news/2006/05/70908.

16) Michael Isikoff, "The Fed Who Blew the Whistle," Newsweek, December 22, 2008, http://web.archive.org/web/20081215105850/http://www.newsweek.com/id/174601.

17) James Risen and Eric Lichtblau, "Bush Lets U.S. Spy on Callers Without Courts," New York Times, December 16, 2005, http://www.nytimes.com/2005/12/16/politics/16program.html.

18) Letter from Attorney General Alberto Gonzales to Senator Patrick Leahy and Senator Arlen Specter, January 17, 2007, http://graphics8.nytimes.com/packages/pdf/politics/20060117gonzales_Letter.pdf.

19) James Bamford, "They Know Much More Than You Think," The New York Review of Books, August 15, 2013, http://www.nybooks.com/articles/archives/2013/aug/15/nsa-they-know-much-more-you-think/?pagination=false.

20) Charlie Savage and James Risen, "Federal Judge Finds N.S.A. Wiretaps Were Illegal," New York Times, March 31, 2010, http://www.nytimes.com/2010/04/01/us/01nsa.html?_r=0&pagewanted=print.

21) Eric Lichtblau, "Senate Approves Bill to Broaden Wiretap Powers," New York Times, July 10, 2008, http://www.nytimes.com/2008/07/10/washington/10fisa.html?pagewanted=print.

22) David Kravets, "House Approves Sweeping, Warrantless Electronic Spy Powers," Wired, September 12, 2012, http://www.wired.com/threatlevel/2012/09/house-approves-spy-bill/.

23) Barton Gellman and Laura Poitras, "U.S., British intelligence mining data from nine U.S. Internet companies in broad secret program," Washington Post, June 7, 2013, http://www.washingtonpost.com/investigations/us-intelligence-mining-data-from-nine-us-internet-companies-in-broad-secret-program/2013/06/06/3a0c0da8-cebf-11e2-8845-d970ccb04497_print.html.

24) Glenn Greenwald and James Ball, "The top secret rules that allow NSA to use US data without a warrant," Guardian, June 20, 2013, http://www.guardian.co.uk/world/2013/jun/20/fisa-court-nsa-without-warrant.

25) Charlie Savage, "N.S.A. Said to Search Content of Messages to and From U.S.," New York Times, August 8, 2013, http://www.nytimes.com/2013/08/08/us/broader-sifting-of-data-abroad-is-seen-by-nsa.html.

26) Charlie Savage, "N.S.A. Said to Search Content of Messages to and From U.S.," New York Times, August 8, 2013, http://www.nytimes.com/2013/08/08/us/broader-sifting-of-data-abroad-is-seen-by-nsa.html.

27) Trevor Timm, "A Guide to the Deceptions, Misinformation, and Word Games Officials Use to Mislead the Public About NSA Surveillance," Deeplinks Blog, Electronic Frontier Foundation, August 14, 2013, https://www.eff.org/deep-

links/2013/08/guide-deceptions-word-games-obfuscations-officials-use-mis-lead-public-about-nsa.

28) Declan McCullagh, "NSA spying flap extends to contents of U.S. phone calls," *CNET*, June 15, 2013, http://news.cnet.com/8301-13578_3-57589495-38/nsa-spying-flap-extends-to-contents-of-u.s-phone-calls/.

29) Peter Beaumont, "NSA leaks: US and Britain team up on mass surveillance," *Guardian*, June 22, 2013, http://www.guardian.co.uk/world/2013/jun/22/nsa-leaks-britain-us-surveillance/print.

30) Barton Gellman and Ashkan Soltani, "NSA collects millions of e-mail address books globally," *Washington Post*, October 14, 2013, http://www.washington-post.com/world/national-security/nsa-collects-millions-of-e-mail-address-books-globally/2013/10/14/8e58b5be-34f9-11e3-80c6-7e6dd8d22d8f_print.html.

31) Eric Lichtblau And James Risen, "Officials Say U.S. Wiretaps Exceeded Law," *New York Times*, April 16, 2009, http://www.nytimes.com/2009/04/16/us/16nsa.html?pagewanted=print.

32) James Risen And Eric Lichtblau, "E-Mail Surveillance Renews Concerns in Congress," *New York Times*, June 17, 2009, http://www.nytimes.com/2009/06/17/us/17nsa.html?pagewanted=print.

33) Barton Gellman, "NSA broke privacy rules thousands of times per year, audit finds," *Washington Post*, August 15, 2013, http://www.washingtonpost.com/world/national-security/nsa-broke-privacy-rules-thousands-of-times-per-year-audit-finds/2013/08/15/3310e554-05ca-11e3-a07f-49ddc7417125_print.html.

34) Kurt Opsahl and Mark Rumold, "Reassured by NSA's Internal Procedures? Don't Be. They Still Don't Tell the Whole Story," *Electronic Frontier Foundation*, June 21, 2013, https://www.eff.org/deeplinks/2013/06/recently-revealed-nsa-proce-dures-likely-ones-found-unconstitutional-fisa-court.

35) Mark Rumold and David Sobel, "Government Says Secret Court Opinion on Law Underlying PRISM Program Needs to Stay Secret," *Electronic Frontier Foundation*, June 7, 2013, https://www.eff.org/deeplinks/2013/06/government-says-secret-court-opinion-law-underlying-prism-program-needs-stay.

36) David Kravets, "Declassified Documents Prove NSA Is Tapping the Internet," *Wired*, August 21, 2013, http://www.wired.com/threatlevel/2013/08/nsa-tap-ping-internet/.

37) Andy Greenberg, "NSA Chief Denies Wired's Domestic Spying Story (Four-teen Times) In Congressional Hearing," *Forbes*, March 20, 2012, http://www.forbes.com/sites/andygreenberg/2012/03/20/nsa-chief-denies-wireds-domes-tic-spying-story-fourteen-times-in-congressional-hearing/.

38) James Bamford, "NSA Chief Denies Domestic Spying But Whistleblowers Say Otherwise," *Wired*, March 21, 2012, http://www.wired.com/threatlevel/2012/03/nsa-whistleblower/.

39) Glenn Kessler, "James Clapper's 'least untruthful' statement to the Senate," *Washington Post*, June 12, 2013, http://www.washingtonpost.com/blogs/fact-checker/post/james-clappers-least-untruthful-statement-to-the-sen-ate/2013/06/11/e50677a8-d2d8-11e2-a73e-826d299ff459_blog.html.

40) "Whistleblower: The NSA Is Lying–U.S. Government Has Copies of Most of Your Emails," *Democracy Now!* April 20, 2012, http://www.democracynow.org/2012/4/20/whistleblower_the_nsa_is_lying_us.

41) Hepting v. AT&T, Public Unredacted Klein Declaration, https://www.eff.org/sites/default/files/filenode/att/Mark%20Klein%20Unredacted%20Decl-Including%20Exhibits.PDF.

42) James Bamford, "The The NSA Is Building the Country's Biggest Spy Center (Watch What You Say)," *Wired,* march 15, 2012, http://www.wired.com/threatlevel/2012/03/ff_nsadatacenter/all/1.

43) Julia Angwin, "U.S. Terrorism Agency to Tap a Vast Database of Citizens," *Wall Street Journal,* December 13, 2012, http://online.wsj.com/article/SB10001424127887324478304578171623040640006.html.

44) "Glenn Greenwald: U.S. Spying on Allies Shows "Institutional Obsession" with Surveillance," *Democracy Now!* October 28, 2013, http://www.democracynow.org/2013/10/28/glenn_greenwald_us_spying_on_allies#.

45) Glenn Greenwald, "NSA collecting phone records of millions of Verizon customers daily," *Guardian,* June 5, 2013, http://www.guardian.co.uk/world/2013/jun/06/nsa-phone-records-verizon-court-order.

46) Cindy Cohn and Trevor Timm, "In Response to the NSA, We Need A New Church Committee and We Need It Now," *Electronic Frontier Foundation,* June 7, 2013, https://www.eff.org/deeplinks/2013/06/response-nsa-we-need-new-church-commission-and-we-need-it-now.

47) Charlie Savage, "N.S.A. Plan to Log Calls Is Renewed by Court," *New York Times,* October 18, 2013, http://www.nytimes.com/2013/10/19/us/nsa-plan-to-log-calls-is-renewed-by-court.html.

48) Jennifer Stisa Granick And Christopher Jon Sprigman, "The Criminal N.S.A.," *New York Times,* June 27, 2013, http://www.nytimes.com/2013/06/28/opinion/the-criminal-nsa.html?pagewanted=all&_r=2&.

49) "NSA Whistleblowers: "All U.S. Citizens" Targeted by Surveillance Program, Not Just Verizon Customers," *Democracy Now!* June 6, 2013, http://www.democracynow.org/2013/6/6/nsa_whistleblowers_all_us_citizens_targeted#.

50) James Risen And Laura Poitras, "N.S.A. Gathers Data on Social Connections of U.S. Citizens," *New York Times,* September 29, 2013, http://www.nytimes.com/2013/09/29/us/nsa-examines-social-networks-of-us-citizens.html?pagewanted=print.

51) James Ball, "NSA stores metadata of millions of web users for up to a year, secret files show," *Guardian,* September 30, 2013, http://www.theguardian.com/world/2013/sep/30/nsa-americans-metadata-year-documents/print.

52) Ellen Nakashima, "U.S. officials dodge questions on scope of surveillance," *Washington Post,* September 26, 2013, http://articles.washingtonpost.com/2013-09-26/world/42417897_1_phone-records-nsa-director-keith-alexander-broad-collection.

53) Glenn Greenwald and Ewen MacAskill, "NSA Prism program taps in to user data of Apple, Google and others," *Guardian*, June 6, 2013, http://www.guardian.co.uk/world/2013/jun/06/us-tech-giants-nsa-data.

54) Barton Gellman and Todd Lindeman, "Inner workings of a top-secret spy program," *Washington Post*, June 29, 2013, http://apps.washingtonpost.com/g/page/national/inner-workings-of-a-top-secret-spy-program/282/.

55) Claire Cain Miller, "Tech Companies Concede to Surveillance Program," *New York Times*, June 7, 2013, http://www.nytimes.com/2013/06/08/technology/tech-companies-bristling-concede-to-government-surveillance-efforts.html?_r=0&pagewanted=print.

56) Ewen MacAskill, "NSA paid millions to cover Prism compliance costs for tech companies," *Guardian*, August 22, 2013, http://www.theguardian.com/world/2013/aug/23/nsa-prism-costs-tech-companies-paid/print.

57) Kevin Poulsen, "Zuckerberg, Page: NSA Has No 'Direct Access' to Facebook or Google Servers," *Wired*, June 7, 2013, http://www.wired.com/threatlevel/2013/06/prism-google-facebook/.

58) Glenn Greenwald and Ewen MacAskill, "NSA Prism program taps in to user data of Apple, Google and others," *Guardian*, June 6, 2013, http://www.guardian.co.uk/world/2013/jun/06/us-tech-giants-nsa-data.

59) Thu-Huong Ha, "Security experts Bruce Schneier and Mikko Hypponen on the NSA, PRISM and why we should be worried," *TED Blog*, July 17, 2013, http://blog.ted.com/2013/07/17/security-experts-on-the-nsas-real-problems/.

60) Barton Gellman and Ashkan Soltani, "NSA infiltrates links to Yahoo!, Google data centers worldwide, Snowden documents say," *Washington Post*, October 30, 2013, http://www.washingtonpost.com/world/national-security/nsa-infiltrates-links-to-yahoo-google-data-centers-worldwide-snowden-documents-say/2013/10/30/e51d661e-4166-11e3-8b74-d89d714ca4dd_print.html.

61) Bruce Schneier, "NSA surveillance: A guide to staying secure," *Guardian*, September 6, 2013, http://www.theguardian.com/world/2013/sep/05/nsa-how-to-remain-secure-surveillance.

62) Bruce Schneier, "Trading Privacy for Convenience," *Schneier on Security*, June 13, 2013, http://www.schneier.com/blog/archives/2013/06/trading_privacy_1.html.

63) "CIA tracks global pulse on Twitter, Facebook," *Associated Press*, November 4, 2011, http://www.cbsnews.com/8301-205_162-57318372/cia-tracks-global-pulse-on-twitter-facebook/.

64) Noah Shachtman, "Exclusive: Google, CIA Invest in 'Future' of Web Monitoring," *Wired*, July 28, 2010, http://www.wired.com/dangerroom/2010/07/exclusive-google-cia/.

65) Ryan Gallagher, "Software that tracks people on social media created by defence firm," *Guardian*, February 10, 2013, http://www.guardian.co.uk/world/2013/feb/10/software-tracks-social-media-defence/print.

66) Andrew Ross Sorkin, "A Database of Names and How They Connect," *New York Times*, February 11, 2013, http://dealbook.nytimes.com/2013/02/11/a-database-of-names-and-how-they-connect/?ref=business.

67) Privacy Impact Assessment, Publicly Available Social Media Monitoring and Situational Awareness Initiative, Office of Operations Coordination and Planning, Department of Homeland Security, June 22, 2010, http://www.dhs.gov/xlibrary/assets/privacy/privacy_pia_ops_publiclyavailablesocialmedia.pdf.

68) Ellen Nakashima, "DHS monitoring of social media concerns civil liberties advocates," *Washington Post*, January 13, 2012, http://www.washingtonpost.com/world/national-security/dhs-monitoring-of-social-media-worries-civil-liberties-advocates/2012/01/13/gIQANPO7wP_print.html.

69) Ibid.

70) Janet Maslin, "Fighting Words Against Big Data," *New York Times*, May 5, 2013, http://www.nytimes.com/2013/05/06/books/who-owns-the-future-by-jaron-lanier.html?_r=0&pagewanted=print.

71) James Risen and Nick Wingfield, "Web's Reach Binds N.S.A. and Silicon Valley Leaders," *New York Times*, June 20, 2013, http://www.nytimes.com/2013/06/20/technology/silicon-valley-and-spy-agency-bound-by-strengthening-web.html.

72) Mike McConnell, "Mike McConnell on how to win the cyberwar we're losing," *Washington Post*, February 28, 2010, http://www.washingtonpost.com/wp-dyn/content/article/2010/02/25/AR2010022502493_pf.html.

73) RASPI, "FSB, Russian police could tap Skype without court order," *Moscow News*, March 14, 2013, http://www.themoscownews.com/russia/20130314/191336455/FSB-Russian-police-could-tap-Skype-without-court-order.html.

74) Vassilis Prevelakis, Diomidis Spinellis, "The Athen's Affair," *IEEE Spectrum*, June 29, 2007, http://spectrum.ieee.org/telecom/security/the-athens-affair.

75) "US caught spying on Greek diplomatic communications in 2004-2005," *WikiLeaks*, September 23, 2013, http://wikileaks-press.org/us-caught-spying-on-greek-diplomatic-communications-in-2004-2005/.

76) Office of the Inspector General, "A Review of the FBI's Use of National Security Letters: Assessment of Corrective Actions and Examination of NSL Usage in 2006," March 2008, http://www.justice.gov/oig/special/s0803b/final.pdf.

77) Kim Zetter, "'John Doe' Who Fought FBI Spying Freed From Gag Order After 6 Years," *Wired*, August 10, 2010, http://www.wired.com/threatlevel/2010/08/nsl-gag-order-lifted/.

78) Declan McCullagh and Casey Newton, "Google offers data on FBI's national-security-related requests for user identities," *CNET*, March 5, 2013, http://news.cnet.com/8301-1009_3-57572634-83/google-offers-data-on-fbis-national-security-related-requests-for-user-identities/.

79) David Kravets, "Microsoft, Too, Says FBI Secretly Surveilling Its Customers," *Wired*, March 21, 2013, http://www.wired.com/threatlevel/2013/03/microsoft-nsl-revelation/.

80) Alexander Abdo, "Google's Report on NSLs: What we still don't know," *ACLU National Security Project*, March 7, 2013, http://www.aclu.org/print/blog/national-security-technology-and-liberty/googles-report-nsls-what-we-still-dont-know.

81) Matt Zimmerman, March 18, 2013, "In Depth: The District Court's Remarkable Order Striking Down the NSL Statute," *Electronic Frontier Foundation*, https://www.eff.org/deeplinks/2013/03/depth-judge-illstons-remarkable-order-striking-down-nsl-statute.

82) Scott Shane And Colin Moynihan, "Drug Agents Use Vast Phone Trove, Eclipsing N.S.A.'s," *New York Times*, September 1, 2013, http://www.nytimes.com/2013/09/02/us/drug-agents-use-vast-phone-trove-eclipsing-nsas.html.

83) "Synopsis of the Hemisphere Project," *New York Times*, September 1, 2013, http://www.nytimes.com/interactive/2013/09/02/us/hemisphere-project.html.

84) Pamela Jones Harbour, "The Emperor of All Identities," *New York Times*, December 18, 2012, http://www.nytimes.com/2012/12/19/opinion/why-google-has-too-much-power-over-your-private-life.html.

85) Mg Siegler, "Eric Schmidt: Every 2 Days We Create As Much Information As We Did Up To 2003," *TechCrunch*, August 4, 2010, http://techcrunch.com/2010/08/04/schmidt-data/.

86) Hearing Before The Committee On Commerce, Science, And Transportation, United States Senate, One Hundred Eleventh Congress, Second Session, July 27, 2010, http://www.gpo.gov/fdsys/pkg/CHRG-111shrg67686/pdf/CHRG-111shrg67686.pdf.

87) Melissa Eddy And James Kanter, "Merkel Urges Europe to Tighten Internet Safeguards," *New York Times*, July 15, 2013, http://www.nytimes.com/2013/07/16/world/europe/merkel-urges-europe-to-tighten-internet-safeguards.html.

88) Statement of Linda D. Koontz, Director Information Management Issues, Testimony.

Before the Subcommittee on Information Policy, Census, and National Archives, Committee on Oversight and Government Reform, United States Government Accountability Office, March 11, 2008, GAO-08-543T.

89) Dominic Rushe, "Zuckerberg: US government 'blew it' on NSA surveillance," *Guardian*, September 11, 2013, http://www.theguardian.com/technology/2013/sep/11/yahoo-ceo-mayer-jail-nsa-surveillance/print.

90) Ellen Nakashima and Dan Eggen, "Former CEO Says U.S. Punished Phone Firm," *Washington Post*, October 13, 2007, http://www.washingtonpost.com/wp-dyn/content/article/2007/10/12/AR2007101202485_pf.html.

91) Andrea Peterson, "A CEO who resisted NSA spying is out of prison. And he feels 'vindicated' by Snowden leaks," *Washington Post*, September 30, 2013, http://www.washingtonpost.com/blogs/the-switch/wp/2013/09/30/a-ceo-who-resisted-nsa-spying-is-out-of-prison-and-he-feels-vindicated-by-snowden-leaks//?print=1.

92) Jared Newman, "Facebook and Yahoo! join motions to disclose national security requests," *PCWorld*, September 9, 2013, http://www.pcworld.com/ar-

ticle/2048434/facebook-and-yahoo-join-motions-to-disclose-national-security-requests.html.

93) Allan Holmes, "NSA Spying Seen Risking Billions in U.S. Technology Sales," *Bloomberg*, September 10, 2013, http://www.bloomberg.com/news/print/2013-09-10/nsa-spying-seen-risking-billions-in-u-s-technology-sales.html.

94) Kevin Poulsen, "Zuckerberg, Page: NSA Has No 'Direct Access' to Facebook or Google Servers," *Wired*, June 7, 2013, http://www.wired.com/threatlevel/2013/06/prism-google-facebook/.

95) Spencer Ackerman, "Fisa court: no telecoms company has ever challenged phone records orders," *Guardian*, September 17, 2013, http://www.theguardian.com/law/2013/sep/17/fisa-court-bulk-phone-records-collection/print.

96) Deborah Davis, *Katharine the Great : Katharine Graham and Her Washington Post Empire*, Institute for Media Analysis, 3rd Edition, 1991, ISBN-13: 978-0941781138.

97) Select Committee to Study Government Operations with Respect to Intelligence Activities, Book I: Foreign and Military Intelligence, U.S. Government Printing Office, 1976, page 192, http://www.aarclibrary.org/publib/church/reports/book1/html/ChurchB1_0100b.htm.

98) Carl Bernstein, "The CIA and the Media," *Rolling Stone*, October 20, 1977, http://www.carlbernstein.com/magazine_cia_and_media.php.

99) Nozomi Hayase, "Wikileaks: Bringing the First Amendment to the World," *Counterpunch*, November 1-3, 2013, http://www.counterpunch.org/2013/11/01/wikileaks-bringing-the-first-amendment-to-the-world/print.

100) Julian Assange, "Google and the NSA: Who's holding the 'shit-bag' now?," *The Stringer*, September 16, 2013, http://thestringer.com.au/google-and-the-nsa-whos-holding-the-shit-bag-now/#.

101) Paul Joseph Watson, "Ex-Agent: CIA Seed Money Helped Launch Google," *Prison Planet*, December 6, 2006, http://www.prisonplanet.com/articles/december2006/061206seedmoney.htm.

102) Edward Wyatt, "Google's Washington Insider," *New York Times*, June 2, 2013, http://www.nytimes.com/2013/06/03/business/susan-molinari-adds-to-googles-political-firepower.html.

103) Eva Gollinger and Julian Assange, "Assange: 'Snowden safe but journalists dealing with him at risk'," *RT*, October 11, 2013, http://rt.com/news/assange-interview-snowden-journalists-079/.

104) Bill Moyers & Company, November 8, 2013, *Heidi Boghosian on Spying and Civil Liberties*, http://billmoyers.com/wp-content/themes/billmoyers/transcript-print.php?post=48454.

105) Seth Rosenblatt, "Microsoft, Google to sue over FISA gag order," *CNET*, August 30, 2013, http://news.cnet.com/8301-1009_3-57600849-83/microsoft-google-to-sue-over-fisa-gag-order/.

106) Amir Efrati, "Google Wins U.S. Contract," *Wall Street Journal*, May 1, 2012.

107) J. Nicholas Hoover, "Military Signs Most Comprehensive Microsoft Contract Yet," *InformationWeek*, January 3, 2013, http://www.informationweek.com/government/enterprise-applications/military-signs-most-comprehensive-micros/240145467?printer_friendly=this-page.

108) Danielle Ivory, "IBM Wins Protest of $600 Million CIA Contract With Amazon," *Bloomberg*, June 7, 2013, http://www.bloomberg.com/news/print/2013-06-07/ibm-wins-protest-of-600-million-cia-contract-with-amazon.html.

109) Glenn Greenwald, "Telecom amnesty would forever foreclose investigation of vital issues," *Salon*, October 15, 2007, http://www.salon.com/2007/10/15/amnesty/.

110) Aliya Sternstein, "The NSA's New Spy Facilities are 7 Times Bigger Than the Pentagon," *Defense One*, July 25, 2013, http://www.defenseone.com/technology/2013/07/nsas-big-dig/67406/print/.

111) Siobhan Gorman, "Meltdowns Hobble NSA Data Center," *Wall Street Journal*, October 7, 2013, http://online.wsj.com/news/articles/SB10001424052702304441404579119490744478398.

112) "NSA $3.2 Billion 'Site M' Expansion Planning Documents Reveal Cyberwar Command Center," *Public Intelligence*, June 14, 2011, http://publicintelligence.net/nsa-site-m-cybercom/.

113) James Ball, Julian Borger, and Glenn Greenwald, "Revealed: how US and UK spy agencies defeat internet privacy and security," *Guardian*, September 5, 2013, http://www.theguardian.com/world/2013/sep/05/nsa-gchq-encryption-codes-security/print.

114) Juliette Garside, "Microsoft Windows performance helps cash reserves grow by $5bn in six months," *Guardian*, January 24, 2013, http://www.theguardian.com/technology/2013/jan/24/microsoft-cash-reserves-grow-5-billion/print.

115) Emily Chasan, "Apple Now Holds 10% of All Corporate Cash: Moody's," *Wall Street Journal*, October 1, 2013, http://blogs.wsj.com/cfo/2013/10/01/apple-now-holds-10-of-all-corporate-cash-moodys/?mod=trending_now_3.

116) Stephen Braun, Anne Flaherty, Jack Gillum And Matt Apuzzo, "Secret to Prism program: Even bigger data seizure," *Associated Press*, June 15, 2013, http://bigstory.ap.org/article/secret-prism-success-even-bigger-data-seizure.

117) *Democracy Now!* "You're Being Watched: Edward Snowden Emerges as Source Behind Explosive Revelations of NSA Spying," June 10, 2013, http://www.democracynow.org/2013/6/10/youre_being_watched_edward_snowden_emerges#.

118) Glenn Greenwald, "XKeyscore: NSA tool collects 'nearly everything a user does on the internet,'" *Guardian*, July 31, 2013, http://www.theguardian.com/world/2013/jul/31/nsa-top-secret-program-online-data/print.

119) *What Is XKeyscore?* http://s3.documentcloud.org/documents/743252/nsa-pdfs-redacted-ed.pdf.

120) Glenn Greenwald, "XKeyscore: NSA tool collects 'nearly everything a user does on the internet,'" *Guardian*, July 31, 2013, http://www.theguardian.com/world/2013/jul/31/nsa-top-secret-program-online-data/print.

121) Richard Esguerra, "Google CEO Eric Schmidt Dismisses the Importance of Privacy," *Electronic Frontier Foundation*, December 10, 2009, https://www.eff.org/deeplinks/2009/12/google-ceo-eric-schmidt-dismisses-privacy.

122) Joe Nocera, "A World Without Privacy," *New York Times*, October 15, 2013, http://www.nytimes.com/2013/10/15/opinion/nocera-a-world-without-privacy.html.

123) *Democracy Now!* "You're Being Watched: Edward Snowden Emerges as Source Behind Explosive Revelations of NSA Spying," June 10, 2013, http://www.democracynow.org/2013/6/10/youre_being_watched_edward_snowden_emerges#.

124) Peter Baker, "After Leaks, Obama Leads Damage Control Effort," *New York Times*, June 28, 2013, http://www.nytimes.com/2013/06/29/us/politics/after-leaks-obama-leads-damage-control-effort.html.

125) Greg Henderson, "Obama To Leno: 'There Is No Spying On Americans,'" *NPR*, August 7, 2013, http://www.npr.org/blogs/thetwo-way/2013/08/06/209692380/obama-to-leno-there-is-no-spying-on-americans.

126) Laura Poitras, Marcel Rosenbach and Holger Stark, "Codename 'Apalachee': How America Spies on Europe and the UN," Der Spiegel, August 26, 2013, http://www.spiegel.de/international/world/secret-nsa-documents-show-how-the-us-spies-on-europe-and-the-un-a-918625.html.

127) Chris Strohm, "Lawmakers Probe Willful Abuses of Power by NSA Analysts," *Bloomberg*, August 24, 2013, http://www.bloomberg.com/news/print/2013-08-23/nsa-analysts-intentionally-abused-spying-powers-multiple-times.html.

128) Barton Gellman, "NSA broke privacy rules thousands of times per year, audit finds," *Washington Post*, August 15, 2013, http://articles.washingtonpost.com/2013-08-15/world/41431831_1_washington-post-national-security-agency-documents.

129) Chris Strohm, "Lawmakers Probe Willful Abuses of Power by NSA Analysts," *Bloomberg*, August 24, 2013, http://www.bloomberg.com/news/print/2013-08-23/nsa-analysts-intentionally-abused-spying-powers-multiple-times.html.

130) Kevin Poulsen, "12 True Tales of Creepy NSA Cyberstalking," *Wired*, September 26, 2013, http://www.wired.com/threatlevel/2013/09/nsa-stalking/.

131) Carol D. Leonnig, "Court: Ability to police U.S. spying program limited," *Washington Post*, August 15, 2013, http://www.washingtonpost.com/politics/court-ability-to-police-us-spying-program-limited/2013/08/15/4a8c8c44-05cd-11e3-a07f-49ddc7417125_story.html.

132) Siobhan Gorman and Jennifer Valentino-Devries, "New Details Show Broader NSA Surveillance Reach," *Wall Street Journal,* August 20, 2013.

133) Amy Goodman, "Owner of Snowden's Email Service on Why He Closed Lavabit Rather Than Comply With Gov't," *Democracy Now*, August 13, 2013, http://www.democracynow.org/2013/8/13/exclusive_owner_of_snowdens_email_service#.

341

134) John Young, "*Wall Street Journal* Secrecy," *Cryptome*, August 22, 2010, http://cryptome.org/0002/wsj-secrecy.htm.

135) Alan Grayson, "On Syria Vote, Trust, but Verify," *New York Times*, September 6, 2013, http://www.nytimes.com/2013/09/07/opinion/on-syria-vote-trust-but-verify.html?pagewanted=print.

136) "Clapper: Fallout over surveillance leaks is 'gut-wrenching,'" *MSNBC*, June 8, 2013, http://video.msnbc.msn.com/msnbc/52144169.

137) *Director of Security Service on MI5 and the Evolving Threat*, Royal United Services Institute, October 8, 2013, http://www.rusi.org/events/past/ref:E5254359BB8F44#.UlRy-RZsfld.

138) Bruce Schneier, "Before Prosecuting, Investigate the Government," *New York Times*, June 11, 2013, http://www.nytimes.com/roomfordebate/2013/06/11/in-nsa-leak-case-a-whistle-blower-or-a-criminal/before-prosecuting-snowden-investigate-the-government.

139) *Democracy Now!* "'On a Slippery Slope to a Totalitarian State': NSA Whistleblower Rejects Gov't Defense of Spying," June 10, 2013, http://www.democracynow.org/2013/6/10/on_a_slippery_slope_to_a#.

140) General Intelligence and Security Service, Ministry of the Interior and Kingdom Relations, *Jihadism on the Web A breeding ground for Jihad in the modern age*, https://www.aivd.nl/english/publications-press/@2873/jihadism-web/.

141) *FBI Intelligence Information Report*, "Use of Gaming Consoles to Conduct MS-13 Operations in Birmingham, United Kingdom, from Los Angeles, California, June 2010," September 13, 2010.

142) Michael Weissenstein, "Mexico's cartels build own national radio system," *Associated Press*, December 27, 2011.

143) *Democracy Now!* "'On a Slippery Slope to a Totalitarian State': NSA Whistleblower Rejects Gov't Defense of Spying," June 10, 2013, http://www.democracynow.org/2013/6/10/on_a_slippery_slope_to_a#.

144) Dominic Rushe, "Lavabit founder: 'My own tax dollars are being used to spy on me,'" *Guardian*, August 22, 2013, http://www.theguardian.com/world/2013/aug/22/lavabit-founder-us-surveillance-snowden/print.

145) Max Frankel, "Where Did Our 'Inalienable Rights' Go?," *New York Times*, June 22, 2013, http://www.nytimes.com/2013/06/23/opinion/sunday/where-did-our-inalienable-rights-go.html.

146) Seymour Hersh, "Huge CIA Operation Reported in US Against Antiwar Forces, Other Dissidents in Nixon Years," *New York Times*, December 22, 1974.

147) Ed Pilkington, "Declassified NSA files show agency spied on Muhammad Ali and MLK," *Guardian*, September 26, 2013, http://www.theguardian.com/world/2013/sep/26/nsa-surveillance-anti-vietnam-muhammad-ali-mlk/print.

148) James Ball, Julian Borger and Glenn Greenwald, "Revealed: how US and UK spy agencies defeat internet privacy and security," *Guardian*, September 5, 2013, http://www.theguardian.com/world/2013/sep/05/nsa-gchq-encryption-codes-security.

149) John Dvorak, "John C. Dvorak on NSA Spying: Are Americans Now the Enemy?" *aNewDomain*, September 6, 2013, http://anewdomain.net/2013/09/06/john-c-dvorak-nsa-spying-americans-now-enemy/.

150) David E. Sanger And Thom Shanker, "N.S.A. Director Firmly Defends Surveillance Efforts," *New York Times*, October 13, 2013, http://www.nytimes.com/2013/10/13/us/nsa-director-gives-firm-and-broad-defense-of-surveillance-efforts.html.

151) Trevor Aaronson, "The Informants," *Mother Jones*, September/October 2011, http://www.motherjones.com/politics/2011/08/fbi-terrorist-informants.

152) Congressional Record – House, H5002, July 24, 2013, http://s3.documentcloud.org/documents/803163/rogers-nsa-speech.pdf.

153) Keith Alexander, *Statement to the NSA/CSS workforce*, Jun 25, 2013, http://www.nsa.gov/public_info/speeches_testimonies/25jun13_dir.shtml.

154) "NSA Confirms Dragnet Phone Records Collection, But Admits It Was Key in Stopping Just 1 Terror Plot," *Democracy Now!*, August 1, 2013, http://www.democracynow.org/2013/8/1/nsa_confirms_dragnet_phone_records_collection#.

155) Shaun waterman, "NSA chief's admission of misleading numbers adds to Obama administration blunders," *Washington Times*, October 2, 2013, http://www.washingtontimes.com/news/2013/oct/2/nsa-chief-figures-foiled-terror-plots-misleading/.

156) *54 Attacks in 20 Countries Thwarted By NSA Collection*, Permanent Select Committee on Intelligence, Democratic Office, July 23, 2013, http://democrats.intelligence.house.gov/press-release/54-attacks-20-countries-thwarted-nsa-collection.

157) Justin Elliott and Theodoric Meyer, "Claim on "Attacks Thwarted" by NSA Spreads Despite Lack of Evidence," *ProPublica*, October 23, 2013, http://www.propublica.org/article/claim-on-attacks-thwarted-by-nsa-spreads-despite-lack-of-evidence.

158) Craig Horowitz, "The NYPD's War On Terror," *New York Magazine*, http://nymag.com/nymetro/news/features/n_8286/index1.html#print.

159) "From Mosques to Soccer Leagues: Inside the NYPD's Secret Spy Unit Targeting Muslims, Activists," *Democracy Now!* September 17, 2013, http://www.democracynow.org/2013/9/17/from_mosques_to_soccer_leagues_inside#.

160) James Risen, "Snowden Says He Took No Secret Files to Russia," *New York Times*, October 17, 2013, http://www.nytimes.com/2013/10/18/world/snowden-says-he-took-no-secret-files-to-russia.html.

161) James Carroll, "The data mine, as computing power grows, so does the threat to personal autonomy," *Boston Globe*, September 2, 2013.

162) Ken White, "Rep. Mike Rogers Angrily Defends Bathroom Spycam," *TechDirt*, October 30, 2013, http://www.techdirt.com/articles/20131030/11223225071/rep-mike-rogers-angrily-defends-bathroom-spycam.shtml.

163) John Markoff, "At Internet Conference, Signs of Agreement Appear Between U.S. and Russia," *New York Times*, April 15, 2010, http://www.nytimes.com/2010/04/16/science/16cyber.html.

164) Public Accountability Initiative, *Conflicts of Interest in the Syria Debate*, October 11, 2013, http://public-accountability.org/2013/10/conflicts-of-interest-in-the-syria-debate/.

165) Daniel E. Geer, "Cybersecurity and National Policy," Harvard Law School National Security Journal, Volume 1 – April 7, 2010, http://harvardnsj.org/2011/01/cybersecurity-and-national-policy/.

166) Steve Henn, "In-Q-Tel: The CIA's Tax-Funded Player In Silicon Valley," *NPR*, July 16, 2012, http://www.npr.org/blogs/alltechconsidered/2012/07/16/156839153/in-q-tel-the-cias-tax-funded-player-in-silicon-valley.

167) Vivian Yeo, "Microsoft OneCare was 'good enough'," *ZDNet*, October 16, 2009, http://www.zdnetasia.com/microsoft-onecare-was-good-enough-62058697.htm.

168) Noah Schachtman, "Russia's Top Cyber Sleuth Foils US Spies, Helps Kremlin Pals," *Wired*, July 23, 2013, http://www.wired.com/dangerroom/2012/07/ff_kaspersky/all/.

169) Donald Kerr, "Remarks and Q&A by the Principal Deputy Director of National Intelligence," 2007 GEOINT Symposium, October 23, 2007, http://www.dni.gov/speeches/20071023_speech.pdf.

170) Ellen Nakashima and Joby Warrick, "For NSA chief, terrorist threat drives passion to 'collect it all,' observers say," *Washington Post*, July 14, 2013, http://www.washingtonpost.com/world/national-security/for-nsa-chief-terrorist-threat-drives-passion-to-collect-it-all/2013/07/14/3d26ef80-ea49-11e2-a301-ea5a8116d211_print.html.

171) Brendan Sasso, "NSA chief pleads for public's help amid push for spying restrictions," *The Hill*, September 25, 2013, http://thehill.com/blogs/hillicon-valley/technology/324499-nsa-chief-pleads-for-publics-help-as-congress-eyes-restrictions#ixzz2g5cAVyzd.

172) Thomas Friedman, "Blowing a Whistle," *New York Times*, June 11, 2013, http://www.nytimes.com/2013/06/12/opinion/friedman-blowing-a-whistle.html.

173) Malte Spitz, "Germans Loved Obama. Now We Don't Trust Him.," *New York Times*, June 30, 2013, http://www.nytimes.com/2013/06/30/opinion/sunday/germans-loved-obama-now-we-dont-trust-him.html?ref=todayspaper.

174) Bruce Schneier, "Protecting Privacy and Liberty," *Nature*, October 25, 2001, http://www.schneier.com/essay-390.html.

Part IV – The Road to Cyber-Security

Chapter 11
The Origins of Cyber-Insecurity

Chapter 12
Cyber-Security for the 99%

Epilogue

The Origins of Cyber-Insecurity

Done is better than perfect.
Move fast and break things.
Carelessness causes security incidents.

– Three different signs posted at Facebook's headquarters[1]

Software flaws account for a majority of the compromises organizations around the world experience

– Shon Harris[2]

As shown earlier in the book, the verdict of *cyberwar* is a misdiagnosis. It implies a military problem, one which consequently lends itself to military solutions. But where does this leave people outside the United States? Cyber-attacks are a global phenomenon. Cyber-security is a universal need. Ivan Arce, the CTO of Core Security Technologies, offers a view from outside:

> The vast majority of the world's population (and proportionally its Internet users) seems to be totally uninterested in giving anything more than passing attention to cyber-security if it is perceived as equal parts U.S. cyber war doctrine and U.S. domestic political debate.[3]

By eschewing the language of war and framing events in terms of cyber-security it's possible to consider more universal solutions, ones that will safeguard us against both the genuine day-to-day threats and hypothetical black-swan events.

A Layered Perspective

To tackle the issue of cyber-security, let's survey the factors that allow an attack to succeed. The hope is that, by doing so, ultimately we'll be able to identify solutions which will make attacks more complicated and expensive.

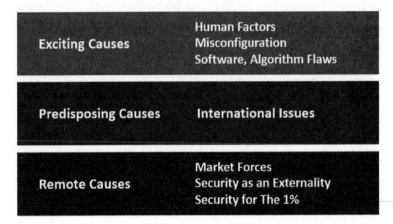

Figure 11-1

When a computer is breached, there's a tendency to seek out simple explanations based on a single source with a direct chain of causality ("for want of a nail, the kingdom was lost," and so on). Despite the aesthetic appeal of such explanations, they're at best an approximation of reality. A more nuanced approach is needed to get a clearer picture of what's happening.

Security incidents usually involve multiple factors that work together in concert on several levels (see Figure 11-1). There are *exciting causes* which lead directly to compromise. There are *predisposing causes* that work to reinforce the exciting causes. Finally there are *remote causes* that have a less immediate connection to what happened, but nevertheless play a role. In this chapter we'll look at factors that exist at all three of these levels and offer potential paths towards remediation.

Exciting Causes

Exciting causes are usually pretty obvious, so obvious in fact that many people often incorrectly perceive them as singular root causes. These factors include careless users, software that's not configured properly, and flawed software (accidentally so or otherwise).

Human Factors

Looking back through Part II of the book, it's clear that users tend to do things they shouldn't, much to the benefit of thieves and spies. This includes visiting web pages that execute a drive-by download, plugging in an infected thumb drive, or opening a booby-trapped attachment in an e-mail. By hook or by crook, malware gains a foothold with the assistance of the user. As you'll recall from the chapter on cybercrime, there's an entire industry of PPI services whose sole goal is to trick users into infecting their computers. Also, looking back through the chapter on espionage, spear-phishing was the attack vector of choice in practically all of the instances that we surveyed.

Then there's the perennial menace of poorly chosen passwords. For example, in the summer of 2012 hackers publicly released a list of almost half a million login credentials for Yahoo!. Of these passwords, over two thousand consisted of a sequential series of numbers (e.g. "123456") and over 700 of these passwords simply used the word "password."[4]

Bad password security also came back to haunt a television station in Montana, KRTV, when mischief makers hijacked the Emergency Alert System (EAS) to broadcast a zombie-attack alert:

> Civil authorities in your area have reported that the bodies of the dead are rising from the grave and attacking the living.

It's believed that the station failed to change the EAS default password that was configured by the factory when the device was shipped. In the wake of the bogus alert, regulators ordered broadcasters to change the passwords on all EAS equipment.[5]

Then there are some users who don't even bother with passwords to begin with. A report published by the Inspector General of the Department of Defense found that 15 out of 48 mobile devices examined at West Point during a spot check didn't even have passwords set up.[6]

Granted there have been efforts to educate users on behalf of government agencies, like the NSA[7] or US-CERT,[8] and public-private sector partnerships, like the National Cyber Security Alliance.[9] These efforts usually consist of publishing a basic guide with a series of tips for users on how to stay safe online.

Misconfiguration

Sometimes problems arise because an organization fails to institute security measures that it knowingly could have. For example, in the aftermath of Operation Aurora, investigators discovered that Google stored its source code, its crown jewels, in an unprotected SCM system. Then there's the TJX Hack, where a retail store relied on a wireless encryption scheme that was known to be insecure. Let's also not forget the Spamhaus DDoS, which was facilitated by a bunch of Internet service providers who failed to implement the recommendations spelled out in Best Current Practice #38.

In March of 2013, researchers posted an announcement on Seclists.org claiming to have commandeered more than 420,000 embedded devices using nothing more than empty or default credentials. Which is to say that people didn't even bother to configure the devices with a password. The researchers stated:

> While everybody is talking about high class exploits and cyberwar, four simple stupid default telnet passwords can give you access to hundreds of thousands of consumer as well as tens of thousands of industrial devices all over the world.[10]

Poorly configured systems are a truly widespread problem. To get a feel for just how pervasive they are, consider a statement made by the director of information security issues at the U.S. Government Accountability Office (GAO) in April of 2012:

> In their performance and accountability reports and annual financial reports for fiscal year 2011, 18 of 24 major federal agencies have reported inadequate information security controls for financial reporting for fiscal year 2011.[11]

One of these "major federal agencies" is the IRS, the steward of vast silos of sensitive financial information. Even an organization like this, with an acute need to maintain security, can get sloppy. Specifically, the GAO reports:

> The agency [the IRS] had not always (1) implemented effective controls for identifying and authenticating users, such as enforcing password complexity on certain servers; (2) appro-

priately restricted access to its mainframe environment; (3) effectively monitored the mainframe environment; or (4) ensured that current patches had been installed on systems to protect against known vulnerabilities.[12]

Often there are political forces at work which compel an organization to adopt a less than optimal security profile. In a university environment, for instance, faculty members have been known to scream "academic freedom" the minute that someone suggests locking down machine settings. Security may also be sacrificed for ideological reasons at an Internet startup company where upper management dictates that everything should be in the cloud.

With regard to promoting appropriate configurations, vendors like Microsoft have made some headway by introducing products, like its web server, which are *closer* to being secure by default. Microsoft has also worked towards establishing baseline configurations and best practices with tools like its Security Compliance Manager.

Buggy Software

Sure, users inadvertently compromise their machines all the time. Sure, people don't always configure their software correctly or patch their computers regularly. But the idea of having individual users shoulder all the blame is unfair; you're just *blaming the victim*.

Even careful users can have their computers breached. This includes systems run by the Department of Defense. Internet folklore has it that if you stick to "safe" web sites then you really don't have to worry about drive-by downloads. In other words, if you've been hacked, it's probably because you've been visiting porn sites or downloading pirated movies. The unpleasant reality is that it's not uncommon for reputable sites, like those belonging to the U.S. Department of the Treasury, to serve up malicious web pages.[13]

Part of the problem is that high-traffic commercial portals often rely on ad networks like MSN and Google subsidiary DoubleClick to serve up web-based advertisements, and these providers can be tricked into placing malicious ad content.[14] Over the six-month period ending in December of 2008, Websense Security Labs conducted a study which concluded:

Seventy percent of the top 100 sites either hosted malicious content or contained a masked redirect to lure unsuspecting victims from legitimate sites to malicious sites.[15]

Highlighting the threat of online advertisements, a similar study conducted by Cisco concluded:

> The notion that malware infections most commonly result from "risky" sites such as counterfeit software is a misconception. Cisco's analysis indicates that the vast majority of web malware encounters actually occur via legitimate browsing of mainstream websites. In other words, the majority of encounters happen in the places that online users visit the most – and think are safe.[16]

It comes down to this: you can educate and train users to the point that they're obsessive-compulsive. You can meticulously impose draconian security settings (e.g. be completely "control compliant") and monitor for the slightest deviation.[17] But *a well-crafted exploit, based on some obscure flaw that the software vendor didn't catch, will sink your battleship every time.*

Renowned bug-hunter Charlie Miller references Stuxnet to underscore this reality:

> You have all of your security software, isolated networks, everything in place, and someone rolls in with 0days and takes you over…. If they can get on an Iranian nuclear site that's not connected and is fully patched, then no one is safe.[18]

At the end of the day, even the most paranoid users huddled in fortified bunkers are at the mercy of bugs, flaws, and weaknesses that they can't really do anything about. End of story. The previous chapters on cybercrime and espionage provide numerous examples of this.

For many system administrators, it's gotten to the point where public-facing servers are like children: they require constant attention, you never stop worrying about them, and the minute you look away they try to do something they are not supposed to. As the head of the NSA's Information Assurance Directorate stated:

> There's no such thing as "secure" anymore.[19]

So what can the security industry do? Security researcher Bruce Schneier points out that it would be wiser to focus on developing software that prevents security problems to begin with:

> We should be designing systems that won't let users choose lousy passwords and don't care what links a user clicks on.[20]

The Software Depression

In the nascent years of the software industry there was talk of a *software crisis*.[21] This concept was based on the observation that the design and implementation weren't on equal footing with established engineering disciplines. The problems that researchers identified are largely still with us today, such that the crisis (which implies a brief duration) could probably be viewed as an enduring depression.

Part of the problem is the attitude that software engineers have towards failure. When a building collapses due to a flawed design it's treated as a *major catastrophe* by all parties involved (the architects, the engineers, the contractors, the owners, etc.). Furthermore, it's unusual for a large-scale structure to be constructed on a design that's based on substandard engineering. Not only will the architects and engineers recast the initial blueprints, they will also question the integrity of other buildings that use a similarly flawed design.

Critical Bugs Are Pedestrian

In contrast to their engineering brethren in more traditional areas, software engineers have a comparatively blasé attitude about failure. Critical flaws, the type of bugs that can be used by attackers to breach the security of a computer, aren't viewed as catastrophic. From the vantage point of the average software developer, critical bugs happen all the time. They simply shrug their shoulders and move on.

Can you blame them? No, this mindset is encouraged from above. As the quotes at the start of this chapter indicate, management seems to think that "Done is better than perfect," and engineers should "Move fast and break things." In a sad fit of cognitive dissonance, these same executives have forgotten that "carelessness causes security incidents."

Bugs are so plentiful nowadays that there are literally automated tools for finding exploitable flaws in software. One proof-of-concept tool designed by researchers, aptly named MAYHEM, not only identifies bugs but also spits out a working exploit.[22] Furthermore, there has been research towards automating the attacks which leverage these software bugs so that the whole process of penetrating a network[23] and wielding exploits to establish a foothold[24] can be executed en masse by a small group of intruders.

Take for example Adobe Reader, a preferred attack vector for black hats who create poisoned PDF documents. In the summer of 2008 Adobe released version 9 of the reader. Since that time Adobe has published well over 30 critical security advisories which describe flaws that could "cause the application to crash and could potentially allow an attacker to take control of the affected system."[25]

The deluge of terminal bugs got so bad that the chief research office at F-Secure, Mikko Hyppönen, advised users to switch to an alternative reader to view PDF documents and commented:

Adobe Reader is the new Internet Explorer.[26]

Hyppönen is, no doubt, referring to Internet Explorer 6, which sported dozens of zero-day exploits over the course of its lifespan.[27]

You'd think that Adobe would learn its lesson after being publicly reprimanded like this. The release of Adobe Reader version X has been followed by a steady stream of similar critical security advisories. In fact, in December of 2011 a zero-day exploit for Reader version X was announced in the press, and reporters indicated that it was being used to breach networks belonging to defense contractors.[28]

The same holds true for Microsoft. While Internet Explorer 6 was a complete disaster from a security standpoint, serious flaws have continued to surface in later incarnations (i.e. versions 9 and 10). Since version 9's release in the spring of 2011, there have been dozens of remote code execution vulnerabilities identified.[29] Three generations after version 6, and drive-by downloads are still an active threat.[30] In fact, while this book's manuscript was being prepared in September of 2013, Microsoft announced an unpatched vulnerability that impacted all supported versions of Internet Explorer.[31]

Keep in mind that a web browser holds a special role as a central channel for information in an increasingly networked world.

It's not just Microsoft's browser either. The company's flagship operating system, Windows 8, is also a ripe target which has been revealing a constant stream of critical bugs. Within days after Microsoft released Windows 8 in late October of 2012, the CEO of VUPEN, Chaouki Bekrar, announced via Twitter that his engineers had already developed the first operational zero-day exploit:

> We welcome #Windows8 with various 0Ds combined to pwn all new Win8/IE10 exploit mitigations ... [32]

Adobe and Microsoft aren't alone. Oracle's Java platform has gained an industry-wide reputation for enabling attacks, as veritable wave after wave of critical flaws have been exposed. In January of 2013 the Java platform's state of insecurity became so severe that the Department of Homeland Security recommended that users disable it.[33] In the wake of this announcement, name brand companies like Apple[34] and Twitter[35] either told users to disable Java or went so far as to disable it automatically. While Oracle rushed to bolster Java's security with an emergency software patch outside of its normal patch release cycle, dozens of new bugs quickly emerged to fill the void.[36] This state of affairs prompted H.D. Moore, the original developer of the Metasploit penetration testing tool, to warn:

> The safest thing to do at this point is just assume that Java is always going to be vulnerable.[37]

Though raw shame goes a long way towards getting holes fixed, it's not unheard of for a bug to go unpatched and ignored for long periods of time, simply because bugs are not viewed as threats by the people who make decisions about bug severity. Or perhaps an intelligence agency has made a special request. Either way, it's also not unheard of for these same bugs to end up being exploited later on by clever attackers.[38]

Even worse, certain software vendors can be reticent about disclosing security problems and have been known to retaliate against researchers who discover them. For example, in the summer of 2011, a researcher named Dillon Beresford was gearing up to give a presentation at a security conference in Texas called TakeDown-

Con. The focus of his talk was to be a series of zero-day exploits he found in PLCs used by Siemens SCADA systems. Both the DHS and Siemens pressured him into canceling his conference appearance.[39]

A few months later, in the fall of 2011, security researcher Charlie Miller unearthed a flaw in Apple's iOS operating system that could be used to download and execute malicious code. As a proof of concept, Miller created a fake stock ticker application that leveraged this flaw and submitted it for distribution at the Apple App Store, which validated the application as legitimate. After Miller disclosed the flaw, Apple revoked his application developer license and suspended him from Apple's developer program.[40]

Machiavelli once examined the power of perception:

> Everyone sees what you appear to be, few really know what you are, and those few dare not oppose themselves to the opinion of the many ... [41]

By silencing the messenger, with legal threats software and retaliation, vendors can maintain the appearance of security and avoid spending money on proactive audits, which is good enough as far as some executives are concerned. The industry as a whole seems to prefer a state of denial, which conveniently pretends that software is secure, and markets it as such ... until some pesky researcher opens his mouth and generates a load of bad press. As you might expect, the underlying reasons are often (but not always) financial.

The Presumption of Security

In criminal trials here in the United States the burden of proof is on the prosecution. In other words, you're innocent until proven guilty. Likewise, our current attitude towards software security infers that users believe software to be secure until proven otherwise. Hence, there's the presumption of security.

The result of this mindset is what's known as the *patch-and-pray treadmill*. Software is viewed as relatively secure until someone publicizes a zero-day exploit and pressures the vendor into admitting there's a flaw and releasing a patch. At this point the software is again presumed to be secure, or *at least you pray that it is*. It's the only alternative, really, because there's no scientific method for conclusively determining if the patched software is any more secure.

Software flaws tend to be like roaches. When you find one you can bet that there are a few dozen that you didn't see. As we have shown, zero-day exploits continue to plague ostensibly mature products. This hints at unsettling systemic problems.

One possible response would be for people to throw up their arms and declare that it's hopeless. To accept that critical software bugs are a fact of life and that society will just have to learn to live with shoddy products. Software vendors like this apology because it absolves them of responsibility. Security software vendors like it because it keeps them in business.

"We can't help it," they shrug, "critical bugs are inevitable, get used to it!"

But to surrender to this perspective is to choose the easy way out and completely negate the likelihood that software engineering, like other fields of engineering, will mature as a discipline. Society does not have to accept low-quality software as the status quo. Software engineering can evolve and advance.

Tools exist that software engineers can use to create secure code.[42] Gary McGraw, a well-known authority on software security, believes that focusing on the tools used to build software may be an attractive starting point.[43] In other words, if you can limit the ability of a tool to create insecure code then you've made solid headway:

> C was a disaster, C++ was a disaster, Java was getting better, .NET was getting even better. You know, we've been moving slowly towards languages that at least have different sorts of vulnerabilities built into them, and make the job of software security easier. So I'd like to see a whole new class of languages that are designed with security right up front. And maybe we can get that accomplished in ten years.

Another way out of the patch treadmill is a formally devised proactive system that recognizes the need to build in security from the ground up. One such solution discussed by Brian Snow, a former technical director at the NSA, is the idea of *assurance*.[44]

From the vantage point of the assurance school of thought, *software is presumed suspect until it is shown to be otherwise.* In other words, a vendor must make users (or an accreditor) sufficiently confident that its product is secure.

How does this happen? According to Snow:

> We analyze the system at design time for potential problems that we then correct. We test prototype devices to see how well they perform under stress or when used in ways beyond the normal specification. Security acceptance testing not only exercises the product for its expected behavior given the expected environment and input sequences, but also tests the product with swings in the environment outside the specified bounds and with improper inputs that do not match the interface specification. We also test with proper inputs, but in an improper sequence. We anticipate malicious behavior and design to counter it, and then test the countermeasures for effectiveness. We expect the product to behave safely, even if not properly, under any of these stresses. If it does not, we redesign it.[45]

Note the emphasis on the design phase. This is not something that gets tacked on at the end of the development cycle to appease marketing executives. Assurance work has to be a part of the development process from the very beginning.

Some of the big vendors have made progress in this direction, or at least the perception of progress. For example, Microsoft has an assurance process it calls the "Security Development Lifecycle" (SDL).[46] Oracle, too, has established an assurance program.[47] To get a broader industry-wide view of where things are headed, you can glance over the Building Security In Maturity Model (BSIMM). BSIMM is a framework for quantifying security practices based on a study of eighty-one software security initiatives executed by forty-two companies (including Adobe, EMC, Google, Intel, Microsoft, and SAP).[48]

Business-types like metrics. They believe that unless you can measure a process you're flying in the dark. Hence the utility of the BSIMM, in theory, is that it establishes universal metrics for the assurance initiatives. Not only that, but it goes beyond mere process to include social and organizational factors. For our purposes the

BSIMM is noteworthy because the mere presence of such a study indicates that the big names in the software industry are starting to realize that security is a vital issue, even if merely on a cosmetic level.

Assurance Is Lacking

Then again, some people may consider it disingenuous for a company to declare its code "trustworthy," and even more dubious to believe that a sexy-sounding development process, whose efficacy has not been scientifically confirmed, can guarantee that code will actually be trustworthy, especially if the NSA has been involved. Certification appears to have taken a back seat to marketing. This is the case because software vendors aren't penalized when they're wrong.

And they still miss the mark, a lot.

Though the term "assurance" has been fashionable for many years and alleged initiatives have sprung up over hi-tech's landscape, critical software bugs persist. In fact, one anonymous corporate hacker who stockpiles zero-day bugs claims:

> In the last few years, every publicly known and patched bug makes almost no impact on us. They aren't scratching the surface.[49]

Take a standard server operating system like Windows Server 2008 R2. Microsoft originally launched its Trustworthy Computing Initiative back in 2001. The company launched the Server 2008 R2 product in the summer of 2009, nearly a decade later (so you'd think they had plenty of time to get things right). Service Pack 1 for this OS, a gigabyte-sized behemoth, was released on the ides of March in 2011. In the months that followed the publication of Service Pack 1, Microsoft issued more than a dozen patches for flaws that could allow remote code execution (an average of more than one per month). Keep in mind that this is *after* Service Pack 1 had plugged two years of existing bugs. So while evangelists may laud the success of their assurance initiatives, the battle is far from over.

This highlights less obvious historical forces. In the years before Microsoft released its first version of DOS, the domain of corporate I.T. was ruled by mainframe vendors like Control Data and IBM. These big iron systems were built from the ground up to be stable and available. It was viewed as a priority by the engineers because customers, who paid large sums of cash to purchase the mainframes, demanded it.[50] Vendors would literally monitor the machines they sold to ensure that they caught problems early so that the machines didn't go down.

Microsoft's early operating systems targeted the low-end of the market. The fundamental strategy was to gain market share by providing cheap software that was "good enough." Even something as basic as application memory protection was nonexistent. If an early Windows machine crashed, the user would shrug their shoulders and reboot.

Contrast this to the high-end arena, where a vendor could expect a prompt phone call from angry executives if their multi-million dollar installation went down. Only in the past ten years, or so, has Microsoft started making inroads into the high-end of the enterprise. Their flagship server products continue to be haunted by the "good enough" mentality which allowed Microsoft to dominate the low-end of corporate computing.

The current situation has gotten to the point where foreign countries have made nontrivial progress towards developing their own national operating systems. China,[51] India,[52] and Russia[53] have all announced plans to develop their own system level software to reduce their dependence on Windows.

Even Germany, presumably an ally of the U.S., has shown qualms about deploying Windows 8 on computers with the latest Trusted Platform Module (TPM) chip. TPM chips store cryptographic keys. These keys are used to verify the integrity of the operating system. According to the Germany's Federal Office for Information Security:

> The use of Windows 8 combined with TPM 2.0 is accompanied by a loss of control over the operating system and the hardware used. As a result, new risks arise for the user, especially for the federal government and for those providing critical infrastructure.[54]

Hence while officials persistently warn of hardware that's been tampered with by foreign intelligence agencies, it appears that other countries are just as concerned about the United States adding some special sauce into the technology that we export to them. As we discussed back in Chapter Six, these suspicions are completely justified. Our intelligence services have long-standing programs with U.S. companies that allow them to embed trap doors in hardware and software.

Inadequate Endpoint Security

As if it wasn't bad enough that software quality falters so badly, the tools that most people rely on to catch malware are also lacking. It's common knowledge that malware authors, as a matter of standard operating procedure, test their creations against a battery of different anti-virus products to ensure that they can evade detection.[55] Recall earlier in the book how F-Secure's chief research officer, Mikko Hypponen, openly admitted that the anti-virus industry was out of its league in its own game.[56]

His sentiments have been echoed by the likes of the NSA's Brian Snow:

> None of the solutions on offer from the AV [anti-virus] industry give us any hope against a determined targeted attack. While the AV companies all gave talks around the world dissecting the recent publicly discovered attacks like Stuxnet or Flame, most glossed over the simple fact that none of them discovered the virus till after it had done its work.[57]

Microsoft's Security Essentials anti-virus technology performs so poorly in tests that the company has adopted what it refers to as a *baseline strategy*. That is, Microsoft suggests that users should only rely on Security Essentials as a backstop and install a dedicated anti-virus package from another vendor for additional protection.[58]

We applaud this sort of honesty, because admitting to a problem is the first step to identifying solutions. Other security vendors have been less forthcoming, but the proof is hard to deny.

In early 2013 there was a flurry of stories about media outlets like the *Wall Street Journal*,[59] the *Washington Post*,[60] and the *New York Times*,[61] being targeted by long-term cyber campaigns. A spokesman for the *New York Times*, in particular, stated that anti-virus software from Symantec was deployed on all of the machines in the company's network, and yet it failed to detect the malware used by the intruders.[62] Symantec released an official statement in response, explicitly claiming that *"anti-virus software alone is not enough."*[63]

To add insult to injury, enterprise security software sold by companies like Symantec and McAfee itself has been known to sport critical bugs which can be leveraged by attackers.[64] Can you imagine entrusting the well-being of a server farm to an expensive security solution only to have intruders turn around and use it to compromise the entire network of machines? It's like a police department led by a corrupt chief.

Predisposing Causes

Another factor that allows cyber-attacks to flourish is their international nature. If operators can find a permissive setting where the law enforcement is willing to turn a blind eye, they can literally operate out in the open. The Koobface gang in St. Petersburg, Russia, is a definitive example. An article in the *New York Times* reported that data found on a command-and-control server run by the gang indicated that they'd made at least $2 million a year for the prior three and a half years.[65] The FBI declines to comments and the Koobface enterprise continues to make money.

Here's another example. In the book *Fatal System Error* the author, journalist Joseph Menn, recounts a story where a detective from the United Kingdom, Andrew Crocker, traveled to the Russian city of Astrakhan in pursuit of a hacker who went by the handle of "Zet." Per standard protocol, Crocker notified the local police chief of Astrakhan, Alexander Petrov, in advance of his arrival, and Petrov was nice enough to take him out to dinner when he arrived. During the course of the greet-and-eat, Petrov insisted that he and Crocker grab some guns and go boar hunting. Petrov, it turns out, was the father of the hacker named Zet.

Remote Causes

While flawed software is arguably the most severe threat that we have discussed, there are aspects of the software industry that encourage this to be the case. The broad proliferation of bugs is actually a function of the market in which software vendors operate. The current state of affairs didn't spontaneously appear. Society's cyber-insecurity is the logical, if not predictable, consequence of economic forces at work.

Market Forces

Enterprise software vendors like Microsoft are corporations. Like any publicly traded corporation, they need to cater to the mandates of Wall Street and turn a profit. Traditionally, Microsoft has targeted the low-end of the computing spectrum, where it has been incredibly successful. Recently Microsoft has been making headway in the mid-range segment with its server software product line. In these zones of the market, users demand two things: cheap software and new features. To survive as a profitable company, Microsoft has had to meet these demands.

There's an old story that Tim Jackson describes in his book *Inside Intel*. It's about a team of software engineers at Intel who identified a snippet of code in Microsoft Excel that, when slightly modified, increased the execution speed 8-fold. They called up the engineers at Microsoft to let them know what they had found so that they could include the improvement. The engineers at Microsoft brushed them off, claiming:

> People buy our applications because of new features.[66]

From a business perspective, this makes sense. Tracking down bugs and conducting the security audits necessary to unearth them is a resource-intensive process. It's so complicated and grueling that guys like Charlie Miller can make their living finding bugs. Why would a profit-driven company devote time and money to securing an existing product, much less supporting an outdated legacy product, when it could just add a bunch of new features and sell it to users as the next edition? Most users have no idea what a zero-day exploit is, anyway, much less how to evaluate the security of a software package.

Thus, unknown critical security flaws can be conveniently overlooked, and the corresponding product miraculously deemed "se-

cure," until an independent researcher comes forward with an unpleasant discovery. This approach effectively outsources the task of
security auditing to a third-party (one who often works at a steep
discount) and turns the user-base into a bunch of glorified beta tes-
ters. But, then again, why spend resources up front finding bugs,
bugs that otherwise might never surface, when it's relatively cheaper to put the marketing folks into damage control mode and issue a
patch? This is the calculus that software companies abide by.

Richard Clarke confides:

> Microsoft insiders have admitted to me that the company re-
> ally did not take security seriously, even when they were being
> embarrassed by frequent highly publicized hacks. Why should
> they? There was no real alternative to its software and they
> were swimming in money from their profits.[67]

Clarke's comments deserve some qualification. Obviously, Microsoft has major competitors in the consumer device market, and
the company does appear to have invested in its Security Development Lifecycle (SDL) assurance program. Conversely, the company continues to churn out new products on a regular basis and
critical security flaws likewise continue to sprout up every month,
lending credence to the notion that aforementioned market forces
continue to prevail.

Negative Externalities

In economics, a *negative externality* is a consequence of production
that damages society as a whole without impacting the bottom line
of the producer. Pollution from manufacturing plants is a common
negative externality in places like China where environmental
regulation is weak. In the software industry, as things stand now,
the costs of cleaning up after security incidents that result from
software bugs are a negative externality.

Companies like Microsoft knowingly release software that's loaded with critical flaws. Instead of making the investment to find them
all, it shifts most of the cost to the customer. Why does it do this?

Well, because it can.

Vendors aren't in business to do the right thing; *they're in business to make money.* To add insult to injury, the resources that both individual users and victimized organizations themselves spend to clean up after incidents don't necessarily make any progress towards fundamentally improving software security.

A Word on Bug Bounties

As an afterthought, software companies have been known to offer rewards for security researchers who identify bugs in their products. This practice generates good press, and helps to create the perception that security is a genuine priority. As such, it can be viewed by more skeptical eyes as a *marketing gimmick.*

For example, Google periodically shells out a wad of cash,[68] sometimes as much as $60,000,[69] to anyone to can find a new way to compromise the company's Chrome browser. Microsoft has also announced that it's willing to pay up to $100,000 for researchers who identify critical bugs in its products.[70]

Bug bounties essentially outsource quality control to independent third parties working at a steep discount. Unfortunately, as we saw earlier in the book, there's a thriving industry devoted to selling zero-day exploits. The very existence of this shadowy global market, which caters to the highest bidder, underscores the reality that *peddling malware is much more profitable than collecting a token reward and a public pat on the head.* It's pretty clear that demand in the black market has outstripped the modest corporate reward system.

According to Christopher Soghoian, a senior policy analyst at the American Civil Liberties Union:

> The bounties pale in comparison to what the government pays.[71]

There are those who suggest that the government step in and leverage its purchasing power to corner the market and hoover up all of the available zero-day exploits.[72] There are several problems with this train of thought.

First, even in this scenario critical software bugs remain a negative externality as far as the software vendors are concerned. The cost of security incidents merely gets shifted from the victims to the taxpayer, failing to provide vendors with an incentive to build better software.

In addition, not every zero-day exploit bought by the government would be used defensively to patch holes in software. Some of the purchased zero-day exploits would be used in offensive operations by U.S. intelligence services. Do you suppose other nations would feel safe if the United States possessed a near monopoly with regard to zero-days? More likely than not, a campaign to hoard zero-day exploits on behalf of the U.S. would merely drive up prices, as arms dealers played one government against another.

Security for The 1%

While accidental bugs are a reality, so are also intentional bugs. Though much of this chapter appears to place the blame for bad security on sloppy engineering, this picture is incomplete. As described earlier in the book, our government plays a role in subverting cyber-security, much to the financial glee of the defense sector.

Back in Chapter Six, we introduced the malware industrial complex; an entire industry devoted to subversion. These companies thrive because of buggy software, flaws and weaknesses that sometimes arise inadvertently and other times are intentionally planted on behalf of intelligence agencies. The products this malware industry sells are used by governments and independent actors to execute clandestine operations.

The growing demand for weaponized exploits provides financial motivations which ensure that software bugs remain secret. This market makes it much more profitable to package and sell flaws as exploits rather than publicize them. Secrecy of this kind makes it less likely that vendors will take corrective action and release patches. Because the flaws aren't addressed, society as a whole is put in a more vulnerable position. All of this occurs on behalf of organizations that want to perform cyber-attacks.

Some government agencies have tried to distance themselves from the seedier elements of the digital arms trade by developing exploits in-house. The problem with this is that the unearthed exploits still remain a secret. Vendors will remain oblivious to the discovered flaw or perhaps be induced by government officials to ignore it on behalf of national security. Either way, the corresponding bugs go unfixed and the bulk of society goes unprotected.

But things get even more twisted. Black market sellers can, in fact, cash out twice by turning around and selling custom detection tools at a hefty premium.[73] Thus, not only do they sell malware, but they sell the tools that detect it. It's like a rogue bioengineer selling a custom bioweapon and the vaccine to cure it, all to the highest bidder.

While politicians and generals often make frenzied accusations about China inserting back doors into hardware and software, this serves only to distract us from U.S. treachery. According to anonymous sources within the government, *thousands of hi-tech companies voluntarily provide sensitive information to U.S. security services* so that they can infiltrate computers belonging to anyone viewed as an "enemy." The list of collaborators, known as "trusted partners," includes big names like Microsoft:

> Microsoft Corp. (MSFT), the world's largest software company, provides intelligence agencies with information about bugs in its popular software before it publicly releases a fix, according to two people familiar with the process. That information can be used to protect government computers and to access the computers of terrorists or military foes.[74]

This puts the behavior of our intelligence officials in a whole new light, because while they're clamoring about cyber-Armageddon on one hand, they're simultaneously neck deep in the black market for weaponized malware, collaborating with vendors to insert back doors, and doing everything they can to sabotage mainstream encryption technology.

Overt admonishments for better security are being contradicted by covert programs that undercut security. The malware-industrial complex is making technology easier to compromise in the midst of an epidemic of cyber-attacks.

The government is actively perpetrating the same acts of economic espionage and sabotage that it publicly disparages. Now perhaps it's clear why India, China, and Russia are working on developing their own operating systems. Furthermore, do you suppose this casts doubt on the viability of global Cloud Services which use platforms based on technology developed by U.S. hi-tech companies?

Stepping back to view this as a whole, it appears that well-funded, or well-connected, organizations enjoy relatively higher levels of security. An essay published by the Electronic Frontier Foundation crystallizes this argument:

> The intelligence community within the government benefits from keeping attacks secret so that they can be deployed against our enemies, and very likely stockpiles zero-day exploits for this offensive purpose. There is then pressure to selectively harden sensitive targets while keeping the attack secret from everyone else and leaving popular software vulnerable. This is *"security for the 1%,"* and it makes the rest of us less safe.[75]

A commentator at the website Cryptome offers a similar analysis.[76] The offensive approach to cyber-security doesn't protect normal citizens; it demonizes them in deference to securing a small group of targets judged worthy of protection:

> It might be fair to say that personal security goes begging in order to maximize national and corporate security wealth protection. A citizen trying to get security against authoritarians is likely to be accused of aiding and abetting national enemies of free markets. The consequence is a campaign to promote the notion that an innocent citizen has nothing to hide from the biggest players in security – governments and their contractors conjoined by agreements to keep the best security highly secret and out of reach of citizens, thereby treating tax-paying and gullible citizens as enemies.
>
> Deliberately crippled personal security is no accident, it is national policy worldwide, cloaked in highest secrecy. If possible, get a top-level secrecy clearance and learn how the best security works and enjoy the privilege.

This is where the offensive approach to cyber-security will take us. Cold War strategies based on massive retaliation will inevitably lead governments to frantically engage in surreptitious malware development and software subversion. The same holds true for strategies that advocate preemptive attacks. Indeed, any approach that revolves around aggressive action will only serve to accelerate the arms race.

Cyber-attacks will proliferate via pricey custom tools and backroom deals with vendors. The malware industrial complex will flourish. The average user, relying on buggy software and commodity security software, will be the primary loser. This top-down model sacrifices security for the 99% by relegating high-security to cabals of spies and criminals.

In private, when they feel they can speak freely, officials will admit what they're really after. In a story published by the *Guardian* which described the NSA's and GCHQ's campaign to undermine strong encryption, the reporters noted:

> Classified briefings between the agencies celebrate their success at "defeating network security and privacy ..."[77]

The intelligence services have admitted that undermining collective security is one of their key goals.

Endnotes

1) Nick Bilton, "Disruptions: New Motto for Silicon Valley: First Security, Then Innovation," *New York Times*, May 5, 2013, http://bits.blogs.nytimes.com/2013/05/05/disruptions-new-motto-for-silicon-valley-first-security-then-innovation/?pagewanted=print.

2) Shon Harris, CISSP All-in-One Exam Guide, Sixth Edition, McGraw-Hill Osborne Media, 2012, ISBN-13: 978-0071781749, page 297.

3) Gary McGraw and Ivan Arce, "Software [In]security: Cyber Warmongering and Influence Peddling," *InformIT*, November 24, 2010, http://www.informit.com/articles/article.aspx?p=1662328.

4) Roger Cheng and Declan McCullagh, "Yahoo! breach: Swiped passwords by the numbers," *CNET*, July 12, 2012, http://news.cnet.com/8301-1009_3-57470878-83/yahoo-breach-swiped-passwords-by-the-numbers/?tag=mncol;txt.

5) Jim Finkle, "Security experts say zombie TV warning exposes flaws," *Reuters*, February 14, 2013, http://www.reuters.com/article/2013/02/14/net-us-usa-zombie-hacking-idUSBRE91D07Z20130214.

6) Spencer Ackerman, "Army Practices Poor Data Hygiene on Its New Smartphones, Tablets," *Wired*, April 1, 2013, http://www.wired.com/dangerroom/2013/04/army-data-hygiene/.

7) *Best Practices for Keeping Your Home Network Secure*, The Information Assurance Mission at NSA, April 2011, http://www.nsa.gov/ia/_files/factsheets/Best_Practices_Datasheets.pdf.

8) *Cyber Security Tips*, United States Computer Emergency Readiness Team, http://www.us-cert.gov/cas/tips/.

9) *Our Shared Responsibility: What Home Users Can Do*, National Cyber Security Alliance, 2011, http://www.staysafeonline.org/sites/default/files/resource_documents/What%20Home%20Users%20Can%20Do%202011.pdf.

10) *Port scanning /0 using insecure embedded devices*, March 17, 2013, http://seclists.org/fulldisclosure/2013/Mar/166.

11) Statement of Gregory C. Wilshusen, Director Information Security Issues, Before Subcommittee on Oversight, Investigations, and Management, Committee on Homeland Security, House of Representatives, GAO-12-666T, April 24, 2012, http://cryptome.org/2012/04/gao-12-666t.pdf.

12) *IRS Has Improved Controls but Needs to Resolve Weaknesses*, United States Government Accountability Office, GAO-13-350, March 2013, http://cryptome.org/2013/03/gao-13-350.pdf.

13) Robert McMillan, "US Treasury Web Sites Hacked, Serving Malware," *IDG*, May 4, 2010, http://www.infoworld.com/d/security-central/us-treasury-web-sites-hacked-serving-malware-624.

14) Dennis Fisher, "Major Ad Networks Found Serving Malicious Ads," *Threat Post*, December 12, 2010, http://threatpost.com/en_us/blogs/major-ad-networks-found-serving-malicious-ads-121210.

15) Websense Security Labs, *State of Internet Security, Q3 – Q4, 2008*, http://securitylabs.websense.com/content/Assets/WSL_ReportQ3Q4FNL.PDF.

16) *2013 Cisco Annual Security Report*, http://www.cisco.com/en/US/prod/vpndevc/annual_security_report.html.

17) Richard Bejtlich, *Control-Compliant vs Field-Assessed Security*, TaoSecurity, July 07, 2006, http://taosecurity.blogspot.com/2006/07/control-compliant-vs-field-assessed.html.

18) Kelly Jackson Higgins, "Apple 'Ban' Gives Miller Time To Hack Other Things," *Dark Reading*, July 10, 2012, http://www.darkreading.com/vulnerability-management/167901026/security/client-security/240003490/apple-ban-gives-miller-time-to-hack-other-things.html.

19) Jim Wolf, "U.S. code-cracking agency works as if compromised," *Reuters*, December 16, 2010, http://www.reuters.com/article/2010/12/16/us-cyber-usa-nsa-idUSTRE6BF6BZ20101216.

20) Bruce Schneier, "On Security Awareness Training," *DarkReading*, March 19, 2013, http://www.darkreading.com/taxonomy/index/printarticle/id/240151108.

21) Peter Naur, Brian Randell, J.N. Buxton (eds.), *Software Engineering: Concepts and Techniques: Proceedings of the NATO Conferences*, Petrocelli-Charter, New York, 1976.

22) Sang Kil Cha, Thanassis Avgerinos, Alexandre Rebert and David Brumley, "Unleashing MAYHEM on Binary Code," *2012 IEEE Symposium on Security and Privacy*, http://www.ieee-security.org/TC/SP2012/papers/4681a380.pdf.

23) Jorge Obes, Carlos Sarraute and Gerardo Richarte, *"Attack Planning in the Real World,"* Core Security Technologies and Instituto Tecnologico Buenos Aires, http://cryptome.org/2013/07/rl-attack-plan.pdf.

24) Carlos Sarraute, Olivier Buffet, and Jorg Hoffmann, *"Penetration Testing == POMDP Solving?"* Core Security Technologies & ITBA Buenos Aires, INRIA, http://cryptome.org/2013/07/pentest-pomdp.pdf.

25) *Security Bulletins and Advisories*, Adobe Reader, Version 9.x, Adobe Systems, http://www.adobe.com/support/security/#readerwin.

26) Erik Larkin, "Ditch Adobe Reader for Better Security," *PCWorld*, April 21, 2009, http://www.pcworld.com/article/163574/ditch_adobe_reader_for_better_security.html.

27) *Vulnerability Report: Microsoft Internet Explorer 6.x*, Secunia, http://secunia.com/advisories/product/11/.

28) Gregg Keizer, "Hackers exploit Adobe Reader zero-day, may be targeting defense contractors," *ComputerWorld*, December 6, 2011, http://www.computerworld.com/s/article/9222454/Hackers_exploit_Adobe_Reader_zero_day_may_be_targeting_defense_contractors.

29) Vulnerabilities, Security Focus, for Microsoft Internet Explorer v.9, http://www.securityfocus.com/vulnerabilities.

30) Ryan Naraine, "Internet Explorer 9 haunted by 'critical' security vulnerabilities," *ZDNet*, October 11, 2011, http://www.zdnet.com/blog/security/internet-explorer-9-haunted-by-critical-security-vulnerabilities/9590.

31) Brian Krebs, "Microsoft: IE Zero Day Flaw Affects All Versions," *Krebs on Security*, September 13, 2013, http://krebsonsecurity.com/2013/09/microsoft-ie-zero-day-flaw-affects-all-versions/.

32) Michael Mimoso, "VUPEN Researchers Say They Have Zero-Day Windows 8 Exploit," *Threat Post*, November 1, 2012, http://threatpost.com/en_us/blogs/vupen-researchers-say-they-have-zero-day-windows-8-exploit-110112.

33) Vulnerability Note VU#625617, Java 7 fails to restrict access to privileged code, DHS Office of Cybersecurity and Communications, http://www.kb.cert.org/vuls/id/625617.

34) Salvador Rodriguez, "U.S. urges users to disable Java; Apple disables some remotely," *Los Angeles Times*, January 11, 2013, http://www.latimes.com/business/technology/la-fi-tn-java-disable-malware-department-oh-homeland-security-20130111,0,6103875.story.

35) Bob Lord, *Keeping our users secure*, Twitter Corporate Blog, February 1, 2013, http://blog.twitter.com/2013/02/keeping-our-users-secure.html.

36) Brian Krebs, "Critical Java Update Fixes 50 Security Holes," *Krebs on Security*, February 13, 2013, http://krebsonsecurity.com/2013/02/critical-java-update-fixes-50-security-holes/.

37) Ms. Smith, "Oracle releases emergency Java patch; experts warn flaws may take 2 years to fix," *Network World*, January 14, 2013, http://www.networkworld.com/community/blog/oracle-releases-emergency-java-patch-experts-warn-flaws-may-take-2-years-fix.

38) Gary McGraw and Ivan Arce, "Software [In]security: Assume Nothing," *InformIT*, April 30, 2010, http://www.informit.com/articles/article.aspx?p=1588145.

39) Kim Zetter, "Fearing Industrial Destruction, Researcher Delays Disclosure of New Siemens SCADA Holes," *Wired*, May 18, 2011, http://www.wired.com/threatlevel/2011/05/siemens-scada-vulnerabilities/.

40) Gerry Smith, "Apple Punishes Researcher Charlie Miller For Finding Potential Security Flaw," Huffington Post, November 8, 2011, http://www.huffingtonpost.com/2011/11/08/apple-charlie-miller-security-flaw_n_1082497.html.

41) Nicolo Machiavelli, *The Prince*, Translated by William Marriot, Project Gutenberg, 2006, http://www.gutenberg.org/files/1232/1232-h/1232-h.htm.

42) John Viega and Gary McGraw, *Building Secure Software: How to Avoid Security Problems the Right Way*, Addison Wesley, 2001, ISBN-10: 020172152X.

43) Gary McGraw, "The Past, Present and Future of Software Security," *ThreatPost*, September 13, 2011, http://threatpost.com/en_us/blogs/past-present-and-future-software-security-091311.

44) Brian Snow, "We Need Assurance!" 2005 Annual Computer Security Applications Conference, http://www.acsac.org/2005/papers/Snow.pdf.

45) Ibid.

46) *Simplified Implementation of the Microsoft SDL*, Microsoft Corp., 2010, http://www.microsoft.com/download/en/details.aspx?displaylang=en&id=12379.

47) *Oracle Software Security Assurance*, Oracle, 2007, http://www.oracle.com/us/support/assurance/software-security-assurance-wp-150395.pdf.

48) Gary McGraw, Brian Chess, and Sammy Migues, *BSIMM3*, September 2011, http://bsimm.com/download/.

49) Roger Grimes, "In his own words: Confessions of a cyber warrior," *InfoWorld*, July 9, 2013, http://www.infoworld.com/print/222266.

50) Thierry Falissard, "Why Mainframes Rarely Crash," *Byte Magazine*, April 1998.

51) "China deploys secure computer operating system," *AFP*, May 12, 2009, http://www.physorg.com/news161355225.html.

52) Spencer Dalziel, "India Plans to Write its Own OS," *The Inquirer*, October 11, 2010, http://www.theinquirer.net/inquirer/news/1741665/india-plans-write.

53) "Russia to create 'Windows rival,'" *AFP*, October 27, 2010, http://topics.dallasnews.com/article/00b9a3kcoo9aR.

54) Glyn Moody, "Windows 8+TPM: Germany Warns of 'Loss of Control,'" *ComputerWorld UK*, August 22, 2013, http://blogs.computerworlduk.com/open-enterprise/2013/08/german-government-warns-of-windows-8-loss-of-control/index.htm.

55) Hiroshi Shinotsuka, "Malware Authors Using New Techniques to Evade Automated Threat Analysis Systems," *Symantec Corporate Blog*, October 28, 2012,

http://www.symantec.com/connect/blogs/malware-authors-using-new-techniques-evade-automated-threat-analysis-systems.

56) Mikko Hypponen, "Why Antivirus Companies Like Mine Failed to Catch Flame and Stuxnet," *Wired*, June 1, 2012, http://www.wired.com/threatlevel/2012/06/internet-security-fail/.

57) Brian Snow, *Your company's security posture is probably horrible (but it might be OK)*, January 29, 2013, http://blog.thinkst.com/2013/01/your-companies-security-posture-is.html.

58) Nicole Kobie, "Microsoft: Security Essentials is designed to be bottom of the antivirus rankings," *PC Pro*, September 25, 2013, http://www.pcpro.co.uk/news/security/384394/microsoft-security-essentials-is-designed-to-be-bottom-of-the-antivirus-rankings.

59) Siobhan Gorman, Devlin Barrett And Danny Yadron, "Chinese Hackers Hit U.S. Media," *Wall Street Journal*, January 31, 2013, http://online.wsj.com/article/SB100014241278873233926104578276202052260718.html.

60) Craig Timberg and Ellen Nakashima, "Chinese hackers suspected in attack on The Post's computers," *Washington Post*, February 1, 2013, http://www.washingtonpost.com/business/technology/chinese-hackers-suspected-in-attack-on-the-posts-computers/2013/02/01/d5a44fde-6cb1-11e2-bd36-c0fe61a205f6_print.html.

61) Jonathan Kaiman, "*New York Times* claims Chinese hackers hijacked its systems," *Guardian*, January 31, 2013, http://www.guardian.co.uk/media/2013/jan/31/new-york-times-chinese-hacked/print.

62) Jordan Robertson, "Symantec After *New York Times* Attack Says Antivirus Isn't Enough," *Bloomberg*, January 31, 2013, http://go.bloomberg.com/tech-blog/2013-01-31-symantec-after-new-york-times-attack-says-antivirus-isnt-enough/.

63) Symantec Statement Regarding *New York Times* Cyber Attack, Symantec Official Blog, January 31, 2013, http://www.symantec.com/connect/blogs/symantec-statement-regarding-new-york-times-cyber-attack.

64) Brian Krebs, "Security Vendors: Do No Harm, Heal Thyself," Krebs on Security, July 13, 2013, http://krebsonsecurity.com/2013/07/security-vendors-do-no-harm-heal-thyself/.

65) Riva Richmond, "Web Gang Operating in the Open," *New York Times*, January 16, 2012, http://www.nytimes.com/2012/01/17/technology/koobface-gang-that-used-facebook-to-spread-worm-operates-in-the-open.html?_r=1&pagewanted=print.

66) Tim Jackson, *Inside Intel Andrew Grove and the Rise of the World's Most Powerful Chip Company*, Dutton Adult, 1997, ISBN-13: 978-0525941415, page 280.

67) Richard A. Clarke, *Cyber War: The Next Threat to National Security and What to Do About It* Ecco, 2010, ISBN-13: 978-0061962233, page 142.

68) The Chromium Projects, Vulnerability Rewards Program, http://www.chromium.org/Home/chromium-security/vulnerability-rewards-program.

69) "Pwnium: rewards for exploits," *The Chromium Blog*, February 27, 2012, http://blog.chromium.org/2012/02/pwnium-rewards-for-exploits.html.

70)Kim Zetter, "Microsoft Launches $100K Bug Bounty Program," *Wired*, June 19, 2013, http://www.wired.com/threatlevel/2013/06/microsoft-bug-bounty-program/.

71) Nicole Perlroth and David Sanger, "Nations Buying as Hackers Sell Flaws in Computer Code," *New York Times*, July 13, 2013, http://www.nytimes.com/2013/07/14/world/europe/nations-buying-as-hackers-sell-computer-flaws.html.

72) Dennis Fisher, "The Case for a Government Bug Bounty Program," *ThreatPost*, May 31, 2013, http://threatpost.com/the-case-for-a-government-bug-bounty-program/.

73) Joanna Rutkowska, "Rootkits vs Stealth by Design Malware," Black Hat Europe 2006, http://www.blackhat.com/presentations/bh-europe-06/bh-eu-06-Rutkowska.pdf.

74) Michael Riley, "U.S. Agencies Said to Swap Data With Thousands of Firms," *Bloomberg*, June 15, 2013, http://www.bloomberg.com/news/print/2013-06-14/u-s-agencies-said-to-swap-data-with-thousands-of-firms.html.

75) Dan Auerbach and Lee Tien, "Dangerously Vague Cybersecurity Legislation Threatens Civil Liberties," *EFF Deeplinks*, March 20, 2012, https://www.eff.org/deeplinks/2012/03/dangerously-vague-cybersecurity-legislation.

76) "Personal Security Weak on Purpose, Fix It," December 2, 2012, http://cryptome.org/2012/12/personal-sec-fix.htm.

77) James Ball, Julian Borger, and Glenn Greenwald, "Revealed: how US and UK spy agencies defeat internet privacy and security," *Guardian*, September 5, 2013, http://www.theguardian.com/world/2013/sep/05/nsa-gchq-encryption-codes-security/print.

Cyber-Security for The 99 Percent

The status quo is unacceptable.
What do we do now? How do we change things?
There really is room for innovation in defensive security.

– Dan Kaminsky[1]

There are a thousand hacking at the branches of evil to one who is striking at the root.

– Henry David Thoreau, *Walden; or, Life in the Woods*

Why should normal citizens suffer the fallout of poor security so that a select group of organizations can launch covert operations? Why should higher levels of security be the sole domain of classified and "critical" networks? Why can't security grow organically from the bottom up? If individual citizens are secure, then aren't nations as a whole more secure? As we've demonstrated, the same cannot be said for the top-down approach. Fortifying a small group of allegedly high-value targets doesn't necessarily do much for Mr. and Mrs. Smith when they go online.

Building Resilient Software

The software industry needs to reorient its mindset towards failure. The never-ending stream of critical software bugs highlights the catastrophic failure of modern software engineering. The design methodologies being used today are insufficient. The industry's only hope is to discover new ways to develop *resilient* software; software that resists attempts at exploitation (robust) and then contains the critical flaws that do emerge (fault tolerance). Truly robust implementations, which possess inherent fault tolerance, are often referred to as *self-healing*.

Resilience, as we'll see, reflects the design priorities of the architects and the engineers who rely on the architect's blueprints. As evidence of this, computer scientist Robert Dewar cites commercial avionics:

> The aviation industry has demonstrated that safe, reliable real-time software is possible, practical, and necessary. It requires appropriate development technology and processes as well as a culture that thinks in terms of safety (or reliability) first.[2]

Prevention versus Response

Defensive measures have traditionally been broken down into two tiers. The first tier aims to prevent breaches, and the second tier aims to detect breaches, and remediate them, after they occur. The first tier is proactive, the second tier is reactive.

There are those who promote reactive measures. But as the DEA can corroborate, a law enforcement approach that focuses on interdiction, apprehension, and harsh sentencing has done little to halt the flow of drugs into the United States. It only leads to a perpetual, and costly, struggle against heavily armed cartels that sprout up in response to poverty on one side of our border and heavy demand on the other. Prevention, education, and treatment are what stifle the demand that fuels the drug trade.

Hence, an ounce of prevention is worth a pound of cure; which is to say that *investing in prevention offers a much higher return on investment* than pouring money into response. Hence, we believe that the first tier needs to be reexamined. To this end there are a couple of strategies that merit attention.

Compartmentalization

In the years following World War II, the Soviet nuclear program was the focus of a vast intelligence campaign on behalf of U.S. intelligence agencies. To counter this effort, the Soviets utilized elaborate, multi-level, denial and deception strategies. According to Mikhail Gladyshev, who was in charge of the plutonium enrichment station at the Mayak complex in the city of Ozersk, compartmentalization of information was very strict:

[W]e put the [plutonium] paste in a box and transferred it to the consumer plant. How much plutonium was in that box we didn't know and it was not recommended for us to know. Even later, when I was the plant's chief engineer, the plans for plutonium production were known only to the facility's director, and all documents were prepared in single copies.[3]

Evgeny Morozov describes a defensive measure in line with this sort of thinking:

In part, then, the solution to cyber-insecurity is simple: if you have a lot of classified information on a computer and do not want to become part of another GhostNet-like operation, do not connect it to the Internet.[4]

Even the bastions of hi-tech fail to heed this advice. Most recently, in October of 2013 Adobe's CSO publicly announced that unnamed black hats had cracked the company's network wide open and absconded with Adobe's primary asset: its source code:

Adobe is investigating the illegal access of source code for Adobe Acrobat, ColdFusion, ColdFusion Builder and other Adobe products by an unauthorized third party.[5]

How's that for embarrassing? Security journalist Brian Krebs helped to break this story. One of his readers made the following astute comment:

You know what is absolutely moronic about this breach? WHY do you have to have trade secrets on network facing equipment? In this day and age with all the breaches and other nasties happening out there, wouldn't most companies think it would be wise to keep their trade secrets on a separate internal network that is not connected to the Internet? How often does the source code have to be accessed?[6]

There are a number of breaches which we've surveyed that probably could have been prevented if *air-gap security* had been implemented. The idea behind air-gap security is simple: relegate sensitive data to a special-purpose network that is physically separated from other networks. The experts trust this approach. For example, Bruce Schneier used air-gap security while working with documents disclosed by Ed Snowden.[7] In ultra-high security environments, machines in air-gapped network are electromagnetically shielded with wire mesh (i.e. what's known as a "Faraday cage") to prevent TEMPEST emanation.

While air-gap security raises the bar that an attacker must surmount, even with an isolated network there's the risk that malware will gain entry when data needs to be exchanged between the isolated network and the outside world. This is exactly how the perimeter of CENTCOM was breached. The same holds in the case of Stuxnet, which propagated in the absence of an outside network connection.

To defend against this, companies like San Francisco-based Cryptography Research have tackled the issue of data exchange using a dedicated USB drive that's wiped clean after each use.[8] To be even more wary, optical media could be leveraged to transfer data in an encrypted format. Obviously as inter-network bandwidth needs increase, this becomes a less efficient solution.

Despite these countermeasures high security air-gap environments still face additional threats. For example, a top-secret document released by French newspaper *Le Monde* lists a series of special terms that appear to represent different ways of surreptitiously collecting data:

HIGHLANDS:	Collection from Implants
VAGRANT:	Collection of Computer Screens
MAGNETIC:	Sensor Collection of Magnetic Emanations
MINERALIZE:	Collection from LAN Implant
OCEAN:	Optical Collection System for Raster-Base Computer Screens
LIFESAFER:	Imaging of the Hard Drive
GENIE:	Multi-stage operation: jumping the airgap etc.
BLACKHEART:	Collection from an FBI Implant
PBX:	Public Branch Exchange Switch
CRYPTO ENABLED:	Collection derived from AO's efforts to enable crypto
DROPMIRE:	Passive collection of emanations using antenna
CUSTOMS:	Customs opportunities (not LIFESAVER)
DROPMIRE:	Laser printer collection, purely proximal access (***NOT*** implanted)

| DEWSWEEPER: | USB (Universal Serial Bus) hardware host tap that provides COVERT link over U.S. link into a target network. Operates w/RF relay subsystem to provide wireless Bridge into target network. |
| RADON: | Bi-directional host tap that can inject Ethernet packets onto the same targets. Allows bi-directional exploitation of denied networks using standard on-net tools.[9] |

Looking through this list, note how Codename GENIE refers to "jumping the airgap" and codename DEWSEEPER describes a process that appears to involve extracting data over ad hoc wireless connections. It would seem that the physical security of an air-gapped machine is just as important as keeping it off the Internet. If a spy can get to your machine and install an "implant," they've sunk your battleship.

To give you an idea of just how insidious and stealthy malware can be, the founder of the *Pwn2Own* hacking competition, Dragos Ruiu, once unearthed a nasty variant of USB-transmitted malware that lurked down in the firmware level of an infected computer. The malware, which Ruiu dubbed *badBIOS*, apparently was able to bridge air gaps using high-frequency sound waves transmitted from the speakers on one system to the microphone on another system.[10] How's that for a covert channel? Even if you flatten an infected computer and re-build it from the vendor's installation DVD, the malware will survive by ducking down into the hardware, where it can communicate with other compromised systems via sound waves and fortify its position.

Poor Man's Tactics

The notion of isolation can also be applied to normal endpoint computers without falling back on full-blown air-gap security. For instance, the American Bankers Association suggests that users rely on a dedicated computer for online banking which is not used for e-mail, recreational web browsing, or anything else.[11] Considering the cost of dealing with a security breach, and recovering from identity theft, the cost of buying a second computer is money well spent.

A less expensive and even more reliable approach is to use a "Live CD." A Live CD is a bootable CD (or DVD) that stores a stand-alone operating system which runs entirely in memory. Instead of launching the native operating system on the computer's local hard drive, a Live CD incites the computer to load and run the operating system stored on the CD. If a computer's local hard drive has been infected with malware, the malware never gets a chance to execute because the computer is relying entirely on files loaded from read-only optical media. Every time a machine is booted using a Live CD it loads a fresh, pristine, copy of the operating system. Furthermore, if an attack takes place while the user is working under a Live CD session, the user can negate the effects of the attack by simply restarting the computer and re-launching the Live CD.

In a nutshell, a Live CD will provide the ability to function securely even if the hard drive of the computer you're running it on has been completely compromised by malware.

There are a multitude of Live CDs in circulation. Journalist Brian Krebs recommends a lightweight, relatively portable, distribution geared towards online banking called Puppy Linux.[12] The Air Force Anti-Tamper Software Protection Initiative (ATSPI) has also developed a Lightweight Portable Security (LPS) Live CD which is used to connect to high-security networks.[13]

Sandboxes and Virtual Machines

So far we've just looked at compartmentalization at the logistical level to give you an intuitive feel for how it works. But what we're actually interested in is compartmentalization within software applications and operating systems themselves.

Given that web browsers are probably *the* attack vector of choice, they deserve special attention. In years gone by, the software architects who designed web browsers placed all of the associated logic (e.g. processing HTML tags, interpreting JavaScript, loading images, etc.) inside of a single monolithic process, one big chunk of computer memory (see Figure 12-1). The basic idea behind this decision was to delegate work to a series of light-weight *threads* (little sub-processes, if you will) within the browser's main process on behalf of performance.

This approach is grounded in historical requirements. When browsers became popular in the mid-1990s, standard hardware (e.g. the Intel 80486) would groan under the weight of loading separate processes into memory. Using threads, which are lightweight sub-processes that execute within an existing process, was less demanding. The problem with using threads is that while it does speed things up, using threads also offers very little protection against malicious code. The walls between threads are extremely porous. Once an exploit corrupts an executing thread and gains a foothold in the address space of the browser, it has free rein to all of the other browser components and can do pretty much whatever it wants.

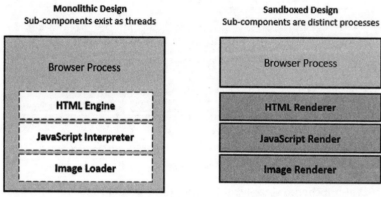

Figure 12-1

Google recognized this problem when it designed its Chrome web browser.[14] In particular, the logic for handling HTML markup, JavaScript, and images is encapsulated in distinct processes known as *renderers*. Each rendering process is placed in its own *sandbox*, a special environment that limits the ability of the contained process to access system resources (e.g. the hard drive, display, network connections, etc.). This way a rendering process that's been attacked by an exploit is constrained in terms of its ability to impact the rest of the browser, allowing it to be shut down gracefully without crashing the browser as a whole.

Joanna Rutkowska has taken this idea of application sandboxing to the operating system level by implementing Qubes OS.[15] Qubes (see Figure 12-2) leverages a compilation of existing open source software (e.g. the Xen open source hypervisor, the X windowing system, and Linux) to create a platform that supports *disposable vir-*

tual machines. Like Google's rendering processes, a disposable virtual machine is limited in terms of what it can do and segmented off from everything else. The difference is that the walls of the sandbox are implemented on a much deeper level, providing better protection. Disposable virtual machines can be launched on a per-document basis and don't have access to persistent storage. This way you can visit a web page or open a PDF and not worry about compromising your computer as a whole. The minute the virtual machine vanishes, any malware that gained entry will likewise be destroyed.

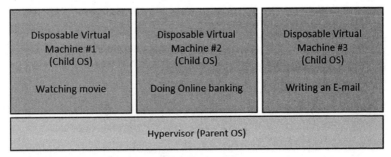

Figure 12-2

Yet another system-level technique to contain attacks is known as *program shepherding,* where control flows of execution within applications are tracked in an attempt to detect corrupted threads of execution. The typical program is defined by a finite collection of logical steps that occur in a given order. Jumps between blocks of code that are out of the ordinary (i.e. requests out of nowhere to alter security privileges) stand out as suspect. One researcher, Piotr Bania, published a paper on a tool that statically altered the kernel-level modules of Microsoft Windows so that control flow transfers could be monitored in this fashion.[16] Bania admits that this approach offers little protection against attacks that overwrite crucial bits of data (e.g. direct kernel object manipulation) or third-party drivers which have their own set of undocumented transfer control paths.

Formal Verification

As we saw in the previous chapter, the goal of assurance is to satisfy the security requirements of the accreditor. The catch is that appeasing an accreditor doesn't guarantee that there won't be a bunch of obscure flaws hidden away in the far corners of the assured software application. In fact, given the steady stream of zero-day exploits, many assurance efforts seem more like marketing ploys that generate a lot of good press.

Compartmentalization also has its limits. If the walls between compartments are imperfect, there's the possibility of an attacker to breach out of the sandbox and wreak havoc. Google's Chrome browser, though an admirable effort, has been defeated on a number of occasions. In March of 2012, Google announced that a researcher named Sergey Glazunov had engineered a full Chrome exploit that successfully bypassed the browser's sandboxing defenses.[17] For his trouble he was rewarded $60,000. Though, with the right connections, he probably could've made much more money selling his exploit in the black market. A few months later, in October, the feat was replicated by a hacker known as "Pinkie Pie," who developed a working Chrome exploit and likewise collected $60,000.[18]

So, rather than assure security to certain extent, or try to contain threats through compartmentalization, an alternative would be to prove absolute security by relying on specialized mathematical tools. This is known as the process of *formal verification*. How does this work?

Let's look at one possible way of doing this. In a previous call for proposals, DARPA provided a basic scheme for creating provable-secure software (see Figure 12-3).[19] Using broad brush strokes, the workflow is as follows: formal specifications, policies, and constraints (i.e. the software's blueprints) are fed into what DARPA refers to as a *synthesizer*. If all goes well, this synthesizer spits out the application's

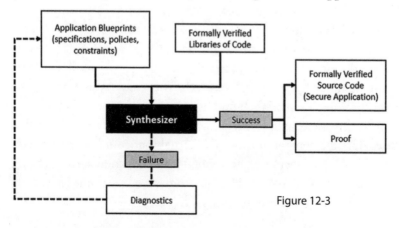

Figure 12-3

code in addition to a mathematical proof which logically demonstrates that the generated code satisfies the original specifications that were fed into the synthesizer. This is why the synthesizer could also be called a *theorem prover*. The proof verifies that the code is bug free.

If the synthesizer fails to do its job, it will produce diagnostics that help isolate the source of failure. To speed up the process, a library of prefabricated code can be used, which has itself been proven secure by this process.

For pedants in the reading audience, the previous approach to formal verification is known as *deductive verification* (i.e. deductive as in logic, as in logical proof). While there are other ways to perform formal verification, like *model checking* and *abstract static analysis*, deductive verification offers the highest level of security assurance. It also requires the greatest amount of effort and expertise.

Cynics may scoff at this idea (bug free software, ha!), but there are implementations in the wild. For example, the Paris Métro Line 14 is fully automated: it doesn't have human conductors operating the train. Certain safety-critical parts of Line 14's control system have been formally verified. The process required generating over 20,000 proofs and entailed 17 man-years of effort.[20]

In November of 2003 formal methods were used to guarantee that the flight control system of the Airbus A340 fly-by-wire system was free of run-time errors. The flight control software in question consisted of 132,000 lines of C code.[21]

Work in the domain of formal verification has also been done at the operating system level. For instance, a European company named SYSGO AG sells a microkernel-based real-time operating system that's been formally verified.[22] The microkernel, PikeOS, targets embedded systems used in industrial settings and was verified using a tool designed by Microsoft Research. The team that performed the verification presented their findings at a conference in 2009.[23]

In this same year, researchers in Australia announced they had developed a general-purpose OS kernel that could be mathematically proven as secure.[24] The verified software, known as the secure embedded L4 microkernel (seL4), consists of 8,700 lines of C code and is based on the pre-existing L4 microkernel.[25]

In case you're wondering, a *microkernel* is a sort of minimalistic operating system that concerns itself with a bare-bones set of operations, relegating other traditional features (e.g. memory management, device I/O, file system management, etc.) to external modules. It's a primordial layer of glue that resides in the bowels of the system, conducting work that's been delegated to the external modules and coordinating their operation to implement a functioning whole that can support applications (see Figure 12-4).

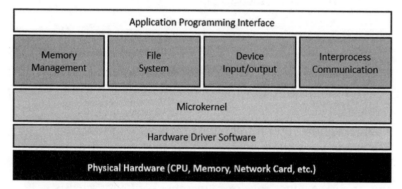

Figure 12-4

According to Professor Gernot Heiser, a senior principal researcher involved in the seL4 project:

> The verification provides conclusive evidence that bug-free software is possible, and in the future, nothing less should be considered acceptable where critical assets are at stake.[26]

There you have it, bug-free software is entirely plausible. The seL4 microkernel is convincing evidence. One of the Holy Grails of software security is becoming a reality. In the future we can say goodbye to buffer overflows, heap overruns, deadlock, you name it. No more zero-day exploits. All we'll need to worry about then would be user errors and misconfiguration.

Cynics may contend that this approach is still not practical (it took a team of about a dozen people four years to complete the proof of seL4), and so the achievement doesn't matter because none of the major vendors are willing to make the investment.

Joanna Rutkowska also points out that a secure microkernel isn't the same things as a much larger, more complicated, operating system:

> There are no general purpose, desktop OSes that would be formally proven to be secure. At the very best, there are some parts that are formally verified, such as some microkernels, but not whole OSes. And what good is saying that our microkernel is formally verified, if we continue to use a bloated and buggy X server as our GUI subsystem?[27]

But this is the very reason why more work needs to be done, because the potential benefits are well worth the investment. The halls of academic research have heard the call for more efficient and flexible formal verification tools. For example, the Why3 deductive verification platform developed by researchers in France[28] is a very pluggable and technically elegant approach. It can be used to process programs written in several different languages (e.g. Java, C, Ada) and can interface with over a dozen different external theorem-proving engines developed by other computer scientists.

The private sector has also heard this call. In October of 2012, Russian security software vendor Kaspersky Lab announced that it would be developing its own operating system from scratch, a stripped down special-purpose implementation intended explicitly for industrial control systems. The company's founder, Eugene Kaspersky, described the planned OS in his personal blog:

> Our system is highly tailored, developed for solving a specific narrow task, and not intended for playing Half-Life on, editing your vacation videos, or blathering on social media.[29]

But it's not just sheer minimalism that will make the OS secure. Instead, Kaspersky Lab plans on mathematically verifying that the proposed system is secure:

> To achieve a guarantee of security it must contain no mistakes or vulnerabilities whatsoever in the kernel, which controls the rest of the modules of the system. As a result, the core must be 100% verified as not permitting vulnerabilities or dual-purpose code.[30]

Echoes of Ken Thompson

You may have noticed that there's an issue that we have been avoiding. In particular, while a vendor may tell you that its enterprise products have been formally verified, how can you be sure that it's telling the truth? After all, Ed Snowden's revelations proved that several big names in hi-tech are cooperating with U.S. spies. As we saw at length in Chapter Six and Chapter Eleven, a myriad of companies have long-standing agreements with national security services to install backdoors outright or provide the information needed to install them, via exploits, once products have been deployed in the field. This set of companies includes (in a betrayal that runs very deep) vendors who sell security products. As John Young has observed, what happened with Crypto-AG (as discussed in Chapter Six) is actually the norm:

> What might be troubling about Snowden's possible revelations that is causing exaggerated surprise of these experts is the disclosure that the dual-uses and dual-roles in spying were more extensive than has been made public. That has been protected by highest secrecy about to be breached, not about the spy agencies but those used to camouflage and assist the spying by downplaying its pervasiveness by selling protection that could never be wholly effective, that the cybersec game was as rigged as gambling.[31]

Hence, the average person has absolutely no reason to trust hi-tech companies.

Public companies exist to maximize profits, not safeguard constitutional liberties, regardless of what their PR spin masters avow. Snowden's disclosures inform on the true mindset of multinational hi-tech corporations: if turning a profit means surreptitiously sticking it to Mr. and Mrs. Smith, then so be it.

Some people might suggest that the industry establish an independent rating agency, a hi-tech incarnation of Standard & Poor's, to evaluate products and pass on its assessments to the general public. But what, exactly, is there to prevent such a rating agency from lying (i.e. silenced by a gag order) just like the enterprise vendors? In the absence of corroborating data, how can the average citizen trust that the resulting assessments are genuinely independent and free of intimidation? Perhaps a global organization of volunteers would have a better chance of evading coercion?

As things stand now, the average citizen, using proprietary technology, is at a loss. Ken Thompson, the original author of the UNIX operating system and lord high alpha geek, can offer some insight. Decades ago in his ACM Turing Award Lecture he concluded:

> You can't trust code that you did not totally create yourself. (Especially code from companies that employ people like me.) ... As the level of program gets lower, these bugs will be harder and harder to detect. A well installed microcode bug will be almost impossible to detect ... [32]

In a nutshell, nothing beats *autonomy*. It's like being a mountain man in the days of the old west. You built your own house, lived off the land, and survived the environments by virtue of your own wits. But achieving total technical autonomy in this day and age can be such a tall order that it resembles a sort of naive idealism. Despite how fictionalized period pieces may convey the romance of life on the frontier, the typical life of a mountain man was dreary, brutal, short and full of bug bites.

Large organizations that have both the necessary resources and the clout can establish a degree of trust by demanding access to source code or simply by building their own software. As mentioned in the previous chapter, the national governments of India, China, and Russia have openly broadcast their plans to roll out their own operating systems.

But where does this leave Mr. and Mrs. Smith?

One alternative would be for the *open source* movement to lead the way by constructing a formally verified system, with all the trimmings, and then releasing all of the related source code to the general public. In this manner a working toolset could be made available to everyone, globally. The potential gains would be enormous. Recall a brilliant medical researcher named Jonas Salk who selflessly gave away the intellectual underpinnings of his polio vaccine, choosing to benefit society instead of pad his wallet. In my mind, this is the most promising long-term strategic path towards cyber-security for the masses.

However, that's just the beginning. Much of what software does with regard to security (i.e. encryption) is based on established technical standards. It's been shown that security standards have been subverted. So it's not enough for standards to merely be publicly available, the process through which these standards are created must be transparent, and once more their theoretical underpinnings must also be made clear so that they can be scrutinized by everyone all over the planet. Committee deliberations over encryption standards like SHA-3 cannot take place behind closed doors, where suspicious changes get made.[33] The development of open standards must also be open.

Richard Stallman, the elder statesman of the *free software movement*, distills the core tradeoffs at play:

> If the users don't control the program, the program controls the users.[34]

On the hardware level, as Ken Thompson notes, things become much more complicated. Semiconductor manufacturing isn't something that everyone can do, much less easily verify. Setting up your own chip fabrication site using front-line technology requires billions of dollars. While the Pentagon does have its own Trusted Foundry Program,[35] it's an exception rather than the rule.

Even if hardware vendors provided the architectural blueprints to their processors, how could users be sure that the chips weren't concealing trap doors short of breaking out an electron microscope and probing the chip? If you ask people who work in chip architecture, they'll tell you that modern processors possess of level of complexity that is mind boggling. There are an endless number of places where trap doors could be concealed. These low-level issues demonstrate why providing trustworthy hardware is the next frontier for the open source movement.

Treating the Symptoms

There are those who believe that all of this work is pointless, that we should simply accept that prevention is always going to fail, and thus engineers and software architects should instead put their energy into detection and response.

However, as we mentioned earlier, our losing battle against the drug cartels indicates just how ineffective this would be. Raw detection and response will do little to stem the current flood of zero-day exploits, and will only lead to a costly struggle to contain the resulting damage (a struggle, no doubt, that *will make many security vendors very wealthy*). Once more, in order to respond to an incident you've got to detect it, and the bad guys have shown time after time that that they've been able to operate with impunity for extended periods of time before being discovered. The contest between attackers and defenders is an arms race, and thanks to buggy software the attackers are usually ahead.

The dividends yielded from avoiding zero-day exploits in the first place, on the other hand, are so high that there's no question that researchers should investigate preventative methods. Undermine the demand for drugs, and the drug trade will wither. Proactively eliminate zero-day exploits, and the effort required to launch a successful attack will become substantially more daunting.

International Cooperation

As noted earlier, nations like China struggle just to collect taxes. If a state-run country like China can't conduct basic administrative tasks that unquestionably benefit the government, how can they be expected to successfully prosecute online criminals or shut down rogue ISPs? You can't expect to eradicate cybercrime in a place where institutionalized corruption is the status quo. To suppose otherwise is wishful thinking.

This goes double for Russia, where the general living conditions have become so hostile that the overall life expectancy is barely higher than Senegal's, and the country suffers from a mortality rate that literally threatens to depopulate the country.[36] The average eighteen-year-old male in Russia has a fifty percent chance of making it to retirement age.[37] If this is indicative of the grave over-arching issues that Russia faces, we doubt that prosecuting cybercrime is high on its current list of priorities.

This is not to say that international teamwork doesn't work. The chapter on cybercrime presents a number of examples where law enforcement agencies were able to work together to take down criminals. Arranging a series of international treaties that collectively work towards establishing global norms of behavior online could go a long way towards making life difficult for online crooks.[38]

It's just that the realities of the global arena, in some instances, put upper bounds on the gains that can be achieved. This is especially true in regions were rule of law is tenuous. Successfully addressing cybercrime internationally often translates into stemming pervasive corruption abroad, and *that's a pretty tall order*.

Espionage is a different story. The utility of international cooperation is even more problematic. The chapter on espionage reinforces this notion. Not only are spies cagey enough to operate out of wild territories, where enforcement is weak, but the countries involved in committing espionage will naturally be indifferent if not outright deceptive.

How can countries genuinely cooperate if they're neck deep in subterfuge?

The answer to this question: they don't. They're more likely to cooperate up to a point to save face, or offer steadfast denials, or, even worse, fabricate convincing evidence that implicates otherwise uninvolved parties.

False-flag and fifth-column operations aren't just an artifact of history and, contrary to what the so-called experts might claim, the existence of sophisticated anti-forensic technology is something to bear in mind whenever someone starts pointing fingers.

Then there's cyberwar, which reveals the same challenges as espionage (only more so). How, specifically, are the provisions of an international treaty to be invoked in the chaos of a genuine attack, if leaders can't even properly identify the country that executed the attack? Hypothetically speaking, if another country was actually going to launch a cyber-assault against a military power like the United States, they certainly wouldn't be foolish enough to openly initiate hostilities from their own backyard. Not unless the attacking country's leaders were suicidal, and indifferent to the possibility of nuclear ICBMs turning cities into parking lots in a matter of minutes.

While international agreements are definitely a significant component of an effective cyber-security strategy, they're hardly a panacea. To rely on this kind of cooperation is to put faith in the underlying integrity and intentions of other global power centers, and sometimes this belief simply isn't warranted. Given the quandary of attribution and the anarchic nature of international relations, policy makers would be well-advised not to lose focus on factors over which they have more direct control.

Managing Externalities

Recall, a central characteristic of the ongoing software depression is the attitude towards failure. In an age when everything is going online, voting machines in particular,[39] critical security flaws need to be viewed, and treated, like catastrophes. If the software industry will not assume this vantage point voluntarily, due to economic imperatives, then society needs to exert sufficient pressure so that they do. This can be done by establishing policies that redirect the cost of bad software back on the organizations that can actually do something about it.

While perfection is possible, as we saw with seL4, for larger implementations it's still more of an ideal that should be aspired to. In other words, while the technology behind code verification matures and efficiencies are achieved, researchers should seek to make critical security bugs rare enough that finding one represents a significant barrier to would-be attackers.

This perspective is in line with how bank safes are rated for insurance purposes. The Underwriters Laboratories (UL), which assigns safe ratings, realizes that there's no such thing as a burglar-proof safe. Given enough time and the right tools, a skilled burglar can crack any safe. Hence, safes are rated in terms of how long it would take to break in:

> There are a dozen different ratings, everything from ATM machines, to gun safes to bank vaults. For example, a safe that bears a Class TRTL-15x6 rating, which might be found in a jewelry store, should resist a hand tool and torch attack for a minimum of 15 minutes. A TRTL-30x6-rated safe, which

would protect important documents or store money, should withstand an attack for 30 minutes. The ultimate safe rating – a TXTL60 – should withstand an hour's worth of attack that includes the use of 8 ounces of nitroglycerin.[40]

There have been rating systems like this for operating systems. It's just that they were based on checklists of security requirements rather than actual trench-level cracking time.

Back in the 1980s, the Department of Defense published a set of manuals that dealt with the evaluation of trusted systems. These books were known as the *Rainbow Series* because their covers were color coded. The Orange Book, entitled *DoD Trusted Computer System Evaluation Criteria* (TCSEC), defined four basic divisions for describing how secure an operating system was. The scale ranged from A to D, with division "A" offering the highest security (i.e. *verified protection*) and division "D" offering the least (i.e. *minimal protection*).

In the 1990s, for example, Microsoft's flagship platform, Windows NT, was ranked in the C division… but only when it wasn't connected to a network.[41] This really doesn't say much for a product that Microsoft was marketing to the public as an enterprise-class network operating system. All told, Windows NT lacked features as basic as a native firewall and support for remote terminal sessions.

The Rainbow Series has been replaced by an international framework known as the *Common Criterion*, which defines Evaluation Assurance Levels (EAL) as a way of gauging a platform's security. Assurance levels range from 0 to 7, with 0 offering almost no security (i.e. *functionally tested*) and 7 offering the most security (i.e. *formally verified*).

Microsoft Windows Server 2008 R2 has a Common Criterion rating of EAL4, which is typical for a commercial operating system. The following link provides the Common Criteria rating for over 100 certified platforms:

http://www.commoncriteriaportal.org/products_OS.html#OS.

Note that, perusing this list of products, there are operating systems that possess higher ratings, like Green Hills Software INTEGRITY-178B real-time operating system. The Green Hills platform has a rating of EAL 6. As a rule, consumers are unaware of these rankings.

The technical aspects of writing better code, however, may well be the easy part. Cyber-security also has aspects that are economic and political in nature. Genuine progress will require changing how vendors view software bugs, so that it makes financial sense for them to eliminate them before they end up in production. This will require altering the legal rules which define the market in which vendors operate. Specifically, we are referring to regulation.

Regulation

Regulation is necessary, particularly in a sector, like the banking sector, which exposes countries and people to a risk.

– Christine Lagarde, head of the IMF[42]

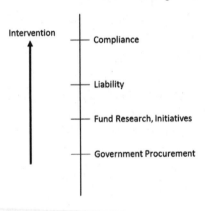

Figure 12-5

Government intervention comes in many forms (see Figure 12-5). Near the bottom of the spectrum are less intrusive measures like the government procurement approach, where, in theory, the federal government uses its clout as a purchaser to incite vendors to write better code. Dan Greer of In-Q-Tel has observed that this is pleasant fiction.[43] To an extent we would agree with him on this. Namely, state-sponsored subversion programs do not tend to incite vendors to focus on better security.

At the other end of the spectrum is the most commonly thought of, and the most intrusive, approach: compliance legislation, where the government would establish security baselines that vendors would need to satisfy in order to operate. The problem with compliance is that the devil is in the details. In the software industry this is particularly true. The effectiveness of compliance-based regulation depends heavily on the nature of its implementation, and Capitol Hill is rife with lobbyists and attorneys who specialize in adding fine print.

Bureaucrats would be faced with the challenges and risks of creating enduring standards for an industry where change is perennial, and pre-existing guidelines are conspicuously absent. That's not to say that it couldn't be done, it's just that it would be extremely resource intensive. In an environment driven by compliance guidelines the goal of developing secure software would take a back seat to the goal of achieving compliance, such that poorly composed guidelines would make matters worse. For vendors, however, there is an upside to this result. Namely, if an incident occurs as a result of bad software, a compliant vendor could point to security guidelines as the culprit (and rightfully so).

For these reasons, we favor liability over compliance.

Liability

Liability is less invasive than federally mandated compliance. Rather than tell companies how to do security right, you penalize them when they get it wrong. This provides greater flexibility because it leaves specific implementation details up to the vendors and puts the government in charge of enforcing the results.

There are different ways that vendors could be held accountable. For example, the government could fine them based strictly on the number of flaws and their severity (e.g. a software tax). Former NSA cryptographer David Rice states:

> Instead of saying all software must be secure, we tax insecurity and allow the market to determine the price it's willing to pay for vulnerability in software. Those who are the worst "emitters" of vulnerabilities end up paying the most, and it creates an economic incentive to manufacture more secure software.[44]

To encourage professionals like Charlie Miller, security researchers who identify and confirm security flaws could be compensated with a bounty that's derived from the fine. Furthermore, this reward would need to be significant enough to attract major-league talent.

Implementing a tax on software bugs would be fairly straightforward but not necessarily evenhanded, as some critical flaws cause a lot more damage than others. Hence, another approach would be to pass on the cost of recovering from incidents to the vendors. Poul-Henning Kamp, a former member of the FreeBSD core team, has fleshed out a skeletal version of this scheme:

Clause 1:

> Consult criminal code to see if any intentionally caused damage is already covered.

Clause 2:

> If you deliver software with complete and buildable source code and a license that allows disabling any functionality or code by the licensee, then your liability is limited to a refund.

Clause 3:

> In any other case, you are liable for whatever damage your software causes when used normally.[45]

It goes without saying that penalties will have to be significant enough to have the desired effect, and it's expected that vendors will seek to limit their exposure through insurance policies. The financial institutions that underwrite these policies will spell out requirements for coverage aimed at minimizing security risks so that their clients in the software industry are less likely to file a claim. These requirements will serve the same basic role as the federal compliance guidelines we saw earlier. The difference is that they'll be maintained by private sector organizations (i.e. the insurers) which will have a strong financial incentive to keep them current, relevant, and substantive.

Opponents will point out that the cost of insurance premiums will be passed along to customers, raising the cost of software. Experts like Bruce Schneier will counter that the public is already paying a pretty high premium for bad security in the form of cyber-crime and espionage:

> Users are already paying extra costs for insecure software: costs of third-party security products, costs of consultants and security services companies, direct and indirect costs of losses. But as long as one is going to pay anyway, it would be better to pay to fix the problem. Forcing the software vendor to pay to fix the problem and then passing those costs on to users means that the actual problem might get fixed.[46]

By placing risk on the shoulders of insurance companies legislators put them in a position where they can directly encourage software vendors to improve the quality of their products. Bad security translates into high premiums, and as David Rice has noted:

> When insecure software starts costing more, people will adjust their behavior.[47]

Catch-22

Government intervention might seem like an entirely plausible approach ... until we recall that the government is part of the problem. How can engineers expect to eliminate technical flaws and weak algorithms if the NSA, bolstered by a horde of private sector malware developers, runs a series of top-secret programs that depend upon, and dictate, the widespread proliferation of technical flaws and weak algorithms?

This reinforces the fact that cyber insecurity has technical, economic, and political aspects. In addressing the unintended flaws (which have technical and economic origins) society must also address the intentional flaws (which have political origins). The public cannot allow the government to try and swim in both directions. To achieve higher levels of cyber-security, the government's policies must change.

Let's look at the institutional scope of the problem. There are those who believe that most of our problems can be attributed to a single government agency, the NSA, which has run amok (i.e. the J. Edgar Hoover phenomenon). This perspective theorizes that General Keith Alexander, who has been portrayed as a cowboy of sorts,[48] is seen as being single-handedly responsible for pushing his organization into dubious territory with limited authorization from above. Mainstream outlets like *The New Yorker* have published pieces that promote this theory.[49]

Secretary of State John Kerry claimed:

> The president and I have learned of some things that have been happening in many ways on an automatic pilot, because the technology is there and the ability is there.[50]

History shows that the rogue agency narrative tends to be refuted. MIT Professor Noam Chomsky notes that intelligence agencies exist in a larger chain of command, such that the notion of a rogue agency actually serves an often unacknowledged institutional need:

> The C.I.A. is basically just an obedient branch of the White House. I mean sure, the C.I.A. has done things around the world – but as far as we know, it hasn't done anything on its own.
>
> There's very little evidence – in fact, I don't know of any – that the C.I.A. is some kind of rogue elephant, you know, off on its own doing things. What the record shows is that the C.I.A. is just an agency of the White House, which sometimes carries out operations for which the Executive branch wants what's called "plausible deniability"; in other words, if something goes wrong, we don't want it to look like we did, those guys in the C.I.A. did it, and we can throw some of them to the wolves if we need to.

The historical record corroborates Chomsky. Under the leadership of Representative Otis Pike, the House Permanent Select Committee on Intelligence (also known as the *Pike Committee*) investigated the illegal activities of the CIA and FBI during the mid-1970s. Parts of the Pike Committee's report were leaked to the *Village Voice* in 1978. On page 189 the Pike report states:

> All evidence in hand suggests that the CIA, far from being out of control has been utterly responsive to the instructions of the President and the Assistant to the President for National Security Affairs.[51]

This organizational view, that the CIA does what the executive branch tells it to, is supported by a Top Secret interview with David Cohen, the former Deputy Director for Operations for the CIA. In this interview, he noted:

> When you take an action on the edge and you don't think leadership will stand with you, you soon decide to stay far from the edge. The DO had many years in which they thought that the White House endorsed action, only to find out that the White House was not supportive in the end. CIA is as risk-taking as the policy environment will support. Just having case officers asked by senior officials, "why did you do this?" sends a message that risk-taking is not supported.[52]

Here's a recent example of this: recall the period leading up to the U.S. invasion of Iraq. When George W. Bush made it clear that he wanted evidence of Saddam's WMD program, George Tenet was Johnny on the spot with his intelligence "slam dunk."[53] Later on, after the various fabrications[54] that led the U.S. to war came to light, the CIA director dutifully fell on his sword.[55]

When the extent of NSA surveillance in places like Germany, France, and Spain became public knowledge, in the fall of 2013, there were intimations that the President was unaware of them.[56] But it didn't take long for DNI James Clapper and General Keith Alexander to publicly insist that the White House knew what was going on.[57]

Meanwhile, evidence shows that the Stuxnet worm was deployed at the behest of the White House and that it leveraged multiple software exploits.[58] In other words, the global campaign to "undermine network security and privacy" is congruent with both the Pentagon's known stance on offensive operations and the President's public statements. Removing General Alexander from his command is a cosmetic solution to a problem that requires sweeping policy changes.

Other Barriers to Change

Let's assume for a moment that somehow government policy could be changed to eliminate intentional security flaws. There's still the matter of all of the accidental flaws, the ones arising from substandard engineering and the associated economic underpinnings. In trying to redirect negative externalities using regulatory tools, i.e. measures which might impact corporate revenue, we encounter yet another political hurdle.

It's no secret that big software companies like Microsoft lobby extensively in Washington. The big vendors have ways to make their voices heard. Richard Clarke spells this out explicitly:

> Microsoft can buy a lot of spokesmen and lobbyists for a fraction of the cost of creating more secure systems. They are one of several dominant companies in the cyber industry for whom life is good right now and change may be bad.[59]

According to the Center for Responsive Politics, during the period starting in 1989 and ending in 2012, Microsoft invested $23 million in political donations (more than double what General Dynamics donated). This puts the company in the OpenSecrets. org top-30 list of all-time donors.

In his book on cyberwar, Clarke describes how Microsoft used its influence to fend off a move by the Pentagon in the late 1990s to migrate to Unix-based platforms, after becoming disillusioned with Microsoft's security problems:

> Microsoft went on the warpath against Linux to slow the adoption of it by government committees, including by Bill Gates. Nevertheless, because there were government agencies using Linux, I asked NSA to do an assessment of it. In a move that startled the open-source community, NSA joined that community by publicly offering fixes to the Linux operating system that would improve its security. Microsoft gave me the very clear impression that if the U.S. government promoted Linux, Microsoft would stop cooperating with the U.S. government. While that did not faze me, it may have had an effect on others. Microsoft's software is still being bought by most federal agencies, even though Linux is free.

Strength in Numbers

Shortly after he was elected, President Franklin D. Roosevelt met with a delegation of labor leaders proposing new programs and he told them:

I agree with you, I want to do it, now make me do it.[60]

This illustrates that political leaders set policy in favor of those organizations that have the capacity to reward or punish them. In line with Tom Ferguson's *Investment Theory of Politics*, these groups are mostly powerful corporate factions.[61]

Powerful forces are moving in directions that undermine cyber-security. The software industry is driven by the need to generate income, and any regulatory measure that threatens revenue streams will be condemned. In addition the defense sector views cyber subversion, as well as the offensive operations that it facilitates, as a growth industry. There are literally hundreds of billions of dollars in funding at stake.

Developing policies that directly tackle the problem of bugs (intentional and unintentional) from a political angle will mean running face-first into the combined clout of moneyed corporate interests. In light of the *Citizens United* decision, money translates directly into political power. *Rolling Stone's* Matt Taibbi describes how wealthy people, driven by their own relentless self-interest, use lobbyists to bend Washington DC to their will:

> They never stop. It's not a war of ideas, it's a war of resources. You march up the Hill with some crazy idea about overturning a bill prohibiting bailouts of companies that engage in risky derivative trades, you get knocked down, and you march up again, then you march up again, and again …
>
> With each successive attempt, you peel off a few more Committee members in the House, slowly but surely weakening resolve. And while you're attacking on the legislative front, you also file a series of lawsuits that tie up the process by targeting reforms in court, and then you also send armies of lobbyists to sit in the laps of regulators during the rule-making process, so that key new laws (like the Volcker rule, designed to separate risky trading from federally-insured depository banking) are either written in reams of industry-friendly language, or delayed altogether.
>
> No matter how bad your ideas are, and how unpopular they are (or, rather, would be, if anyone in the general public

understood them and/or cared enough about them to complain to their congressional reps), you can still score huge wins just by continually attacking and chipping away.[62]

Given the staggering success with which the moneyed elite have used this approach to gain control of Washington, the end result is difficult to ignore. Even a former President, Jimmy Carter, has recognized the suspension of democracy:

America does not at the moment have a functioning democracy.[63]

While corporate state capture is generally a fact of life in our political system, it doesn't mean that public opinion can universally be ignored. There is hope. If public opinion didn't matter, how would you explain the immense effort undertaken by the elite to manipulate it: countless think tanks, public relations firms, and corporate-funded news outlets?

This is society's trump card. Recent events show that sufficient public uproar can still effect change. Despite intense pressure from members of the Deep State (e.g. Saudi royalty, elite financial interests, arms manufacturers, neocon hawks and the American Israel Public Affairs Committee) the United States has opted for diplomacy in regard to dealing with Syria.[64]

The public needs to mobilize and show politicians they they're not going to tolerate policies that undermine cyber-security. On a broader scale, they need to show that they won't allow big money to *manage* our republic. As we've seen the larger problem enables the smaller one. Rest assured that when the public finally embarks on this necessary uprising, the forces of the Deep State will act to quell the disruption.[65]

Endnotes

1) Kim Zetter, "Everyone Has Been Hacked. Now What?," *Wired*, May 4, 2012, http://www.wired.com/threatlevel/2012/05/everyone-hacked/all/1.

2) Robert Dewar, "Wall Street and the Mismanagement of Software," *Dr. Dobbs*, August 08, 2012, http://www.drdobbs.com/architecture-and-design/wall-street-and-the-mismanagement-of-sof/240005196.

3) Oleg A. Bukharin, "The Cold War Atomic Intelligence Game, 1945-70," *Studies in Intelligence*: Volume 48, Number 2, 2004, https://www.cia.gov/library/center-for-the-study-of-intelligence/csi-publications/csi-studies/studies/vol48no2/article01.html.

4) Evgeny Morozov, "Cyber-Scare: The exaggerated fears over digital warfare," *Boston Review*, July/August 2009, http://bostonreview.net/BR34.4/morozov.php.

5) Brad Arkin, "Adobe Secure Software Engineering Team (ASSET) Blog," *Adobe*, October,2, 2013, http://blogs.adobe.com/asset/2013/10/illegal-access-to-adobe-source-code.html.

6) Brian Krebs, "Adobe To Announce Source Code, Customer Data Breach," *Krebs on Security*, October 3, 2013, http://krebsonsecurity.com/2013/10/adobe-to-announce-source-code-customer-data-breach/.

7) Bruce Schneier, "Want to Evade NSA Spying? Don't Connect to the Internet," *Wired*, October 7, 2013, http://www.wired.com/opinion/2013/10/149481/.

8) Elinor Mills, "How one company stays safe with two networks," *CNET*, March 30, 2010, http://news.cnet.com/8301-27080_3-20001391-245.html.

9) CLOSE ACCESS SIGADS, September 10, 2010, https://s3.amazonaws.com/s3.documentcloud.org/documents/807030/ambassade.pdf.

10) Dan Goodin, "Meet "badBIOS," the mysterious Mac and PC malware that jumps airgaps," *Ars Technica*, October 31, 2013, http://arstechnica.com/security/2013/10/meet-badbios-the-mysterious-mac-and-pc-malware-that-jumps-airgaps/.

11) Byron Acohido, "Online banking warning surprises some experts," *USA Today*, January 4, 2010, http://content.usatoday.com/communities/technologylive/post/2010/01/online-banking-precaution-for-small-and-mid-sized-businesses-draws-attention-/1.

12) Brian Krebs, "Banking on a Live CD," *Krebs on Security*, July 12, 2012, http://krebsonsecurity.com/2012/07/banking-on-a-live-cd/.

13) Lightweight Portable Security, http://www.spi.dod.mil/lipose.htm.

14) Barth, A., Jackson, C., Reis, C., and Google Chrome Team. 2008. *The Security Architecture of the Chromium Browser*, http://crypto.stanford.edu/websec/chromium/chromium-security-architecture.pdf.

15) Joana Rutkowska and Rafal Wojtczuk, *Qubes OS Architecture*, Invisible Things Lab, January 2010, http://qubes-os.org/files/doc/arch-spec-0.3.pdf.

16) Piotr Bania, *Securing The Kernel via Static Binary Rewriting and Program Shepherding*, 2011, http://www.piotrbania.com/all/articles/pbania-securing-the-kernel2011.pdf.

17) Don Reisinger, "Chrome hacker wins $60,000 for finding 'full' exploit," *CNET*, March 8, 2012, http://news.cnet.com/8301-1009_3-57393337-83/chrome-hacker-wins-$60000-for-finding-full-exploit/?tag=txt;title.

18) Dan Goodin, "Google Chrome exploit fetches "Pinkie Pie" $60,000 hacking prize," *ArsTechnica*, October 10, 2012, http://arstechnica.com/security/2012/10/google-chrome-exploit-fetches-pinkie-pie-60000-hacking-prize/.

19) High-Assurance Cyber Military Systems (HACMS), DARPA-BAA-12-21, February 23, 2012, http://cryptome.org/2012/03/darpa-hacms.pdf.

20) Lars-Henrik Eriksson, "Industrial use of formal methods," Uppsala University, February 4, 2013, https://www.it.uu.se/edu/course/homepage/pvt/vt10/OH-bilder%20formella%20spec.pdf.

21) The Astrée Static Analyzer, http://www.astree.ens.fr/.

22) Christoph Baumann, Bernhard Beckert, Holger Blasum, and Thorsten Bormer, Ingredients of Operating System Correctness, Lessons Learned in the Formal Verification of PikeOS, http://www-wjp.cs.uni-saarland.de/publikationen/Ba10EW.pdf.

23) Christoph Baumann, Bernhard Beckert, Holger Blasum, and Thorsten Bormer, *Better avionics software reliability by code verification*, In Proceedings, embedded world Conference, Nuremberg, Germany, 2009, http://www-wjp.cs.uni-saarland.de/publikationen/Ba09EW.pdf.

24) Tom Espiner, "Researchers Prove Kernel is Secure," *CNET*, August 15, 2009, http://news.cnet.com/8301-1009_3-10310255-83.html.

25) Gerwin Klein, Kevin Elphinstone, Gernot Heiser, June Andronick, David Cock, Philip Derrin, Dhammika Elkaduwe, Kai Engelhardt, Rafal Kolanski, Michael Norrish, Thomas Sewell, Harvey Tuch and Simon Winwood.

seL4: Formal verification of an OS kernel, Proceedings of the 22nd ACM Symposium on Operating Systems Principles, Big Sky, MT, USA, October, 2009.

26) "Code Breakthrough Delivers Safer Computing," *Communications of the ACM TechNews*, September 30, 2009, http://cacm.acm.org/news/43696-code-breakthrough-delivers-safer-computing/fulltext.

27) Joanna Rutkowska, "Introducing Qubes 1.0!," *Invisible Things Lab*, September 03, 2012, http://theinvisiblethings.blogspot.com/2012/09/introducing-qubes-10.html.

28) http://why3.lri.fr/#documentation.

29) Eugene Kaspersky, "Kaspersky Lab Developing Its Own Operating System? We Confirm the Rumors, and End the Speculation!," *Nota Bene*, October 16, 2012, http://eugene.kaspersky.com/2012/10/16/kl-developing-its-own-operating-system-we-confirm-the-rumors-and-end-the-speculation/.

30) "Securing Critical Information Infrastructure: Trusted Computing Base," *SecureList*, October 16, 2012, http://www.securelist.com/en/analysis/204792248/Securing_Critical_Information_Infrastructure_Trusted_Computing_Base.

31) John Young, "Snowden Induced Mea Culpas," *Cryptome*, August 24, 2013, http://cryptome.org/2013/08/snowden-mea-culpas.htm.

32) Ken Thompson, "Reflections on Trusting Trust," *Communication of the ACM*, Vol. 27, No. 8, August 1984, pp. 761-763, http://cm.bell-labs.com/who/ken/trust.html.

33) Lily Hay Newman, "Can You Trust NIST?," *IEEE Spectrum*, October 9, 2013, http://spectrum.ieee.org/telecom/security/can-you-trust-nist/.

34) Richard Stallman, "Why Free Software Is More Important Now Than Ever Before," *Wired*, September 28, 2013, http://www.wired.com/opinion/2013/09/why-free-software-is-more-important-now-than-ever-before/.

35) John Markoff, "Old Trick Threatens the Newest Weapons," *New York Times*, October 26, 2009, http://www.nytimes.com/2009/10/27/science/27trojan.html.

36) Nicholas Eberstadt, "The Dying Bear: Russia's Demographic Disaster," *Foreign Affairs*, November/December 2011, http://www.foreignaffairs.com/articles/136511/nicholas-eberstadt/the-dying-bear.

37) Grace Wong, "Russia's Bleak Picture of Health," *CNN*, May 19, 2009, http://edition.cnn.com/2009/HEALTH/05/19/russia.health/index.html.

38) Peter Singer and Noah Shachtman, "The Wrong War: The Insistence on Applying Cold War Metaphors to Cybersecurity Is Misplaced and Counterproductive," *Brookings Institute*, August 28, 2011, http://www.brookings.edu/articles/2011/0815_cybersecurity_singer_shachtman.aspx.

39) Brad Friedman, "Diebold voting machines can be hacked by remote control," *Salon*, September 27, 2011, http://www.salon.com/2011/09/27/votinghack/.

40) Underwriters Laboratories (UL), *Ten things you did not know about UL's safe testing*, http://ul.com/global/eng/pages/corporate/newsroom/storyideas/urbansafetymyths/safes/.

41) Microsoft Developer Network, *Windows NT Security Systems*, 1998, http://msdn.microsoft.com/en-us/library/ms953175.aspx.

42) "Christine Lagarde: Facing down worldwide recession," *60 Minutes*, November 20, 2011, http://www.cbsnews.com/8301-18560_162-57326856/christine-lagarde-facing-down-worldwide-recession/?tag=contentMain;cbsCarousel.

43) Dan Greer, "Cybersecurity and National Policy," *Harvard Law School National Security Journal*, January 10, 2011, http://harvardnsj.org/2011/01/cybersecurity-and-national-policy/.

44) Andy Greenberg, "A Tax On Buggy Software," *Forbes*, June 26, 2008, http://www.forbes.com/2008/06/26/rice-cyber-security-tech-security-cx_ag_0626rice.html.

45) Poul-Henning Kamp, "The Software Industry IS the Problem," *ACM Queue*, September 8, 2011, http://queue.acm.org/detail.cfm?id=2030258.

46) Bruce Schneier, "Information Security and Externalities," *Schneier on Security*, January 18, 2007, http://www.schneier.com/blog/archives/2007/01/information_sec_1.html.

47) Andy Greenberg, "A Tax On Buggy Software," *Forbes*, June 26, 2008, http://www.forbes.com/2008/06/26/rice-cyber-security-tech-security-cx_ag_0626rice.html.

48) Shane Harris, "The Cowboy of the NSA," *Foreign Policy*, September 9, 2013, http://www.foreignpolicy.com/articles/2013/09/08/the_cowboy_of_the_nsa_keith_alexander.

49) Hendrik Hertzberg, "Obama's Game of Telephone," *New Yorker*, November 1, 2013, http://www.newyorker.com/online/blogs/comment/2013/11/how-much-did-president-obama-know-about-the-nsa-eavesdropping-on-angela-merkel.html.

50) Dan Roberts and Spencer Ackerman in Washington and Paul Lewis, "US surveillance has gone too far, John Kerry admits," *Guardian*, November 1, 2013, http://www.theguardian.com/world/2013/oct/31/john-kerry-some-surveillance-gone-too-far/print.

51) Philip Agee and Louis Wolf , *Dirty Work: The CIA in Western Europe*, 1978, pp. 17-28, http://cryptome.org/dirty-work/cia-myths.htm.

52) Top Secret Interview with David Cohen, Prepared by Gordon Lederman, June 21, 2004, http://cryptome.org/nara/cia/cia-04-0621.pdf.

53) PBS Frontline, *The Dark Side*, June 20, 2006, http://www.pbs.org/wgbh/pages/frontline/darkside/themes/tenet.html.

54) Martin Chulov and Helen Pidd, "Defector admits to WMD lies that triggered Iraq war," *Guardian*, February 15, 2011, http://www.theguardian.com/world/2011/feb/15/defector-admits-wmd-lies-iraq-war/print.

55) William Branigin, "CIA Director Tenet Resigns," *Washington Post*, June 3, 2013, http://www.washingtonpost.com/wp-dyn/articles/A12296-2004Jun3.html.

56) Siobhan Gorman and Adam Entous, "Obama Unaware as U.S. Spied on World Leaders: Officials," *Wall Street Journal*, October 28, 2013.

57) Mark Landler And Michael S. Schmidt, "Spying Known at Top Levels, Officials Say," *New York Times*, October 30, 2013, http://www.nytimes.com/2013/10/30/world/officials-say-white-house-knew-of-spying.html.

58) David Sanger, "Obama Order Sped Up Wave of Cyberattacks Against Iran," *New York Times*, June 1, 2012, http://www.nytimes.com/2012/06/01/world/middleeast/obama-ordered-wave-of-cyberattacks-against-iran.html.

59) Richard A. Clarke, *Cyber War: The Next Threat to National Security and What to Do About It* Ecco, 2010, ISBN-13: 978-0061962233, page 143.

60) John Nichols, "How to Push Obama," *Progressive*, January 2009, http://www.progressive.org/mag/nichols0109.html.

61) "How Money Rules Washington," *Moyers and Company*, May 17, 2013, http://billmoyers.com/wp-content/themes/billmoyers/transcript-print.php?post=31390.

62) Matt Taibbi, "Deja Vu on the Hill: Wall Street Lobbyists Roll Back Finance Reform, Again," *Rolling Stone*, May 21, 2013, http://www.rollingstone.com/politics/blogs/taibblog/deja-vu-on-the-hill-wall-street-lobbyists-roll-back-finance-reform-again-20130521.

63) Alberto Riva, "Jimmy Carter: US "has no functioning democracy,"" *Salon*, July 18, 2013, http://www.salon.com/2013/07/18/jimmy_carter_us_has_no_functioning_democracy_partner/.

64) Matt Stoller, "The radical constitutional change everyone missed," *Salon*, September 19, 2013, http://www.salon.com/2013/09/19/the_radical_constitutional_change_everyone_missed/.

65) Leonard Downie and Sara Rafsky, "The Obama Administration and the Press, Leak investigations and surveillance in post-9/11 America," *Committee to Protect Journalists*, October 10, 2013, http://cpj.org/reports/2013/10/obama-and-the-press-us-leaks-surveillance-post-911.php.

Epilogue

It is part of the general pattern of misguided policy that our country is now geared to an arms economy which was bred in an artificially induced psychosis of war hysteria and nurtured upon an incessant propaganda of fear.

– General Douglas MacArthur, 1951[1]

The "Pentagon system" – diverting public finance into hi-tech industries and a state-guaranteed market – largely through arms production. It is essentially public subsidy for private profit – and they call it "free enterprise." That can only be done by inciting fear in the minds of the public.

– Noam Chomsky[2]

An institution takes a situation and tries to extract value from fear, and this is what is called securitization: transform a situation into a threat to security, and later propose that the institution can save you from the threat. Okay. Securitization is what the Pentagon does every day.

– Julian Assange[3]

He [General Keith Alexander] is the only man in the land that can promote a problem by virtue of his intelligence hat and then promote a solution by virtue of his military hat.

– Former Pentagon Official[4]

Over the past few years a chorus of legislators, former government officials, and think-tank fellows has wielded cyber doomsday metaphors in the arena of public debate. We've witnessed several examples: *Electronic Pearl Harbor, Cyber-Katrina, Cyber 9/11,* etc. While some of these people go so far as to declare that a cyberwar has already broken out, nearly all of them warn that if the United States fails to implement the measures that they endorse, civilization will face a digitally inflicted Armageddon. The resulting perception of risk has been used to justify policy decisions at the federal level in addition to the development of offensive cyber capabilities.

Figure E-1

The Hazards of a Misdiagnosis

But is this view of reality correct? Does it provide us with an accurate diagnosis of what's transpiring? Is there really a cyberwar in progress? Is a Cyber-Armageddon truly imminent? And even more importantly, are the prescribed courses of treatment being put forth appropriate? We've argued that the cyberwar pundits are *wrong on all counts*: that their diagnosis is incorrect and their proposed solutions are equally flawed.

To this end we presented accepted definitions of war, terrorism, espionage, and crime. This classification scheme allowed me to survey reported cyber incidents and place them into appropriate categories. The result of this cataloging process speaks very loudly. Crime and espionage are pervasive on the Internet. Genuine incidents of war, however, are practically nonexistent. This underscores the fact that the cyberwar dogma conflates threats in a manner that blurs the lines between espionage, crime, and war so that events can be rendered to fit a particular picture of reality.

By framing society's cyber-insecurity in terms of a war, marketing consultants are tacitly guiding the public towards military solutions. In the mind's eye of these corporate executives, every emerging global phenomenon is a nail to be hit with the hammer of the defense industry. As Assange noted, this is *securitization* is practice.

Securitization In-Depth

The core mechanism behind securitization can be seen as an instance of the "Hegelian Dialectic." Hegel's dialectic is a philosophical model, developed over a century ago by German philosopher Georg Wilhelm Friedrich Hegel. It can be used to describe how history evolves. According to Hegel's framework, history occurs through conflict between opposing forces.

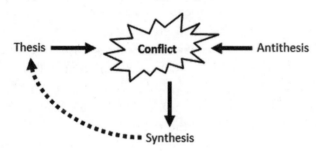

Figure E-2

The dialectic model entails three stages of development: thesis, antithesis, and synthesis (see Figure E-2). The emergence of an initial event, the *thesis,* incites an opposing response known as the *antithesis.* The thesis and antithesis then duke it out to produce a *synthesis* which inevitably gives rise to a new thesis.

Why is this abstraction relevant? Hegel's dialectic illustrates that if you can control the nature of the conflict between the thesis and antithesis then you can manage the nature of the synthesis. Or, put crudely, nothing beats a fixed fight.

This very approach was leveraged by Russian security services in the early 1920s to ferret out monarchists and anti-Bolsheviks. The

Red spymasters ran a campaign called "Operation Trust," where they silently commandeered a mock opposition group during the Russian Civil War. The movement was built upon an existing structure of genuine anti-Bolsheviks and royalist sleepers who were left behind. Russian spies found that the most effective way to control the opposition is to organize it yourself.[5]

Hegel's dialectic can be used to understand the logic behind the "strategy of tension" applied by Operation Gladio, a NATO "stay-behind operation" in Europe that was established in the final days of World War II. Gladio agents launched a series of bloody false-flag attacks (the thesis) aimed at innocent civilians which were staged in such a way that they appeared to be the work of communists. The intention was that the carnage would lead to public outcry (the antithesis) which would in turn provide a pretext to increase state power and isolate the political left (the synthesis).[6]

Another documented example can be found in 1962, when the U.S. Joint Chiefs of Staff, the top leadership of the Department of Defense, authorized a series covert programs known as "Operation Northwoods."[7] The plan, as it was drafted, called for the CIA to execute acts of terrorism (the thesis) against innocent civilians, where attackers would be disguised as Cuban agents in an effort to manufacture public uproar (the antithesis) that would lend support for an invasion of Cuba (the synthesis).

Yet another, more recent, example of Hegel's dialectic appeared in the *Los Angeles Times* in October 2002. An article by William Arkin described a proposal by the Pentagon to create an organization called the *Proactive, Preemptive Operations Group*, (P2OG).[8] The proposal stated that P2OG would provoke terrorists and states possessing weapons of mass destruction into launching attacks on innocent people (the thesis), who would clamor for security (the antithesis), providing the pretext for a U.S. military response (the synthesis).

The strategy of tension may very well be at play in Greece as the country buckles under austerity measures. Five senior police officials in Greece were moved to other posts in the wake of an inquiry that looked into connections between the police and the ultra-right Golden Dawn political party.[9] There are also allegations under investigation that sympathetic elements with the Greek armed forces have been training Golden Dawn hit squads.[10] According to Greek investigative journalist Dimitris Psarras:

> The Golden Dawn's strategy today is exactly that [strategy of tension]... They want to force the other side's hand into committing similar violent acts, just like during the strategy of tension in Italy in the '70s.

Applied to the practice of securitization, officials don't explicitly create a threat. Instead they frame events in a manner that lends itself to the public's perception of a threat (thesis) and gives rise to an emotional response on behalf of the public (antithesis), thus enticing them towards a preconceived, and lucrative, solution (synthesis) that they might not otherwise accept (see Figure E-3).

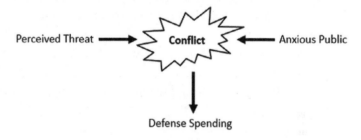

Figure E-3

As noted in one of this chapter's opening quotes, there is a small group of influential bureaucrats who have the ability to both *create the appearance of a threat* and simultaneously *propose solutions*.

Threat Inflation

> *Anyone who thinks cyberwar is a significant problem compared to what afflicts a very visible portion of American lives daily is a fool worth only your contempt.*

> – George Smith[11]

The absence of historical data makes it nearly impossible to analytically calculate the probability of a genuine Cyber-Armageddon. This means that the public is left with expert opinion, and even then the experts don't agree. For example, at a 2010 security conference held in Estonia, Charlie Miller claimed:

> It would take two years and cost less than 50 million dollars a year to prepare a cyberattack that could paralyze the United States.[12]

Other acknowledged experts, like Howard Schmidt, have qualms about the ease of a crippling attack:

> Catastrophic failure is still the part that I don't believe is likely, and anybody who intends to try to do that is probably going to meet more resistance than they're prepared for.[13]

Nobody, and we mean nobody, truly knows what the exact likelihood of Cyber-Armageddon is. Yet despite the noticeable scarcity of hard numbers the threat is conveyed by cyberwar pundits as being "imminent." As if it could be predicted with *absolute certainty*. To compound matters, cyberwar hyperbole focuses almost entirely on how terrible the digital apocalypse will be when it happens.

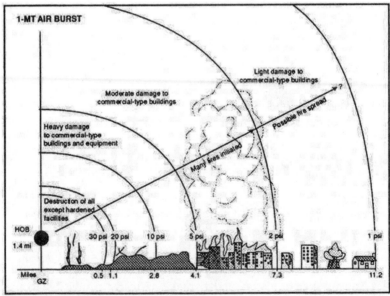

Figure E-4

The core message of cyberwar isn't designed to appeal to reason. It's disseminated in a manner that appeals to emotion.

As during the run-up to the invasion of Iraq, the technique of *Threat Inflation* is being used to alter the public's perception of risk. The end result of this emotional coercion is a pronounced sense of anxiety, a crisis mentality which makes people so apprehensive that they'll pay any price to feel safe again. And hence they're receptive to preconceived solutions that benefit specific sectors of our economy.

Just because there are several types of insurance doesn't mean consumers should go out and buy all of them. *Prudent buyers won't pay any price to be safe*, they purchase coverage shrewdly and only after a careful evaluation their position. The same mindset is required when considering cyber-security.

By blindly accepting predictions of the apocalypse, the public risks spending resources and yielding civil liberties to protect itself at a very high cost, and relinquishing the opportunity to invest those resources on measures that will do a much better job at a potentially lower cost without giving up their rights.

Nigel Inkster, the former MI6 agent, summarizes this idea concisely:

> We need to be wary of rebuilding our world to deal with just one problem, one which might not be by any means the most serious we face.[14]

And it's not like we don't have serious problems to contend with, one of which was identified by President Franklin D. Roosevelt on April 29, 1938:

> The liberty of a democracy is not safe if the people tolerate the growth of private power to a point where it becomes stronger than their democratic State itself. That, in its essence, is fascism – ownership of government by an individual, by a group or by any other controlling private power.[15]

Ever widening inequality[16] observed by mainstream economists like Thomas Piketty and Emmanuel Saez indicates the emergence of what Princeton professor Sheldon Wolin calls *inverted totalitarianism*.[17] This is what happens when corporate factions, driven by their own self-interest, achieve state capture and re-shape the ground rules by which society operates for their own benefit.[18]

The Folly of Deterrence

While the diagnosis of cyberwar is incorrect, the same holds true for the remedies that cyberwar proponents have recommended. In terms of solutions, there are those who would have our leaders look to the Cold War for direction. Specifically, they recommend that we utilize the strategy of deterrence to discourage cyber-attacks with the threat of massive retaliation. This approach would necessitate heavy investment in offensive technology, a financial shot in the arm for U.S. defense contractors: a business sector which is the largest in the world and accounts for more than half of the world's total arms sales.

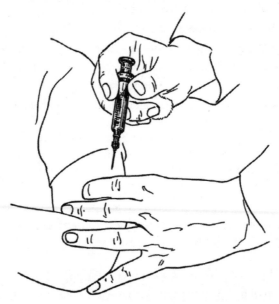

Figure E-5

In Search of Enemies

But what real use would all of this offensive weaponry be if our military and security services can't determine who attacked them? Can officials actually identify the offenders behind cyber-attacks?

Traditionally the Chinese Government has been cast as the culprit of choice without recognizing that a broad plurality of different operators inhabit China's lawless networks. Organized crime, foreign intelligence officers, rogue bureaucrats, and corporate spies all ply their trade freely thanks to rampant corruption: corruption which blossoms on behalf of poorly implemented economic reforms and hobbled bureaucratic oversight. A nation like China, which faces severe internal problems, cannot be expected to eradicate bullet-proof server hosting.

Furthermore, is it even realistic to assume that the threat from the Chinese government is existential? China is a major trading partner of the United States and it owns a substantial amount of U.S. foreign debt. What, pray tell, would China stand to gain by destroying the United States infrastructure?

We find it ironic that while the Pentagon conjures up apocalyptic daydreams for local consumption, just around the corner the bureaucrats in the State Department are desperately trying to get China to purchase high-end aircraft manufactured by U.S. defense contractors. Given the saber rattling that goes on in both nations, it might be possible to conclude that the Chinese and United States military are keeping each other in business.

American Hypocrisy

Nobody hacks as prolifically and aggressively as the two countries who most vocally warn of the dangers of hacking.

– Glenn Greenwald[19]

The alleged Chinese threat and the ensuing strategy of deterrence is a pretext. While our military officials erupt in fits of righteous indignation over alleged intrusions by China, the United States is actively developing its own malicious software payloads (Stuxnet, DuQu, Flame, Gauss, etc.) and furtively infiltrating thousands of networks all over the world. As we saw in Chapter Six, these operations involve a substantial amount of economic espionage.

In a sentence, it's hypocrisy in its purest form.

New York Times columnist Joe Nocera sums up the state of affairs:

> If you are going to lecture the world about right and wrong
> – and if you're trying to stop bad behavior – perhaps you
> shouldn't be engaging in a version of that behavior yourself.[20]

There was uproar when the PLA allegedly spied on media outlets, and yet the U.S. government seems to have no qualms about covertly monitoring the American press.

Officials have warned stridently of the Chinese putting back doors into their technology while U.S. intelligence services have long-standing and pervasive programs to do just that.

Most security professionals erroneously concluded that the government lost the crypto war when the Clipper Chip's key escrow plan was scrapped during the Clinton years. Unfortunately the NSA simply ducked under the radar, subverting literally everything they could get their hands on.

Generals claim that they'll focus on retaliatory responses, but the U.S. government has been involved in conspicuous first use on countless occasions.

This consistent double standard highlights the fact that while there are an untold number of actors on the global stage conducting cyber-attacks, the United States is investing hundreds of billions of dollars to assume the role of the Internet's principal aggressor.

Figure E-6

James Bamford, an investigative journalist who has traced the evolution of the NSA for three decades, echoes this notion:

> The NSA has been coming out with all these charges against
> China going after our secrets, our information, and so forth.

416

It's caused the Congress to give enormous amounts of money to NSA, this money for defensive use against the Chinese and so forth. What never comes out is the U.S. offensive capability against the rest of the world. The U.S. – there's nobody that can even compare to the U.S. We've got an enormous Cyber Command. They're expanding NSA's secret city by a third to accommodate 14 new buildings, 10 parking garages, a new enormous supercomputer center – all this for this new, very secret Cyber Command. And it's dedicated largely to offensive, to creating wars, not preventing wars.[21]

Our leaders tend to paint the United States as being an innocent victim. However, more often than not *the United States is a perpetrator*. As the documents leaked by Ed Snowden confirmed, the focus of CYBERCOM isn't on deterring attacks, it's about launching them. In many instances these attacks are launched to acquire a strategic economic advantage and impose U.S. dominion abroad.

In the end, it's probably safe to assume that everyone is spying on everyone else. They always have and probably always will. Though at the same time, it's also important to recognize that not all espionage programs are the same, and that scale matters. Given the amount of tax money our leaders throw at it, the United States, with its army of private sector contractors, steals secrets on a level both domestically and internationally that is unsurpassed. When it comes to breaking into networks and collecting sensitive information the United States is admittedly in a class all by itself. Journalist Glenn Greenwald elaborates on the repercussions of this fact:

That the U.S. government – in complete secrecy – is constructing a ubiquitous spying apparatus aimed not only at its own citizens, but all of the world's citizens, has profound consequences. It erodes, if not eliminates, the ability to use the Internet with any remnant of privacy or personal security. It vests the U.S. government with boundless power over those to whom it has no accountability. It permits allies of the U.S. – including aggressively oppressive ones – to benefit from indiscriminate spying on their citizens' communications. It radically alters the balance of power between the U.S. and ordinary citizens of the world. And it sends an unmistakable signal to the world that while the U.S. very minimally values the privacy rights of Americans, it assigns zero value to the privacy of everyone else on the planet.[22]

This double standard has serious consequences. It illustrates that U.S. leaders are unwilling to adhere to the values and principles that they claim to represent. Whistleblowers have exposed our political elite as untrustworthy. Having lost its moral authority in this domain, the United States cannot hope to name and shame cyber offenders. The ethereal bindings of soft power have dissolved, leaving only a dangerous example that other nations can follow.

Subverting Attribution

As things stand now there are a lot of players on the field. A worldwide market for sophisticated mass interception tools and weaponized malware reflects this state of affairs. To make matters even more confusing, hundreds of independent operators have rushed out on to the scene.

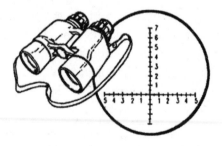

Figure E-7

As the chapter on espionage demonstrates, attribution is often useless when facing an organized attacker, the kind of attacker capable of prolonged multi-stage operations. We don't see this changing any time soon. Why? Because governments like *the United States, driven by the desire to execute covert operations, have ensured that this is the case* by developing, and investing in, anti-forensic tools that subvert the process of attribution.

Given that tools for "operational non-attribution" are available to anyone with the cash to buy them, or the skill build them, coupled with the sheer number of actors on the global stage, it would be unwise to conclude that attribution can be achieved with any degree of accuracy – *the wilderness of mirrors*.

In fact, history has shown that there's a very real danger that investigators will identify the culprit of an attack incorrectly. This in turn highlights the futility of deterrence and arms-control treaties.

Turning to Big Brother

Unable to educate millions of children adequately, unable to provide health care for millions of adults, with infrastructure crumbling in many parts of the country and a moribund economy, we nonetheless spend immense sums on an ever-growing spying industry ...

– Letter to the Editor, *New York Times*[23]

Some people believe that if they simply capture and analyze enough data, they can overcome the problems of cyber-security. They literally avow that "we need an invasive NSA."[24] This is the core stance of officials like General Keith Alexander, who believes that the answer to terrorism and cyber-attacks (which he views as the greatest threats facing the United States) is expanded computer monitoring.[25]

This book shows in graphic detail that he's wrong on all counts. The doctrine of mass interception will only serve to push society towards that envisioned by George Orwell in his book *1984*, where no one except the Thought Police has any freedom.

Figure E-8

A *surveillance state* is one where rulers are in a position to compile various lists[26] of people that they view as political threats.[27] In historic terms, society has never witnessed anything as intrusive or ubiquitous.

The surveillance state is the leading edge of something much worse. Given the corrupting nature of power, the next evolutionary step in this progression may be a *police state*. This is where things go from bad to worse. As in China during Mao's Cultural Revolution, the authorities take their compiled lists, round up everyone on them en masse, and conduct re-education, brainwashing,[28] torture, genocide, etc.

We don't live in a police state, yet. Otherwise this book would not have been published. But according to whistleblowers from the NSA, the United States is already well on its way. The public has cheerfully embraced mobile devices, which may as well be mobile telescreens if corporate data hoarding is any indication.[29] This trend is being accelerated though widespread use of social media, giving security services another way to monitor the public by trawling the web. People are literally *opting into surveillance* when they should be doing just the opposite.

> [There is] no more effective protest than to refuse to validate the rigged voting machine. Millions, billions of disappearing users could scare the shit out of investors and, believe it or not, governments exploiting the Internet to propagandize sanctimony of national security secrets.[30]

Leaders try to reassure us: never mind the warrantless wiretaps, the historically unprecedented explosion of corporate data silos, national security letters, or the appalling fixation on secrecy (secret courts, secret laws, secret interpretations of public laws, etc.), a trend which threatens our Republic on a fundamental level.

Wolfgang Schmidt, a former lieutenant colonel of the East German Stasi, made the following remark regarding the mass interception systems being leveraged by U.S. intelligence:

> You know, for us, this would have been a dream come true…. So much information, on so many people.[31]

Decision makers have put into place the mechanisms needed to make us all into Winston Smiths, with not much more than flimsy policies, many of them secret, to prevent abuse. Individual liberty in the United States is disintegrating right before our eyes. It does so primarily in the name of counterterrorism.

Inside our borders, the NSA's panopticon is archiving mountains of data on the empire's self-confessed *adversaries*: the public. Outside our borders, mass interception is a tool, in strategic terms, primarily for influencing foreign political systems abroad and shoring up the economic primacy of the elites.

To further the reach of Big Brother, the public is being presented with a sales pitch based entirely on a false dichotomy:

> Hand over privacy or you can't have security.

This is a notion, by the way, that Founding Father Benjamin Franklin saw as abhorrent:

> They who can give up essential liberty to obtain a little temporary safety, deserve neither liberty nor safety.

People don't have to yield privacy to gain security. It's possible to have both simultaneously. The United States doesn't need to revert to China's Chongqing model to protect national security. Society doesn't benefit from the authoritarian, top-down, approach to security. Society needs the opposite methodology, where individual users are empowered and have access to strong technology, so that they don't have to sacrifice liberty or security.

Root Causes of Cyber-Insecurity

This becomes clear when digging down to the roots of cyber-insecurity. What allows cyber-attacks to succeed? While it's true that users make poor decisions and misconfigure their computers, placing responsibility solely on their shoulders becomes a counterproductive exercise in *blaming the victim*. Hard data supports the conclusion that users are being put at significant risk by technical defects and systemic weaknesses that they can't do anything about. This is why attacks have been successful even in purportedly high-security environments.

A network populated by hyper-vigilant users with meticulously configured computers will still be breached by attackers who are in the know. Put up all the barriers and sensors that you want, a seasoned attacker will leverage defective technology (e.g. zero-day exploits, intentional design flaws, concealed back doors, hobbled cryptography) to walk right through them. Even anti-virus vendors have openly acknowledged that they're completely outgunned, such that the false sense of security that they peddle is akin to snake oil.

The hi-tech industry is in the midst of a quality control depression, which is in many ways self-inflicted, and the current nods towards assurance have done little to stem the flood of bugs. The current top-down approach, where a small subset of targets judged worthy of protection is endowed with relatively higher levels of security, isn't making things better. It's making things worse.

Cyber-Security for the 1%

I'm a big believer that – the best defense is an offense.

– Stewart Baker, Former NSA General Counsel[32]

In the end reliable cyber-security is an illusion for the average user. Hi-tech vendors knowingly engage in sub-optimal engineering practices on behalf of the bottom line. Many of these same vendors also collaborate with U.S. intelligence services to subvert the products that they sell. The fruit of this clandestine public-private alliance enables global dragnet surveillance, targeted espionage by Advanced Persistent Threats, covert acts of sabotage, and ensures a steady flow of cash to the malware-industrial complex. In other words, bad security isn't accidental.

This subversion runs deep: deliberate architectural flaws, carefully disguised back doors, and weakened technical standards. All of these tactics undermine our collective security. It's as if the NSA went around and weakened the locks on every front door in the world.

Bruce Schneier comments:

> This is much worse than what we're accusing China of doing to us. We're pursuing policies that are both expensive and destabilizing and aren't making the Internet any safer.[33]

But then again insecurity is what enables Big Brother to "protect" us. Poorly secured networks and easily penetrated systems facilitate spying. Recall how journalists at the *Guardian* observed this when they waded through secret documents leaked by Ed Snowden:

> Classified briefings between the agencies celebrate their success at "defeating network security and privacy ..."[34]

To make matters worse, this state-sanctioned campaign creates holes that can be leveraged by anyone who knows how to use them, crooks as well as spies. Once a trap door is discovered, it doesn't care who's using it.

Even if the U.S. government could be convinced to end its covert hi-tech subversion, there are still significant negative repercussions from assuming an offensive stance. Offense requires a steady stream of bugs, and this kind of demand is what's spurring a flourishing market for zero-day exploits. The black market for exploits undermines the ability of vendors to patch unintended bugs, as there are financial incentives for the bugs to remain secret. There's an awful lot of money in selling a freshly unearthed exploit to the wrong people. High-minded bug bounties can't even come close.

These factors work in concert to bestow the privilege of higher-security to a select few: the people with access to secrets, the people who know about the trap doors. *Intelligence officers and thieves win, everyone else loses.*

This is security for the 1%, and it's a recipe for disaster.

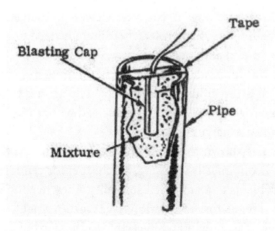

Figure E-9

Instead what's needed is an approach that starts at a grass roots level, one that focuses on building resilient high-security software and makes it openly available to everyone. This is security for the 99%.

Cyber-Security for the 99%

Taking a good hard look at cyber insecurity, there are specific technical, economic, and political forces at work that undermine cyber-security. Furthermore genuine progress on technical and economic fronts will be unlikely until the excruciating political issues have been addressed.

On a technical level, there should be a renewed emphasis on prevention. Sure, detection and response are valuable. It's just that they fail to strike at the root. If software engineers fail to come to grips with the mess being created by poorly designed software, society will be engaged in a perpetual (not to mention costly) struggle to contain the ensuing damage. Prevention offers a higher return on investment than response. As the bloodshed in Mexico can confirm,[35] failure to stifle demand for illicit drugs merely leads to a destructive, unending fight against well-armed cartels.

Rather than just trying to deal with the consequences of bad software, after the fact, which is what most of the computer security industry is focused on, why not look for ways to encourage vendors to make software that eliminates problems preemptivel?

Critical software bugs need to be viewed as the catastrophes that they are. Engineers and researchers literally need to go back to the drawing board and devise new ways to develop resilient software using techniques like compartmentalization and formal verification. While the industry has often paid lip service to this goal, software security will need to be perceived as the main priority rather than just a marketing stunt.

History has shown that software vendors won't do this independently. Economically speaking, it's cheaper for vendors to treat security problems as a negative externality. They need to be given financial and regulatory motivation to get security right. There are well-founded reasons why architects must adhere to building codes and the engineers who design cars must satisfy vehicle safety standards. The free market has failed to solve these problems.

Society is being exposed to significant risk. Hence, a regulatory structure is needed to ensure that software companies don't engage in shoddy engineering techniques that pass on the costs of that risk to society. When the vendors realize that it's in their best interest to create secure software, they will no doubt find ways to do so. It's a matter of enforcing the right priorities.

But for the government to enforce the right priorities, its own policies have got to be consistent. A regulatory program established in the name of better cyber-security would be useless if intelligence services are running an industry-wide program of subversion on behalf of the Deep State. The government can't work towards diverging goals like this and expect cyber-security to improve. It's not going to happen. The public needs "radical transparency" that covers the gamut from standard development to implementation. Anything less will provide inroads to subversion.

Once more, the regulation that's put in place has to have teeth. If the banking reform that followed the financial collapse of 2008 is any indication, as long as Washington is controlled by big money, moves towards regulation will be cosmetic gestures. Politicians will opt for legal band-aids that appease Main Street without threatening their powerful constituents in Wall Street. For example, the retirement of General Keith Alexander[36] and squabbling about leadership responsibilities within the military[37] are mere cosmetic gestures. The same institutional forces that created the problem endure.

In a nutshell, better security means fewer bugs, intentional or otherwise. It may sound straightforward, deceptively so, but declawing the intelligence services and instituting meaningful regulation within the hi-tech sector will oblige massive political shifts. In both cases these initiatives (neutering spies and regulating hi-tech) will run up against profound sources of influence outside the government.

Agents for better cyber-security will encounter the Deep State. Or, as the chairman of the European Parliament's foreign affairs committee recently described it, *a creepy state within a state.*[38] The United States has become an empire of corporate interests.

Our leaders contend that mass interception is indispensable.[39] This means that implementing change will require mobilization. Recall how FDR told labor leaders to "make me do it." Despite the growing power of corporate money, there have been groups of ordinary people in the past who have challenged, and overcome, entrenched power structures through a combination of public awareness, litigation, and non-violent direct action. These groups were ultimately able to realize their goals in terms of tangible legislation, like the 19th Amendment of the Constitution, the Wagner Act of 1935, the G.I. Bill of 1944, or the Civil Rights Act of 1964. In doing so, broad segments of society were given entry to, and subsequently able to benefit from, economic and political participation that hadn't previously existed.

In a system that's currently beholden to oligarchic factions, it's conceivable that people could regain a voice by organizing. As a group, the American public could develop the *infrastructure* necessary to nurture domain knowledge, create new channels of communication that foster accountability, coordinate sustained action across multiple fronts, and maintain the sort of logistical continuity that allows an organization to learn from its mistakes.[40] In a nutshell:

> Despite the murmurings there recurs calls for "cut the cowardly shit, let's fight."[41]

Endnotes

1) Edward T. Imparato, *General MacArthur Speeches and Reports 1908-1964*, Turner, 2000, ISBN-13: 978-1563115899, page 206.

2) Noam Chomsky, "Hidden Power and Built Form: The Politics Behind the Architecture," *Architecture MPS*, Volume 3, Number 3, October 1, 2013, http://architecturemps.com/2013/10/01/v-3n-2/.

3) Pedro Miguel, "Assange on Securitization, Politics, and the Survival of Wikileaks," International Boulevard, July 3, 2013, http://internationalboulevard.com/europe/116-united-kingdom/249-assange-on-securitization-politics-and-the-survival-of-wikileaks.

4) Ellen Nakashima and Joby Warrick, "For NSA chief, terrorist threat drives passion to 'collect it all,' observers say," *Washington Post*, July 14, 2013, http://www.washingtonpost.com/world/national-security/for-nsa-chief-terrorist-threat-drives-passion-to-collect-it-all/2013/07/14/3d26ef80-ea49-11e2-a301-ea5a8116d211_print.html.

5) Richard B. Spence *Trust no One: The Secret World of Sidney Reilly*, Feral House, 2003, ISBN 0922915792.

6) Ed Vulliamy, "Secret agents, freemasons, fascists... and a top-level campaign of political 'destabilisation'," *Guardian*, December 5, 1990, http://www.cambridge-clarion.org/press_cuttings/vinciguerra.p2.etc_graun_5dec1990.html.

7) David Rupper, "U.S. Military Wanted to Provoke War With Cuba," *ABC News*, May 1, 2001, http://abcnews.go.com/US/story?id=92662&page=1#.TxsGQG_Ox2B.

8) William Arkin, "The Secret War," *Los Angeles Times*, October 27, 2002, http://articles.latimes.com/2002/oct/27/opinion/op-arkin27.

9) "Greece: Police Under Scrutiny," *Associated Press*, September 23, 2013, http://www.nytimes.com/2013/09/24/world/europe/greece-police-under-scrutiny.html?_r=0.

10) Helena Smith, "Greece launches inquiry into claims Golden Dawn trained by armed forces," *Guardian*, September 23, 2013, http://www.theguardian.com/world/2013/sep/23/greece-inquiry-golden-dawn-armed-forces/print.

11) George Smith, "Failed State (continued)," *Escape From Whitemanistan*, September 19, 2013, http://dickdestiny.com/blog1/?p=16284.

12) "Time to wake up to cyber threat: experts," *Agence France-Presse*, June 18, 2010, http://www.physorg.com/news196079983.html.

13) Josephine Wolff, "Interview With Cyber-Security Czar Howard Schmidt," *Daily Beast*, December 21, 2010, http://www.thedailybeast.com/newsweek/2010/12/21/interview-with-cyber-security-czar-howard-schmidt.html.

14) Lewis Page, "Top MI6 spy: Terrorism less serious than bird flu," *The Register*, February 11, 2009, http://www.theregister.co.uk/2009/02/11/mi6_spy_rubbishes_terrorism_fear/.

15) Franklin D. Roosevelt: "Message to Congress on Curbing Monopolies.," April 29, 1938. Online by Gerhard Peters and John T. Woolley, *The American Presidency Project*, http://www.presidency.ucsb.edu/ws/?pid=15637.

16) Annie Lowrey, "Incomes Flat in Recovery, but Not for the 1%," *New York Times*, February 15, 2013, http://www.nytimes.com/2013/02/16/business/economy/income-gains-after-recession-went-mostly-to-top-1.html.

17) Sheldon Wolin, "Democracy Incorporated: Managed Democracy and the Specter of Inverted Totalitarianism," Princeton University Press, 2010, ISBN-10: 069114589X.

18) Moyers & Company, *On Winner-Take-All Politics*, January 13, 2012, http://billmoyers.com/wp-content/themes/billmoyers/transcript-print.php?post=2389.

19) Glenn Greenwald, "Various items: NSA stories around the world," *Guardian*, September 23, 2013, http://www.theguardian.com/commentisfree/2013/sep/23/various-items-nsa-india-belgium/print.

20) Joe Nocera, "This Isn't How to Stop Hacking," *New York Times*, June 14, 2013, http://www.nytimes.com/2013/06/15/opinion/nocera-this-isnt-how-to-stop-hackers.html.

21) "James Bamford on NSA Secrets, Keith Alexander's Influence & Massive Growth of Surveillance, Cyberwar" *Democracy Now!* June 14, 2013, http://www.democracynow.org/2013/6/14/james_bamford_on_nsa_secrets_keith#.

22) Glenn Greenwald, "The NSA's mass and indiscriminate spying on Brazilians," *Guardian*, July 6, 2013, http://www.guardian.co.uk/commentisfree/2013/jul/07/nsa-brazilians-globo-spying/print.

23) David Hayden, "A Surreal Spying Industry," *New York Times*, November 4, 2013, http://www.nytimes.com/2013/11/05/opinion/a-surreal-spying-industry.html.

24) Jack Goldsmith, "We Need an Invasive NSA," *New Republic*, October 10, 2013, http://www.newrepublic.com/node/115002/print.

25) David Sanger and Thom Shanker, "N.S.A. Director Firmly Defends Surveillance Efforts," *New York Times*, October 12, 2013, http://www.nytimes.com/2013/10/13/us/nsa-director-gives-firm-and-broad-defense-of-surveillance-efforts.html.

26) Jo Becker and Scott Shane, "Secret 'Kill List' Proves a Test of Obama's Principles and Will," *New York Times*, May 29, 2012, http://www.nytimes.com/2012/05/29/world/obamas-leadership-in-war-on-al-qaeda.html.

27) Joe Sharkey, "Jumping Through Hoops to Get Off the No-Fly List," *New York Times*, February 14, 2006, http://www.nytimes.com/2006/02/14/business/14road.html.

28) Alfred McCoy, "The CIA's secret history of psychological torture," *Salon*, June 11, 2009, http://www.salon.com/2009/06/11/mccoy/.

29) Claire Cain Miller and Somini Sengupta, "Selling Secrets of Phone Users to Advertisers," *New York Times*, October 6, 2013, http://www.nytimes.com/2013/10/06/technology/selling-secrets-of-phone-users-to-advertisers.html.

30) John Young, "Privacy and Cybersecurity Illusions Have to Go," *Cryptome*, October 6, 2013, http://cryptome.org/2013/10/privacy-cybersec-illusions-go.htm.

31) Matthew Schofield, "Memories of Stasi color Germans' view of U.S. surveillance programs," *McClatchy*, June 27, 2013, http://www.mcclatchydc.com/2013/06/26/v-print/195045/memories-of-stasi-color-germans.html.

32) "Secret weapon against hacking: College students," *PBS News Hour*, October 26, 2013, http://www.pbs.org/newshour/bb/science/july-dec13/cylab_10-26.html?print.

33) Bruce Schneier, "US Offensive Cyberwar Policy," *Schneier on Security*, June 21, 2013, http://www.schneier.com/blog/archives/2013/06/us_offensive_cy.html.

34) James Ball, Julian Borger, and Glenn Greenwald, "Revealed: how US and UK spy agencies defeat Internet privacy and security," *Guardian*, September 5, 2013, http://www.theguardian.com/world/2013/sep/05/nsa-gchq-encryption-codes-security/print.

35) Damien Cave, "Mexico Updates Death Toll in Drug War to 47,515, but Critics Dispute the Data," *New York Times*, January 11, 2012, http://www.nytimes.

com/2012/01/12/world/americas/mexico-updates-drug-war-death-toll-but-critics-dispute-data.html.

36) Warren Strobel and Mark Hosenball, "U.S. eavesdropping agency chief, top deputy expected to depart soon," *Reuters*, October 16, 2013, http://www.reuters.com/article/2013/10/16/us-usa-nsa-transition-idUSBRE99F12W20131016.

37) Brendan Sasso, "NSA chief likely to lose cyber war powers," *The Hill*, November 4, 2013, http://thehill.com/blogs/hillicon-valley/technology/189036-nsa-chief-likely-to-be-stripped-of-cyberwar-powers.

38) Alison Smale, "Amid New Storm in U.S.-Europe Relationship, a Call for Talks on Spying," *New York Times*, October 26, 2013, http://www.nytimes.com/2013/10/26/world/europe/fallout-over-american-spying-revelations.html.

39) David Sanger, "As U.S. Weighs Spying Changes, Officials Say Data Sweeps Must Continue," *New York Times*, November 4, 2013, http://www.nytimes.com/2013/11/05/world/as-us-weighs-spying-changes-officials-say-data-sweeps-must-continue.html.

40) Chris Hedges, "The Sparks of Rebellion," *Truthdig*, September 30, 2013, http://www.truthdig.com/report/item/the_sparks_of_rebellion_20130930.

41) John Young, *Political Cypherpunks Trumps Apolitical Cryptography*, September 8, 2013, http://cryptome.org/2013/09/cpunks-crypto.htm.

Index